Praise for Books from PlanningShop

PlanningShop

❝ PlanningShop has been invaluable to our organization. We use PlanningShop materials for our entrepreneur classes because the content is comprehensive and constantly updated.❞

— *Ken Freeman, Director Small Business Development Center, Yuba Community College District*

Bringing the Cloud Down to Earth

❝ No matter how you refer to it, working in the Cloud is a fundamental business practice these days and Abrams has done a terrific job of making this sometimes confusing subject relevant and practical for businesses of all shapes and sizes.❞

— *John Jantsch, author of* Duct Tape Marketing *and* The Referral Engine

Successful Marketing: Secrets & Strategies

❝ Successful Marketing encourages students to think through standard marketing concepts while applying them directly to their business idea.❞

— *Meredith Carpenter, Entrepreneurship Instructor, Haywood Community College*

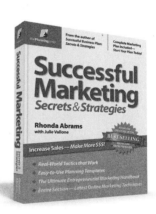

Successful Business Research

❝ At last, a straightforward book that demystifies the process behind conducting effective business research … gives business practitioners and students an incredibly useful tool to enable them to find accurate and timely information for business plans, academic papers, and other business uses.❞

— *Molly Lavik, Practitioner Faculty of Marketing, Graziadio School of Business and Management, Pepperdine University*

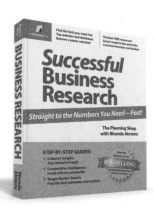

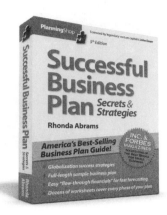

Successful Business Plan: Secrets & Strategies

❝ [*Successful Business Plan* is] user-friendly and exhaustive…highly recommended. Abrams' book works because she tirelessly researched the subject. Most how-to books on entrepreneurship aren't worth a dime; among the thousands of small business titles, Abrams' [is an] exception. ❞

— *Forbes Magazine*

❝ There are plenty of decent business-plan guides out there, but Abrams' was a cut above the others I saw. *Successful Business Plan* won points with me because it was thorough and well organized, with handy worksheets and good quotes. Also, Abrams does a better job than most at explaining the business plan as a planning tool rather than a formulaic exercise. Well done. ❞

— *Inc. Magazine*

❝ We are again using *Successful Business Plan* in my business honors course this semester. Must be working, as Penn State was just named (by Kaplan and *Newsweek* magazine) as the 'hottest school in the U.S. for student entrepreneurs!' ❞

— *Greg Pierce, Penn State University*

❝ *Successful Business Plan* enables my Entrepreneurship students at the University of Vermont to develop really great business plans. The book's easy-to-follow, step-by-step format makes preparing a plan logical and understandable. Over the years…several students have actually launched their businesses successfully. Our son used the book at St. Michael's College in Vermont to develop a plan for airport fitness centers, winning the school's annual business plan competition for business majors…with a hefty cash prize! His plan was so thorough, especially the financials, that he was flown to the West Coast to present his plan to a prospective buyer. The bottom line, there is no better road map to business plan success than *Successful Business Plan*! ❞

— *David Kaufman, University of Vermont*

❝ *Successful Business Plan* was an excellent learning tool for me at the University of Vermont and proved to be incredibly valuable as I started my own business after graduation. The step-by-step guidance through business planning ensures that you have all your bases covered before investing time and money in a new enterprise. The book helped me start a promotional products business and I have since recommended this book to dozens of other entrepreneurs who have used it for everything from restaurants to fashion boutiques. If you are considering starting your first, second, third or tenth business you need to look at *Successful Business Plan*! ❞

— *Issa Sawabini, University of Vermont, '99*
   Partner, Monitor Premiums LLC

" If you'd like something that goes beyond the mere construction of your plan and is more fun to use, try *Successful Business Plan: Secrets and Strategies,* by Rhonda Abrams…this book can take the pain out of the process. **"**

— *"Small Business School," PBS television show*

" *Successful Business Plan* is easy to follow and comprehensive. From the first chapter to the last, it guides you through the business planning process with a proven systematic approach. **"**

— *Sean S. Murphy, Ernst & Young LLP*

" As a 20 plus year veteran SBDC director, consultant and entrepreneurship instructor, I have assisted thousands of individuals and business owners through the planning process. Having reviewed tens of thousands of plans and critiquing hundreds of planning texts, programs and tools, *Successful Business Plan: Secrets & Strategies* remains my hands-down favorite text/workbook/guide. The content and construction is comprehensive, practical and 'do-able' for the serious small business owner/entrepreneur. **"**

— *David Gay, Illinois Small Business Development Center at College of DuPage*

" In my opinion, your book is the definitive guide for successful business plans. I particularly appreciate and recommend the use of the Flow-Through Financial worksheets. Each is a great device to illustrate the connection between the qualitative and quantitative elements of a plan. **"**

— *Gene Elliott, Business Consultant, New Mexico*

" I've been using and promoting *Successful Business Plan* since 1993, and it's great! I've taught business plan writing in several local SBDCs, as well as nationally, through the Neighborhood Reinvestment Training Institute. My course is designed and delivered around your book. **"**

— *Ransom S. Stafford, Business Consultant, Twin Cities, MN*

" One of the best books on business planning. The overall quality of this book is excellent, but three things make it stand out: First, it contains worksheets that walk you through the information gathering process. Fill them out, and even the financials—always the hardest part of a plan—will fall right into place. Second, it has a sample plan that reads like a real business plan, written by a real person for a real business. You can use much of the wording in your own plan. Third, it has tips from successful managers, leaders, and business owners, large and small. I was especially fascinated reading the tips from ex-49'er head coach Bill Walsh. You can't go wrong following his advice on planning and organizing! **"**

— *Economic Chamber of Macedonia*

❝ *Successful Business Plan* is thorough, well-organized, and a very useful tool for business planning and development. It's an excellent guide to the details involved with creating a solid, useful business plan. ❞

— *Jim Jindrick, The Institute of Electrical and Electronics Engineers and the University of Arizona*

❝ I chose *Successful Business Plan* because of its ease of use, its clarity, and its good examples. I have used the book for a number of years now. ❞

— *Jean Morris, The Culinary Institute of America*

❝ It has a clearly defined, comprehensive approach. ❞

— *Zane Swanson, Emporia State University, KS*

❝ Here at the SBDC we offer clients an eight-week business planning counseling program called Business Plan Expedited (BPE). BPE is structured around *Successful Business Plan*—the end result is a well-written business plan that can be used as a part of a business loan application package. I specifically chose this text because I used it, per recommendation from my graduate school advisor, for my MBA project in graduate school 13 years ago! ❞

— *Indria Gillespie, Sierra College SBDC*

❝ Your book has been both an inspirational read as well as a comprehensive guide for starting my business. Being relatively inexperienced with entrepreneurship, your book has not only given me the ability to create a solid roadmap for planning, but has also provided an encouraging and easy way to cope with the enormous amount of information and organization needed. I particularly enjoy the various quotes from business professionals who have had experience in business planning. They give precious insight and different viewpoints that I would not have seen. Thank you for writing this book! ❞

— *Simon Lee, entrepreneur*

❝ It combines, in a very clear way, both aspects of business planning and effective writing of business plans. The book is very well written. The forms are very useful. ❞

— *Eyal Yaniv, Bar Ilan University, Israel*

PlanningShop
Palo Alto, California

en·tre·pre·neur·ship

A REAL-WORLD APPROACH

Hands-on Guide for Today's Entrepreneur

Rhonda Abrams

PlanningShop:

facebook.com/PlanningShop

twitter.com/PlanningShop

Entrepreneurship: A Real-World Approach

© 2012 by Rhonda Abrams

Published by PlanningShop

FREE BUSINESS TIPS AND INFORMATION:

To receive PlanningShop's free email newsletter on starting and growing a successful business, sign up at www.PlanningShop.com.

PLANNINGSHOP:

555 Bryant Street, #180
Palo Alto, CA 94301 USA
650-364-9120
Fax: 650-364-9125
Email: info@PlanningShop.com
www.PlanningShop.com

PlanningShop is a division of Rhonda, Inc., a California corporation.

ACKNOWLEDGMENTS:

Contributing writing and research: Alice LaPlante
Editing: Anne Marie Bonneau
Proofreading: Mark Woodworth
Cover and interior design: Diana Russell, www.DianaRussellDesign.com
Indexing: Sandi Schroeder, Schroeder Indexing Services
Project Manager: Rosa Whitten

ISBN 10: 1-933895-26-8 (print)

ISBN 13: 978-1-933895-26-0 (print)

Library of Congress Control Number: 2012909939

"This publication is designed to provide accurate and authoritative information in regard to the subject matter covered. It is sold with the understanding that the publisher and author are not engaged in rendering legal, accounting, or other professional services. If legal advice or other expert assistance is required, the services of a competent professional person should be sought."

— *from a Declaration of Principles jointly adopted by a committee of the American Bar Association and a committee of publishers.*

Printed in the United States of America

10 9 8 7 6 5 4 3 2 1

About the Author

Entrepreneur, author, and nationally syndicated columnist **Rhonda Abrams** is widely recognized as a leading expert on entrepreneurship and small business. Rhonda's column for *USA Today*, "Successful Strategies," is the most widely distributed column on small business and entrepreneurship in the United States, reaching tens of millions of readers each week.

Rhonda's books have been used by millions of entrepreneurs. Her first book, *Successful Business Plan: Secrets & Strategies*, is the best-selling business plan guide in America. It was named one of the top 10 business books for entrepreneurs by both *Forbes* and *Inc.* magazines. She is also the author of more than a dozen other books on entrepreneurship and has sold more than a million copies of her books. Rhonda's other books are perennial best sellers, with three of them having reached the nationally recognized "Top 50 Business Best-Seller" list.

Rhonda not only writes about business—she lives it! As the founder of three successful companies, Rhonda has accumulated an extraordinary depth of experience and a real-life understanding of the challenges facing entrepreneurs. Rhonda first founded a management consulting practice working with clients ranging from one-person start-ups to Fortune 500 companies. An early web pioneer, she founded a website for small business that she later sold. Today, Rhonda is CEO of the publishing company PlanningShop, which focuses exclusively on the topics of business planning, entrepreneurship, and new business development. PlanningShop is America's leading academic publisher in the discipline of entrepreneurship.

A popular public speaker, Rhonda regularly addresses leading industry and trade associations, business schools, and corporate conventions and events. Educated at Harvard University and UCLA, Rhonda lives in Palo Alto, California.

Rhonda Abrams:

facebook.com/ RhondaAbramsSmallBusiness

twitter.com/RhondaAbrams

Table of Contents

Build-Your-Business Worksheets

CHAPTER 1

What Is Entrepreneurship?

learning objectives

In this chapter, you'll learn how to:

- Understand the importance of entrepreneurship
- Recognize the positive contributions of entrepreneurship to society
- Describe the characteristics of successful entrepreneurs
- Recognize the various aspects of change and learn to embrace and leverage them
- Understand the positive aspects of failure
- Define the advantages and disadvantages of entrepreneurship
- Determine personal goals and a company vision

Entrepreneurship paves a road to personal wealth

On a personal level, entrepreneurship can make an incredible economic impact. Being successful in starting your own business can be a road to financial freedom. In fact, according to the U.S. Federal Reserve, equity in unincorporated businesses—typically the smallest of independent businesses—makes up the second largest share of total household wealth in America, second only to home equity.

Understanding Entrepreneurship

Do you dream of one day owning your own **business**? Do you have an idea for a new or improved product or service that you hope to turn into a reality—something that people will want, buy, value, and even love?

Do you feel a need to be in control of your own life? To have the opportunity to act on your ideas? Do you want to be your own boss?

Are you able to motivate yourself to work hard, to do well, even without a boss, or teacher, or parent looking over your shoulder? Do you have the persistence to stick with something until you can make it a reality?

Are you willing to risk security—of a job, a paycheck, a manager guiding you, the structure of a workplace—for the excitement and possibility of creating your own company? For the chance to perhaps make a fortune or at least earn a good living?

Are you willing to learn how to handle failure in return for the possibility of independent business success?

Then what you are dreaming about is "entrepreneurship."

The origin of the word is "entreprendre"—French for "to undertake." Take a look at that word—"undertake." Notice that it emphasizes an attempt to act, and not the outcome of that action. You *undertake* something.

This implies that what matters is that you have begun something; you've started on a journey. And although traveling on that journey may not always be a smooth ride, at least you're in the driver's seat.

Entrepreneurs change the world

Entrepreneurs make enormous contributions to societies around the globe. Fast-growing entrepreneurial **ventures** transform entire economies. Even smaller enterprises make tremendous contributions to the health and stability of their communities.

Entrepreneurial companies produce far more than just money. They also provide:

■ **New ideas and innovation.** Although some large corporations have research and development departments, overwhelmingly, new products and services are created and introduced by new small companies. This is certainly true in technology, but it's also true in the entire spectrum of products and services. Many Fortune 500 companies—from computers to cars, cola to cartoons—were started by entrepreneurs with little more than a new and better idea.

■ **New jobs.** Total new-job creation in the United States is a result of new businesses. In fact, America relies on new businesses to offset the job losses from bigger and older corporations. The Small Business Administration (SBA) estimates that small businesses create 65 percent of all new jobs in the country. Worldwide, substantial job creation is largely a result of new business formation, especially in emerging economies.

Out with the old, in with the new

The average lifespan of the 500 largest companies—commonly referred to as the "Fortune 500"— is merely 30 years. Only 71 of the 1955 Fortune 500 companies still existed 55 years later. By 1983, one-third of companies listed in 1970, only 13 years earlier, had disappeared. So new companies are continually replacing the old.

en·tre·pre·neur·ship **key terms**

Business
An entity organized for the purpose of buying and selling a product, service, knowledge, or other thing of value; a company set up with the intention of making a profit; an activity established to provide income and financial well-being for the person running the business.

Entrepreneur
An individual who, through their own initiative and hard work, launches a new undertaking—typically a business—that involves risk and uncertainty. Ordinarily, entrepreneurs seize on opportunities, innovate, experiment, and pioneer to bring to market a new, better, less expensive, or somehow improved product or service, or to open up new markets. Many entrepreneurs also aim to advance social goals in their ventures.

Entrepreneurial thinking
Applying the characteristics of entrepreneurs—such as innovation, creativity, risk-taking, the willingness to accept failure, and fast response time—to other endeavors, such as corporate enterprises, education, and social programs.

Risk
In entrepreneurial terms, risk involves uncertainty, with the possibility of encountering unexpected setbacks, suffering losses, and even resulting in failure. New ventures present various types of risk, such as market risk in that target customers may not be ready for the product or service; or technology risks in that the necessary technology may not be able to be developed in an acceptable time frame; or execution risks, in that the planned activities may not be able to be carried out.

Start-up
A term often used for a young business; most often applied when the business has the intent or potential to grow to substantial size.

Venture
An entrepreneurial undertaking, usually referring to a new business.

Vision
The ability for an entrepreneur to conceive a company, product, or service that doesn't yet exist, typically in response to a specific need in the market and often in somewhat great detail. A visionary is one who can see possibilities where others do not.

REAL-WORLD RECAP

How entrepreneurs change the world

- New ideas and innovation
- New jobs
- New industries
- Middle class income
- Flexibility
- Old values

- **New industries.** Entrepreneurs not only create new businesses, but when they're incredibly successful, they may even end up creating entire new industries. In recent years, for example, the success of a few social media companies—like Facebook—has fostered the generation of a whole ecosystem based around those companies. This leads to an immense explosion of jobs in related businesses.

- **Middle class income.** In many areas—including rural areas, developing countries, and older regions in the United States—there are no large corporations to provide decent jobs. There, the only path to a middle class lifestyle (or better) is through the creation of one's own business.

- **Flexibility.** Smaller companies can open, close, move, and change focus much more quickly than big corporations. Typically, smaller companies are the first to respond to changing market needs and conditions, and often provide a testing ground for big corporations to learn how they themselves will need to adapt. The smaller companies offer the job opportunities and new products our society needs until big firms figure out how to catch up.

- **Old values.** Big companies get distracted by things such as keeping Wall Street happy, arranging mergers and acquisitions, and rewarding executives with huge bonuses. Newer companies, by contrast, concentrate on the basics: cash flow, profits, providing high-quality products and services, and serving and retaining their customers. Perhaps even more important, owners of newer or smaller businesses know their employees are people, not "human resources," and need to be treated as such.

Entrepreneurs, in short, make a huge difference. They innovate, pioneering new industries and producing new products. They provide vital services. They support their communities. They create wealth, for the entrepreneurs, the investors, and society. Most important, they create jobs. And when you create jobs—good jobs, with fair pay and good working conditions, where people can take pride in their work and be treated with respect—you change their world, your world, and the world in general.

Growth of entrepreneurship

Humans have been engaged in entrepreneurial endeavors for thousands of years. It's nothing new for someone to see something that people want to buy and then figure out a way to sell it. It may be part of human nature to be able to identify an opportunity and wish to seize on it, and, through hard work, be motivated to make money in the process.

While it's true that entrepreneurship has been around for a long time, we are now in a golden age of entrepreneurship. Throughout the world, entrepreneurs are making a greater impact than ever before, and gaining the recognition that comes from that impact.

Although much attention is paid to technology-based **start-ups**, especially in places like Silicon Valley in California, the truth is entrepreneurship is flowering in *all* industries and geographic locations around the world. Even concepts that once were the sole province of philanthropists and charitable organizations have now become the interest of entrepreneurs who aim to apply their innovative and strategic thinking to solving some of the globe's most pressing problems.

Indeed, since the earliest part of the 21st century, there has been a ground shift. The best and the brightest in our society, who before might have gone to work for big corporations, now want to start their own ventures, at younger and younger ages. Some of the growth in entrepreneurial desire has certainly come from seeing the example of those who have succeeded—especially young entrepreneurs—who have created whole new industries, transformed the way we live and work, and made fortunes along the way. Seemingly overnight, entrepreneurs have become millionaires—even billionaires—as a result of launching innovative businesses.

Of course, most entrepreneurs never become millionaires. Yet the chance to act on your ideas, to make your own way, to create new products, to invent new services, and to make a difference in the world, has encouraged record numbers of people to become entrepreneurs.

Factors driving the growth of entrepreneurship

Besides the example of successful entrepreneurs, what's propelling the rapid growth of interest in launching one's own businesses?

- **Less job stability.** The days are long gone when people assumed they would work for one company all their lives. For starters, a large number of businesses today run extraordinarily "lean." Rather than hiring full-time permanent employees, many businesses opt for part-time personnel or either temporary or contract workers. There has also been a cultural shift in how people view their employment and careers. Most people expect to—want to—change jobs. A person born in the later years of the "baby boom" (1957–1964) held an average number of 11 jobs just between ages 18 and 44.[1] Younger people today are likely to have as many different jobs, if not more. Indeed, it's typical for people in developed countries, especially the United States, to have two, three, or even more "careers" over the course of their lifetimes as their interests change and evolve. With less job stability, there's more opportunity—and more need—to start your own business.

- **Lifestyle driving career choices.** Want to live in the mountains so you can ski, or by the beach so you can surf? Be home in the afternoon to raise your kids? Increasingly, people want their careers to mesh with their lifestyle goals. Entrepreneurship allows much more flexibility to create an income in a way that meets personal goals. You can create businesses in locales where the kind of job you want doesn't exist, have more flexibility in work hours, and spend less time commuting and more time on family,

Global entrepreneurship by the numbers

- 400 million entrepreneurs in 54 countries
- 163 million of them are women
- 165 million of them are young (18–25 years of age)
- 69 million offer innovative products or services
- 18 million sell internationally

(source: Global Entrepreneurship Monitor, 2011 Report)

---

1. U.S. Department of Labor, Bureau of Labor Statistics.

hobbies, or other interests. The desire for a lifestyle that a traditional job can't satisfy is one key reason that people choose an entrepreneurial path.

- **Technology infrastructure.** It has become cheaper and easier than ever to start a businesss. Businesses that once required a huge upfront investment in infrastructure, equipment, and staff can now do a lot more for a lot less. Many of the daily administrative and office tasks can easily be automated; a huge array of companies exists to provide technology solutions to small and new businesses. Web design firms, search marketing specialists, third-party IT services providers, and all sorts of consultants represent merely a few of the new types of business opportunities that have emerged. It's possible to build a fairly substantial business with only a virtual team, especially for technology needs.

- **Technology opportunities.** New technology creates new business opportunities. The Internet, in particular, over the last few decades has created entire new industries—mobile, cloud, and social media. Advances in technology and science have led to an explosion in biotech, genetics, and medical equipment and other health care–related industries. "Green" technology is providing significant new prospects in a wide range of environmentally related businesses. In virtually every category, the rapid changes in underlying technology have opened up great possibilities for entrepreneurs.

- **Government support for entrepreneurs.** Throughout the world, governments have increasingly recognized the importance of new ventures and small businesses for their economic growth and health. National governments are setting up agencies to assist entrepreneurs, lessening regulation and red tape for starting new businesses, and providing tax benefits. Even state, regional, and local governmental entities are getting in on the act, helping to make it easier for new business formation. Officials realize that without new businesses economies stagnate.

- **Mature financing environment.** Investors have become more and more comfortable with putting their funds into new and risky ventures. The unbelievable financial success of those who have invested in entrepreneurial ventures since the last two decades of the 20th century and during the first decade in this century has led to the growth of a large pool of investors willing to take risks on entrepreneurs and new ventures. There's now a mature, sophisticated, and well-funded investing community in a few key regions of developed countries. And, even in smaller communities and less developed areas, many more private investors—"angel investors"—are willing to support entrepreneurs. The availability of more venture capital means the possibility of many more new businesses launching.

- **Financial considerations.** Many people simply don't feel they can meet their financial goals by working for an hourly wage or even a professional-level salary. This is especially true in areas with few high-growth and professional opportunities, as well as in many developing countries. The notoriety given to young multimillionaire founders and early employees of high-tech start-ups has fueled many people's dreams. No surprise, then, that many people feel that they can achieve their financial goals more fully and easily if they choose to become self-employed—or to build their own business and employ others.

Thinking like an Entrepreneur

Can you learn to be an entrepreneur, or must you be born with an entrepreneurial spirit? While some people are naturally more oriented toward an entrepreneurial lifestyle, and feel more comfortable with the uncertainty that comes with entrepreneurship, it's definitely possible to work on developing some of the key attitudes and attributes of those who start and grow successful businesses.

Many business books and experts assert that there's just *one* kind of person who can be a successful entrepreneur—someone who's a risk taker, extroverted, a natural salesperson, a leader and a visionary, someone willing to work around the clock.

It's a great list, but it's just not true. There's a whole range of personalities who become successful entrepreneurs. The key is to find the right type of business to suit *you*.

Of course, someone who, by nature, needs an extremely high level of security, guidance, and reassurance might be a poor fit for an entrepreneurial lifestyle. But the idea that you must relish **risk**—be an emotional skydiver—is often overstated when describing the types of people who make good entrepreneurs. Many people who don't think of themselves as embracing risk become entrepreneurs. The key is that although a successful entrepreneur takes risks, those risks are *measured*. While entrepreneurs frequently go out on limbs, the ones that make it generally test that limb first to make sure it has a good chance of bearing their weight.

Great entrepreneurs expect change

Change is inevitable, but one thing that sets successful entrepreneurs apart from others is their willingness to adapt to, embrace, even leverage change for their own gain. Many entrepreneurial companies, especially those involved in technology, have change at the very core of their existence. Still, for every business, change is inevitable.

Even companies that were created on the basis of innovation often become staid over time. Once they have established customers, channels, business units, and models, it's easy for them to get complacent. Their employees become used to doing things the way they always did. When companies are mired down in doing things the same old way, they're viewed as rich targets for newer, entrepreneurial companies to go after.

Small businesses by the numbers

According to the Small Business Administration (SBA), small businesses in the United States:

- **Represent 99.7 percent of all employer firms**
- **Employ half of all private-sector employees**
- **Are responsible for 43 percent of total private payroll**
- **Generate 65 percent of new jobs annually**
- **Hire 43 percent of high-tech workers**
- **Produce 16.5 times more patents per employee than do large businesses**
- **Account for 97.5 percent of exporters**

The best entrepreneurs—the ones who succeed over decades—recognize that they must keep responding to change, reinventing their companies, continually innovating.

In planning for change, keep in mind the kinds of conditions that will affect your business's future.

■ **Technological changes.** It's impossible to predict the exact technological developments that will affect your industry, but you can be sure that you'll be faced with such changes. Even if you are making old-fashioned chocolate chip cookies, you'll find that advancements in oven design, food storage, and inventory control software will place competitive pressures on your business. Competitors' technological advances may cause significant downward pricing pressures on you.

■ **Sociological changes.** Evaluate demographic and lifestyle trends in light of their potential influence on your business. In the cookie business, for example, consumer interest in natural foods or the number of school-age children in the population may influence the number and kind of cookies you sell. What sociological factors have the greatest impact on your company? Keep your eye on trends that represent true change; be careful not to build a business on passing fads.

■ **Competitive changes.** New businesses launch every day. How hard is it for a new competitor to enter the market, and what are the barriers to entry? The Internet has made it possible for companies all over the world to compete against each other, increasing the number and type of competitors you may face.

■ **Market and marketing changes.** Consider how your company deals with these outside changes. Also anticipate major internal changes, such as growth, the arrival or departure of key personnel, and new products or services. No business is static. Planning a company to be agile and responsive to change will make the inevitable changes easier.

Great entrepreneurs know how to fail

One critical key to **entrepreneurial thinking** is to learn how to think differently about "failure." True, nobody wants to fail, but, for most entrepreneurs, some failure is inevitable. Or at least it is if you ever hope to succeed. Virtually all success depends on trying things that may fail.

Successful entrepreneurs possess the ability—or rather, the determination—to view failure as an opportunity to learn and then apply that lesson to their next business attempt. Indeed, many venture capitalists say they prefer to finance entrepreneurs who've already failed in at least one business, because they've learned a lot from failure. "Let them learn on someone else's nickel," one VC once said, recognizing that the best entrepreneurs learn from their setbacks.

BUILD-YOUR-BUSINESS WORKSHEET

Think like an Entrepreneur

The most successful entrepreneurs possess numerous key characteristics. Not all entrepreneurs have all of them, of course. But check the traits that apply to you. Work on developing the ones you're missing.

☐ You see opportunities where others see problems. When you encounter a need that isn't filled or a flaw in a product, service, or even our society, you look to see if there's a way to solve it.

☐ You are driven to succeed. You're so motivated to achieve your goals that you're prepared to overcome obstacles that would likely discourage or stop others.

☐ You are a self-starter. Rather than waiting for someone to issue instructions, you can take initiative. When you're interested in something, you don't need others to tell you what to do.

☐ You are persistent. You don't give up on things easily. You can handle setbacks and keep on going.

☐ You are innovative. You can think "outside the box" when attempting to meet challenges.

☐ You are energized by challenges. The idea of having to solve a problem, create something new, or build something from nothing, spurs you rather than deters you.

☐ You take control of your own destiny and bear responsibility for your own actions. You don't blame others for what happens to you in life. You can honestly accept responsibility for the results—both positive and negative—of decisions you make and actions you take.

☐ You are willing to give up the security blanket of a "regular" job. You don't mind working without the safety net of a regular paycheck or the benefits and social structure that an established employer provides.

☐ You accept and embrace change. Change is inevitable, yet in the entrepreneurial world, change comes even faster and more frequently. But rather than fearing it, you welcome it and enjoy the excitement of the ride.

☐ You can be a team player. No great entrepreneurs succeed on their own. You're able to work with others to achieve a common goal. You're capable of listening to others' ideas and incorporating the good ones into your own thinking.

☐ You understand the importance of making a profit. You know that all your best intentions and actions are for naught if you aren't actually making a profit—that is, bringing in more money by selling a product or service than it costs you to provide it. You're not embarrassed by the idea of making money.

Does failure mean you've failed?

History is filled with stories of entrepreneurs who've failed at first. Bill Gates and Paul Allen started—and failed at—a computer company before they started Microsoft. Steve Jobs was fired from Apple; went on to start a new company, NeXT, that was widely considered unsuccessful; then was brought back to Apple and led it to become the most valuable company in the world. The founder of FedEx, Frederick W. Smith, while a student at Yale, got a "C" on a business paper outlining his idea.

Great entrepreneurs are good at failing. But there are different ways to fail. To succeed, try to fail the *right* way:

- **Fail fast.** Try new things without obsessing about perfection. Develop things quickly, then get them out the door. You need real-world feedback from customers, users, and partners, to be able to fix your mistakes. Google's product development mantra reflects this reality: "Experiment, Expedite, Iterate." Other companies that grew quickly also embraced this kind of failure. One of Facebook's mottos is "Move fast and break things." To fail fast, give employees the authority to make decisions and act on them independently. They will make mistakes—fail. If things don't work out, move on quickly—without a lot of criticism. Start, fail, change. Fast.

- **Fail forward.** If you're going to fail—and you will—fail in a way that moves your company, products, or services in a new direction. Failure only leads to success if you're stretching yourself, trying new things, innovating. Remember, innovation doesn't require perfection. It's now a "version 1.0" world. There's great tolerance for new products and services that aren't perfect at first. Move fast and forward.

- **Fail smart.** You don't learn much, or gain much, if you fail because you're doing something stupid and avoidable: partnerships imploding because of a lack of communication, employees unmotivated because they're treated poorly, or management not taking care of business fundamentals, such as getting contracts signed or sending out invoices. Failure is only useful if you're learning something from it.

- **Fail cheap.** Try to keep your financial losses from a failure as minimal as possible. One way to do this is to start "lean"—try new things with the least amount of investment, to test the concept. The idea is to launch the "minimal viable" version of whatever you're trying. Remember, it doesn't usually have to be perfect to test a concept.

- **Fail with integrity.** Character matters. Even if you fail, there's a very good possibility that people who worked with you before—even invested in you—will be willing to team with you again in the future. But that's possible only if you've proven to be a person they trust and respect. If you've failed because you are dishonest, because your word is not reliable, or because you cheat, then your one failure is likely to become permanent failure. Experienced and intelligent people will forgive your failures if they're honest attempts to accomplish something.

Keep in mind, an unexamined failure is just a plain failure. You've got to learn from your mistakes and failures to grow.

The Advantages and Challenges of Entrepreneurship

It seems cool to be an entrepreneur. Movies are made about young entrepreneurs, portraying them as contemporary heroes. Being an entrepreneur seems exciting. The possibility of becoming fabulously wealthy is enticing. It seems easy to create the next big thing.

Yet, as in all things in life, there are advantages and challenges to entrepreneurship. And it's wise to understand both as you consider becoming an entrepreneur.

Advantages

The advantages of entrepreneurship fall into three general categories: personal, professional, and financial.

PERSONAL BENEFITS

Many people focus on the financial rewards of being an entrepreneur, but much of the payback that people get from their entrepreneurial ventures is personal, increasing the possibility that you'll derive greater satisfaction from your working life than you would as someone else's employee.

First and foremost is the ability to do something that interests you. You almost certainly will choose to start a business in some field that attracts your attention. It may not be "sexy" to others—perhaps you're finding a new way to crunch data, to manage mobile networks, or even to improve cleaning supplies—but it holds interest for you. It's a great personal benefit to have the opportunity to do something you have a passion for, rather than spending the majority of your waking hours performing tasks in which you have little real interest.

Next, you get to create something of your own making. Being able to make something from nothing brings tremendous satisfaction. It can be something as simple as a food truck or a corner bakery, even being a self-employed consultant, but the idea of having created a job and a business yourself is highly rewarding and empowering and will give you a tremendous sense of pride.

You also get more personal choice over where, when, and how you work. Many people want to live in a particular geographic area—say, close to the mountains or by the ocean—or perhaps in a place where there aren't an abundance of jobs. Creating your own business enables you to have more location choice. Having the independence and flexibility to make time for family, hobbies, or other activities is another huge draw to the entrepreneurial life.

Most important, you're your own boss. The idea of not having a boss is intensely appealing for many. You have no one to answer to, no one to judge you, and no one who can fire or transfer you. If you've only had bad bosses, not having a boss can be a huge draw.

Oprah OWNs up to failure

Hopes were sky-high when the extraordinarily popular TV personality Oprah Winfrey launched her own television network—OWN—in January 2011. But by the end of the first year, OWN was, by virtually any measure, a failure. Winfrey was committed to the long-term success of the network, however, and took a realistic view of her entrepreneurial failure, saying, "Who hasn't made mistakes? The beauty is you can say, 'I learned from that.' I don't worry about failure. I worry about, 'Did I do all I could do?'"

PROFESSIONAL BENEFITS

You'll also reap extensive professional benefits from your entrepreneurial endeavors. For starters, you can advance more rapidly than you would in a traditional office setting. You won't be held back because you lack experience or seniority or by office politics. You won't be limited by what your boss thinks of you. You'll succeed or fail on your own merits.

You'll also be able to fully leverage your creativity and ingenuity. Rather than simply carrying out other people's ideas or implementing their **visions**, you reap the professional benefits of any exciting insights or "ahas!" you get. You can aggressively pursue exciting new ideas for products and services. When you have a good idea, you can act on it—instead of waiting for a committee or encountering bureaucratic opposition.

You get to choose the people you work with. When you're in charge, you can hire a team that works well together, with people you respect and like. You're not stuck with the other employees whom some boss hires. Your only limits on whom you can hire are your company needs, your cash, the available labor force, and labor laws.

Finally, you'll thrive because of the sheer adrenaline factor. Entrepreneurs are challenged and surprised every day, and because of this they grow at a much faster rate, professionally, than their counterparts in traditional employment situations. And because you're the boss, you can invest in further education and training as you want or need it.

FINANCIAL BENEFITS

The financial benefits of running your own firm can be substantial. Research performed by Thomas Stanley and William Danko for their book *The Millionaire Next Door* found that self-employed businesspersons were *four times* more likely to be millionaires than those in traditional employer-employee roles. Your earning potential is theoretically unlimited: You can go as far as your business idea will take you. You also benefit directly from your success. The fruits of your labors belong to you. You can take as much or as little out of your business as you choose. And you're untethered from the economic ups and downs—and whims—of a traditional employer. You make, and reap, the financial rewards of your own hard work.

Challenges

You'll inevitably confront and surmount a number of challenges on your entrepreneurial journey. Among other challenges, you'll need to find ways to manage the following realities.

YOU'LL FACE RISK

There's a chance—a very good chance—that whatever business or enterprise you start may fail. Reports of the percentage of entrepreneurial failures are often overstated, but nevertheless there's a high likelihood that you'll end up having to (or choosing to) close up shop. With failure comes loss—loss of pride, loss of time, financial loss. The stress of dealing with a failing business puts tremendous strains on personal and professional relationships. Your family may not understand the pressure you're under. You may have friends and family who have invested their money, and their hopes, in you, and they may not be as understanding or patient as you'd like. And you may feel guilt and shame at disappointing them. Failure is never easy.

Even when you don't fail, you have a greater sense of risk in an entrepreneurial undertaking than by being someone else's employee. Sure, you may get laid off from a job, but generally, there isn't the day-to-day understanding of the reality of risk as there is when you own a business. And when you're the one in charge, especially when you have others dependent on you for their livelihood, this can put you under a tremendous amount of pressure.

YOU'LL DEAL WITH FINANCIAL INSTABILITY

When you own a business, expect your income to fluctuate considerably. Frequently, business owners experience an economic roller coaster, with great highs and deep lows in income. This is far different than having the comfort of a steady paycheck. What you sell to customers or bill clients is what you get. You'll inevitably experience dry spells or go through times when your resources are stretched. And you may need to look beyond your own means for the cash to grow your business or even to keep your doors open if times get tough.

Moreover, when you have employees, you get paid last. By law, you must pay employees what you owe them—and by ethics, you'd want to make sure you're paying your employees on time. That means that when the coffers are low, you're the one who has to make do, who goes without a paycheck, who gives up income.

And you don't get benefits. Want a vacation? Sure, you can take one anytime you like, but it's not a "paid vacation." While you're away, you lose any income you would have made. Need health care insurance? When you start your own business, you have the same kind of decisions to make as the largest publicly traded companies: What kind of health benefits will you be able to afford—both for yourself and for any others you employ? Which insurance company (or companies) will provide them? How will you fund these benefits? Likewise for retirement savings—both your own and for any employees. Will you contribute to a 401(k) plan?

YOU'LL WORK HARD AND DRIVE YOURSELF

This is a given of the entrepreneurial life: Self-employed individuals tend to work longer hours than the typical employee. There's no such thing as a "typical" workday—you'll often find yourself working nights and weekends, on family holidays, during vacations. You don't get paid for the time you're not working. This means that you will lose revenue for each day you

REAL-WORLD RECAP

Challenges of entrepreneurship

- **You'll face risk**
- **You'll deal with financial instability**
- **You'll work hard and drive yourself**
- **You must cope with constant change**
- **The buck stops with you**

are sick and for vacation days, so it's likely you'll find yourself taking fewer days away from work. Moreover, many entrepreneurs have to continue doing their "day" jobs until their entrepreneurial ventures are established. So expect long hours for many years.

You also have to be a self-sufficient worker. You must be a disciplined self-starter. No one assigns you tasks—that may seem liberating at first, but it may also feel burdensome when you don't know which way to turn. Depending on the type of business you start, you may be working on your own most of the time. You won't have the traditional "network" of coworkers to turn to for support or assistance. If your computer breaks down, you'll have to figure out how to get it up and running again—either yourself or by hiring outside help. You'll either do your own books or find a good accountant. And you won't have the built-in social structure of the traditional workplace.

YOU MUST COPE WITH CONSTANT CHANGE

The one constant you face is change. And just when you think you have everything under control, something new will come along—count on it. You'll need to develop your capacity for rolling with the punches. Nimble companies that can quickly evaluate and respond to changing conditions will most likely succeed.

Therefore, you must be a fast learner. Unless you're a most unusual person, you will be largely jumping into the great unknown when you start your business. You may have a deep understanding of your professional field— nursing or engineering or culinary arts—yet it's a given that you will be confronted regularly with unanticipated challenges. Your ability to learn the ropes and pick up on things quickly will be one of the prime determinants of your success.

THE BUCK STOPS WITH YOU

As an entrepreneur, you'll be faced with a constant barrage of decisions you need to make—how much to charge a customer? how much to pay an employee? what kind of equipment to purchase? where to locate your office? what new products to develop? which ones to phase out? And on and on.

Good entrepreneurs learn how to delegate many decisions to others, yet at the end of the day the final decisions always rest with you. You establish and maintain the company culture. You are the final voice on all major or critical decisions. Your choices are the ones that matter most. Being in charge is a huge burden.

Your Goals, Ideas, and Vision

Now that you have a general understanding of entrepreneurs and entrepreneurship, it's time to take a closer look at your own motivations and vision. *Why* do you want to be an entrepreneur, and what *kind* of entrepreneur do you want to be? When you think of creating your own company, what do you envision that company to be?

The Four Cs

When you start out, it's important to understand your personal goals. Some entrepreneurial ventures fail and others flounder precisely because their founders or executives are uncertain of what they really want to achieve. They don't structure the company and their responsibilities in ways that satisfy their personal needs and ambitions.

Most entrepreneurs' personal goals can be summed up by the Four Cs: *creativity, control, challenge,* and *cash.* Of course, everyone wants all four of these, to some degree, but knowing which ones you most want or need can help you structure your company to best achieve your goals.

Which of the Four Cs motivates you most?

- **Creativity.** Entrepreneurs want to leave their mark. Their companies provide not only a means of making a living but also a way for them to create something that bears their stamp. Creativity comes in many forms, from designing a new "thing" to devising a new business process or even coming up with an innovative way to make sales, handle customers, or reward employees.

  If you have a high need for creativity, make certain you remain involved in the creative process as your company develops. You'll want to shape your business so it's not simply an instrument for earning an income, but beyond that a way for maintaining your creative stimulation and making a larger contribution to society. But don't overpersonalize your company, especially if it's large. Allow room for others, particularly partners and key personnel, to share in the creative process.

- **Control.** Many people start businesses because they want more control over their lives. Perhaps you'd like more control over the way your good ideas are implemented. Maybe you want, or need, greater control over your work hours or conditions so that you can be more involved in family, community, or hobbies. Control is a major motivation for most entrepreneurs—usually more important than money. But how much control you need—especially day to day—directly influences how large your company can be.

  If you need or want a great deal of control over your time, you'll most likely need to keep your company smaller. In a large company, you have less immediate control over many decisions. If you're a person who

What's your chance of success?

When you start a business, you'll often hear one statistic repeated over and over: "Fifty percent of all new businesses fail within five years." The facts are actually somewhat different.

About 50 percent of all new businesses still exist after five years, and about 50 percent will have closed. Those may have closed for many reasons: The owner found a good job, moved, decided to pursue another line of business, and so on. "Failure"—meaning the business couldn't make a profit—may have been only one of many causes.

needs control, you can still grow your business larger. You'll simply need to structure communication and reporting systems to ensure that you have sufficient information about and direction over developments, thus meeting your needs. If you seek outside funding in the form of investors, understand the nature of control your funders will exert and be certain you're comfortable with these arrangements.

- **Challenge.** If you're starting or expanding a business, it's clear you like challenge—at least to some degree. You're likely a problem-solver and risk-taker, enjoying the tasks of figuring out solutions to problems or devising new undertakings. Challenge-hungry entrepreneurs can be some of the most successful businesspeople, but they can also be their own worst enemies—flitting from one thing to another, never focusing on one long enough to succeed.

  If you have a high need for challenge in your business life, it's important to develop positive means to meet this need, especially once your company is established and you've met the initial challenge of starting a company. Otherwise, you may find yourself continually starting new projects that divert attention from your company's main goals. As you plan your company, establish goals that not only provide you with sufficient stimulation but also advance—rather than distract from—the growth of your business.

- **Cash.** Every entrepreneur wants to make money. Perhaps it's just enough money to provide a decent income; perhaps it's so much money that you can buy a jet. How much you want, or need, affects how you'll develop your business. Will you require investors and, if so, when? Will you sacrifice control to grow the business quickly?

Keep in mind there are trade-offs between personal goals. For example, wanting more cash often means having less control, while staying at the center of the creative process can necessitate having a partner or growing slowly—once again trading off control or cash.

The size of your vision

Once you've considered the Four Cs, you must continue to define other aspects of your vision. A good way to proceed is to identify how large a business you hope to launch—and how big you intend it to become. You have several options.

SELF-EMPLOYMENT

The greatest number of all businesses fit into this classification. These are one-person ventures that provide critical income for the entrepreneur—and often the *only* source of income for the entrepreneur's family.

Solo sustainer businesses represent the classic self-employment business model—frequently called "sole proprietorships." These businesses are owned by one person and are typically nonincorporated. Self-employed accountants, physicians, and others who provide professional services fall into this category.

BUILD-YOUR-BUSINESS WORKSHEET

The Four Cs

Use this worksheet to help determine which of the Four Cs are the most important to you.

	Extremely Important	Somewhat Important	Somewhat Unimportant	Not Important
CREATIVITY				
Determining the design or look of products/packaging	☐	☐	☐	☐
Creating new products or services	☐	☐	☐	☐
Devising new business procedures/policies	☐	☐	☐	☐
Identifying new company opportunities	☐	☐	☐	☐
Creating new business materials	☐	☐	☐	☐
Devising new ways of doing "old" things	☐	☐	☐	☐

Other: _____

	Extremely Important	Somewhat Important	Somewhat Unimportant	Not Important
CONTROL				
Over own work responsibilities	☐	☐	☐	☐
Over own time, work hours, etc.	☐	☐	☐	☐
Over company decisions and directions	☐	☐	☐	☐
Over products/services	☐	☐	☐	☐
Over other employees	☐	☐	☐	☐
Over work environment	☐	☐	☐	☐
Over social/environmental impact of products/services	☐	☐	☐	☐
Over own future and business's future	☐	☐	☐	☐

Other:_____

	Extremely Important	Somewhat Important	Somewhat Unimportant	Not Important
CHALLENGE				
Long-term problem solving	☐	☐	☐	☐
Critical problem solving ("putting out fires")	☐	☐	☐	☐
Handling many issues at one time	☐	☐	☐	☐
Continually dealing with new issues	☐	☐	☐	☐
Perfecting solutions, products, or services	☐	☐	☐	☐
Organizing diverse projects & keeping the group goal-focused	☐	☐	☐	☐

Other: _____

CASH

List approximate dollar ranges for each of the following. Measure wealth as the value of stocks or the company.

Income needed currently_____   Wealth desired in 2–5 years_____

Income desired within 12–24 months_____   Wealth desired in 6–10 years_____

Income desired in 2–5 years _____   Wealth desired in 10+ years_____

Businesses in the self-employment group share these characteristics:

■ Income from the business is critical to maintaining the lifestyle of the entrepreneurs and their families.

■ The entrepreneur generally works alone (or sometimes with the aid of part-time administrative assistants or independent service providers, such as attorneys, IT consultants, webmasters, and bookkeepers).

■ The business generates current income for the entrepreneur, rather than creating ongoing income streams that could continue even if the entrepreneur were to leave the business.

In other words, in solo sustainer businesses, the business sustains the entrepreneur, while the entrepreneur sustains the business. Once the entrepreneur stops working, the business stops—period. In essence, the entrepreneur is the "product" that the company sells, and is the sole income generator for the business. There is no "business" independent of the entrepreneur.

SMALL BUSINESS

When someone uses the term "small business," they usually mean a business that's intended to grow to a reasonably healthy size and stay there. The goals of the venture's founders typically include:

■ The business is designed to be a career for the owner.

■ The business also provides jobs for others.

■ The business is designed to produce ongoing, annual income for the entrepreneur.

■ The business may be capable of building value independent of, and lasting longer than, the entrepreneur's personal involvement.

■ The business is small enough for the owner to be able to control it, yet big enough to be able to support growth.

Ideally, a business like this will develop value in addition to the annual income it produces for the owner and the paychecks it generates for employees. With good planning and development, many of these businesses can be sold to others when it comes time for the entrepreneur to retire. They can also be passed down to family members or employees. Most independent, one- or two-location businesses fall into this category, such as restaurants, construction companies, auto repair shops and dealerships, retail stores, and small business or personal service firms.

Smaller businesses such as these may seem far less exciting than high-growth start-ups, although they're also less risky. They tend to use proven business models, and they can reach out to established support networks, such as industry associations and consultants, for assistance.

HIGH-GROWTH START-UPS

The entrepreneur who starts this kind of venture has a different kind of ambition than those who launch other types of businesses. Yes, they may start small, but their vision doesn't stop there. These entrepreneurs have plans to grow *big*. Their goal is to develop a company that will expand into a major enterprise—one worth many millions of dollars. They envision a company so substantial that perhaps it will become a household name, with publicly traded stock. Or they may hope that an even larger corporation might acquire the business in the future.

Google founders Larry Page and Sergey Brin right from the beginning hoped to make it really big by creating search technology that would harness the chaos that was the early Internet. Ray Kroc saw the possibilities in a small hamburger-franchise and grew the McDonald's empire from a single burger stand, based on his vision of applying mass production concepts to a service industry (food preparation). And every day, venture capitalists are presented with business plans from would-be entrepreneurs whose definitions of success go well beyond merely earning a decent living.

High-growth start-ups are the types of new companies that get a lot of press. They are exciting, innovative businesses that aspire to new heights and strive to break new ground. They're also risky. Since an entrepreneur creating a visionary venture wants to build a company with huge potential, they often have to put personal considerations—such as the business's ability to generate current income for them or provide them with financial stability—second to the need to find a concept that can support the growth of a large enterprise.

Because visionary ventures inevitably involve finding and securing big markets—or developing new products or technologies—they typically require a great deal of money to get started. This means that the entrepreneur not only has to spend a lot of time seeking financing, but they also will probably need to give up a significant portion of the company's ownership to investors.

Your business vision

Now that you've determined the level of importance of each of the Four Cs, and figured out which of them suits you, you can start thinking at a fairly high level about the type of company you want to build and run.

- **How big a company do you want to build?** As you begin to think about your business, keep in mind that the business itself may dictate the size. Some people deliberately keep their business vision small: They want to be sole proprietors and have no interest in employing others or growing a business that requires more than their particular input. Those with professional skills like accounting or business consulting often fall into this category. Big ideas often require big companies to make them come to fruition. It would be impossible to run a furniture manufacturer that has mass-market reach with just three employees. A lot of this comes back

Social responsibility and social entrepreneurship

Increasingly, entrepreneurs want to achieve more than simply profits with their companies. They want to do something positive for the environment or for humanity. Where once they might have formed a nonprofit organization, they now want to harness the energy and efficiencies of a profit motive to achieve positive social goals. See Chapter 17 for more on this topic.

to control. It's hard to maintain a high degree of control over a larger company—although some people certainly try.

■ **Do you want to work by yourself or with others?** This is a critical question. You may be a self-sufficient type who prefers being in control of every aspect of your business over delegating responsibility or partnering with others. Or you may be gregarious and socially inclined and need others to support you, to bounce ideas off, and to socialize with. Or your business may absolutely require others with complementary skills to make it a success. Your preferences in this regard will determine the type of business you'll start.

■ **What business values or corporate culture do you want to create?** What's important to you about the nature of the business you build? How will you treat your employees? Interact with your community? Relate to the world in general? What code of ethical conduct will you adhere to when doing business? Management style plays into this: You may prefer a buttoned-down, traditional workplace. Or you might want to foster a more fun environment that includes scooters, video games, and even nap rooms. Here's where your commitment to socially responsible behavior comes into play, as does your vision of how you want to be viewed by others in your organization. Do you want to create a role for yourself as a traditional authoritarian boss or to nurture a more collaborative, "flat" organizational culture? Some companies are committed to valuing families, allowing four-day workweeks and guaranteeing that employees can leave at 5 p.m. Your business values represent an important aspect of your business vision.

■ **What are your business skills?** What are your leadership and management qualities or other personality traits that stand you in good stead when pursuing your passion? Do a careful inventory of your business skills at this point, because it will determine whether and how you should bring in other individuals to complement your skills, or what additional education or training you need if you hope to go it alone. Can you motivate others? Can you communicate well? Are you willing to learn these skills if you don't currently possess them? Keep in mind that your inventory of business skills should include not only the ones you have now, but also the vital ones you're willing to work on or develop.

From dream to reality

If you're like most entrepreneurs, you probably have many dreams for your future. Dreaming is vital. The first step in starting your business is to be able to imagine a new reality. It can be a truly unique reality: a zero-emission sports car such as the Tesla, for example. Or it can be a down-to-earth reality: starting a retail auto-parts company that enables you to earn a decent living while creating respectable, long-term jobs for your employees.

BUILD-YOUR-BUSINESS WORKSHEET

Your Business Vision

Now it's time to focus on the vision you have for your business. After completing this exercise, you will have a better idea of what your business goals are and what you need to do to achieve them.

How big a company do you want to build? _____

_____

Do you want to work by yourself or with others? _____

_____

What are your business values? What kind of corporate culture do you want to create? _____

_____

_____

_____

_____

_____

_____

Which of your leadership or management qualities or other personality traits will stand you in good stead when pursu-

ing this passion? _____

_____

_____

_____

_____

_____

_____

What business skills are you willing to develop to make your venture a success? _____

_____

_____

_____

_____

_____

_____

_____

Most—if not all—successful businesses start with a dream. Yet there's a difference between those who merely dream and those who make their entrepreneurial dreams come true.

The steps that move from dream to reality make up the entrepreneur's "dream scale"—from the least-achievable stage of dreaming to the most achievable and action-oriented one.

1. **Fantasy.** These concepts are impossible or highly unrealistic to achieve. Hucksters make fortunes off people who fantasize about getting rich in their spare time. Whether it's an infomercial, a weekend real-estate seminar, or a multilevel marketing program, what most of these people sell is the fantasy that you can make money without hard work or risk. Most of these schemes drain money and time away from achievable goals, such as going back to school or starting a realistic business.

2. **Dream.** Although these concepts are potentially achievable, at this stage, you see only the positive side. Most people have a dream business they'd like to run—a bed-and-breakfast, a wine bar, a fantastically successful social-networking site. Are these fantasies? No. Some people *do* run delightful B&Bs on Cape Cod; others start Facebook or Twitter. However, the reality is that it's very difficult and expensive to succeed at most of these businesses. But at this stage, all you see is the upside.

3. **Concept.** At this stage, you have achievable ideas but you also bring the downsides and difficulties of your dream into focus. You're willing to challenge your own assumptions and the claims of those who promise to make your dreams come true. You're not afraid to look at the costs, limitations, or work required, and you're willing to begin evaluating realistically your chances of success.

4. **Goals.** At this stage, you make a specific, realistic evaluation of what you personally want to achieve and what you're willing to sacrifice to achieve it. Even practical visions involve trade-offs: If you want a large business, you may need investors who would exercise some or all the control over your company. Make sure you're comfortable with these trade-offs.

5. **Business plan.** Finally, you're ready to develop a thorough, thoughtful, step-by-step road map to success. This is where you actually figure out how to make your vision and goals a reality. You examine your industry, study the competition, and research your market. You identify the best strategies for success and detail your action items, milestones, marketing, and operations. This is your business road map. For more on business plans, see Chapter 4.

BUILD-YOUR-BUSINESS WORKSHEET

Moving from Dream to Reality

Using your business idea, fill out the following worksheet to distinguish the achievable from the dream.

Business Idea: _____

Stage	Description	Details
Fantasy	Difficult-to-achieve concepts	
Dream	Achievable, but you only see the upside	
Concept	Closer look at costs, limitation, work required, and chances of success	
Goals	Realistic evaluation of what you really want	

Entrepreneurs Make a Difference

Finally, most people who choose the entrepreneurial life wouldn't have it any other way. They recognize how difficult it can be; they may complain about the number of hours they put in, the vacations they've missed; they may have suffered the ups and downs of income. Their business—or businesses—may even have failed. But in the end, they're sustained by how engaging and challenging being an entrepreneur can be.

As you start on your entrepreneurial journey, aim to make a difference. Businesses only succeed when they meet a real need. Yet those needs can be petty and small: Think of those who've created reality shows about housewives in New Jersey. Instead, look to fill needs that are important; make your contribution positive. Do something—create something—that has an impact. It doesn't have to be world-changing. You need not invent a miracle medical device or devise a way to feed the world's poor. But whatever you choose to do, try to make a beneficial impact on the world you inhabit.

Entrepreneurs change the world—*you can be one of them.*

CHAPTER 2

Opportunity Identification and Feasibility Analysis

learning objectives

In this chapter, you'll learn how to:

- Understand the factors that contribute to a successful business concept

- Identify the factors that differentiate a company from its competitors

- Distinguish between a practical, viable business and a highly successful one

- Recognize business opportunities within specific industries

- Articulate a concept for an actual business

- Choose a business model

- Conduct a feasibility analysis—the opportunity to ask yourself some tough questions, and to modify, refocus, or change your idea if necessary

- Develop a product prototype

The Successful Business Concept

The basis of all business is meeting needs and wants. You can devise a wonderful new product, or create a fantastic new service, but if it doesn't address some real and, ideally, important need or desire, people won't buy it and inevitably, your business will fail. Even Thomas Edison recognized this fact when he said, "Anything that won't sell, I don't want to invent."

Of course, great companies have been built on what seems to be totally new ideas—things that people didn't know they needed or wanted until someone created them. No one knew that it would be absolutely critical to walk around with 10,000 songs available at all times until the invention of the iPod, right? Yet, there had been MP3 players before that, and Sony Walkmans even earlier. Indeed, the desire for music is as old as humankind. What the iPod represented was a substantially improved, enjoyable, and intuitive way to meet a longstanding need and wish for music-on-demand.

Some entrepreneurial businesses turn out to be far more successful than others. What sets those apart? What do highly successful companies do—or seize on—that gives them greater growth?

A company is more than its concept. Success also depends on a concept's execution—management, marketing, financial management, and many other operational considerations. Increasingly, however, a company's values and corporate culture contribute to its long-term viability and its appeal to customers and employees alike.

Factors of a successful business concept

As you develop your business concept, keep in mind that successful businesses incorporate at least one of the following factors that are basic to a successful business concept.

■ **Innovation.** The most exciting, and often most risky, entrepreneurial companies are innovative companies. They bring something to the market that either is new or significantly alters and improves on an existing offering. It can mean developing and deploying new technology. But more often, it involves building on an existing product or service, or improving on it, or finding a new use for it. For example, search engines existed long before Google. The company's founders, Larry Page and Sergey Brin, came up with a new, more effective way of ranking search results (an algorithm based on how many other pages linked to a page and their importance) that searchers found more reliable. Innovation is not limited to technology. Many successful companies innovate in low-tech, no-tech, or services industries.

■ **Underserved or new market.** Many entrepreneurial companies succeed by bringing a proven product or service to a market for which there is greater demand than competitors can currently satisfy, establishing a location that has been overlooked by competitors, or identifying a market that has not yet been served or dominated by a competitor. These can be new markets, such as introducing a product or service to a new country. At other times, markets are growing, and there just aren't enough competitors in the same geographic location. Markets can also become underserved when large

Better, faster, cheaper

In business, "better, faster, cheaper" is the mantra for how to differentiate your product or service from other similar products or services. (In the high-tech industry, it's often "smaller, faster, cheaper" because more-compact size is highly desirable in components.)

The beauty of this mantra is its simplicity: People indeed always look for a better, cheaper product. And "faster" can apply to how the product works or performs, or how a customer gets it, or how quickly you get it to market.

Remember this phrase as you assess the viability of a business opportunity. In other words, ask yourself: Will your product be better, faster, or cheaper than the competition's?

en·tre·pre·neur·ship **key terms**

B2B
A business that sells a product or service to another business, either for that company's own use or for that company to resell to consumers.

B2C
A business that sells a product or service directly to the consumer or end user.

Business model
Describes what a company does and the structure it puts into place to make money. Business models include designing and manufacturing a product that is sold to other businesses (B2B); providing access to a software application online and selling it on a subscription basis; or providing a marketplace online for people to sell their products or services and charging a commission on sales.

Feasibility analysis
A preliminary study undertaken to determine whether something is viable, and whether to proceed.

Niche
A specialized, clearly identifiable group within a larger target market that a company chooses to focus on and serve.

Prototype
The initial design that will become the standard for your production.

Shared ownership model
With this type of business model, a company provides a product, a service, or information to a group of customers who do not need access to the commodity so frequently that they need or want to own their own personal version. In other words, several people "share" one commodity.

companies abandon or neglect smaller portions of their current customer base. Sometimes an innovative company leads the way and others follow once the innovators have built or created customer demand. This often leads to "me-too" businesses that can achieve remarkable success. For example, after SuperCuts built acceptance for low-cost hair services, other companies, such as Great Clips, came in and followed on that success. Great Clips now has more than twice as many locations as SuperCuts.

■ **Lower price.** Customers often are tempted by lower cost options, and being a low-cost leader is a time-honored strategy for a business concept. Unless you have some sort of strategic advantage, though, such as a unique production or distribution method, secret supply sources, or arrangements with partners that make your own costs *consistently* lower, this can be a strategy difficult to sustain in the long term. If your only key differentiator is that you provide a cheaper product or service, it is fairly easy for someone else to beat you at your own game. SuperCuts, for instance, was able to be profitable with low-cost hair care services because it standardized procedures, enabling the company to serve customers faster and with lower-paid stylists, thus giving it an ongoing cost advantage.

■ **Higher quality.** Often innovation comes in the form of higher, or different, quality. An entrepreneur may recognize an opportunity because of a lack of high-quality offerings in an otherwise robust market, or may notice customers expressing dissatisfaction with current options. For example, many people like the convenience and price of fast food, but often find it not terribly healthy. In 1993, Steve Ells, a culinary-taught chef working at one of the best restaurants in America, decided to open a fast food Mexican restaurant based on high-quality, often organic, ingredients. His company—Chipotle—became the forerunner of a new trend in the prepared food industry, later reaching a market value of over $10 billion.

■ **Convenience.** Making a product or service available in a more convenient way for customers can create a viable business opportunity. A neighborhood hardware store might have higher prices, say, or a mobile pet-grooming service that goes to pet owners' homes might provide the same products or services as a storefront service but far more conveniently, thereby attracting and retaining customers. Enterprise Rent-A-Car, for example, picks up customers at their residence or place of business, for free. This added convenience sets Enterprise apart from the competition.

■ **Service.** A number of highly successful companies seized business opportunities made possible by the opportunity to provide better service than competitors. "Better service" can be defined in various ways. The obvious way is to give customers more personal attention—the department store Nordstrom, for one, has staked out a competitive advantage based on its high quality of service, particularly its return policy and its ample sales staff. Another type of better service is to take care of customers faster. FedEx founder Fred Smith pioneered a way to deliver mail and packages overnight—thus combining service with innovation.

■ **New delivery system or distribution channel.** Often, you don't need to sell anything much better or differently than your competitors—you simply have to sell it by different methods or through different channels. Some successful companies have been founded by creating or using new sales channels. Tupperware pioneered in-home parties to sell food storage containers. One of the earliest companies to see the possibilities in the Internet as a sales channel was Amazon.com. Because wholesale book distribution companies already existed that could deliver individual copies of books to customers, Amazon did not need to buy inventory to open what it claimed to be "the world's largest bookstore." Amazon leveraged that operational advantage to use a new channel to reach customers.

■ **Increased integration.** Integration refers to a situation where a company controls more steps in the design, production, and sale of its product or services rather than relying on outside suppliers. This can create a competitive advantage because it gives the company more power to oversee the quality at every stage of a product's life, and also because there may be increased profit margins. Vertical integration may be particularly useful for companies that want to gain a competitive advantage based on quality—such as Apple or Starbucks, both companies that maintain control over more stages of design, production, and sales than other electronics companies or coffee shops. Still, it is often difficult for one company to manage all the various functions well, and often vertically integrated companies do not benefit from suppliers' ingenuity or cost-cutting methods.

Characteristics of *highly* successful businesses

You know you have a great business idea—but does it have the potential to become *highly successful*? You may be satisfied with running a one-person show that provides a comfortable income. But if you have dreams of a company that will become a household name, employ thousands of well-paid workers, make an initial public offering (IPO) of company stock, and make you rich, your business should have *most* of the following traits:

■ **Compelling, executable business idea.** The basis for the business itself must be rock-solid. You must have a truly effective and impressive product or service that fills a real need in the market. And you must be able to build a business around it, over a reasonable period, with a reasonable amount of money.

■ **Large market and potential for high or rapid growth.** Certain businesses that you could come up with might offer a great product or service and become successful enough to provide a very high income for you. But you need to have a sizable and expanding market to grow large, as well as to attract the kind of investment you'll require to expand. If you want to be the next Google, you need investors, and they will look for a speedy, high return on the funds they put into your business.

If you build it, will they come?

One of the biggest mistakes entrepreneurs make is focusing more on their product or service than on understanding their customers. You could have what you think is the coolest new idea on the planet, but if no one is interested in buying it, then you don't have a business.

During the Internet boom of the late '90s, Webvan's concept of delivering virtually everything to people's homes—from groceries to prescriptions, dry cleaning, and movie rentals—seemed like a brilliant one, and it received over three-quarters of a billion dollars in funding!

It turned out that customers were used to going to their favorite grocery store and liked picking out their own produce and meat; not enough of them were willing to pay for the convenience of delivery. The company's demise was one of the most spectacular during the so-called "dot-com bust."

- **Growing industry.** You'll have far better luck building a highly successful company in a healthy, growing industry than in one that is flat or shrinking. Yes, some businesses do grow significantly in old, mature industries, but it's easier to grow when your industry is growing too.

- **It's a business, not just a product.** Many would-be entrepreneurs dream up great ideas and devise wonderful new products. But some are destined to be "inventors," not "entrepreneurs." Often, one good product idea is not sufficient to support an entire business. A song is a product and may have a short shelf-life; a music publishing company is a business, in for the long haul.

- **Capable entrepreneur and strong team.** One of the most important contributors to business success is a company's management. Being a visionary entrepreneur, or having one at your right hand, isn't enough; you have to be able to assemble a quality team, capable of both developing the product and managing the company.

- **Original idea, but not completely new one.** Most widely successful companies build on concepts and markets pioneered by others. But why not just implement your own truly new and groundbreaking concept? Because a novel product or invention typically requires a very large budget, to educate customers on how the concept works and why they need it. That takes time and money, so sometimes it pays *not* to be first. Many people have become fabulously wealthy by letting the first or second company in the market invest in developing demand and proving the concept—and *then* coming up with an improved version.

A company's values and integrity

Every company must make money. You can't stay in business unless you eventually earn a profit. Yet studies of business success over time have shown that companies that emphasize goals in addition to making money succeed better, and survive longer, than companies whose sole motivation is profit.

As you develop your business concept, keep in mind those values that you want your company to embody. These values can be aimed externally, at achieving some business, social, or environmental goal. Or they can be aimed internally, at creating a certain type of workplace or quality of product or service. Or they can be aimed at both.

Articulating your company's values to employees, suppliers, and even your customers can strengthen their commitment to your business. Values-driven companies often achieve greater success in attracting and retaining good employees, and they can usually better weather short-term financial setbacks because employees and management share a commitment to goals in addition to financial rewards.

A company is likewise strengthened by maintaining integrity in all aspects of its dealings—with employees, customers, suppliers, and the community. Certainly, you will face situations where it appears that you will be at a disadvantage if you're more honest than your competitors or fairer than other employers. Nevertheless, the long-term benefits of earning and keeping a reputation for integrity outweigh the perceived immediate disadvantages. A clear policy of honesty and fairness makes decision-making in difficult situations easier, inspires customer and employee loyalty, and helps avoid costly lawsuits and regulatory fines. It's also the right thing to do.

Recognizing Business Opportunities

Business opportunities are all around you. You may be impatiently standing in line waiting for a service, or frustratingly using a product you think is inferior, or working for a big corporation you feel overlooks potential customers, and suddenly you realize—"there must be a better way." And there's your business opportunity.

Interestingly, most solid, profitable businesses are developed from rather mundane ideas. While it might take a Levi Strauss to invent blue jeans or a Steve Jobs and Steve Wozniak to create a personal computer, many other businesses are required for selling jeans or providing services, software, and components for computers. That could lead you to start a company like the Gap (which began by only selling Levi's) or Adobe Software (used by scads of graphic designers who also loved Mac computers). Many great business opportunities are to be found building on others' concepts, and they do not require strikingly new ideas.

Granted, if you're looking for a huge investment from professional venture capital firms, you'll probably need a big, bold, market-changing idea. Those ideas create and change industries, and economies depend on entrepreneurial inventiveness. If you've got a great, new idea, you may be able to change the world.

But you don't have to be the most inventive or original person to become a highly successful entrepreneur. Planning a business around a totally new concept can be more risky than building an enterprise on more commonplace possibilities. After all, many business opportunities lie out there.

What is a business opportunity?

A business opportunity occurs when you see a chance to provide a product, service, or information to other people. What you provide can be something new. Or it can be a better or cheaper version of an existing product or service, or just a more convenient way of delivering an existing product or service. In its most basic form, an opportunity means that something is missing from current market choices, and that circumstances are ripe for taking advantage of that lack.

Are you an industry insider?

Precisely because they are so immersed in a particular product or service industry, some people see opportunities that others less familiar with the territory would miss. For example, no one would be in a better position to know what types of new kitchen utensils would be useful for restaurants than a working chef. Likewise, a manager of rock bands might see the need for better software to track bookings and billings than would a software engineer. No matter what your industry or area of expertise, you should be constantly looking to spot these kinds of opportunities.

Lots of business opportunities exist, but that doesn't mean they're all viable. To be viable, an opportunity must lead to a sustainable business, one that

1. Is profitable, that is, it can bring in more money than it costs to operate

2. Reaps profits of sufficient volume to meet your financial goals

There are a lot of business ideas that simply can't be made profitable, or that are profitable but don't generate sufficient income to support the entrepreneur, much less employees. This is frequently the case for solo inventors or craftspeople, who may create a small and much-needed or desirable product or service but find the market too small or too expensive to reach to generate enough revenue to make producing it worthwhile.

Where does inspiration come from?

In looking at where business ideas come from, entrepreneurs usually report that their business inspiration came from one or more of the following.

- **Previous work experience.** Many entrepreneurs get their inspiration when they realize that they could offer something new or better in a field they already know. Often they've worked in a company where they've felt frustrated that their employer has not responded to changing conditions or has neglected customers. The better you know an industry, a product, or a market, the more likely you may realize how you can fill an unmet need. Consider some of the needs of former customers that weren't met, some of the skills you developed that might be transferable to another industry, or some things your former employers did poorly that you think you could do much better.

- **Hobbies or personal interests.** Many people dream of turning their hobby or interests into a business. As with previous work experience, being involved with a personal interest often sparks ideas for businesses. There may be a product or service you wish you had; you may recognize that there are products or services you want that are not conveniently or affordably available. You might even have already made contacts at suppliers, identified potential customers, or found good distribution channels. Moreover, you know you like your idea, and you may be able to work in an environment you enjoy (whether it's outdoors, or in foreign locations, or in a space close to home where you can take your dog to work). Inevitably, though, having to earn money doing something changes the way you feel about it. Before you forge ahead with a business based on a hobby, examine the pros and cons.

- **Someone else's work experience.** Often the work experience of a family member or close friend can spark an idea. Familiarity with an industry or existing business gives you some knowledge of potential opportunities, just as your own work experience or hobbies do.

- **Systematic research.** Activities such as undertaking market research or attending business opportunity seminars have sparked ideas for a number of entrepreneurs. For example, you may be interested in a growth field such as green energy. To start a new business in the field, you could immerse yourself in data and information to discover what's needed or missing.

■ **An "Aha!" moment.** Most of us have at some time in our life encountered a personal need, a business situation, or an idea when fiddling around with equipment or technology, and instantly thought up a way to approach it better. Of course, most "Aha!" moments are likely based on past experience and expertise, even though we may not be consciously aware of the connection at the time.

It's helpful to learn about where other successful entrepreneurs got their inspiration, but that doesn't mean it will determine your path. Thousands of different kinds of businesses, products, and **niches** beckon you when you widen your horizons. Be assured that every industry in every sector has opportunities for entrepreneurs like you.

Opportunities in old industries

New industries clearly offer a great many business opportunities that attract entrepreneurs. After all, they're exciting and they're in the news. Because new industries often grow rapidly, opportunities abound for innovative businesses and brand-new concepts.

But, old industries also often hold entrepreneurial opportunities. Here's why: As industries age, big corporations tend to dominate them. That should mean it's extremely hard to compete in old industries. And it is, usually. However, once these big companies get huge, they often start to neglect or eliminate some of their smaller—but still profitable—customers or market niches.

Huge corporations regularly jettison customers, product lines, or even entire divisions that don't meet certain revenue levels—often in the tens or even hundreds of millions of dollars. Or, as companies expand, they develop increasingly bureaucratic procedures that alienate many of their long-time customers. Yet that doesn't mean those customers or product lines couldn't be profitable for smaller, hungrier companies.

For example, when the first supermarkets opened in the '30s and '40s, these stores, relatively small by today's standards, bought out local grocers, bakeries, and butcher shops, often shutting down neighborhood stores. The trend toward consolidation continued throughout the '50s and '60s, and as more and more people moved to the suburbs, increasingly large supermarkets sprang up there to serve them. The dawn of the "superstore" in the '70s and '80s led to the rise of big discount stores, such as Walmart and Target, and some of these stores eventually carried groceries as well, eliminating more neighborhood grocers. This consolidation of supermarkets, which continues today, has created opportunity for more specialty grocery stores, both large, such as Trader Joe's and Whole Foods, and small, such as bakeries, butcher shops, farmers markets, and other innovative food suppliers, like CSAs (community supported agriculture that delivers organic food directly

REAL-WORLD RECAP

Where does inspiration come from?

■ Previous work experience

■ Hobbies or personal interests

■ Someone else's work experience

■ Systematic research

■ An "Aha!" moment

to homes)—many of the types of stores that supermarkets put out of business decades before.

Apply technology in non-technology industries and markets

New technologies often create whole new industries, leading to an explosion of new businesses. Whenever a technology or device is invented—let's say television, the computer, or the Internet—the first, often huge, business opportunities come from making and selling those specific technologies. The second wave comes from making and selling peripheral products or support services for those technologies.

But there's a third wave of very real business opportunities—when entrepreneurs begin to make, sell, and implement those new technologies in processes and equipment for specific industries. For example, the first wave of "cloud"-based applications (applications based in the Internet) was designed for the general corporate market (such as Salesforce CRM, an Internet-based customer relationship application) or for the general consumer market (such as Google Docs). Then, entrepreneurs seized on these new technologies to develop cloud-based solutions for specific industries, creating many new successful businesses.

Traditional to entrepreneurial

Virtually any skill that has historically been harnessed to fulfill a traditional job can be turned into an entrepreneurial venture. Here are some examples of how traditional jobs and skills can be applied to entrepreneurial goals.

TRADITIONAL JOB/HOBBY	ENTREPRENEURIAL APPLICATION
Skilled cook/baker	Open a restaurant, bakery, catering company; start a line of specialty food products
Associate in law firm	Set up a legal practice; develop software for the legal industry in an area you see as lacking
Fashion salesperson or apparel buyer	Start a clothing design or manufacturing company; create a website to sell apparel
Engineer in large manufacturing company	Found a start-up based on a new idea in your field; become a consultant to manufacturing companies
Sports enthusiast	Develop new equipment for your sport; open an online sporting goods store; offer personal training services; start a sports camp
Animal lover	Establish a chain of doggie daycare facilities; develop a new line of pet food products

What Is Your Business Model?

Now that you've articulated a vision for your business idea, you need to consider a number of other factors as you begin to ground your vision in reality. These real, practical, nuts-and-bolts aspects of running a business will ultimately determine your success. No matter how brilliant the idea, execution in business is everything!

One of the first things you will do is identify your **business model**.

The term "business model" describes what your company does and how you make money. For example, will you make a product? If so, how will you sell it? To wholesalers? To consumers? If to consumers, will you sell directly or use intermediaries? If you use intermediaries, will you use distributors or retailers to reach consumers, or will you open your own brick-and-mortar storefront or e-commerce website? Or perhaps you won't sell your product to consumers at all, but lease it to them. And how will you make your product? Will you design and manufacture it yourself, or will you outsource manufacture and then assemble components?

If you sell a service, will it be for a flat fee, on an hourly or time-and-materials basis, or perhaps via a subscription? Will you provide the service yourself or engage others to work for you? Or perhaps you won't sell a product or service at all, but be an intermediary—a broker of some type between buyers and sellers.

In other words, what structure are you putting in place to make your money? What's your business model?

Thinking through and deciding on your business model is critical, because it's fundamental to your company's viability. Even the best concept will have a hard time succeeding if it's not supported by the right business model.

You have many different types of business models to choose from. By figuring out your own best model, you'll begin providing more definition and structure to your business concept.

Understanding your business model thoroughly is critical for planning the activities of your business. You have to know how you intend to make money to determine who your real customer is, how to set prices, what kinds of profit margins you can reasonably expect, what kind (if any) of customer service to provide, and the like.

For example, many online companies make money the traditional way: by selling something directly to customers at a profit—a conventional e-commerce company. Other companies behave more like "land-based" media companies, making money through advertising. Some online companies bring people together, acting as brokers, such as online dating or vacation rental sites. Subscription-based software applications that operate in the cloud, such as customer relationship management (CRM) software, are yet another model.

Find your niche

One way to seize a business opportunity is to specialize in a single or a few specific, clearly defined, narrow—or niche—markets.

When selling a consumer product or service, a good way to choose a niche is to focus your marketing efforts on a specific demographic group. For example, certain companies make cell phones designed for easy use by seniors or children. These companies wouldn't be able to compete with huge producers of cell phones for the greater and more technically savvy consumer market, but they *can* get a piece of the pie by specializing in these narrow market groups.

Companies selling to businesses may often adapt a product or service for a specific industry. Specializing in a niche market significantly increases the reach and effectiveness of your marketing dollars. And being a specialist often allows you to charge higher fees, too.

For an in-depth discussion on defining a niche, see pages 129–132.

Business Opportunities

Answer the following questions to come up with possible business opportunities. Use both common and unconventional ideas. Use the business idea(s) you come up with here as a basis for some of the other exercises throughout this book.

An industry/demographic group/hobby I'm interested in: _____

Biggest trends in this industry/demographic group/hobby: _____

A product or service I wish were available: _____

A product or service others have asked about: _____

A product or service that could improve the field: _____

A product or service I personally need or want now: _____

A product or service I personally wanted or needed within the last year: _____

A product or service that someone in my family needs or wants: _____

A product or service that someone I know needs or wants: _____

A product or service that needs improving: _____

A product or service lacking in a particular industry or trade: _____

A product or service that exists elsewhere but isn't available in my geographic area:_____

A product or service that will be needed because of population trends: _____

A product or service that will be needed because of changing technology:_____

A business or service that seems like something I'd enjoy: _____

A business or service that I think I'd be good at:_____

A business or service my friends or family suggested I'd be good at:_____

A business or service using some of the things I enjoy working with:_____

A business or service located in a place where I enjoy spending time: _____

Other business idea: _____

_____

_____

_____

_____

_____

_____

_____

_____

_____

BUILD-YOUR-BUSINESS WORKSHEET

Your Bright Idea

Use this space to record your initial business ideas. This will become a starting point for defining your business concept.

What is your business idea? _____

_____

_____

_____

_____

_____

_____

_____

_____

How did you come up with it? _____

_____

_____

_____

_____

_____

_____

_____

_____

_____

What excites you about it? _____

_____

_____

_____

_____

_____

_____

_____

_____

_____

Basic Business Concept

Using this worksheet as a guide, outline your business concept as you presently conceive it.

Is yours a retail, service, manufacturing, distribution, or Internet business? _____
_____

What industry does it belong to? _____
_____

What products or services do you sell? _____
_____

Who do you see as your potential customers? _____
_____

What is your basic overall marketing and sales strategy? _____
_____
_____

Which companies and types of companies do you consider to be your competition? _____
_____
_____

List your competitive advantages, if any, in each area listed below.

New products/services: _____
_____
_____

Improved features/services and added value: _____
_____
_____

New or underserved markets reached:_____
_____
_____

New/improved delivery or distribution method: _____
_____
_____

Methods of increased integration: _____
_____
_____

While most business models have been around for a long time—selling products directly to customers, for instance—business models continuously evolve. This is particularly true as new technologies, especially those spawned by the Internet, create new ways to bring customers and people together. And new business models will certainly yet develop. Perhaps you'll invent one for *your* business!

Types of business models

WHAT YOU DO

- Design physical products/merchandise

- Manufacture physical products/merchandise

- Sell physical products/merchandise

- Create information/content/data

- Aggregate or distribute information/content/data

- Provide personal or business services

- Provide expert advice/consultation

- Provide money/financing

- Provide labor/human resources

- Transport products/people

- Provide infrastructure/telecommunications

- Provide a marketplace—physical or online—for others to sell goods or services

HOW YOU SELL IT

- **Direct sales to consumer/end user.** Either as "**B2C**" (business to consumer) sales as a retailer, on the Internet, in-person, and so on; or "**B2B**" (business to business) or "**B2G**" (business to government) by selling directly to other companies or governmental entities

- **Wholesale sales.** Using intermediaries, whether brick-and-mortar or online retailers, distributors, and so on, to reach customers

- **Brokering.** Bringing others together for transactions; taking a commission on sales (such as in real estate or financing), or providing your service on a subscription basis (such as with online dating sites), or charging a flat or hourly fee

- **Leasing.** Providing your product, service, or information to customers for a set period of time for a fee but without their taking ownership of the asset

- **Shared ownership.** Providing your product, service, or information to a group of customers who do not need access to it so frequently that they

One of the first decisions you'll make
Thinking through and deciding on your business model is critical, because it's fundamental to your company's viability. Even the best concept will have a hard time succeeding if it's not supported by the right business model.

Barriers to entry

Certain obstacles will stand in the way of a company—either yours or a competitor's—attempting to enter a given market. Significant barriers to entry make it harder to succeed in an entrepreneurial venture. But once you're established, these same barriers to entry stand in the way of competitors coming after you:

- Substantial initial investment required
- Limited distribution channels
- Entrenched customer loyalty to existing offerings
- High "switching costs" for customers to move to new offerings
- Aggressively low prices from competitors
- Intellectual property protections, such as patents
- Government regulations, tariffs, trade restrictions
- Language or cultural differences
- Market saturation and oversupply

For more on barriers to entry, see pages 124–126.

need or want to own their own personal version; in other words, several people "share" one commodity

- **Subscription service.** Providing your product, service, or information to customers on an ongoing basis

- **Per use fee.** Charging customers to use your product, service, or information each time they use it, without an ongoing commitment or set period

- **Advertising/sponsorships.** Receiving payment from other businesses that make their company or products known to your customers

- **Licensing/franchising.** Allowing others to use your content, brand, design, or business practices in their own companies for a period of time

- **Auction.** Selling the product or service to the highest bidder

- **Donations/grants.** Receiving funds from others without their receiving goods or services in return, done because they support your cause or efforts; this is primarily a business model for not-for-profit, charitable businesses, but for-profit social ventures might also receive these

It is very likely that you will employ more than one business model. For instance, let's say you have an e-commerce, transaction-based, website that sells yoga clothing and accessories (made by other companies) directly to consumers. If your website is successful—one that attracts a lot of users—you may also want to sell advertising on that site to manufacturers of yoga clothing or other items that appeal to a yoga clientele. If you're highly successful, you might decide to also open brick-and-mortar stores, design some of your own yoga products, or even offer yoga retreats.

It's also probable that your business model will change over time. But it's important that you have a clear sense of which business models will be primary at the time you launch your company.

If you are submitting your business plan for an online business to a potential investor, include a clear statement of your business model, specifying what percentage of your income will come from which business models.

Feasibility Analysis

At this early stage, when you are just fleshing out your business concept and business model, you will certainly not have all the information you need to know whether your business can be successful, whether you can execute on your idea, or how much money you can reasonably expect to make. You will not, for instance, have done a financial analysis at this point, so you won't know what your costs and profits are likely to be. To do that, you'll develop a complete business plan—a critical step in your entrepreneurial process.

Nevertheless, a **feasibility analysis** is a chance to begin to flesh out your initial business idea, see which components are already in place to make it possible, see which are not, and do a quick assessment of whether you can pull this off. Before you develop the in-depth, specific components of your business plan, take time to see if it seems feasible—and identify the road-blocks you'll likely face.

Doing a feasibility analysis is a chance to open your eyes, ask yourself some tough questions, then determine whether your idea, as originally conceived, needs to be modified, refocused, or changed dramatically. (Or perhaps even scrapped altogether. It's better to drop an unworkable idea early on and move on to pursuing one of your other, potentially more successful, ideas.)

How involved your feasibility analysis is will depend a bit on how unusual your idea is or how hard your market is to reach. The more novel your concept, or the more unproven your marketing and sales channel, the more investigation you'll need to do to figure out whether the necessary building blocks are available to you or whether you'll have to create those too.

Let's say you've got an idea for an entirely new product—tasty meals that come in packages that are self-heating, no microwave required. You originally plan first to sell them in airports so passengers can carry hot meals on board to eat while they fly. There are a lot of things you can look at fairly quickly to test the feasibility of this idea. Does such packaging already exist and is it proven? Would airlines allow such packages on planes? How expensive is it for you to get space in airports to sell these? That's on top of the bigger question: Would flyers even *want* this? Doing a quick feasibility analysis, you might realize that, even if the concept of self-heating meals is workable, you'd be better off introducing them to college students, both because of the complications of dealing with airports and airlines, and because a younger target market might be more open to novel products.

But if you're doing something more proven—let's say you're opening an Italian restaurant on a street that's already a major destination for diners—your feasibility analysis will be much less involved. Is there space available in that neighborhood? Are the rents too high to operate profitably? Do you personally have the restaurant experience necessary to make this a success? Can you find a great Italian cook?

With every feasibility analysis, start by evaluating yourself. Are you really suited to run a business? Do you yourself have the knowledge and skills to pull this off? Can you assemble a winning team?

A feasibility analysis is only a beginning to your business plan—*and* to your questioning and exploring. You should continually challenge your assumptions. It's the entrepreneurs most willing to ask themselves the tough questions who are most likely to succeed.

A feasibility analysis vs. a business plan

How does a feasibility analysis differ from creating a full-fledged business plan? Think of developing and planning your business as entailing a few components:

1. **VISION.** Identifying and articulating your business idea and concept.

2. **FEASIBILITY ANALYSIS.** Challenging your concept, identifying which components are in place to make it realistic to easily execute, recognizing the biggest obstacles you'll likely face.

3. **BUSINESS PLAN.** Clarifying your business strategy in detail, describing how you're going to execute on your vision, developing the major components of your business, projecting detailed financial forecasts.

4. **MARKETING/OPERATIONS/ TECHNOLOGY PLANS.** Describing in detail and developing budgets for the internal aspects of how you'll run your business day-to-day.

The Feasibility Analysis worksheet on pages 44–45 helps you evaluate your basic business concept. You'll need to do some basic business research to fill it out. See Chapter 3 for more on research.

Creating a Product Prototype

If you are creating a product, one of your first steps is to actually design and build at least one sample product (unless the costs are substantial even for the first one). This will be your product **prototype**—the initial design that will become the standard for your production. The process of completing a prototype helps you work through a number of critical issues. Think of this as part of your feasibility analysis for a product-based business.

It may be likely that you'll have to build many models before you get to a final prototype. Even after you've come to your "final" prototype, there will be changes as you get to production.

For example, take one of the simplest examples of developing a prototype: one for a new packaged specialty food item, let's say pasta sauce. The designer—in this case, the chef—would keep trying many recipes until they came up with their prototype: that is, the sauce they want to eventually bottle and sell. At that point, some evaluation should be made of how realistic that recipe is to produce on a mass scale. Even so, once dealing with production, the entrepreneur or business owner might realize certain ingredients are too expensive to include or they will have too short a shelf-life to be viable as a commercial product, and the actual production model will have to be changed.

Likewise, let's say you are developing a new cloud-based software application. Building the entire application and coding all the functionalities of your site will be hugely expensive—making it financially impossible to build a complete working prototype. In fact, you'll need to raise substantial money from investors even to build your site. But you still need a prototype to show to your investors. In such a case, you might design a prototype site primarily with images, to demonstrate what kind of functionality will eventually be programmed once you receive financing.

Even during the prototype phase, you should begin to look at cost and pricing. This is critical information to discover during this phase, and it involves doing some initial research into what your raw materials and production costs will be and what the market will bear with regard to your product's pricing. If your product is truly unique, you'll have to make your best educated guess as to what price you can command. Always overestimate your costs and underestimate the price you will get. Remember, as you'll learn in later chapters, your product's profitability will depend not only on the cost of raw goods and production, but also on labor costs (including your own time), overhead (things such as rent, utilities, and salaries), and the shipping and distribution costs involved in selling the product.

In many cases, you need to take into account design considerations that will affect the manufacturing of the product. Design is more than the "look and feel" of a product. You must also consider how the various components of your product will integrate with each other and how they can be designed to reduce cost and complexity in manufacturing. If the ears designed for the teddy bear you plan to manufacture are too complicated to be sewn on easily, or the new amplifier you're designing doesn't integrate seamlessly with the rest of the off-the-shelf components you plan to use in your high-end stereo systems, you need to catch the problem in the prototype stage—otherwise you risk losing a ton of money after you go into production.

Finally, although you may think you have the expertise to design the product yourself, and the desire to manufacture the product in your own company, actually attempting to fabricate a prototype will put this notion to the test. If you lack the skills to do it yourself, you may have to hire an outside design firm to get you through the prototyping stage. This will cost you money—depending on the product in question, sometimes a substantial amount. And building production facilities can be extremely costly and time consuming, requiring you to raise additional money for your entrepreneurial venture and taking even more time before you can get your product into the marketplace. Unless you're a craftsperson turning out one-of-a-kind goods, or are making limited quantities of something you can assemble using standard or off-the-shelf components, making a product usually requires outside providers at some stage of the process—whether in design or manufacturing or both.

As you develop your prototype, focus particularly on the following issues:

- **Will the product work?** Most importantly, you need to test whether the product actually functions as you've envisioned. Does it work? And work well? If you're building a mechanical, electrical, or electronic product in particular, the product must be perfectly functional from an engineering standpoint.

- **Can it be produced in sufficient quantities/bulk?** If you will be manufacturing the product in bulk, you'll need to judge whether you can ensure consistent quality of both components and the final product when made in large quantities.

- **Can you afford to make the product?** You might be capable of making the product, but can you do so in such a way that you make a profit? Can it be made efficiently and cost-effectively? Can you use standard, easily available components that will reduce costs? Is it likely that you can command a price that enables you to make a profit?

- **Will you need to create the product on your own?** Will you need to eventually develop a production facility? Or are there contract manufacturers who can produce the product for you, thus lowering your costs and increasing the speed with which you can get to market?

The benefits of prototype production

Building a prototype accomplishes many things: It helps you work out the design and functions, clarifies the steps and components going into your product, identifies problem areas, gives you a better indication of costs, produces something to show funders and potential customers, and helps make your business concept seem real.

Importantly, you'll save yourself a great deal of time and money by producing prototypes before submitting orders to suppliers or sending design specifications out for manufacturing.

Feasibility Analysis

Complete this worksheet after conducting your initial research to identify which areas of your business are the strongest and which are likely to present major challenges. Rate each of the following areas on a scale of 1–10 — with 1 being "not at all" to 10 being "completely." The higher your scores in each area, the less risk you are likely to face. Those areas with very low scores will probably make it more difficult for your business to be developed and, ultimately, successful. You will need to spend more time on those areas as you develop your complete business plan.

Your Industry

_____ Is economically healthy.

_____ Is new, expanding, or growing signficantly.

_____ Is characterized by a large number of competitors rather than a few entrenched, large companies.

_____ Is able to withstand downturns in economic cycles.

_____ Has positive forecasts for significant growth in the immediate future.

Your Product or Service

_____ Is proven and not unique.

_____ Is already in demand.

_____ If unique, there are significant barriers to keep others from competing with you.

_____ Is currently developed or can be developed in the near future.

_____ Has a clear source of suppliers for the necessary materials or inventory.

_____ Can be produced at a cost significantly lower than the future sales price.

_____ Is not burdensome — in terms of cost or time — for new customers to convert to.

_____ Is consumable — meaning customers will use your product or service repeatedly.

Your Market

_____ Is clearly identifiable.

_____ Is large enough to be able to support your business.

_____ Is small enough to be able to be reached affordably for marketing purposes.

_____ Has shown they are already interested in your product or service.

_____ Is growing.

_____ Has forecasts for significant growth in the immediate future.

_____ Has existing sales channels to sell to your customers.

Your Competition

_____ Exists.

_____ Is clearly identifiable.

_____ Has market share that is widely distributed and is not dominated by a few major companies.

_____ Does not have deep pockets to come after you.

Your Operations

_____ Do not entail significant initial capital investment.

_____ Do not require the purchase of substantial, expensive inventories.

_____ Do not require new or unproven technologies.

_____ Are not reliant on one or two suppliers or distributors.

_____ Do not entail unusual production or operational challenges.

_____ Have a ready source of skilled labor.

_____ Do not require expensive insurance or entail significant liability.

Your Leadership Abilities

_____ You have started or run a company previously.

_____ You have had training in entrepreneurship and/or business management.

_____ You have previous experience in this industry.

_____ You are open to suggestions and guidance from others.

_____ You are able to be flexible and change course if the situation demands.

_____ You have prior experience leading a team.

_____ Others naturally find you to be a leader.

_____ You have the personal capability to develop your product or service.

_____ You have the personal capability and willingness to go out and make sales.

_____ You have a good credit history.

Your Management Team

_____ You have identified and/or secured others with the capability to develop your product or service.

_____ You have identified and/or secured others who can make sales.

_____ You have clearly identified/secured others to be part of your team.

_____ Members of your team have previous industry experience.

Financial/Business Model

_____ You will be able to finance all start-up costs and become profitable without any outside funding.

_____ There exist funding sources (angel investors, venture capitalists) who actively invest in your industry.

_____ The business does not require high start-up costs.

_____ The business does not require high annual operating costs.

_____ You will be able to be profitable within the first 12 months.

_____ You are able to forecast continued, significant growth for at least 36 months.

_____ A clear, proven business model already exists on how you'll charge customers for your product or service.

Entering a Mature Industry: How Zipcar Created a New Business Model

challenge

Innovate in a mature and overcrowded market

solution

Introduce a new business model

When Henry Ford invented the Model T in 1906, he launched more than merely the automobile industry. Within a decade after the first Model T took to the road, the rental car industry began. More than 100 years later, a few large corporations own the handful of leading rental car brands. Mature industries such as this are notoriously difficult for new competitors to penetrate. But Zipcar did—by introducing a new business model.

In 1999, Robin Chase sat in a café in Cambridge, Massachusetts, with her friend Antje Danielson. Danielson had just returned from Berlin where she saw the success of a new concept in rental cars—"car-sharing." It was the height of the dot-com boom, and Chase, a serial entrepreneur and 42-year-old mother of three, was eager to start her own company. Not long after that conversation in the café, Chase would launch her own car-sharing company—Zipcar.

The idea was simple in concept: Allow people to use cars only when they needed them, just for the amount of time they needed, if only for an hour or a few hours. They'd be spared the expense of owning and maintaining an automobile. Millions of Americans need a car, but the economics of owning one simply aren't there for them, especially in urban areas where they can use public transportation. Many more people do invest in automobiles, but grossly underuse these expensive assets. And too many cars choke U.S. roadways, causing traffic jams, creating delays, and accelerating global climate change.

Of course, people could always turn to a traditional rental car service, but those require rentals of a minimum of a day, and the cost and inconvenience to rent a car simply to pick up groceries, visit a big-box store to buy things in bulk, or drive to a party in the suburbs doesn't make much sense.

Car-sharing is a concept born of the Internet Age. Although the concept of sharing ownership of an expensive resource like an automobile has been around for decades, the logistics of scheduling, figuring out charge rates, tracking locations, and making cars conveniently available to people scattered over a large geographic area meant that executing the concept wasn't feasible. Robin Chase immediately saw that the convergence of technology, economics, urban culture, environmental concerns, and young people increasingly accustomed to sharing over the Internet would open up a tremendous business opportunity. The time was right.

Starting in Cambridge, the company bought a small fleet of cars and offered to rent them by the hour to city residents. To be eligible, people had to first join Zipcar by paying an annual membership fee, have their driving record checked, and then obtain a personalized electronic "Zip-

card." They could reserve cars by the hour, 24/7, 365 days a year. They were directed to the Zipcar parked closest to their neighborhood, and would use their Zipcard to unlock the door and start the engine. Zipcar paid for the car, the insurance, the maintenance, the gas, and the parking.

First and foremost, what made Zipcar viable was a new business model—in essence, a "subscription" to share cars. Customers are not merely "renters," they are "members." The second factor was cost. While Zipcar's daily rates compare to rental car agencies' prices, members can rent by the hour and pay far less than a daily rate. But, from Zipcar's point of view, renting a car for 15 single hours at $8 an hour nets them far more than renting that same car for a day at $80.

The third factor was convenience. Zipcar purchases parking rights in multiple locations throughout urban areas, with the goal of putting a Zipcar within a 10-minute walk of any member. Finally, technology. Each Zipcar windshield is equipped with an RFID transmitter, which sends the signal to members' Zipcards, allowing them to unlock the car. An automated system tracks the time the member has the car and the mileage they accumulate. Each car also has a GPS system installed. Zipcar doesn't track customer locations, but in the rare instance when a car goes missing, the GPS can locate it. Each car can also be made nonoperational by using a central "kill" command to prevent theft, stopping the car in its tracks.

"Our core idea was to make cars consumable by the hour; everything else stemmed from that,"[1] Chase said. That was the basis for her business, yet it also creates positive environmental results. Fewer people in the cities Zipcar serves now need to own individual cars, and the ones who rent from the company use the cars more sensibly than do private car owners, the company believes. "Once people pay by the hour, they use cars in a totally very rational (and therefore greatly reduced) way."[2]

Zipcar has a fanatically loyal customer base. It spends very little on marketing, as most new business comes from word of mouth. Chase noticed early on that the car-sharing model fostered a genuine sense of community. Zipcar members who lived in nearby neighborhoods grew to recognize each other. Some cities even have local Zipcar gatherings where people who "share" the neighborhood Zipcar fleet socialize.

Zipcar has grown rapidly, becoming the leading car-sharing service in the United States. On June 1, 2010, Zipcar made its initial public offering (IPO), for $75 million. Today, many other competitors and imitators of Zipcar have emerged, and the legacy car rental agencies have launched their own car-sharing services. ■

questions

1. Robin Chase first targeted college students and urban dwellers for Zipcar; how do you think this contributed to her success?

2. Shared ownership is an increasingly popular business model; what other products and services do you think would suit this business model?

3. How do you think Zipcar can compete effectively, now that large rental car companies have entered the field?

4. What other companies have introduced new business models?

1. "How Robin Chase Built Zipcar, the Largest Car-Sharing Service in the World," by Erin Bury, March 30, 2011, *Sprouter.com*.

2. Ibid.

WOULDN'T IT BE NICE IF...?

Goal:

Learn to spot and begin to evaluate new business opportunities.

What to Do:

1. Working either alone or in groups, recall a time when you needed or wanted a product or service but you couldn't find something that met your needs or wants. Perhaps it had to do with a hobby or sporting activity; perhaps a household or office task; perhaps a personal product or service. It doesn't have to be something entirely new—it could be a significant improvement on an existing product or service. To help brainstorm ideas, remember all the times you, or others, have said, "Wouldn't it be nice if…" regarding a product feature or service they would love to have.

HINT: When brainstorming, don't worry about how realistic or feasible these ideas are. Merely come up with as many ideas as you can. The more "out there" your ideas are, the better.

2. Pick the two ideas you believe are the most promising. At this point, consider issues such as whether the product or service can realistically be created, how much it would cost to be produced, whether it could be sold at a profit, how strong the competition is, whether there is an existing sales and distribution channel, and so on.

3. Make a list of all the strengths of each of the top two ideas.

4. Make a list of the challenges of implementing each of the top two ideas.

5. Begin to analyze how feasible each idea is by writing down a potential—ideally, a realistic—solution for each challenge you identified.

6. Present your best idea (most profitable, most feasible) to the rest of the class.

CHAPTER

3

Basic Business Research

learning objectives

In this chapter, you'll learn how to:

■ Conduct business research for a new or existing company

■ Distinguish between primary and secondary research

■ Distinguish between quantitative and qualitative research

■ Determine which key issues to look for when conducting industry research

■ Determine which key issues to look for when conducting market research

■ Conduct basic primary market research, through surveys and interviews with prospective customers

■ Determine which key issues to look for when researching major competitors

■ Develop research questions that will help garner the best data

■ Select the most relevant data

■ Organize the vast amounts of data involved in business research

Why Research Is Important

Knowledge is power, especially for entrepreneurs or aspiring entrepreneurs. Entrepreneurs are, naturally, enthusiastic about their ideas. With accurate information at your fingertips, you can better judge whether your ideas are likely to bear fruit—and whether the opportunity you've identified is a viable one.

The only way to get this information is through research. The word "research" doesn't have to be frightening. Research can be as simple as interviewing people who are potential customers or talking with other entrepreneurs who've already done what you hope to do. Perhaps it involves looking up facts about your particular industry online. It's a good idea to find out what's going on in your chosen field or industry. What are the trends? What's hot and what's not?

Think of research as a reality check that will align your vision with what's actually happening in the world. Research helps you identify opportunities, set prices, adjust your marketing, and improve your product or service.

You don't need to be exhaustive in your research efforts; it's neither necessary nor possible. You are merely looking for information that will answer key questions about the particular opportunity you have identified. At the same time, your research must be thorough enough to give you insight into whether you should proceed along the path you have chosen, or investigate other options.

Types of Business Research

How will you go about gathering the information you need? Will you conduct your own research, or will you rely on information that's already out there? Will that research be based on cold, hard numbers and facts, or will it come from opinions and observations? Before you get started on your research efforts, it's useful to understand the meanings of some key research terms.

Primary vs. secondary research

Two of the basic types of research available to any business information seeker are primary and secondary.

■ **Primary research.** Original research done by collecting data directly, typically from research subjects (such as target customers). For example, the U.S. Census Bureau conducts **primary research** when it sends out tens of thousands of census takers to count every person in the country. Industry associations often collect data from association members to compile information about industry trends, pricing, and other issues. Professional polling companies and research organizations often do original—or primary—research. You might do your own primary research by surveying prospective customers or interviewing others in your field.

Primary research is particularly useful for gathering information from prospective customers for a new product or service. However, since primary research entails gathering data directly from subjects, conducting it can require a great deal of time and money. Nevertheless, primary research is often necessary when no other data is available, and it can provide you with valuable insights into customer preferences.

en·tre·pre·neur·ship key terms

Beta testing
The testing of a product or service before its official release. Customers or clients who take part in beta testing provide feedback on how a company can improve its products or services and make them more appealing to consumers.

NAICS codes
Developed by the governments of the United States, Canada, and Mexico as a way to standardize industry categorization, numerical NAICS codes classify every type of business in North America. Providing this code when searching for business information makes locating that data much faster and easier and produces more accurate results.

Primary research
Original research done by collecting data directly, typically from research subjects.

Qualitative information
Generally, subjective information, frequently expressed in words, not numbers.

Quantitative information
Data that is expressed in numbers.

Secondary research
Research that compiles, analyzes, or compares data collected from others who conducted their own original research.

■ **Secondary research.** Research that relies on data collected from others who conducted their own original research. This type of research often compiles, analyzes, or compares existing data.

As an entrepreneur collecting information to help you make good business decisions, you'll rely most on **secondary research**. Many sources of primary research data are government agencies (which often provide it for free), industry associations, or private research companies (typically specializing in certain industries) that may charge substantial sums of money for the data they gather, such as Gartner or Forrester for technology-related research, Gallup for consumer behavior, and so on.

An important business skill is the ability to find and use information that has been collected by others and is already available in thousands of libraries, websites, and online databases.

PRIMARY VS. SECONDARY RESEARCH

PRIMARY RESEARCH	SECONDARY RESEARCH
Data collected by government agencies or research companies (for instance, U.S. Census Bureau or IRS data)	Reports based on analyzing and evaluating data collected by others
Data collected through consumer surveys, polling, focus groups, beta tests, and taste tests	Graphs and charts created based on data collected by others
Financial data included in corporate annual reports	Compilations of data from a number of sources
Original reports, created by the collectors of data gathered using any of the methods above, perhaps including tables, graphs, or charts	Articles based on interviewing those who conducted primary research
	Books that evaluate or analyze data collected by others

Quantitative vs. qualitative research

When conducting business research, you'll look for cold, hard facts: the size of your market, the historic growth rate of your industry, and the annual revenues of companies in your industry. You'll also dig for insight and analysis: why customers behave a certain way, or which trends will likely affect your industry in the future. In other words, you need both quantitative *and* qualitative information.

■ **Quantitative research.** Data that is expressed by numbers. Examples of **quantitative information** include the total amount consumers spent on a product in a year, past growth rates of an industry, the market share distribution of major competitors, and numerical results of consumer surveys. You're more likely to find this kind of data in reports from government agencies and research companies, library databases, industry associations, and consumer surveys.

- **Qualitative research.** Generally, subjective information, frequently expressed in words, not numbers. Examples of **qualitative information** include experts' observations about what motivates consumers, forecasts of future industry trends, customer views of major competitors, and comments consumers make about a product. You're more likely to find this kind of information in news reports and articles from industry and general-interest publications, as well as by conducting your own research.

Numbers add believability to a business plan, marketing plan, or other business report because they reflect how the market or industry actually works and has behaved in the past. Numbers show you've done your homework. But there is no reliable quantitative data about the future. So you'll need qualitative information to give insight into what might happen in the years to come.

Don't underestimate the value of qualitative data when conducting business research. Whether you're trying to convince investors to finance your business, figuring out whether to launch a business or product, or planning a marketing campaign, you'll have more success and can present a stronger, more compelling case by combining both types of information.

Critical Areas to Research

When thinking about launching an entrepreneurial venture—or any business—the three basic areas of research you'll want to look at are:

- Industry

- Market

- Competition and company

Certainly, you'll want to research other issues that are important for your particular business. For instance, if you manufacture a product, you'll want to research suppliers and distribution channels. If you develop a technology product, you may need to research technical standards. In many businesses, you'll need to research governmental regulations.

Start your research process by figuring out exactly what you need to look for. Begin by answering two questions:

1. What is the primary question I want my research to answer?

2. How will I use the information I find?

A good way to begin your research is by asking a fundamental question that challenges the basis—or underlying assumption—of your business (or a portion of it). For example, if you plan on opening a chain of environmentally friendly, low-cost dry cleaning establishments in a large city, you might ask, "Is there likely to be substantial demand for a new, environmentally friendly dry cleaners throughout the city of Laurelwood?" Or, if you plan on developing online applications for the management of medical records nationwide,

Research resources

To research your company and complete the worksheets and exercise in this chapter, be sure to refer to Chapter 20 on pages 463–480 for a comprehensive list of research resources. You'll find resources for researching your industry, your target market, your competition, and more.

you might ask, "Is the U.S. market for medical records management applications large enough for me to succeed?"

In the case of the dry cleaners, your question would lead to other questions, such as the number of dry cleaners in Laurelwood now, the nature and strength of competitors, the number of potential customers in Laurelwood based on information about the demographics of people who use dry cleaners, and so on.

Industry

No matter how good your idea, you never build a business in a vacuum. Trends affecting your industry affect your business, too. If your industry is booming, your business has a better chance of succeeding than if your industry is shrinking or in trouble. Knowing what's happening in your industry enables you to better compete and to anticipate structural issues that will likely confront you.

In addition to educating yourself about your specific industry, it's a good idea to look at the health of the broad economic sector to which your industry belongs (for example, manufacturing, retail, transportation, information, or services). Information about past performance in this broad economic sector, and growth projections for it, gives you a sense of the economic environment in which your industry operates. If you want to open a bookstore, for example, it's useful to find out what's happening in the entire retail sector in your area.

Still, the most important data you can collect concerns your specific industry. After all, even if the retail sector as a whole is thriving, bookstores may face unique pressures.

Finding industry data helps you:

- Understand conditions and trends your business may encounter, so you'll be better prepared to deal with them

- Gather solid facts and figures to help you prepare a more realistic business plan and build a stronger company

- Demonstrate to potential financing sources (investors and lenders) that you have a good grasp of external business conditions as well as a realistic plan for your business

TIPS FOR FINDING INDUSTRY INFORMATION

1. Begin with an industry overview by reading a few articles that give you a sense of an industry's history and trends. Good sources for overviews like this include general business media websites and publications, industry-specific publications, and industry analyst reports. Remember to refer to Chapter 20 on pages 463–480 for research resources.

Types of Industry Information to Research

From this list of suggested industry topics, select which issues you will focus on.

☐ General industry overview and analysis

☐ Key technological, sociological, distribution, or other factors dramatically affecting your industry

☐ Current and historical financial performance of the industry, including:

— Total revenues, overall and by product lines, if possible

— Total number of units sold, by product lines, if possible

— Total profits and average profit margins

— Growth rates over the past few years

☐ Companies in the industry, including:

— Total number of companies

— Leading companies in the industry

— Total employment in the industry

— Market share distribution of each company

☐ Industry's performance in relation to your target market (geographic and demographic), including:

— Total revenues and profits from that target market

— Number of companies serving that target market and market leaders

— Trends relating to that target market

☐ Impact of seasonal changes and economic cycles on the industry

☐ Trends and forecasts, especially the projected future growth rate of the industry

☐ Industry resources, including major suppliers and vendors, trade publications, associations, and research companies

Searching by NAICS codes

Every type of business in North America has been assigned a numerical code, called a NAICS code. NAICS (pronounced *nakes*) stands for the North American Industry Classification System. NAICS was developed by the governments of the United States, Canada, and Mexico as a way to standardize industry categorization.

You'll often be asked to provide a NAICS code as part of a search for business information. Knowing the NAICS code for the industry you're interested in makes searching for, and finding, data about it much faster and easier—and produces more accurate results.

2. Find the **NAICS code** for your industry. Knowing the numerical code that identifies your specific industry makes it much easier to find information, especially statistical data. To find the NAICS code for your industry, go to www.census.gov/eos/www/naics.

3. Make a list of terms that can be used to describe your industry or its key aspects. Most industries can be identified in more than one way. A dairy, for instance, can also be called a "milk producer" or be referred to as "cattle farming." Having a variety of relevant terms at your fingertips to describe your industry will help when you conduct keyword searches.

4. Check out your industry's trade association. Trade associations are good places to find statistical data, projections of industry trends, and links to other sources of information. A list of many trade association websites is available at www.planningshop.com/associations.

   When exploring a trade association website, look for tabs or topics such as:

   — Press/media, or news

   — Research

   — About the industry

   — Industry publications

5. Use the "Types of Industry Information to Research" worksheet on page 55 to make a list of key statistics and information about the industry you're researching.

Market

Understanding your customers is essential to business success. You need to know who they are, where they are, what they want, how they behave, and what they can afford. Most important, you have to know that they exist—and in numbers big enough to support your business.

If you're seeking financing for your company, anticipate that your investors will grill you about the size of your potential target market. They'll want to know that this market is large enough to sustain your business, even in the face of existing competition.

Your target market may consist of either consumers (in which case yours is a B2C, or business-to-consumer, business) or other businesses (a B2B, or business-to-business, business). In either case, before you begin to research your target market, you must narrow the market definition even more by identifying the particular market segment you want to reach.

Finding information about your market and your potential customers helps you:

■ Determine the size of a market and whether it's large enough to sustain your business

- Understand the characteristics of your potential customers, what motivates them, what they buy, and where and how they buy

- Gain insight into the trends affecting your target market so you'll be better prepared to respond to future changes in the market

- Become more aware of your customers' preferences, actions, and tastes, especially in response to your specific product or service

Market research

"Will the dog eat the dog food?" This well-known quote comes from famed entrepreneur and venture capitalist Eugene Kleiner, one of the founders of Silicon Valley. In short, Kleiner's question asks: Will customers actually *buy* what you sell? You must find out what dogs like, meaning put the bowl in front of Fido. You must do some market research.

While the term "market research" most often applies to original research about potential or current customers, you engage in market research anytime you seek data about your target market. For example, you conduct market research when you look for census data about the geographic area in which you're planning to run a business or launch a product.

From a business perspective, conducting primary market research—by interacting with prospective customers directly—often provides critical insight into whether customers truly want your product or service. If you plan to introduce an organic dog food, for instance, you could do a great deal of secondary research and still not find crucial information. You could determine the number of dogs in the market, the sales figures for all dog food, the sales figures and trends for organic pet food, and so on. But you'd still want to know, "Will the dog eat my dog food?"

HOW TO CONDUCT YOUR OWN MARKET RESEARCH

Some of the most important information you need will not be available from any published source, particularly information that's quite specific to your market or new product. To obtain this data, you will have to undertake your own primary research. You have several means to choose from.

- **Personal observation.** One fundamental way to gather information—and also one of the easiest—is through personal observation. Watching what goes on in other businesses or the way people shop gives you insight into factors affecting your own business. You can observe automobile-traffic and foot-traffic patterns near a selected location, how customers behave when shopping in businesses similar to yours or for similar products, and how competitors market or merchandise their products or services. You can also observe research subjects interacting with your product by inviting individuals to try your product before launch. Technology companies typically have user labs to find out how customers actually use their products. Personal observation is a vital tool in your planning process and is applicable for almost every business, large or small.

Know thy customers

Early in your entrepreneurial venture, you need to *clearly* define your customers, as many of the decisions you make about your business will follow from knowing who they are. Chapter 5, which focuses entirely on the topic of customers and target markets, provides further, in-depth guidance to help you identify your customers.

REAL-WORLD RECAP

Primary market research methods

- Personal observation
- Informational interviews
- Surveys
- Focus groups
- Beta testing, samplings, and taste tests

■ **Informational interviews.** The second principal method of market research is informational interviewing. Since the amount of information you can garner from personal observation is limited and colored by your own perceptions, you should talk with as many people as possible who can provide you with information relating to your business.

Some of these interviews may be highly structured. For instance, you might make personal appointments with those you want to interview and prepare a list of questions. In other cases, such as when you go into a competitor's store and chat with a salesperson, your questions will appear to be more casual.

■ **Surveys.** If you decide you need information from a large number of people, you may want to conduct a survey, whether by phone, mail, online, or in person. Surveys are a good way both to spot trends and to assess customer needs and desires. You can conduct in-person surveys by going to an appropriate location and interviewing subjects on the spot. Develop a questionnaire of the most important concerns to ascertain from interview sources. Don't make your survey too long, or people will refuse to participate. Many online tools and apps make conducting online or mobile surveys easy and inexpensive.

■ **Focus groups.** A popular form of market research is the focus group, a small gathering of people brought together to discuss a product, business concern, or service in great detail. For example, a few joggers might be brought in to examine and evaluate a new pair of running shoes. Focus group participants are often paid a small fee.

Focus groups typically evoke candid opinions. Market research firms conduct focus groups for businesses, bringing together the participants and leading the group discussion in a room with a one-way mirror, so that the participants can be observed. However, if you lack the funds to hire a market research firm, you still might consider assembling a focus group of your own, perhaps a group of potential consumers. Try, though, to find focus group participants you don't know personally, to get objective results.

■ **Beta testing, samplings, and taste tests.** One fast and easy way to get real-world feedback on your new product is to ask prospective customers or clients to try out your product or service and give you feedback before you release the product or service or offer it for sale to others. In the technology world, this is typically referred to as **beta testing**. (Originally, "alpha testing" was internal testing of a software product, and "beta," or second, testing was done by those outside the company. The term "beta testing" has become more broadly used for most outside testing of prerelease technology products or services and has even crept into nontechnology products and services.) Giving samples of your product to potential customers, or conducting taste tests or other kinds of trials

BUILD-YOUR-BUSINESS WORKSHEET

Types of Target Market Information to Research

From this list of suggested market topics, select which issues you will focus on.

☐ General size of market

— What is the approximate size of the target market?

— What is the historic rate of growth of the target market?

— What changes are occurring that could affect the size of the market (including income levels, need for product/service, social values)?

— What are forecasts for market growth?

☐ Demographic characteristics of consumer customers

— Age range

— Income level

— Educational level

— Home ownership

— Marital status/household size

— Ethnic/religious group

— Occupation

☐ Demographic characteristics of business customers

— Industries

— Revenue level

— Number of employees

— Business stage/age

New data is often better data

All other factors being equal, the best data is the newest. A great deal can happen in even a few years, so it's generally better to present data from the last year or two, if you can find it. Some exceptions exist, though. U.S. Census data is considered to be useful and authoritative, yet it often lags a few years because such a large amount of data is collected and analyzed.

while your product or service is still in development, can give you valuable information about what you need to do to improve it or to make it more attractive and useful to customers.

TIPS FOR FINDING MARKET INFORMATION

1. A great place to start looking for target market data is one of the U.S. Census Bureau's websites. Start at www.census.gov. Refer to Chapter 20 on pages 463–480 for other research resources.

2. The most detailed insights about target markets are often compiled by private research firms. Their data can be expensive to acquire, though some resources are available free through many college or university libraries.

3. If your target market consists of businesses in a specific industry, you can usually gather a good deal of information from the trade association serving that industry. For instance, if you sell commercial kitchen equipment, your target market may be restaurants, and you can find information about the number and growth rate of restaurants at the National Restaurant Association's website.

4. If your target market consists of individuals with specific demographic characteristics, such as members of a particular ethnic group or religion, you can often find associations serving that group. If your market consists of consumers with specific interests or hobbies, such as gardening or travel, you can typically find associations serving those consumers, as well. These social organizations often have access to statistics about the size and growth rate of their constituents.

5. Many media outlets (including magazines, newspapers, and radio and television stations) that serve a specific market offer details about their target markets in their information for advertisers. Check their websites.

6. Try talking to people who are in the same industry or business as yours in a different city; they're an excellent source of information. In addition, large banks and universities frequently maintain information about the health of the local economy and particular industries. They are a good and reasonably reliable source of future-growth forecasts. Don't overlook real estate agents, as they often have more up-to-date information about neighborhood trends at their fingertips than any other source.

7. Sometimes you can even talk to your competitors. In many industries and professions, and in instances where there's more work than the market can handle, your competitors may be willing to talk with you directly.

8. Suppliers, distributors, and independent sales representatives can give you a great deal of information about industry trends and what your competition is doing, without violating confidentiality. Because they're in touch with the market, they know which products and services are in demand.

Competition and company

Conducting research about individual companies offers you many benefits, from identifying your biggest or toughest competitors to determining whether a potential customer is creditworthy. If you're seeking funding for a business, prospective investors will certainly want to know about the health and performance of your major competitors.

Finding information about specific companies can often be difficult; after all, they don't necessarily want their competitors to know what they're up to. Nevertheless, quite a bit of data is available on publicly traded companies (that is, businesses that sell their stock on a public stock exchange). In the United States, such companies are required by law to regularly disclose financial information to the Securities and Exchange Commission.

As well, investment analysts track publicly traded companies for their investor clients, and you can access many of their reports on some of the databases listed in this book. These companies are usually of interest to the financial press, too, and you can also find articles about their performance in media archives.

While locating information about private and smaller companies is more difficult, it's not impossible. Often you can collect information from industry publications and associations, local media in a company's home community, research firms such as Dun & Bradstreet, and even a company's own websites or customers. Be sure to refer to Chapter 20 on pages 463–480 for other research resources.

Finding information about a company helps you:

- Learn which products and services a company offers and, often, how much they charge

- Estimate the revenues and profits of a company, sometimes including revenues for specific product lines

- Gather background information about prospective customers and suppliers

- Investigate potential strategic alliances by finding companies whose services or products complement yours

TIPS FOR FINDING COMPANY INFORMATION

1. Determine the correct name or names of the company, including:

   Its official corporate name. A company's corporate name may be different from the one you're familiar with. For instance, the corporate name for United Airlines is UAL Corporation.

   The name of its parent or its subsidiary company or companies. Some corporations own many subsidiary companies. Bloomingdale's department store, for instance, is a subsidiary of Macy's—its parent company.

Forms of competition

Competition comes in the following forms:

- **DIRECT COMPETITION:** Companies most like yours

- **LARGE COMPETITION:** The Walmarts and the Home Depots

- **ONLINE COMPETITION:** Online sellers that may operate from anywhere in the world

- **INDIRECT COMPETITION:** Other products and services your customers may buy instead of yours

- **FUTURE COMPETITION:** Competitors that may enter the marketplace in the future.

When researching your competition, you'll focus mostly on your direct competitors.

Types of Company Information to Research

From this list of suggested company topics, select which issues you will focus on.

☐ Names of the company:

— Official corporate name

— Parent/subsidiary companies

— Product names

— Trademarks

☐ Company information:

— Headquarters and locations

— Names of officers, executives, and staff

— Press releases

— Product announcements

☐ Products/services of a company:

— Leading product lines

— Pricing

— Features

— Distribution methods

— Patents/copyrights and other intellectual property

☐ Financial condition of the company, including:

— Current revenues and profit figures

— Historical sales, financial performance, and growth rate

— Stock performance/market value

— Sales by product lines

☐ Other key issues:

— Is the company publicly traded?

— Customers/client list/testimonials

— Legal/regulatory compliance issues

Its brand/product names. Often you will know a product's name but not the name of the company that makes it. For example, Crest toothpaste, Tide detergent, and Iams pet food are all made by Procter & Gamble.

2. Make sure you spell any names correctly when entering them into keyword searches.

3. Check the company's website. Look for an About Us section and a Press/Media section, which usually feature background information about the company and its officers, press releases, and recent news articles. Also look for product information and lists of clients and customers or testimonials.

4. Learn whether the company you're researching is public or private.

5. Identify the U.S. state in which the company is legally incorporated (if applicable). You can typically find the names of corporate officers and company contact information through the Secretary of State's office in the state where the company you're researching is incorporated.

6. Use the "Types of Company Information to Research" worksheet on page 62 to make a list of key statistics and information about the companies you're researching.

Evaluate Your Data

You now have a *lot* of data—perhaps more than you can actually use. How do you select the information that's most relevant and most accurate and that will best help you meet your goals?

For instance, you may find one source that says an industry is growing at 5 percent each year, another that says it's growing at 2 percent, and another claiming the industry is actually shrinking. How do you know which piece of data to trust—and to use?

Don't imagine that you can choose to present only the data that supports your conclusions. That's not only a terrible way to make business decisions; it's also likely that an investor will have access to the same data as you and will be quick to point out that things may not be as rosy as you make them seem. Prove that you've done your homework by showing the range of data available, even if it's not always as favorable as you might like. Your thoroughness and honesty will add credibility to your plan.

You must apply some critical analytical skills when you evaluate the data you've collected. For every piece of information you collect, you must consider: 1) the source and 2) the time period.

Consider the source

Contrary to popular belief, sometimes numbers *do* lie. That's why, when evaluating data, you must always consider its source. Remember, the source is not

5 tips for organizing your data

1. Use the most recent data you can find; printed information is often at least two years old, and a lot can change in that time.

2. Translate data into units rather than dollars or other currency whenever possible. Due to inflation, financial information may not give you consistent information from year to year.

3. Give the most reliable source the most credence. Generally, the larger the group sampled for information, or the more respected the organization that conducted the research, the more trustworthy the numbers you collect.

4. Integrate data from one source to another in order to draw conclusions. But make sure the information comes from the same time period and is consistent; small variations can lead to vastly inaccurate results.

5. Use the most conservative figures. Naturally, you'll be tempted to paint the brightest picture possible, but such information often leads to bad business decisions.

Research Questions

Formulate a general research question about the type of business you plan to start. As guidelines, look at the two examples of the environmentally friendly dry cleaners and the medical records management applications (see pages 53–54). Now, make a list of questions for each of the following areas that logically follow or challenge that statement. Use the questions below as a guide.

General research question: _____

_____

Industry/Economic Sector

What is the size of the industry of which your business is a part? _____

_____

What has the growth rate of that industry been over the last few years? _____

_____

What is the projected future growth rate of that industry? _____

_____

What are the leading products/services in that industry? _____

_____

What are typical profit margins in that industry? _____

_____

What are the key trends/developments affecting that industry? _____

_____

Is the industry dominated by a few major companies, or are there many healthy competitors? _____

_____

Other: _____

Other: _____

Target Market

What are the demographic characteristics of your target customers? (That is, age, gender, marital status, income, education level, type of business, and so on.) _____

_____

_____

_____

What is the size of your potential market in your specific geographic area in terms of revenue? _____

_____

_____

_____

What has the growth rate of that market been over the last few years?_____

_____

_____

_____

What is the projected growth rate of that market? _____

_____

_____

_____

How many other companies in your type of business currently serve the target market? _____

_____

_____

_____

Other: _____

Other: _____

Continued

BUILD-YOUR-BUSINESS WORKSHEET

Research Questions (continued)

Company

Which companies are the leading competitors in your industry? _____

_____

_____

Which companies are the leading competitors in your specific geographic target market? _____

_____

_____

How is market share divided? _____

_____

_____

What products/services do your leading competitors offer? At what price? _____

_____

_____

How are your competitors perceived in the marketplace? _____

_____

_____

Who are some potential customers for your products/services? What are the names of key personnel and what is their contact information? _____

_____

_____

Who are some potential suppliers of products/services that you need? How do their current customers rate them? ___

_____

_____

Other: _____

necessarily the website or database where you found your information but rather the entity that did the primary research and compiled the data you found.

One of the first things to look for when examining a data source is whether any potential bias or hidden agenda is influencing the data. Imagine that you are searching for data on cigarette sales to minors. You find several studies on the issue, drawing quite different conclusions. Which source do you believe offers the most reliable data?

- A government agency
- A tobacco industry association
- An antismoking advocacy organization
- A private, for-profit research company
- A university research study

Any one of these sources might have an agenda other than simply reporting the facts. For instance, though both the tobacco industry association and the antismoking organization might have special expertise on the topic of cigarette sales, their particular points of view could lead to inherent bias in their research results. The private, for-profit research company may well be conducting the study for a client with a special interest in the issue (such as the tobacco industry), and this could also skew the results.

Remember, the types of questions a researcher asks, the size of the survey sample, the composition of those surveyed, and the methodology for compiling the data can all dramatically influence the results produced.

Generally, the most accurate sources are considered to be:

- **Government data.** Data from government sources, particularly from the U.S. Census Bureau, is generally regarded as fairly accurate, as it's drawn from large samples. Also, it's expected that such data is free from inherent bias.

- **Private research company data.** Private research companies charge large sums of money to gather data relating to an industry. Since their primary income derives from the sale of such data, its accuracy is directly related to their ability to stay in business.

- **Studies conducted by universities.** Generally, studies conducted by university faculty and researchers are highly regarded. Such studies typically undergo academic review and are likely to follow accepted research procedures. Ideally, such studies are relatively free of bias.

- **Studies using large samples.** The greater the number of respondents, the more likely it is that the information they supply reflects reality.

In many situations, finding information about the methods used to collect data can help you evaluate its credibility. For instance, trade associations may be an excellent source of data, since many of them collect information about

Check the time

It's important to look not only at how recent the data is but also at the time period the data covers. For instance, here are two headlines adapted from real newspaper stories reporting on the same study:

- "VC funding falls to 7-year low"
- "VC funding increases by 7 percent"

Both headlines were completely accurate. Both reported on the same study. Yet the first focused on data for only one quarter of the year; the second article reported on the total amount of funding for the entire year compared to the year before. So look for data that covers reasonable time periods.

THE GOOD VS. THE BAD

GOOD SIGNS	BAD SIGNS
Data was collected by an independent research firm	Study was funded by a private company or association with a political or profit agenda
Large sample size	Small sample size
Large percentage of those polled responded	Small percentage responding
Objective, neutral questions were asked	Questions were skewed to elicit particular responses

Data with an agenda

Be particularly cautious when evaluating data from certain types of sources. This can include:

- Statistics from individual companies, which may have manipulated data to increase sales
- Data from politically or economically motivated organizations, which may have had a special agenda and used research techniques that support the message they want to send
- Data from studies with very small samples, which may not represent reality

their own industries. Still, this data may be either highly reliable (when it comes from those associations that are careful and objective in their research) or highly unreliable (when, for example, an association uses data for political or marketing purposes).

Organize your data and avoid plagiarism

As you comb through dozens of databases and various resources looking for the information you need, you'll find you may lose track of where you spotted a particular statistic. So, when you're ready to prepare your business plan, marketing strategy, or business proposal, you may discover you have no idea of the source of some of your data. This can create some very unfortunate results.

Readers of business plans and other business documents will want to know the sources of the information in your work. You may be questioned about your conclusions, therefore you need to be able to cite the sources of your data. Many entrepreneurs have had their business plans rejected by investors because they couldn't support claims about the size of their market or their potential profit margins.

Appropriate citations are particularly important in academic papers. Plagiarism can result in your failing a class or facing disciplinary action. The business world, too, views plagiarism as a sign of untrustworthiness. Potential investors or partners will avoid doing business with you if they suspect you of such behavior. Even when no one suspects you of behaving unethically, failure to keep track of your sources is sloppy—and dangerous.

To avoid these types of problems, carefully organize your findings, and always note sources and resources while doing your research. As you collect data, be certain to note where you found it, the source of the data, the URL of the website and access date (if you found it on the Web), or the database, book, or research report it's from.

To help you keep track of your data, a worksheet is provided on page 69 for use as a guide. Keep notes on the information found, source, date, and so on—as you gather information from each source.

BUILD-YOUR-BUSINESS WORKSHEET

Organizing Data Sources

As you do your research, use this worksheet to organize your research sources.

Data found: _____
_____
_____

Resource used to locate data (database, website, or print source): _____
_____
_____

Location of resource (Web address, name of database, call number, or issue date): _____
_____
_____

Original source of data (name of study): _____
_____
_____

Original source of data (name of individual/organization originating data): _____
_____
_____

Data found: _____
_____
_____

Notes/comments: _____
_____
_____
_____
_____

Luxury Doesn't Just Happen: The Ritz-Carlton Hotel Company

The president of the United States gives only one award for quality in business—the prestigious Malcolm Baldrige Award. So it's a big deal to win it. The Ritz-Carlton Hotel Company did so in 1999. How did they do it? Research! When the U.S. Department of Commerce selected Ritz-Carlton for the award, it cited the premium hotel chain's extraordinarily detailed understanding of its customers and operations as a primary reason for giving the award.[1]

"What we get from data is essential," said John Timmerman, vice president of operations for the luxury hotel chain.[2] But the Ritz isn't interested in numbers for numbers' sake. It wants to turn the numbers into actionable behaviors that improve the customer experience. "To be agile in any marketplace, especially one that changes as rapidly as ours, means being a learning organization," said Timmerman. "If you can't define it, you can't control it, you can't measure it, and you can't improve it."[3]

Ritz-Carlton is fanatically detail-oriented, so the data it collects is broad and deep. It identifies and documents procedures for quality improvement (QA) and problem solving, makes sure that experts review all its methods of data collection and analysis, and establishes high standards for success. It uses three types of comparative data: 1) comparisons to its industry and foremost competitors, 2) benchmarks established by the industry, and 3) benchmarks established within the company.[4]

One of its ongoing research tasks is to identify problems before they occur. According to its application for the Baldrige Award, by 1999, the Ritz had identified no fewer than 970 potential problems that could arise during interactions with overnight guests and 1,071 potential issues that might occur during interactions with meeting-event planners. Each potential issue is flagged, a solution is created, and all employees are trained how to handle the situation should the potential ever become actual.

Even the most subjective data is collected and used—data that other businesses would ignore as *too* subjective. For example, subtle reactions of guests to specific decor, services, or entertainment are noted and fed

challenge

Remain at the top of an industry in the face of fierce competition and a volatile global economy

solution

Carefully research every aspect of customers and industry

1. "1999 Baldrige Award Recipient, Ritz-Carlton Hotel Company, L.L.C.," Oct. 5, 2010. *National Institute of Standards and Technology*.
2. "How the Ritz-Carlton Manages the Mystique," by Jennifer Robinson, Dec. 11, 2008. *Gallup Management Journal*.
3. Ibid.
4. www.quality.nist.gov/PDF_files/RCHC_Application_Summary.pdf.

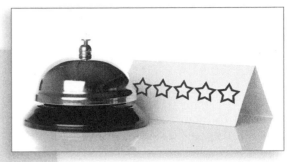

into the river of data that is used to establish business priorities. "As a result, the hotel can pick up on information that might have been easily missed," said Timmerman.[5]

Sometimes, the results of its research contradict conventional wisdom. In a Forbes.com interview, Ritz-Carlton President Simon F. Cooper said, "A breakthrough in our thinking was understanding that we are not a hotel brand but a lifestyle brand."[6] This was a hugely inspirational realization for Ritz-Carlton, because, for a hotel company, growth relies on developing new properties in new places. That puts limits on growth. But as a lifestyle brand, Ritz-Carlton can offer any number of products and services. Suddenly the possibilities were endless—and as researching the lifestyles of its customers was something it had been doing for years, it had amassed a wealth of data to back up new strategies. So it launched vacation packages, spa "experiences," and executive gifts and incentives.

Of course, many if not most companies make some attempt to research their markets, survey customer satisfaction, and measure employee engagement. But where Ritz-Carlton truly excels is not merely in the amount of data it acquires, but also in how it disseminates results throughout the organization in ways that actually drive the business forward. Data isn't just kept in reports on some executive's desk. Instead, Ritz-Carlton analyzes the ocean of data and incorporates its understanding of changing customer and market requirements into business decisions—and then involves the entire workforce to take action. This information is disseminated in a variety of ways: through formal classes, electronic communications, and printed materials, but most commonly through face-to-face interactions.

For example, at the Ritz, every employee in every location participates in a daily preshift meeting in which the top priorities and goals are presented and discussed. Result: Everyone is always informed, and on board, with the latest strategy. Most important, all employees understand the particular ways that they, personally, contribute to reaching the goals.

Through research, the Ritz-Carlton clearly leaves little to chance. By knowing its customers, its industry, and its markets, it ensures that it maintains a competitive edge. ∎

questions

1. What types of information do you think would be most useful to a luxury hotel company to improve its performance and profitability?

2. How does research for an existing company differ from the kind of research needed for a prelaunch venture?

3. Why is it important that the results of research be shared throughout a company?

4. Can you think of examples of other companies at which doing research on customers' lifestyles might affect their choice of product offerings?

---

5. Ibid.
6. "How Ritz-Carlton Stays at the Top," by Robert Reiss, Oct. 30, 2009, *Forbes.com*.

EXERCISE: critical thinking

WHAT DO YOU NEED TO KNOW?

Goal:

Think through the information you must acquire before deciding whether your business idea is viable.

What to Do:

You have an idea for a new business—to run a travel service, specializing in luxury and active adventures, and combining first-class accommodations and food, while enabling guests to pursue an active pastime, such as scuba diving on the Great Barrier Reef, bicycling in Provence, or hiking in Yellowstone National Park.

1. In this exercise, either alone or working with others, identify the questions you need answered in order to evaluate whether you have a viable business idea. Make a list of *all* the types of informa-tion and data that would be important to know before you invest significant time and money in your idea. What research should you undertake to help make your endeavor successful?

In particular, identify what you need to know about:

a. The competition

b. The potential market for your services

c. The industry you'd be part of

d. The labor and operational aspects of your venture

e. The financial prospects—in terms of both profitability and getting funded

2. Rank the data items in order of importance to your venture.

learning objectives

In this chapter, you'll learn how to:

- Recognize the importance of a business plan

- Evaluate the purpose of a business plan for an entrepreneurial venture

- Develop a successful, compelling business plan

- Apply key business success factors to the business planning process

- Determine what to include in a business plan and what to omit

- Understand, analyze, and prepare a sources and use of funds sheet and an assumption sheet

- Apply best practices when preparing financial forms

- Determine the recipients of a business plan

- Conduct a business plan presentation, both in person and electronically

- Develop and execute an effective elevator pitch

- Define a winning strategy for business planning classes and competitions

Whose money do you want?

When you need money for your business, don't just seek a wealthy person with a checkbook. In most cases, you're tied to your investors for the life of your business. So research and spend time getting to know potential investors. Find out where they've invested in the past, and speak with other entrepreneurs who've worked with them. For an in-depth look at financing see Chapter 8.

Why You Need a Business Plan

In this day and age, everyone's in a hurry. In a world of 140-character tweets, can you really expect anyone to read a 30-page written business plan? Is a business plan even necessary to raise money today? Perhaps not, if you're one of the founders of Google or eBay and you have another good idea. In that case, you may be able to raise millions just sketching your idea out on a napkin.

Still, virtually all entrepreneurs can benefit from developing a business plan, which requires thinking through the issues critical to their success and identifying the strategies to help them reach their goals. And if you're trying to raise money from investors, you can expect funders to say, "Send me your business plan." Even if funding sources say all they want is a few slides and some financial projections, you'll benefit from having gone through the process of developing a business plan. Why? Because you can certainly expect that when you finally get that all-important pitch meeting with prospective funders, they'll grill you on every aspect of your business. If you haven't developed a thorough business plan, you won't have good, polished answers to give them.

Developing a business plan can be a critical factor for successfully starting a company. A highly regarded study from the Illinois Institute of Technology that followed would-be entrepreneurs over a three-year period showed that individuals who intended to start a business were six times more likely to actually launch a business if they completed a business plan.

However, just because you need a business plan, that doesn't mean you have to spend a huge amount of time writing, editing, and polishing a long written document. It's the planning and not the physical plan that's truly important. The process of developing your business plan is the biggest benefit—examining the critical aspects of your business, researching factors and trends affecting your success, asking yourself the tough questions.

While developing a business plan, you'll likely change some aspects of your business. You may even conclude that your concept isn't viable and decide to scrap the idea entirely. That's what planning is all about. Now's the time to make those kinds of mistakes—on paper instead of in the real world.

Business plan success factors

Creating your business plan provides a means of crystallizing your ideas and challenging your assumptions. The ultimate purpose of developing such a plan is to establish a successful business. The following factors play the biggest part in business success, so use them to guide your planning and thinking.

- **Formulate your business concept.** Your business concept is about meeting needs. In fact, meeting needs is the basis of all business. You can devise a wonderful new machine, but if it doesn't address a real and important need or desire, people won't buy it and your business will fail. Your business plan should clearly and succinctly lay out your business concept and explain how it will offer the market something it won't be able to resist.

- **Understand the market.** It's not enough to have only a great idea or a new invention as the basis of your business. You must also identify a market that's sufficiently large, accessible, and responsive. If your market isn't big enough, you can't succeed. If it's too big, you won't be able to reach it efficiently. If it

How you'll use your plan

Most likely, you want to use your business plan as one or more of the following:

- **A tool for raising funds (either investments or loans)**
- **An internal document to guide your company's development**
- **A recruitment tool for key personnel**

en·tre·pre·neur·ship key terms

Assumption sheet
A statement that briefly outlines the information a company used to come up with its financial projections, such as market size, profit margins, and key expenses.

Company description
A section of the business plan that describes the basic details of a business, such as legal status, ownership, products or services, company mission, and milestones achieved.

Digital presentation
A computer presentation, also referred to as a "slide" show, a "deck," or a "preso" (each frame of a computer presentation is called a "slide").

Elevator pitch
A concise summary of a company's service, business, or product idea that can be delivered in a very short time.

Executive summary
Highlights the most important aspects of a business, summarizing key points of its business plan.

Sources and use of funds
A one-page description of a company's sources of money and how that money will be used.

isn't ready for you, your business will fail, no matter how good your concept. Your business plan must contain an overview of the market you intend to enter and an explanation of why it's ripe for receiving your product or service.

- **Investigate industry health and trends.** Generally, your company is subject to the same conditions that affect your overall industry. If consumer spending declines nationally, there's a good chance your new consumer product will also experience poor sales. Thus, as you develop your plan, you need to respond to industrywide factors that will affect your own company's performance. Although it's certainly possible to make money in an industry that is experiencing hard times, you can only do so if you make a conscious effort to position your company appropriately. For example, if you plan to start a construction business and the number of new-home starts is down, you may want to target the remodeling market or the commercial real estate market rather than the new-home construction market. But you need to be aware of industry conditions and be able to address them in your business plan.

- **Create a consistent business focus and clear strategic position.** Key to creating any successful business is developing a clear, strategic position that differentiates you from your competition—and then maintaining focus on that position. All too often, businesses fail because management loses sight of the central character of the enterprise. Defining a clear, strategic position enables you to capture a particular place in the market and distinguish yourself from your competitors. Different companies may sell a similar product, yet each may have a quite different sense of what its business is really all about.

- **Hire capable management.** Perhaps more than any other factor, competent management stands out as the most important ingredient in business success. The people in key positions are crucial in determining the health and viability of your business. Moreover, because of the importance of capable management to business success, many investors and venture capital firms place the single greatest emphasis on this factor when evaluating business plans and deciding on loans or investments. They'll review the management section of a business plan with special scrutiny. Your business plan must inspire confidence in the capabilities of your management, so you should put your management team together carefully.

- **Attract, motivate, and retain employees.** A company is only as good as its people. The ability to attract and retain outstanding employees and managers is crucial to a company's long-term viability and competitiveness. Your company's reputation for treating employees well directly enhances both the number and the quality of job applicants and your company's ability to retain employees once hired.

- **Take control of your finances.** Key to any business is the way it handles money. Not fully anticipating start-up costs can immediately place impossible pressures on a new business. And poor cash flow management can bring down even a seemingly thriving enterprise. Things always take longer and cost more than anticipated. Build financial cushions into your plan to allow for unanticipated expenses and delays.

- **Anticipate and adapt to change.** Change is inevitable, and the rate of change grows ever faster. In today's world, your company needs to anticipate and quickly respond to change, and also to train its employees to be adaptable. Companies that are nimble and able to quickly evaluate and respond to changing conditions are most likely to be successful.

- **Emphasize company values and integrity.** Every company must make money. You can't stay in business unless you eventually earn a profit. However, studies of business success have shown that companies whose management is driven by significant goals in addition to making money (such as social goals, the drive for innovation, or the desire to create a great place to work) succeed better and survive longer than companies whose sole motivation is monetary.

As you develop your business plan, keep in mind those values you wish to express or achieve in the company you're creating or expanding. These values can be aimed externally, at achieving some business, social, or environmental goal, or they can be aimed internally, at achieving a certain type of workplace or quality of product or service, or both.

What Goes into Your Plan?

Your business plan includes the following basic components:

- **The executive summary.** Highlights the most important aspects of your business, summarizing key points of your business plan.

- **Company description.** Features the basic, factual details about your business, such as your legal status, ownership, products or services, company mission, and milestones achieved to date.

- **Industry analysis and trends.** Evaluates your industry and shows potential investors that you understand external business conditions.

- **Target market.** Identifies the types of people or businesses most likely to be your customers, details the size and trends of that market, and explains their needs and wants.

- **Competition.** Evaluates other companies offering a similar product or service or filling a similar market need.

- **Strategic position and risk assessment.** Differentiates your company from the competition. It shows where you stand in the marketplace, what makes you compelling to customers, and what advantages you have over the competition.

- **Marketing plan and sales strategy.** Outlines how you'll reach your customers, convey a positive message about your products or services, build a brand, and secure orders or make sales.

Do the right thing

A company is strengthened by integrity. In the long run, when you deal with everyone—customers, suppliers, and employees—with fairness and honesty, you create a more sustainable and successful business. Integrity inspires customer and employee loyalty, helps avoid lawsuits and fines, and makes decision-making easier.

- **Operations.** Explains how you run your business and actually produce your goods or services, and outlines the day-to-day factors that may give you an edge over your competition.

- **Technology plan.** Outlines what technology you'll use and how you'll use it.

- **Management and organization.** Describes the key people running your business and how your company will be structured from a personnel point of view.

- **Community involvement and social responsibility.** Details your company's values and how you'll act on those values; identifies how you'll be a good corporate citizen.

- **Development, milestones, and exit plan.** Shows where your business will be in several years' time, how you'll get there, and the milestones you plan to reach along the way; indicates potential strategies for making liquid the financial investments in the company.

- **The financials.** A set of financial statements showing the current financial status and future predicted income and expenses of your company.

When evaluating a business plan, experienced business plan readers generally spend the first five minutes reviewing it in this order: first, the executive summary; second, the financials; third, the management section; and next, the exit plan or terms of the deal, if applicable.

The **executive summary** is the most important portion of your business plan if you're seeking financing. Only a clear, concise, and compelling condensation of your business right up front will persuade readers to wade through the rest of your plan. No matter how beneficial your product, how lucrative your market, or how innovative your manufacturing techniques, your executive summary alone must persuade a reader to spend the time to find out about your product, market, and techniques.

Preparing Your Financials

For the financial portion of your business plan, the three most important forms you'll prepare are:

- **Income statement.** Shows whether your company is making a profit, by delineating the income and expenses for the period covered.

- **Cash flow statement.** Shows whether the company has the cash to pay its bills.

- **Balance sheet.** Shows how much the company is worth overall.

Chapter 7 covers these three forms in depth.

Other forms to include in your business plan are:

- **Break-even analysis.** Shows the point at which sales exceed costs and you begin to make a profit. Advisable for internal planning. See pages 161–163 for more information on this analysis.

- **Start-up costs.** For a new business, shows the initial investment necessary to begin operations. Base this form on the "Start-Up Costs" worksheet on page 193.

- **Sources and use of funds.** Shows where you'll get financing for your business and how you'll spend the money invested or lent. A potential investor or loan officer will want to see this.

- **Assumption sheet.** Shows those reading your financial statements how you determined the figures used. A good adjunct to other forms.

Sources and use of funds

If you're seeking outside financing, either through loans or investors, those contemplating giving you money will naturally want to know what you're going to do with the money you raise. They'll also want to see what other sources of money you have, if any, and whether you have contributed any of your own funds.

To provide such information, devise a one-page description of the **sources and use of funds**. This can go in the business plan itself or can be sent with the cover letter to potential financing sources. It should tell a potential investor that you have specific plans for the money you raise, that you're not taking on debts or giving up equity thoughtlessly, and that you'll use the funds to make your business grow.

The worksheet "Sources and Use of Funds" on page 81 is particularly helpful to you with investors or lenders if you already have some commitment of financing from respected sources (which shows that other people believe in your company) and are committing significant personal funds (which shows that you believe in the project enough to take substantial personal risk). A sources and use of funds sheet also demonstrates that you're using your funds to start or expand a business, rather than to offset existing debts (a use that investors notoriously dislike).

In your sources and use of funds statement, you should include both funds you've received to date and the amounts you're now seeking, clearly delineating each. In preparing your statement, consider the following issues and terms:

- **Funding rounds.** The number of development stages at which you'll seek financing from the investment community.

- **Total amount.** Amount of money sought in this round of financing, from all funding sources.

Predicting the future

In a business plan, you typically make guesses about what will happen in the future. But they shouldn't be wild guesses. Your forward-looking projections should be conservative. Base your assumptions on the belief that will things take longer and cost more than you originally expect.

- **Equity financing.** Amount you'll raise by selling ownership interest in the company.

- **Preferred stock.** Outstanding stock for which dividends will be paid, before other dividends can be paid for common stock or before other obligations of the company are paid; investors often want preferred stock.

- **Common stock.** Stock for which dividends are paid when company is profitable and has paid preferred stock dividends and other obligations.

- **Debt financing.** Amount of money you'll raise by taking out loans.

- **Long-term loans.** Loans to be paid back in more than a year's time.

- **Mortgage loans.** Loans taken out with property as collateral.

- **Short-term loans.** Bridge loans, credit lines, and other loans to be paid back in less than a year.

- **Convertible debt.** Loans that are later convertible to stock, at the funder's option, giving both the security of a loan and the potential of stock.

- **Investment from principals.** Amount of money that you or other key employees are contributing to the company; this can be in the form of cash or property.

- **Capital expenditures.** Purchase of necessary equipment or property.

- **Working capital.** Funds to be used for the ongoing operating expenses of the business.

- **Debt retirement.** Funds used to pay off existing loans or obligations.

Assumption sheet

Financial forms are merely meaningless numbers unless you base them on decisions and facts. Your potential financing sources want to see how you arrived at your numbers and must be convinced that your assumptions are reasonably accurate. If, for instance, you have indicated your sales at a certain amount, investors want to see what size you assume the market is and what percentage of the market you assume you can secure. If those figures seem realistic, you increase your credibility; if those assumptions seem based on inaccurate numbers or overly optimistic projections, investors will look skeptically at the rest of your plan.

It's good discipline for you, as well, to learn to develop an **assumption sheet** whenever you do financial projections. Otherwise, you can be too easily tempted to write down figures that look good on paper but have little to do with reality.

If you have worked through the business planning process, putting together an assumption sheet should be a relatively easy task. You have already asked yourself most of the questions called for on this form and have the answers available to you.

BUILD-YOUR-BUSINESS WORKSHEET

Sources and Use of Funds

Complete the following form to describe how much money you are seeking and how you will use the funds raised. Be as specific as possible: If you know what equipment you are going to buy, list it; if you have a loan from a bank, state the name of the lending institution, amount, and terms.

Number of funding rounds expected for full financing: _____

Total dollar amount being sought in this round: _____

Sources of Funds

Equity Financing: _____

Preferred Stock: _____

Common Stock: _____

Debt Financing: _____

Mortgage Loans: _____

Other Long-Term Loans: _____

Short-Term Loans: _____

Convertible Debt: _____

Investment from Principals: _____

Uses of Funds

Capital Expenditures: _____

Purchase of Property: _____

Leasehold Improvements: _____

Purchase of Equipment/Furniture: _____

Other: _____

Working Capital: _____

Purchase of Inventory: _____

Staff Expansion: _____

New Product Line Introduction: _____

Additional Marketing Activities: _____

Other Business Expansion Activities: _____

Other: _____

Debt Retirement: _____

Cash Reserve: _____

Think visually

As you work on your business plan, look for the kind of information and statistics that you can convey in graphic form, to make a greater impact and keep readers' attention. As you do your research, capture any charts and graphs that will be helpful. Even consider "infographics" that display data in interesting fashion. Help your business plan come alive.

An assumption sheet should list purely straightforward information; it doesn't require substantial detail or explanation. You don't even need to use sentences; simply provide the data in each category. Be familiar with these assumptions so that you're ready to defend your assumptions when meeting with investors.

Complete the "Assumption Sheet" worksheet on page 84, and include a finished assumption sheet at the conclusion of your financial forms in your business plan.

Guidelines for preparing your financial forms

In preparing your financial forms for your business plan, you'll almost certainly have questions as to how to attribute certain expenses. You might wonder whether you should ascribe sales commissions to cost of goods sold or to operating expenses. Accounting practices differ, so follow these guidelines:

- **Be conservative.** Avoid the tendency to paint the rosiest picture possible; doing so reduces your credibility.

- **Be honest.** Experienced financing sources will sense dishonest or manipulated figures; expect to be asked to justify your numbers.

- **Don't be "creative."** Use standard formats and financial terms; otherwise you look inexperienced to financing sources.

- **Get your accountant's advice.**

- **Follow the practices used in your industry.**

- **Choose the appropriate accounting method.**

- **Be consistent.** Make a decision and stick with it for all your accounts, otherwise you can't compare one year's figures to another.

Historical performance of your company

If you run an existing business (not a newly established one), you also need to gather historical data about your own company. In particular, you should examine your past internal financial records. Here is some of the financial information you may need to locate:

- Past sales records, broken down by product line, time period, store, region, or salesperson, depending on size of your business

- Past trends in costs of sales

- Overhead expense patterns

- Profit margins on product lines

- Variations from budget projections

If you cannot easily gather this information, change your reporting system so that in the future you'll be able to have the data you need for adequate planning.

If you've created business plans or set goals or objectives in the past, you should also track how well your business has performed in terms of meeting the objectives set in those previous plans. Have you consistently underperformed, or perhaps exceeded your goals? Have you reached key milestones within the time period originally projected?

Preparing Your Plan

The most important aspects of your plan must jump out at even the most casual reader. Even if your plan is intended for internal company use only, it will be more effective if it's presented in a compelling, vivid form. Highlighting specific facts, goals, and conclusions makes your plan easier to review, more effective as a working document, and more likely to make a positive impact.

Keep in mind that funding sources primarily look for answers to the following questions concerned with the heart of the plan:

- Is the business idea solid?

- Is there a sufficient market for the product or service?

- Are the financial projections healthy, realistic, and in line with the investor's or lender's funding patterns?

- Is the key management described in the plan experienced and capable?

- Does the plan clearly describe how the investors or lenders will get their money back?

Within the first five minutes of reading your business plan, readers must perceive that the answers to *all* these questions are favorable.

Length of the plan

Although no magic number exists for the perfect business plan length, here are some general guidelines:

- Limit the plan (not including the financials and appendices) to about 15 to 35 pages; 20 pages are enough for most businesses.

- Only a plan for a complicated business or product should exceed 30 pages (not including the appendices).

- Anything less than 10 pages seems insubstantial.

While they provide a good way to present additional information, appendices should be no longer than the plan itself.

Tailoring the plan for your recipients

Once you've researched your potential funders, you should organize your cover letter and executive summary to highlight those aspects of your business most likely to fit the needs and interests of each funder.

Is the venture capital firm particularly interested in patentable new technology? Will the bank fund only those companies established for more than three years? If so, discuss these areas in the first paragraph of your cover letter, or place greater emphasis on them in your summary.

Assumption Sheet

Use this worksheet to show how you arrived at the numbers in your financial statements.

SALES

Product Line	Year $	Units	Year $	Units	Year $	Units	Annual Growth Rate %
Total							

Describe the projected increase/decrease in selling price of each product line/service. _____
_____
_____

PERSONNEL/MANAGEMENT

Describe the number of employees and assumptions regarding total payroll projected in the financial forms. _____
_____
_____

Describe key management positions to be added, and timing. _____
_____
_____

GROSS PROFIT MARGIN

List the projected gross profit margin for each product line or service. _____
_____
_____
_____

Describe any major changes in cost of goods that are projected to affect gross profit margin. _____
_____
_____
_____

KEY EXPENSES

Describe the timing and costs of key projected expenses.

Plant Expansion or New Branches _____

_____

Major Capital Purchases_____

_____

Major Marketing Expenses _____

_____

Research and Development _____

_____

Other Key Expenses _____

_____

FINANCING

Describe any financing debt (loans) that are projected to be added or retired.

_____

_____

_____

Describe the interest rates assumed to be in effect for these financial projections.

_____

_____

_____

OTHER

Describe any other major developments that are assumed in creating your financial projections (such as strategic partnerships, competitive situation, etc.).

_____

_____

_____

_____

_____

_____

_____

Five crucial minutes

Although you may spend five months preparing your plan, the cold, hard fact is that an investor or lender can dismiss it in less than five minutes. If you don't make a positive impression in those critical first five minutes, your plan will be rejected. Only if it passes that first cursory look will your plan be examined in greater detail.

Language that conveys success

Convey realistic optimism and businesslike enthusiasm by following these guidelines:

- Employ a straightforward, even understated, tone.

- Avoid formal, stilted language; be natural, as if you were speaking to the reader in person.

- Use clear, active language.

- Avoid passive verbs and jargon.

- Always be professional.

- Avoid slang, and don't be "chatty."

- Instead of using superlatives like "the best" or "terrific," provide specific information that proves you're doing something right.

- Use positive comments from third-party sources, if possible.

- Use business terms.

Distributing and Presenting Your Plan

Whether the plan is intended for internal or external use, you must consider how you can best distribute it for greatest impact and how to make the finished plan an effective instrument for achieving your aims. Although a banker will probably be satisfied with only a written plan, an investor or strategic partner will probably want a **digital presentation**, such as a PowerPoint, as well.

A word about confidentiality: Nondisclosure agreements

Although most new entrepreneurs are probably overly concerned about issues of confidentiality, you may want to draw up a "nondisclosure agreement," or NDA, for the recipient to sign before receiving your plan. However, many professional investors—particularly venture capitalists—don't sign NDAs. They see so many plans in so many related industries that they would inevitably have a conflict.

The best way to protect your information is to be selective about to whom you send your plan. Research your recipients to make certain they're not already funding a competitor. Check their reputations for honesty and discretion. Deal only with reputable people. On top of that, limit the number of copies of your plan in circulation, and omit from your plan highly technical, sensitive information. You can provide that information later to only the most serious sources of potential funding.

For a sample NDA, see page 388.

Preparing a digital presentation

Most investors now expect to first see your business plan's basic info and highlights in digital form. Expect to be asked for your "slides" and financials. However, you still need a written plan, either to be reviewed before you're granted a meeting or to leave behind after you meet with potential investors.

In some cases, you won't present your plan in person. Many investors will likely ask for your slides before they'll even consider looking at your plan. In that case, you'll send your presentation electronically. For this reason, you must create a presentation that's compelling enough to stand on its own without a presenter.

Consider embedding video or audio into your slide show. Your content can include a prototype if you have one, a demonstration such as how your service will be performed, a look at your location, or anything else that will make your plan more comprehensible and exciting. You can link to a password-protected YouTube video if you have one. You may also choose to put the slides online on a password-protected site.

Of course, the presentation should contain all the major points of your business plan. You need not present them in the exact order of the written plan, but you may have to explain some elements before other points will be understandable. If you make your presentation in person, the investors will interrupt you to ask questions, challenge your assumptions, and so forth, so make certain you get to your most important points early in your slides.

Adjust the content of your slides according to the knowledge base of your audience. You don't want to bore them with information they already know (or don't need to know), such as the nitty-gritty details of your day-to-day operations. You can, however, include background information for those recipients who need it. And do your homework. Some quick research on your potential investors can reap big rewards. If you include some of this information in your presentation, your credibility increases dramatically.

Remember, your slides are meant to whet their appetite. While there's no exact number that will be right for every business, you should be able to convey all the key details of your company in 12 slides. If you have too many and you are presenting in person, you're going to feel as if you have to rush through your presentation to get to them all. The text of each slide should be primarily in short, bulleted points. You rarely need whole sentences. Put no more than three to five bullet points on a slide.

If you present your slides in person, practice first. Make certain you feel comfortable working with the computer and the software so that you're not distracted during your meeting.

Nine surefire ways to ruin your business plan

1. **Make basic mistakes**
2. **Underestimate the competition**
3. **Overestimate sales**
4. **Plan more than one business at a time**
5. **Build your business alone**
6. **Use made-up numbers**
7. **Forget a sources and use of funds statement**
8. **Don't include an exit strategy**
9. **Lie**

12 CRITICAL SLIDES

SLIDE NUMBER	SLIDE NAME	SLIDE DESCRIPTION
1.	Title Slide	Your company's name, a short company description, name of presenter(s) if presenting in person
2.	Your Elevator Pitch	A succinct description of your products or services, market, and competitive advantages; use vibrant language; if possible, embed audio or video to demonstrate your product or service
3.	Size of Opportunity	Investors want to know the potential size your company can grow to and your plans for future development
4.	Your Specific Target Customers	Who they are and the customer needs that your product will meet
5.	The Market Size	Numbers and dollars, past growth, growth forecasts
6.	The Competition	Division of market share, how your product compares to theirs, your value proposition in comparison to the competition's, and barriers to entry
7.	Your Team	Who they are, past successes and experience, and why they're qualified to do the job
8.	The Business Model	How you'll distribute your product, pricing strategies, how you'll reach your customers
9.	The Time Line	When you expect to reach key milestones
10.	Financials	A brief summary of key points from your income statement, balance sheet, or cash flow projections
11.	Funding	How much you're asking for in this round, how many future rounds are expected, how much you'll request during those rounds, and how the funds will be used
12.	The Investment Opportunity	Potential exit strategies and financial return for investors

Your elevator pitch

Before considering a prospective investment, venture capitalists and other investors often want to hear what they call the **elevator pitch**. This is the concise description of a company—its product or service, its market, its competitive advantages—that an entrepreneur could give in the time it would take to ride up an elevator (and not an elevator in a skyscraper!). An elevator pitch shows that you understand your business. (If you're unclear on your strategic position, you'd still be mumbling as you pass the fifteenth floor.)

Your elevator pitch doesn't have to be made in an actual elevator to be useful. You'll find you'll use it often: in emails to prospective financing sources, to introduce yourself and your company at networking events, and to deftly and briefly describe your business to potential customers.

It takes some thinking to decide which aspects of your business to mention in an elevator pitch. Even more frustrating, you have to decide which parts of your company to leave out. Often, these can be the things you're most excited about—a new technology, a great location, and the fact you get to go to Europe on buying trips. But if they're not central to the core of your business, they don't belong in an elevator pitch.

Your elevator pitch must not only be short, it must be clear. Unless you're in a highly technical field, your neighbor or grandmother should be able to understand your business well enough to be able to describe it to someone else. A good elevator pitch offers the following information:

- **What your business makes or does.** This should be very brief: "My company manufactures water- and weather-proof, solar-powered outdoor lights."

- **What market you serve.** You should be very specific about this: "Fifteen- to 30-year-old males who daily play video games" or "Small businesses with five to 10 employees."

- **How you plan to make money.** This is very important if you're giving your elevator pitch to potential investors. Because they'll want to know how you will earn a profit, you need to be very explicit about the business model you plan to employ. For example, "We will charge a monthly subscription ranging from $5 to $25 per user."

- **How your business compares to other, familiar businesses.** If you compare your business to other similar businesses, people may more easily understand what your product or service is all about. For example, a new social networking site for lawyers might be described as "Like Facebook for law-firm employees." Or a new airline might be described as "A discount carrier with more frequent service than XYZ regional airline."

- **Why you will succeed.** What are the market conditions that make your idea a surefire success? You need to use all your powers of persuasion here. If you have any hard numbers to back up your assertions, so much the better: "Census figures show that families with young children are moving into this area at a rapid pace (up 27% over the previous decade), and those families will require housing."

- **Your ultimate goals for the business.** Do you want to eventually run a multinational corporation, or do you want to keep it relatively small and contained? You should be prepared to articulate your vision for the business's size and reach.

BUILD-YOUR-BUSINESS WORKSHEET

Your Elevator Pitch

Use this worksheet to develop the main components of your elevator pitch. Then edit your responses to fewer than 100 words. Remember to keep your pitch short. Focus on what customers get, not on what you do. And make your pitch easy to remember.

Company name:_____
_____

Does: _____
_____

Serves this market: _____
_____

Makes money by: _____
_____

Is like these other companies: _____
_____

But is special because: _____
_____

It will succeed because: _____
_____

Aims to achieve: _____
_____

Final elevator pitch: _____
_____
_____
_____
_____

Classes and Competitions

You may prepare a business plan for a class assignment or to enter a business plan competition (often with significant cash awards). One major difference in preparing a business plan for a class or competition is that you're much more likely to be working with a team—as equals—rather than having one entrepreneur with a vision driving the process and making the final decisions.

Another major difference from the "real world" is the way your plan will be judged. Professors and competition judges typically place more emphasis on the quality of the written plan itself than potential funders do. And in the "real world," potential funders will base far more of their decisions on the capabilities of the key founders than competition judges or professors will.

The team process

One of the major challenges of developing a business plan for a class or competition is working with a team. Mastering the dynamics of working together in a group—how to reach decisions, allocate tasks, communicate, and so forth—will help prepare you for the very real situations you'll be in when developing an actual business. The following key steps will help you manage your competition process.

- **Choose your team.** Your people determine your success. Unlike with an actual business, you don't always have the option of jettisoning members of your class or competition team. So choose carefully, and look for balance among the functional areas you'll put in your plan: Having four great marketers may be overkill, leaving you without sufficient depth in operations, technology, or finance.

- **Make decisions.** The first decision any group must make is to decide how they're going to make decisions. Devising a clear and fair decision-making process makes every other decision easier and the group interaction more pleasant. The important thing in devising a decision-making process is that all team members "buy in" to the process.

- **Choose your project.** How do you decide which business you're going to plan? Some classes or competitions may limit the kinds of businesses you can select as a project, but more often you have a universe of options from which to choose. You'll probably start your selection process with a brainstorming session of team members, to come up with a list of possibilities. In fact, some professors require you to submit a number of potential business plan projects. Refer back to Chapter 2 to help you focus your selection process.

- **Identify key issues.** Once you've decided which business you're going to plan, you need to identify the key issues you'll have to address in developing that plan. Go over the "Basic Business Concept" worksheet on page 38. Be critical: Don't be afraid to tear your business idea apart. Ask yourself all

REAL-WORLD RECAP

The team process

The following key steps will help you manage your competition process:

- Choose your team
- Make decisions
- Choose your project
- Identify key issues
- Assign tasks
- Reevaluate assumptions
- Integrate the work
- Prepare and present the plan

Special considerations for classes

Generally, the issues for preparing a successful business plan for a class—and getting a good grade—are the same for preparing any business plan. Still, professors and teachers will particularly look for:

- Well-integrated plan sections
- Well-documented sources of information
- An accurate assessment of the real-world situation
- A clear statement of assumptions
- An adequate assessment of risks
- Clear writing and presentation

In a class, you'll also likely be judged by how well the team has worked together, so pay particular attention to your group dynamics.

the tough questions that a reader—whether a professor, judge, or potential funder—will inevitably ask.

- **Assign tasks.** When apportioning tasks, you can choose to either divide up tasks based on functional areas or share all tasks among team members. Because it's generally helpful to have one key person act as the focal point for reporting in, setting meetings, and so on, you'll also need to choose a group leader. The group can then decide the nature and extent of the leader's responsibilities.

- **Reevaluate assumptions.** Toward the end of the planning process, before putting the written plan and presentation together, reassemble the group to reevaluate your original assumptions and readjust your business concept or strategy. As a result of your research and data into the industry, market, and competition, you'll have a much better idea of what might actually succeed. Take the time to do this step, and be willing to change as well.

- **Integrate the work.** Even after each member of the team has completed their section of the plan, you're far from finished when they turn their sections in. You'll likely find that you have a very uneven document: some sections more thorough than others, some more clearly written than others. Put one team member, or at most two, in charge of completing the written plan. It's difficult to write an excellent document by committee.

- **Prepare and present the plan.** Finally, decide who'll be giving the presentation of the plan, if an oral presentation is required or is an option (take it!), and then practice that presentation. You don't want to be caught fumbling at the last minute, figuring out who's going to stand up.

Tricks for improving your chances in business plan competitions

Although each business plan competition has its own rules and requirements, you can improve your odds at winning by adopting these strategies.

- **Understand the nature of the competition.** A competition sponsored by M.I.T. will have a different emphasis than one sponsored by a business association that helps launch small businesses.

- **Find team members with complementary backgrounds and skills.** Judges often look at your depth of expertise. If your background is in marketing, balance your team with team members skilled in other functions, such as technology, operations, or finance.

- **If possible, talk to past winners or entrants for insights.** If the competition sponsor shares examples of previous years' winning plans, look at a number of entries—not just at the first-prize winner; you'll get a better feel for how they distinguish among entries.

■ **Research the judges.** What areas of interest and expertise do they have? If they're investors themselves, what types of businesses do they invest in? Such information gives you a sense of the level of industry and technology knowledge they'll bring to their judging.

■ **For university competitions, call on alumni members for advice or information.** In fact, this may be the perfect opportunity to get a personal meeting with a potential funder (or employer) who happens to be an alumnus or alumna of your school.

■ **Be real.** Unless the competition specifically seeks plans for visionary businesses and groundbreaking concepts, judges are much more likely to be impressed with a concept that has a good chance of succeeding in the real world.

BUILD-YOUR-BUSINESS WORKSHEET

Who's on Your Team?

Functional Area	Tasks	Team Member(s) Responsible

Business Planner Plans for Survival

Based in Palo Alto, California, the heart of Silicon Valley, PlanningShop—the publisher of the book you're reading—didn't start out as a publisher at all. It was an Internet pioneer, providing content and resources for small businesses. Yet business planning has been the key to its survival.

In the late 1990s, the company, then called "RhondaWorks," had gotten off to a strong start. Founded by Rhonda Abrams, the company secured partnerships with Microsoft, FedEx, and Hewlett-Packard. These were the heady days of the dot-com boom, and the company looked like it was headed straight for huge success.

Previous to launching her Internet company, Abrams had written the best-selling business plan guide in the United States, *Successful Business Plan, Secrets & Strategies*. In early 1999, she gained the rights to publish that book herself, which she did on the side while building RhondaWorks.

RhondaWorks had been initially funded by angel investors. By fall 2001, the money was running out. Luckily, RhondaWorks was about to ink a big deal with Compaq Computer, providing a much-needed influx of cash and keeping RhondaWorks forging ahead. Another Fortune 100 company was also close to signing a deal.

Early on the morning of September 11, 2001, Rhonda and her team were at Compaq Computers in Houston, about to sign their names to the deal. On TV monitors in the lobby, they watched live images of the Twin Towers falling. Everything stopped. Reeling and in shock, the team headed back to their hotel. Needless to say, the deal was off. On September 12, Abrams heard word from the second company that nothing would happen for at least six months to a year.

With U.S. airspace shut down and flights grounded, Abrams and her team were stuck in Houston. Sitting in their hotel room, they realized their company was in trouble. Money was about to run out. All deals were on hold.

With some rough calculations scribbled out in that hotel room—and a fierce sense of loyalty—Abrams realized that for one year, based on the side business of her book sales, she could keep two key employees, Deborah Kaye and Arthur Wait, on the payroll. After that year, though, she wouldn't be able to promise anything. It was time to come up with a new business plan—and a new company.

Later, back in Palo Alto, Abrams, Kaye, and Waite spent two full days creating a business plan for a publishing company. They looked at the entire publishing industry—the market, industry health and trends, the competition, and so on. They pondered what kind of strategic position they could carve out in the marketplace, what competitive advantage they could achieve, their finances and marketing. They took nothing for granted. PlanningShop was born.

challenge

Find ways to survive in a rapidly changing economic and business environment

solution

Through annual business planning, identify opportunities and threats, then explore ways to adapt

Their business planning didn't stop there. Abrams—who had been a business plan consultant for over a decade—knew the company needed annual business planning sessions to make sure they could grow and respond to any changes in the industry or market. After all, it's easy to become so involved in the day-to-day operations of running a business that you miss out on opportunities or fail to notice threats gathering on the horizon.

During an annual business plan session in the early 2000s, Abrams realized that about *90 percent* of her company's income came from one single book distributor. Not only was she totally reliant on the distributor, she was legally tied to it for sales to the entire bookstore channel. "I remember saying," Abrams noted, "that if I was advising a client who was so dependent on one income stream, I would tell them to diversify immediately. They're way too vulnerable if something happens." That issue became a key focus of their business plan that year. She and her team investigated where their other 10 percent of sales were coming from. Their answer was a surprise—the academic market.

Schools around the country were using *Successful Business Plan* in a variety of business classes—MBA capstone classes, entrepreneurship classes, business planning classes, and others. Without PlanningShop doing any marketing of its own, universities and colleges around the country had found PlanningShop. It was now time for PlanningShop to find them.

Abrams and her team devoted resources to pursue the academic channel. It was a smart move. At the end of 2006, the distributor on which PlanningShop had been so dependent went belly up. The income from that channel was frozen and could be gone. Fortunately, the company had diversified. PlanningShop stayed afloat as a direct result of their annual business planning process.

As with any business, the ups and downs didn't stop there. In 2008, when the economy fell off a cliff, publishing fell hard along with it. Book sales plummeted. In January 2009, PlanningShop held another "all-hands-on-deck" planning session to decide how to respond to a complete change in book-buying behavior and a terrible economy. What became clear was that there would *be* no clarity. Their approach? What they'd call "the spaghetti year." The company would throw everything it had against the wall—and see what stuck. This meant business would be chaotic and everyone would have to work *very* hard.

Fortunately a lot of things "stuck." The years 2010 and 2011 were two of the best years in the company's history.

What does the future hold? For one, PlanningShop now sees itself as a "content creation company" as the publishing industry undergoes a huge transformation, transitioning not merely from physical books to digital, but also in consumer buying behavior, channels, and business models. But PlanningShop will continue to plan—and adapt to new conditions. You can plan on it. ■

Rhonda Abrams, Owner, PlanningShop

questions

1. When do you think planning is most crucial? Do you think it's necessary when business is booming?

2. PlanningShop survived by diversifying its sales channels. For other companies, diversification of products or services helps survival and growth. Diversifying can also lead to lack of focus. When is it a good idea to diversify, and when is it not? Are there types of businesses where diversification is extremely difficult or not feasible? Which, and why?

3. PlanningShop had lots of setbacks. When do you know it's time for your business to throw in the towel? Can you ever know for sure?

HOW TO SPEND $100,000

Goal:

Plan where you will spend your resources.

What to Do:

Working alone or in groups, imagine that you run an online job recruiting service specializing in first-time job placement for new college graduates. In addition to listing job openings (for which companies pay you a fee), you also provide free webinars and regularly updated information to first-time job hunters on topics ranging from resume and cover letter writing, to what to expect in an interview, to how to negotiate a salary.

You have a team of seven employees—three IT people, two salespeople, an office manager, and an administrative assistant. You have grown slowly but steadily over the last three years since starting up, but want to grow substantially more in the coming year. You have a number of ways you could do this: Launch an aggressive marketing campaign, add new services, create an online community for first-time job seekers, and so on.

You remember reading about annual planning in this book in college, and you decide to schedule a two-day planning session with your entire staff to determine in which direction you'll take the company. By the end of the two days, you've come up with several different ideas—more than you can possibly execute. You give each member of the team, including yourself, an imaginary $100,000 to spend anywhere they would like in the business. Answer the following:

1. What plans for growing the business can you come up with? List as many as you can.

2. How would you divide up the $100,000 and spend it? Go through your list and allot dollar amounts from $0 to $100,000 for each idea. (Don't go over your total $100,000 imaginary budget!)

3. For each expenditure, explain your reasoning behind it and how you think it will benefit the company.

5 Your Customers and Target Market

learning objectives

In this chapter, you'll learn how to:

- Recognize who the customers are

- Determine whether a market exists

- Distinguish between customer categories such as purchasers, end users, and distributors

- Define customer needs and wants

- Identify and describe the target market

- Evaluate the size of the target market

- Analyze the trends affecting the market

- Recognize viable market niches

Your Customers: Who Are They?

Before you can begin marketing to your prospective customers, you first have to know who they are. Are they old or are they young? Do they live in the city or in the suburbs? Are they more concerned about price or about quality? If you're selling to businesses, are they big companies or small? What industries are they in? How quickly do they make their buying decisions?

This information may not immediately seem important, especially when you're just launching an entrepreneurial venture. After all, you need every customer you can find. But narrowing in on exactly the type of customers you'd most like to reach—and the kind that are most likely to be willing, eager, and able to buy from you—is a key building block to success in marketing. Defining your **target market** gives focus to all your marketing and sales activities, helps you craft your advertising messages (and images) and choose where and when to advertise, influences which distribution channels you use, and perhaps even helps you decide on the color of your employees' uniforms or the type of music playing in your store.

It's critical to clearly, and early, define your customers, because many of the other decisions you make about your business will follow from knowing who they are. If you don't know who your customers are—their age, location, interests, spending habits, income level, and the like—you won't know how to tell them about your product or service or how to get it to them. You could waste money placing ads on the wrong websites, sending direct mail to the wrong people, or participating in the wrong social media. Without knowing who your customers are, you could easily misjudge the price your customers are willing to pay. *Know thy customers* should be one of your business mantras from Day One. It's important to understand both who makes up your target market and the characteristics and motivations of that market.

Are customers really out there?

First, you need to figure out if potential customers actually exist. Companies have been built—and have failed—on the false premise that customers for a given product or service are, in fact, out there. You can assess whether your customer base actually exists in a number of ways.

The best way to know whether customers are out there is, paradoxically, if you have competition—if direct competitors are already selling the same or similar product or service. The fact that real customers are already paying real money for what you intend to sell provides the strongest indication that you're likely to find a willing customer base. While novice entrepreneurs often are scared off by the fact that they have competition, the fact that you have healthy competition means customers are out there. Indeed, many investors in entrepreneurial companies like to see healthy competitors. Of course, if your competition is very strong and their customers extremely loyal, it may be difficult to attract these customers to your offerings. But, in general, the rule is that "it's easier to get a piece of an existing market than to create a new market."

Still, most entrepreneurs either are introducing something new, improved, or different—or are trying to reach a new market. That means you need to *attempt* to determine whether you'll find receptive customers.

Target markets and established businesses

Even if you've been in business for years, you still need to do market research. That's because customers change and evolve. What was true about your customer base when you first built your business may no longer be accurate. What's going on with them now may not be what originally motivated them to buy from you.

Learning more about your present customers can help you keep them. Your research may suggest that you might need to modify your marketing activities—perhaps even your products and services. You'll also learn how to bring in more new customers.

en·tre·pre·neur·ship key terms

Consumer
The individual who will actually use the product or service; this term is especially applied to goods and services aimed at individuals, rather than business customers.

Demographics
The description of a market by the most basic, objective aspects of the customer base. These details are the specific, observable traits that define a target market, such as age, income, gender, and occupation for consumers, or company size, revenue, and industry affiliation for business customers.

End user
The actual user of a product or service, which may differ from the actual buyer of the product. This term is especially applied to goods and services aimed at business, rather than consumer, customers.

Market segmentation
The process of dividing a market into sections or "niches" that are perceived as having something in common—either they behave in similar ways, or they have similar

requirements. The goal of market segmentation is to tailor a product or service to appeal to each segment. This "tailoring" can include marketing, pricing, or distributing differently, or adding or deleting features.

Psychographics
Characteristics of a target market based on attitudes, values, lifestyle, desires, business style, and behavioral characteristics that may affect the buying decisions of customers.

Purchasing patterns
The typical buying habits of customers, such as number of times they purchase, interval between purchases, amount of product or service purchased, time required to make purchasing decision, where and how customers purchase product, and method of payment.

Target market
The people, businesses, and organizations most likely to buy a product or service; the people, businesses, and organizations a company tries to reach so these groups will purchase its goods or services.

Who's in the bull's-eye?

When defining your target market, keep the image of an actual target in mind. The outermost ring of the target is the entire universe of potential customers—everyone who might ever possibly be interested in your product or service. As you get closer to the center of the target, narrow in on the customers who are more likely to actually make a purchase. The group at the center should be those whom you would most like to have as customers, whom you can reach and sell to affordably, and who are most likely to buy.

To do so, you can start with basic market research—progressing through customer surveys, sampling, testing, or interviewing potential customers in focus groups (for more on research, see Chapter 3). These activities will tell you what actual members of your target customer base think about what you're planning to offer. Or you can start testing in small markets to see the response to your offering. McDonald's does this all the time: It offers new specialty sandwiches at a number of selected restaurants in a few locations, to gauge market reaction.

Notice the word *attempt* in the earlier paragraph. It's important to understand that you may not be able to judge whether you have potential customers, based on traditional methods of market research. This is especially true if you offer a truly innovative product or service. The more innovative it is, the longer it will take for customers to become familiar with it, grow comfortable with it, and begin to buy it. It's much easier to market ballpoint pens, for example, than to convince people to purchase a new device that allows them to input text into a computer without typing.

And there's the fact that customers don't always know what they want until they try it. Once, if you'd tried to sell bottled water to the mass market, they'd have laughed all the way to the kitchen tap. And almost certainly, if asked whether they would pay $70-plus a month to have a mobile phone, the vast majority of Americans would have answered with a resounding *no*. Even savvy businesspeople make mistakes of this kind. Every market test that 3M conducted of Post-it notes predicted failure—and now they're indispensable. The newer something is, the longer it takes to catch on.

A target is something you aim at

There's a reason it's called a *target* market—because you are defining exactly whom you're trying to reach. The clearer the image of your target is, the more likely you are to hit it.

Let's say you're selling a new kind of energy bar. You know it would be good for a whole range of people: health buffs, office workers who can't get away for lunch, serious athletes, people who are sick and need more calories, harried moms who don't have time to stop for a meal, and just about anyone else who could use a quick, healthy pick-me-up.

If you tried to sell to everyone who might buy your product, you'd need a huge marketing budget to make them all aware of you. You'd probably have to spend a fortune on advertising. And even then, you'd have to decide what you would say in your ads and what kinds of people and images you would feature.

Instead, you need to select one or two market segments to pursue, especially since yours is a new company, with limited resources. But whom should you sell to? How do you target your market? You have to narrow in on the factors that best make you able to compete and to reach—and sell to—a specific type of customer. These are some of the factors you need to consider in closing in on the "bull's-eye" in your target market:

- **The features and benefits of your product or service.** Which group is your energy bar best suited to?

- **The competition.** Is there a segment of the market that other energy bar makers are not reaching, or are underserving?

- **Market trends.** Is there a part of the overall market for energy bars that's growing?

- **Most motivated buyers.** Which part of the market has the most immediate need or desire to purchase energy bars?

- **Greatest ability to purchase.** What type of customer is most likely to have the disposable income to spend on energy bars?

- **Ease of reaching your prospects.** Is there a part of the market that's easiest to tell about your energy bars, because of trade shows, media (such as magazines), or other communications directed specifically at them?

- **Ease of selling to your prospects.** Are there any existing distribution channels (such as specific stores, websites, or wholesalers) that will make it easier or less expensive for you to reach one part of your market?

In your case, let's say you've developed your energy bar to have particular benefits for people engaged in sports. It happens that you're located in a college town, filled with athletes on college teams: football, baseball, soccer, swimming, field hockey, and more. The town has even more recreational athletes: runners, swimmers, snowboarders, cyclists, skateboarders, and hikers.

Your research reveals that athletes on the college's athletic teams are the easiest and fastest to reach. After all, if you can only convince the coaches of each team that your energy bar can improve their players' performances—perhaps even giving each team samples to introduce them to your products—you may be able to get their teams to make large, repeated purchases. If they like your energy bars, the star players may endorse them when you start to market to recreational athletes. And you may be able to get other college (and high school and professional) teams all over the country to buy your energy bars, too. (That's basically how Gatorade launched in 1965. It was promoted as an energy drink for athletes, and it now serves a much broader market.)

End user vs. actual customer

If you were asked to say *precisely* who your customers, or potential customers, are, how would you answer? You might say that your customers are all the people who purchase and use your product or service—but you'd be wrong. You must be careful to distinguish between your customer and the **end user** or **consumer** of your product or service. You may be selling directly to your end users. Or you may be selling to an intermediary—and that intermediary may well have other intermediaries.

Are you a B2C or B2B?

One key component of your company's business model—the basic structure of how you will make money—is whether you will be selling "B2B" or "B2C."

- **B2C (BUSINESS TO CONSUMER):** You sell a product or service directly to the consumer or end user.

- **B2B (BUSINESS TO BUSINESS):** You sell a product or service to another business, either for the company's own use or for that company to resell to customers.

In your marketing, you will want to emphasize different features, depending on whether yours is a B2C or a B2B business. With a B2C business, you'll focus entirely on the *personal* benefits the end user will get from purchasing the product or service. With a B2C business, you'll also have to emphasize the broader benefits the company will reap, especially when it resells your products or services to others. The focus will include how you meet a *business need*, such as through increased efficiency or improved profits.

Primary and secondary customers

Your primary customers are the ones you spend the most time (and money) targeting. For example, if you're an outdoor apparel manufacturer, your primary customer could be a snowboarding or surfing enthusiast. Yet you might also have "secondary" customers—customers you wouldn't necessarily expect to be interested in your product.

Many outdoor product manufacturers have strong secondary markets among people who aren't active in a particular sport but are attracted by the brand image. Surfboard maker O'Neill, for example, has a strong secondary market selling T-shirts displaying the company logo to the general population, who aren't surfers but perhaps wish they were!

Let's continue with the energy bar example. Who's your customer? Is it a coach purchasing the energy bars for an entire team? They'll want to know not only whether it will improve performance but how much bulk purchases will cost. Or is it the end user (the "consumer") of your product—the college athlete—who will actually eat it and get the burst of energy needed to score that winning goal? They'll be interested in the taste, as well as how it makes them feel.

Or is your customer the snack foods buyer at the grocery store? This person's concerns are down to earth: how much money you're going to spend on advertising, how quickly you'll replenish inventory, and whether you'll pay the store a "stocking fee" to obtain shelf space.

Recreational athletes and other consumers won't have a chance to buy or eat your energy bars if you don't meet the supermarket buyers' needs first. On top of that, if you don't have your own sales and distribution force to sell to snack shops and supermarkets, it's likely you'll first have to find a distributor and convince them to carry your product.

The coach. The athlete. The store buyer. The distributor. That's a lot of "customers" you have to satisfy with each energy bar. You'll give yourself a competitive edge by thinking of each of these "customers"—and planning for their needs and motivation.

Being responsive to the details that are important to distributors, retailers, sales representatives, and others helps you plan your marketing materials, operations, packaging—and even the nature of the product itself. If yours is an industry in which sales reps must purchase their samples, for instance, you can set yourself apart by supplying free samples. If retailers can fit more square packages on a shelf than round packages, you'll be more competitive by choosing a square package.

Even if you think you'll market "directly to consumers" on the Internet, you'll discover that there are still many entities between you and your "customer" in cyberspace. In the case of the energy bars, your intermediary might be the online grocery store, a health food site, a sporting goods store, a gym, or a search engine that will help customers find you. So you'll still have more than simply athletes to please.

The same thing goes for services. For example, you might run a spa that does a booming business in gift certificates, where the target market is not solely composed of the people who will actually get the massage or facial, but also of the spouses and friends who will be giving the gift. In such a case, your marketing campaign could stress the gift's power to impress the recipient.

BUILD-YOUR-BUSINESS WORKSHEET

Who Are the Customers?

If you sell a product—one that you either develop or resell—you should identify your customers in each of the following categories. You'll find that the number of customers in each category grows, the closer you get to the end user.

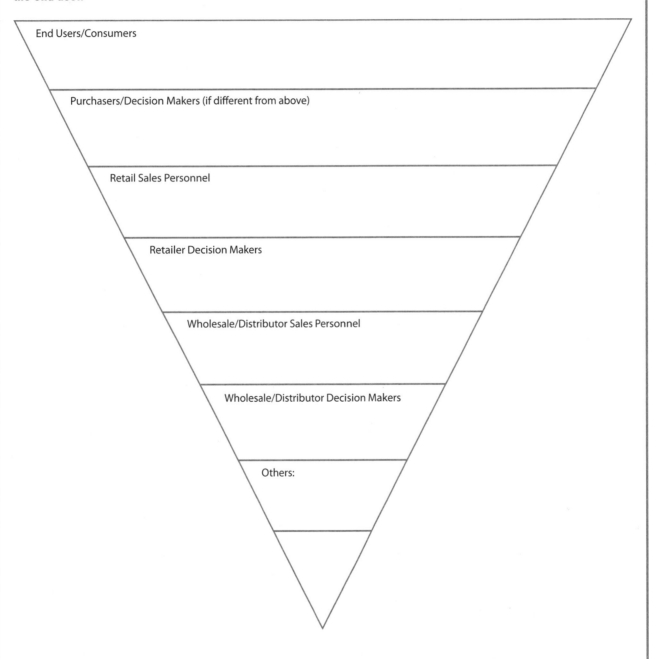

End Users/Consumers

Purchasers/Decision Makers (if different from above)

Retail Sales Personnel

Retailer Decision Makers

Wholesale/Distributor Sales Personnel

Wholesale/Distributor Decision Makers

Others:

Large or hard-to-reach markets

Certain markets cost more to reach, so you're going to need a bigger marketing budget for these. If the market is very large (such as all new parents in the United States), your media costs will be high.

If your market is diffuse, with many different characteristics (say, all young adults between the ages of 22 and 35), you'll have to try to reach them in many different ways, which is costly.

If you target other businesses (B2B) and they're not well aggregated (for instance, not in a specific industry that conducts a trade show, or not in a specific geographic location), then plan on spending more on marketing to identify and reach these customers.

Know Your Customers: Understanding Market Characteristics

Essential to business success is a thorough understanding of your customers. After all, if you don't know who your customers are, how will you be able to assess whether you are meeting their needs? Since success depends on your ability to meet customers' needs and desires, you must know who your customers are, what they want, how they behave, and what they can afford.

As you begin to define your customers (both end users and intermediaries), you should have a good idea of their various attributes: age, location, industry, **purchasing patterns**, buying sensitivities, and **psychographics** (what motivates them). Although you might not have enough research data at this stage to fully understand all aspects of your customer, you should have some idea of whom you're targeting with your product or service.

Of course, not all products and services require that you know everything about a customer. If you're a software engineer with a new add-on to a web browser, for example, you don't need to know the age and sex of your target customers—you merely need to know that they use that browser and are looking for functionality of the kind you can provide. Still, it's good to guesstimate what your "typical" customer might look or act like before you actually start making your product or planning your service.

The most important way in which you need to understand your customers, however, is to determine what they need and want. Ideally, you will fulfill a need that is currently unaddressed—or at least addressed ineffectively—by existing products or services. These wants and needs should be directly related to your key differentiators (what sets your products or services apart from those of the competition).

Defining your target market

You may be tempted to describe your market in the broadest possible terms, choosing to include all those who might potentially use your product or service. Doing so gives you the comforting sense that you have a huge market to exploit. Unfortunately, this gives you little genuine information on which to base your business decisions. You could end up defining the market for furniture as everyone who lives indoors—hardly helpful if you're trying to come up with a marketing plan for your furniture manufacturing company!

Instead, you need to identify the particular market segments you wish to reach. These segments describe distinct, meaningful components of the overall market and give you a set of specific characteristics by which to identify your target market.

Let's say you want to launch an online computer training company. You plan to take a piece of the growing online market for computer training for businesses with high computer use. Thus, you might define your target market in these terms: *"Primarily businesses with at least 50 employees, high employee turnover, a high dependence on computers, and the desire to keep their employees 'on site.' These businesses have annual revenues of at least $5 million and are in the following industries: government, accounting, insurance, financial/ banking, education, engineering, medicine, and transportation."* You then need to determine whether your market has enough potential customers who fit this profile to support your business.

To be a useful planning tool, the definition of your target market must meet these criteria:

- **Definable.** It should have specific characteristics identifying what the potential customers have in common.

- **Meaningful.** The characteristics must meaningfully relate to the decision to purchase.

- **Sizable.** It must be large enough to profitably sustain your business.

- **Reachable.** Both the definition and the size must lead to affordable, effective ways to market to your potential customers.

Once you have defined your market, you should then assess its size and trends, evaluate your competitors for that particular market, and finally probe the market for strategic opportunities.

Demographic description

Begin describing your market by the most basic, objective aspects of the customer base. These details are the specific and observable traits that define your target market.

Demographics are particularly useful when devising your marketing plan. Many marketing vehicles—such as media outlets, publications, mailing lists, radio, and TV—accumulate this kind of data about the market they reach. Thus, you're better able to judge whether such vehicles are appropriate for your company.

Remember, you want to define those characteristics of your target market that meaningfully relate to the interest, need, and ability of the customer to purchase your product or service.

In the previous definition of the target market for the computer training company, for instance, the definition "a high dependence on computers" relates to the need for computer training; "high employee turnover" relates to the fact that there is an ongoing need to train new employees; "on site" is important because trainers need to deliver the training at the customer's office; and "annual revenues of at least $5 million" relates to the customer's ability to pay for computer training services.

Geographic description

Next, define the primary geographic area or areas you intend to serve. This definition should be as concrete as possible, indicating whether your business serves a particular neighborhood, city, state, region, nation, or portion of the international market.

Also, look at the density of the area—whether urban, suburban, or rural—and, if customers will be coming to your place of business, indicate whether the location is in a mall, strip center, business district, or industrial area, or will be a standalone facility. Some businesses define their geographic market by climate, serving only cold-weather (say, skiing areas) or hot-weather (such as surfing) locations.

If you make your product or service available globally—especially on the Web—you may be tempted to view the entire world as your geographic target market. However, even online, there are limitations as to which geographic areas are your primary target markets. These limits may be due to issues of fulfillment (e.g., shipping goods), language, licensing, or legal matters, and there are certainly limits of realistic market demand from different areas.

Lifestyle/business-style description

You also need to grasp a sense of the concerns and interests of your customers. How do they spend their time? What issues are they facing in their lives or businesses? With whom do they associate? How do they relate to their employees and community?

Your natural instincts and experience with customers give you some sense of what your customers are interested in. It's logical, for instance, to assume that receptive targets for your expensive specialty food product are fairly likely to subscribe to food magazines, read online "foodie" blogs, and might belong to local food and wine organizations. Or, if the market for your business service is law firms, you would naturally assume that their lawyers belong to the local bar association.

A little research can help you identify other aspects of your target market's lifestyle or business style. Observe customers in places where they shop or live. What other products or services do they buy? What kinds of vehicles do they drive? What types of clothes do they wear?

Review the media you think your target customers interact with. What other companies are advertising? What are the programs, articles, blogs, or postings about? Survey your customers, whether online, in person, by mail, or on the phone, and ask them about some of their activities.

What kind of people or businesses need or want your product or service? Do they go to the movies, watch TV, or rent videos? Do they entertain at home? If so, for whom? What other kinds of products or services would be used in the same setting with yours?

Develop a mental picture of your customer's entire week. Be creative, but logical and realistic. You want to relate to your customer as a whole, which makes you more responsive to their needs and gives you ideas for marketing vehicles and approaches. The "Target Market Characteristics" worksheet on page 109 helps you achieve this.

Psychographic description

In addition to the observable, objective characteristics of your market, less tangible but equally important psychological factors also influence your targeted customers' purchasing decisions. These are aspects of self-image: how customers see, or want to see, themselves. Some of these are fairly self-conscious attributes—for example, homemakers priding themselves on being smart shoppers. Some are less conscious, perhaps being status-seeking or gadget-happy. Marketing experts segment consumers into various psychographic and lifestyle groups. Some of these segments become well known; for instance, the term "early adopters" is widely used for those consumers who are eager to be among the first to try new technologies.

Business customers as well as consumers can be described in psychographic terms. Some companies view themselves as being on the cutting edge of technology, others as fiscally responsible, and still others as socially responsible. These distinctions can help you determine marketing efforts and positioning of your product or service.

Purchasing patterns description

In planning, it's particularly important to understand the buying patterns of your customers. For instance, if Fortune 500 companies are your target market, you must recognize that these large companies have slow decision-making processes and, due to their size, resist change even when presented with compelling facts. You must keep these realistic constraints in mind when forecasting your sales to this market.

Buying sensitivities description

What factors are most important to your customer when deciding to buy? Of course, all customers would say that they want the highest quality, best service, and greatest convenience, all at the lowest price. But in reality, customers know they have to make trade-offs: paying a little more for extra features, driving farther to get a lower price. What aspects are your customers least willing to give up? What are the areas of their greatest sensitivity?

Target Market Size and Trends

Once you have defined the characteristics of your target market, you must then assess the size of this market and evaluate the trends likely to influence both market size and customer behavior in the near future.

Early adopters

According to communications scholar Everett Rogers' "Diffusion of Innovations" theory, five types of people adopt new products or services, and they do so at different speeds. They range from "innovators," who leap into the unknown and are the first to line up when something new appears, to "laggards," who are generally fearful and cautious of trying new things. "Early adopters" tend to be on the faster end of the spectrum, which also includes "early majority" and "late majority" kinds of people.

High-tech consultant Geoffrey Moore's "Crossing the Chasm" theory builds on this theory and hypothesizes that marketers should focus on one group of customers at a time, using each group as a base for marketing to the next group. The most difficult step is the transition between visionaries (early adopters) and pragmatists (early majority). This is the chasm he refers to. If a firm can create a bandwagon effect that builds momentum from group to group—from innovators down to laggards—its product has a chance of being a market leader.

Market size

Surprisingly, you generally will *not* want your target market to be either too small or too large. Markets that are too small obviously present trouble from the start, as you won't have enough customers. (The exception: Niche markets may be quite small, serving a limited number of customers with a very specific need, but can still be lucrative and able to support a well-defined business if the product or service meets a highly specific need and has substantial profit margins. See more on niche markets on pages 129–132.) Extremely large markets, by contrast, invite numerous well-financed competitors, require extremely expensive marketing campaigns, and are typically difficult to penetrate for new, entrepreneurial companies (the exception being if you are developing a large, well-financed business).

For some businesses, particularly smaller retail operations, determining whether your market is sufficiently sizable will be mostly a matter of intuition and observation. You needn't do a scientific study. But if you are unsure about your market, or need to convince investors, you must gather data to support your plan.

Ever wonder why there are three or four fast-food joints at the same intersection? Or why, all of a sudden, not one but three big office-supply stores open in a community? The answer is they're all relying on similar statistics to analyze a market. They look for certain factors: population density, characteristics of nearby residents (age, gender, income), and the number and type of local businesses (among many other factors).

BUILD-YOUR-BUSINESS WORKSHEET

Psychographic Description

Go through the lists below and check off the psychographic traits that characterize your target customers.

Consumer	Business
☐ Technically adept	☐ Technically advanced
☐ Status seeking	☐ Industry leader
☐ Trend-setting	☐ Innovative
☐ Conservative/responsible	☐ Conservative/responsible
☐ Socially responsible	☐ Socially responsible
☐ Environmentally conscious	☐ Environmentally conscious
☐ Smart shopper	☐ Smart business operator
☐ Family-oriented	☐ Fiscally prudent
☐ Fun-seeking	☐ Good manager of employees
☐ Good housekeeper	☐ Influenced by leading companies
☐ Other:_____	☐ Other:_____

BUILD-YOUR-BUSINESS WORKSHEET

Target Market Characteristics

Use this worksheet to identify the major characteristics of your target market.

What are the demographic characteristics of your target market? (For individuals, list age, gender, marital status, income, education level, and so on. For businesses, list years in business, annual revenue, and industry.)_____

_____

_____

_____

Describe the geographic area you are targeting. (Country, region, state or province, city, suburb, zip codes, and so on.)

_____

_____

_____

How do your customers spend their time? For businesses, how do they relate to their employees and community? Describe their lifestyle/business style. _____

_____

_____

_____

What are some of the psychographic aspects of your customers? (Their motivations, based on emotions, desires, lifestyle, and values.)_____

_____

_____

How and where do your customers make their purchases? How long do they wait between purchases? _____

_____

_____

What factors are most important to your customers when deciding to buy? What kind of trade-offs are they willing to make? What trade-offs will they absolutely resist?_____

_____

_____

Big corporations hire consulting firms to compile these statistics. Luckily, you've got an even bigger consulting group doing it for you—free! The U.S. government, particularly the Census Bureau, compiles all sorts of information that's useful for businesses, and it has put much of that information online. The table on page 111 outlines some of the more useful websites for target market research. You'll also find demographic and geographic information through local governmental agencies, real estate brokerages, chambers of commerce, and business directories. For more information on conducting research, see Chapter 3.

Market trends

Equally important as estimating the size of your current market is evaluating the trends that may affect that market in the coming years. Doing so will give you a sense of your company's continuing viability, the strategic opportunities the market presents, and how your company must plan to respond to changing customer behavior.

Preparing for change is not so much a matter of predicting the future as it is analyzing the recent past. Much of your analysis can be based on observable changes in demographics and customer behavior. For instance, let's say your product is designed to appeal to retired individuals in the American Southwest. You can analyze increased population figures for that age group in particular states and membership trends in organizations such as the AARP. This will provide you with a sense of how the market size is changing. Studies of new hobbies, disposable income growth, and altered buying habits for the age group will give you indicators of the issues and opportunities your company will face in the near future.

Identifying Market Segments and Niches

Market segmentation is the process of dividing a market into sections—or segments—that are perceived as having something in common. For example, either these segments behave in similar ways or they have similar requirements. The goal of market segmentation is to tailor your product or service to appeal to each segment. This "tailoring" can take the form of adding or deleting specific features or of marketing, pricing, or distributing the product or service differently. For example, Nike segments its shoes into several categories of customers, depending on the sporting activity they engage in: running, basketball, baseball, and so on. Likewise, automobile manufacturers segment their marketing messages to appeal to different age groups.

Find your niche

A niche market is a group, or subset, of customers within a larger target market who have specialized needs or who can be identified easily by objective factors such as industry, age, life stage, activities engaged in, and so on. Finding a niche—and marketing to customers in it—provides a simple, fast way

BEST U.S. GOVERNMENT WEBSITES FOR TARGET MARKET RESEARCH

RESOURCE	WEBSITE	DESCRIPTION
Fedstats	www.fedstats.gov	The main portal for finding government statistics. The government has tried hard to make this accessible, but if you don't know what you're looking for, you may find it difficult to find at this site.
U.S. Census Bureau	www.census.gov	This site gives you access to all census data, including facts about people, businesses, trade, and much more.
County Business Patterns	www.census.gov/econ/cbp/	If you want to know what's going on in your hometown, this is the place to go. This easy-to-use database provides detailed information about businesses in any area, down to zip code level.
Quick Facts	http://quickfacts.census.gov/qfd/index.html	This is an easy way to access a wide variety of information about population characteristics at the state or county level.
American FactFinder	http://factfinder2.census.gov	The gateway site of the Census Bureau to specific information on people, housing, and economic and geographic data.
U.S. Economic Census	www.census.gov/econ/census07/	Compiled every five years, the Economic Census gathers highly detailed information on business activity, by industry and subsectors of industries, down to zip code. This site can provide you with very specific information for your target area.
Census Bureau's State Data Centers	www.census.gov/sdc/	The U.S. Census Bureau maintains this site, linking to each state's main statistic site.

For more research resources, see Chapter 20 on pages 463–480.

of distinguishing yourself from competitors and generating greater awareness of your business.

Specializing may also enable you to charge more for your products and services. That's because many customers are willing to pay more for goods specially tailored for them, especially if those products or services are hard to find. Niche products and services also often generate powerful word-of-mouth activity. Just because the word "niche" is used doesn't mean the market has to be small, but rather that it's specialized and identifiable.

Market Size and Trends

Use this worksheet to describe your market size and trends likely to affect customer behavior in the next few years.

What is the current approximate size of your target market? _____

_____

_____

What is the rate of growth of the target market? _____

_____

_____

What changes are occurring in the makeup of the market? _____

_____

_____

What changes are affecting the ability to afford the product/service? _____

_____

_____

What changes are affecting the need for the product/service? _____

_____

_____

How are customers changing the use of the product/service? _____

_____

_____

What changes in social values and concerns are affecting the product/service? _____

_____

_____

Examples of niche marketing:

- Promoting a line of hair care products for curly hair

- Developing accounting software for one-person businesses

- Creating bedding for people with allergies

When choosing your niche, keep these factors in mind:

- **Define your niche objectively.** A niche should relate to a very specific, clearly defined group that members of that group can easily see themselves as belonging to. For example, if your hair salon targets people who want "extra-gentle haircuts in a fun atmosphere," it's not clear whom that targets. But if you spell out your niche demographic—your salon offers haircuts for kids—it's clear whom you're trying to appeal to.

- **Make sure your targeted niche is large enough to sustain you.** Some niches can be too small to grow a business successfully, depending on the geographic area you serve. For example, a chain of "cat-friendly" hotels probably won't provide a big enough market, but a chain of specifically *pet*-friendly hotels, which welcome guests' dogs as well as cats (and other pets), might be able to appeal to the large numbers of people who like to travel with their furry or feathery companions.

- **A niche market can still be a big market.** Just because you carve out a specific segment of a market to target doesn't mean it's necessarily a small market, just that it is clearly a subsection of a larger market. For example, the car maker Toyota clearly targeted its Venza SUV to "empty nesters"—Americans over the age of 50 with no children at home: a huge demographic group but one that's not usually targeted for SUVs.

- **Serving a niche doesn't mean you can't serve a larger market as well.** Choosing to target a niche does not mean you only have to serve that market segment, just that you're clear about your niche when marketing to it. For example, if your law firm specializes in real estate transactions, you'll focus the bulk of your marketing and sales activities toward your services to real estate companies and professionals. But if others come to you for additional legal services, such as writing up contracts or wills, you can offer those, too.

For more on niches, see pages 129–132.

Whether you call your target market a niche, a market segment, a target demographic, or your ideal customer, it's critical that you define your preferred customers as clearly as possible. Most of the decisions you'll make about your business—especially your marketing—follow from knowing your customers in as much depth and breadth as possible. The more you understand your potential customers, the more able you will be to reach them, meet their needs, and make sales.

Know Thy Customer:
The Secret of Trader Joe's Success

Conventional wisdom says that the grocery business is one of tiny profit margins, dominated by huge stores, patronized by notoriously disloyal customers who'll go wherever discount coupons take them. It's a tough, tough business.

Monrovia, California–based Trader Joe's confounds all these truisms… and boasts some of the highest profit margins in the industry. Its secret? Focus on a very specific customer niche, understand those customers extremely well, and create products and a company personality that clearly appeals to that particular customer base.

The origin of Trader Joe's is remarkably humble. It began as a small chain of convenience stores in Southern California in the late 1950s named Pronto Markets. Rexall Drug launched Pronto in 1958, when convenience stores were just gaining a foothold in the American retail landscape. When the 7-Eleven chain entered the California market, Rexall decided to leave the field rather than compete. The relatively young (early 30s) head of the Pronto division, Joe Coulombe, recognized an entrepreneurial opportunity. With bank financing, he arranged a buyout.

So, Coulombe now owned a small chain of stores, but he faced the same dilemma that stymied his former bosses at Rexall—how to compete with 7-Eleven. He realized that he couldn't. Not directly. He'd have to find a different way to succeed.

Soon after taking ownership, in 1967, Coulombe changed the name of one store to "Trader Joe's" (perhaps because he had recently returned from an extended trip to the Caribbean) and began experimenting.

Coulombe himself was a well-educated, avid reader. From his reading and research, he learned that a higher percent of Americans were attending college, and they were becoming more sophisticated in their food choices. Moreover, increasingly affordable jet travel was creating a segment of Americans who came home from international travel with more venturesome tastes.

From the beginning, Coulombe knew exactly the type of customer he was trying to reach. "I wanted to appeal to the well-educated and people who were traveling more," he explained in a 1989 issue of *Forbes*, "like teachers, engineers, and public administrators. Nobody was taking care of them."[1]

Coulombe recognized that merely because his potential customers were well-educated, they weren't necessarily swimming in cash. That meant offering quality, interesting food at low prices. One of his early decisions was to search out unique, high-quality, often-international food products; negotiate hard with suppliers directly; and put the store's name on the products. By eliminating intermediaries and big brands, he cut

challenge

Find a way to differentiate when competition is stiff, profits are small, and cash is scarce

solution

Develop a sharp focus on a clearly defined target market

---

1. "Brie, but no Budweiser," by Ellen Paris, Oct. 2, 1989. *Forbes*.

most of the costs out of the distribution chain, and passed those savings on to customers.

Coulombe also realized that these customers bought liquor—a highly profitable business. At first, Trader Joe's offered virtually every California wine made. In the late 1960s and early 1970s, this wasn't difficult: Napa Valley hadn't yet permeated the consciousness of the nation's wine drinkers, and California wine was considered second-rate. Indeed, many mocked Trader Joe's for carrying such a low-rent product. (It still does. The company's $1.99 wine, affectionately known as "Two Buck Chuck," is a highly popular, and mocked, offering.)

Trader Joe's also recognized that its target market, though not all "health food nuts," was showing a growing interest in health foods. The company has never touted itself as an organic or natural food store, yet it was the first grocery store chain to stock large selections of these products.

Operationally, Coulombe decided to limit his customers' choices. Go into a Safeway, Kroger, or any large supermarket, and you'll find at least a dozen types of ketchup. Trader Joe's offers just one. The idea, of course, is that Trader Joe's offers the best ketchup. To give you an idea of how radical a strategy this is, the average grocery store carried 38,718 different products in 2010, according to the Food Marketing Institute. Trader Joe's has about 4,000; and 80 percent of those items carry a Trader Joe's private label.

With fewer products, Trader Joe's could operate much smaller stores. The company knew customers preferred small stores they could enter and leave quickly. The average supermarket in 2010 was a gargantuan 46,000 square feet. A Trader Joe's is about 6,000 square feet. By deliberately keeping stores small, Trader Joe's has retained its appeal as a cozy, unique store, and not some big impersonal superstore. All of this—plus its friendly and helpful employees, garbed in loud Hawaiian shirts—appeals to the self-image of a well-educated professional, eschewing a more "common" supermarket.

Privately held Trader Joe's (it was bought by the German food retail giant Albrecht family in 1979) is now the grocery industry's poster child. Revenues were estimated at approximately $8 billion per year in 2011. And, as of that year, the company was estimated to rake in more than $1,750 in merchandise sales per square foot, more than *double* the amount Whole Foods achieves, despite its targeting essentially the same niche market. It's little wonder that Trader Joe's is one of the hottest retailers in the United States.

Most important, Trader Joe's keeps a close eye on its target customer base. Before opening a store, it carefully monitors demographics in a market by salary, education, and even such indicators as subscriptions to gourmet food and health magazines.

Communities and consumers aggressively lobby the chain to open stores in their areas. A Trader Joe's not only brings good jobs, its presence in your community also serves as an affirmation that you and your neighbors are worldly and smart. After all, that's exactly the type of customer Trader Joe's targets. ∎

questions

1. In what other ways could Joe Coulombe have changed his convenience stores to be able to survive when 7-Eleven entered the market?

2. What other market segments could have been—or could be now—a good customer base for Trader Joe's?

3. As Trader Joe's keeps expanding, can it continue to be perceived as a store aimed at a narrow market segment, especially one that considers itself special?

4. What can large supermarkets do to grab a piece of Trader Joe's market?

WHAT SIZE WILL YOUR LOAF OF BREAD BE?

Goal:

Identify the specific needs of a market segment and how to exploit those needs.

What to Do:

Read the following summary of the grocery industry:

"In addition to traditional grocers, there are now dozens of different types of retailers attempting to gain their share of the food wallet. It is estimated that shoppers spend over $500 billion annually on food in various store formats. The conventional supermarket and food/drug combination stores typically associated with grocery shopping have lost a great part of their market share to retailers like Wal-Mart Supercenters, Sam's Club, Costco, and a variety of Dollar Stores....In 2001, Wal-Mart became the largest seller in food.... Major demographic and consumer lifestyle changes have affected not only how consumers shop, but also where they choose to shop and eat their meals. Traditional supermarkets have seen a decline in how much shoppers spend and how frequently they shop in a particular store. While some supermarket operators continue to attempt to cut costs so they can offer reduced everyday prices, they find this to be a tough approach when competing with low-cost operators like Wal-Mart and Costco.... Many shoppers are turning to 'destination stores' in search of a different shopping experience. These specialty grocery stores offer more personalized service, higher-quality fresh products, expanded wine and cheese selections, and takeout gourmet foods. Shoppers are encouraged to 'hang out,' eat, and have fun." (MSDN Library, May 2006)

1. Imagine that you're a supermarket industry consultant, hired to come up with a new store concept that would target a specific demographic market as a way to competitively differentiate itself from large grocers like Safeway, Kroger, Publix, Walmart, Target, Costco, and others.

2. Choose a niche demographic that you think is underserved or that could be well-served by a targeted offering. (For example: two-parent families with young children and both parents employed; single professionals; or an ethnic group.)

3. Make a list of all their food-related issues, challenges, wishes, and needs. (For example: Two-income families are typically rushed for time and must shop during evenings or weekends; professional singles want smaller portions of high-quality food; both may want more ready-to-eat food.)

4. Brainstorm a new grocery store concept to appeal to that specific niche. Answer the following:

   a. What are the defining characteristics of the brand? (Upscale? Friendly? Inexpensive? Organic? Gourmet?)

   b. What types of products will you sell? (Canned goods? Dairy? Meats? Fish? Alcoholic beverages? Takeout? Local, organic? Gourmet?)

   c. How will prices compare to competitors?

   d. What is the quality of the products?

   e. Will you offer anything but food and beverages? (For example: household products, baby clothes, office supplies, electronics?)

   f. Could you offer any unique services or features? (Babysitting? Massage? Singles mixers?)

   g. Where will your stores be located? (Malls? Near schools? In urban centers?)

   h. How large will your stores be?

   i. What will significantly distinguish you from the competition?

   j. What other features, products, or services will you offer?

5. Present your grocery store concept to the class.

CHAPTER 6

Competitive Analysis, Strategic Positioning, and Risk Assessment

learning objectives

In this chapter, you'll learn how to:

- Define a specific strategic position in the marketplace

- Outline a clear and sustainable competitive advantage

- Evaluate the competition thoroughly and honestly

- Understand the importance of existing competition

- Distinguish between the various types of competitors

- Recognize the factors that can affect a competitive position

- Identify the dominant companies in a given market

- Analyze the barriers to entry in a specific market

- Recognize various competitive advantages and their pitfalls

- Define a niche market

- Evaluate the risks that a company faces

Reality check

Today's business reality is that customers have easy, convenient access to many of your competitors, some of whom may sell the same or similar products or services for lower prices. In this environment, you have to develop a distinct impetus for your customer to keep doing business with you.

What Makes Your Business Special?

Is your business special? Distinct? Sure, *you* think it's absolutely amazing, but can customers easily discern what makes you unique? How do you differ from competitors? Is it just price? Or the product mix you offer? The colors on your website? Are those differences really important? And can you sustain them over time?

To be successful in business, you have to know what makes your company distinct from all the other companies offering similar products or services. What makes customers want to buy from you? What are your unique competencies that, over time, give you an edge?

In short, what is your specific strategic position in the marketplace, and what is your sustainable competitive advantage?

You have to understand your competition if you're going to be an effective competitor yourself. But you must also examine your own company and develop a strong sense of your **strategic position**—your strengths and weaknesses in terms of your values, your core competencies, your management, your resources, and your assets. While it's important to understand what (or whom) your business is up against and to understand your competitive environment, the competition is not likely to be the primary issue determining your company's long-term viability. Success for an entrepreneur depends much more on what *you* do than on what your competition does.

Nevertheless, one of the most important aspects of formulating your business concept is being aware of the alternatives available to your customers. In other words, how else can they acquire the products or service you offer? You also need to understand one very critical point: Whatever your **key differentiator** is—that is, whatever you do better than your competitor—it will have to evolve over time. Your competitors will not stand still; you can't either. You must remain flexible and responsive, yet know what your core competencies are.

Many start-up companies are tightly focused on their competition. Although big businesses spend millions of dollars fighting over each percentage point of market share (just think of Coke vs. Pepsi, Ford vs. GM, and so on), this isn't necessarily productive for new companies. Still, that does not mean that you can simply ignore the competition. You need to know who's out there, what they offer, and what they charge. If you approach your competitive analysis as an opportunity to learn, you may find ways to enhance your own products or services—or at least to improve your marketing.

Know What You're Up Against— Your Competition

Famed baseball player Satchel Paige used to say, "Don't look back; someone may be gaining on you." But in business it is imperative to see who's gaining on you. It is far better to know what you're up against than to be surprised when your sales suddenly disappear to an unexpected competitor.

en·tre·pre·neur·ship key terms

Barriers to entry
Conditions that make it difficult or impossible for new competitors to enter the market. Two examples of barriers to entry are patents and high start-up costs.

First-mover advantage
The first company to gain a reasonable foothold in a new market. Having a market to itself for even a brief period may enable a company to define the product, set standards, establish key strategic partnerships, capture customer attention, or in other ways gain dominance.

Key differentiators
Characteristics that differentiate one company from another. Key differentiators motivate customers to buy from one company rather than either choosing another

company or not buying at all. Key differentiators are price, quality, convenience, selection, and socially conscious policies or products.

Niche
A specialized, clearly identifiable group or market segment that a company chooses to focus on and serve within a larger target market.

Strategic position
A company's distinct identity that separates it from the competition and helps it focus on its activities.

Switching costs
Barriers for customers that make it difficult to switch from one product or service to another.

Comparing competitors' pricing

When assessing your competition, you'll certainly want to know what they charge. After all, setting prices is one of the most difficult aspects of starting a new business. This is especially true in service industries, where prices can vary greatly from one provider to another. For more on pricing, see pages 221–223.

Every business has competition. Those currently operating a company are all too aware of the many competitors for a customer's dollar. But many people new to business—excited about their concept and motivated by a perceived opening in the market—tend to underestimate the actual extent of competition and fail to properly assess the impact of that competition on their business.

You may believe that your business idea is completely unique—that you've come up with a brand-new idea. And, it may be that you have come up with a fresh approach to meeting a need in the market. But remember this: One of the very worst statements you can make in thinking through your business or creating a business plan is, "We have no competition."

If you believe you have no competition, that indicates that either 1) you haven't fully examined the realities of your business and the competitive environment, or 2) your concept actually has no market.

You can see this with any seemingly "new" invention, no matter how innovative it seemed at the time. Take the photocopier, for example. When the first one was introduced, no competition existed from other makers of photocopiers, of course. But competition still came from many sources, including suppliers of carbon paper and mimeograph machines. There was a demonstrated demand for making copies of documents. If no competition truly existed at the time the photocopier was invented—if people weren't duplicating documents by some means—it would have meant that no market for photocopiers existed.

Honestly evaluating your competition will help you better understand your own product or service and give investors a reassuring sense of your company's strengths. It enables you to know how best to distinguish your company in the customer's eyes, and it points to opportunities in the market.

Learn from your competition. The basic concept of competition is responsiveness to customers. Watching your competitors can help you understand what customers want.

As you begin your competitive assessment, keep in mind that you need to evaluate only those competitors aiming for the same target market. If you own a fine French restaurant in midtown Manhattan, you don't have to include the McDonald's next door in your competitive evaluation: You're not aiming for the same customer at the same time. By contrast, if you plan on opening an online store for sporting equipment, you have to look far afield at any retail stores and franchises, both in your area and nationally, as well as at mail order dealers and other Internet stores from around the world, since that's where your potential customers now shop.

When conducting a competitive analysis, identify the following:

- Who your major competitors are
- On what basis you compete
- How you compare
- Potential future competitors
- **Barriers to entry** for new competitors

More than a better mousetrap

It's tempting to want to judge your competition solely on the basis of whether your product or service is better than theirs. If you have invented a clearly superior widget, it's comforting to imagine that widget customers will naturally buy your product instead of the competitors' and the money will roll in.

Unfortunately, many other factors determine your success in comparison to other widget manufacturers. Perhaps their brand name is already well-known. Perhaps their widgets cost much less. Perhaps their distribution system makes it easier for them to get placement in stores. Perhaps they have a bigger marketing budget. Maybe customers just like the color of your competitors' packages better. Or maybe they are comfortable with what they're using now and don't feel a need to change.

The objective features of your product or service may be a relatively small part of the competitive picture. In fact, all the components of customer preference, including price, service, and location, are only part of the competitive analysis. You'll need to examine many other factors, not the least of which is the strength of your competitors' companies. In the long run, companies with significant financial resources, highly motivated or creative personnel, and other operational assets will prove to be tough, enduring competition.

Types of competition

Competition comes in many forms, including:

- **Direct competitors.** These companies offer the same or similar product or service mix, try to reach the same target market, and typically have close relationships to their customers. They're the ones you first think of when you hear the word "competition"—and who keep you up at night. Most markets have enough business to go around, but you'd better know what your direct competition is doing.

- **Large competitors.** The Walmarts, Home Depots, and Lawyers 'R' Us— national companies or franchises with huge marketing budgets. Don't just dismiss these as being inferior because they're big. A lot of them have adopted customer service practices that used to be the hallmark of small businesses. These are very real competitors to you, particularly if you plan to compete on price.

Truth or fiction?

"If a man can write a better book, preach a better sermon, or make a better mousetrap, than his neighbor, though he build his house in the woods, the world will make a beaten path to his door."
— *Ralph Waldo Emerson*

REAL-WORLD RECAP

Sources of competition

Competition comes in many forms, including:

- Direct competitors
- Large competitors
- Online competition
- Indirect competition
- Future competition

- **Online competition.** If yours is a brick-and-mortar operation selling physical goods, you'll almost certainly face stiff competition from Internet sellers. They most likely offer lower prices, may be able to charge few or no taxes, and perhaps even provide free or highly discounted shipping. Don't be surprised if customers use you as a "showroom" and then shop online. Competing effectively is a challenge, requiring you to provide a unique product mix, high customer service that engenders loyalty, and an experience that brings customers in.

- **Indirect competition.** It's important to understand that you can face a great deal of *indirect* competition—that is, rather than having another company compete head to head against your product or service, you compete against other types of products or services that your customers might spend their funds on rather than yours. For example, if you run a lakeside resort for family vacations, your competition would include not only the resort on the other side of the lake, but also Disney cruises, mountain cabins for rent, and vacation packages to Hawaii.

- **Future competition.** You must make a few reasonable predictions of what the competition will look like in the future. New competitors enter markets all the time, and sometimes current competitors drop out. So don't take comfort in the fact that other companies have overlooked a particular product or service. Once you show you can succeed, someone will want to take a piece of that market from you. Who are your new competitors likely to be? How long will you have the field to yourself before other competitors jump in?

In most situations, though, when assessing the competition, you'll concentrate your energy on looking at what your direct competitors are doing—who they are, what their competitive strengths and weaknesses are, and how much they charge.

You can identify these direct competitors by looking at directories (online directories, trade association directories, even the Yellow Pages) and advertisements. You can also ask suppliers and distributors to name the major competition in your area. See if your competitors are exhibiting at trade shows. And you can survey potential customers, asking them to name your competition. Indeed, identifying whom your customers are considering as an alternative to you is one of the best types of market research you can do.

Other factors affecting your ability to compete

In addition to your competitors, many other factors can affect your competitive position.

- **First-mover advantage.** In new industries or new market segments, the first company to gain a reasonable foothold in the market can often leverage being early into a significant competitive advantage. Having a market to oneself for even a brief period may enable a company to define the product, set standards, establish key strategic partnerships, capture customer attention, or in other ways gain dominance. This rush to market, however, does not guarantee success, and many industries have instances of early market leaders being overtaken by later-stage competitors.

- **Installed user base and switching costs.** One big challenge in introducing a new product or service—especially one involved with technology or electronics—is assessing whether that product is compatible with existing products or what the **switching costs** will be for customers who "switch" from their current product or service to yours. If a sizable portion of the market currently uses a product or service that performs a similar function to yours but is incompatible with your new product or service, customers may resist the cost and inconvenience of making the transition, even if your offering appears superior.

  For example, switching from videocassettes to DVDs took consumers a long time because it involved replacing a pricey machine as well as personal libraries of movies, while switching from DVDs to streaming video took far less time because many consumers already had cable boxes or DVRs that could accommodate the technology. With business customers, the time, energy, and disruption it takes to deploy new technology often keeps companies from moving to improved technology, even if it is cost effective.

- **The Web.** Using the Internet substantially lowers barriers to entry in many industries, and in some cases it allows competitors to operate at very narrow profit margins or increase their operating efficiency significantly. The Internet also arms customers with considerably more purchase information, sometimes even wholesale prices. Companies that previously may have been able to compete effectively in a particular geographic area likely now face worldwide competition.

- **Inertia.** Sometimes your biggest competition comes from consumers' simple lack of motivation to change their ways, try a new product, or investigate a new service. In such cases, you may have to devise unique marketing plans to light a fire under them.

Market share distribution

Some competitors are more important than others, due entirely to the fact that they command a large percentage of the sales. Although these companies may not necessarily provide the best product or best service at the best price, they nevertheless represent a crucial component in evaluating your competitive position.

Companies that generate a significant portion of all sales to the target market must be carefully considered, because they:

- Generally define the standard features of the product or service

- Substantially influence customers' perception of the product or service

- Usually devote considerable resources to maintaining their market share

Consider the playing field

It's generally easier and less expensive to enter a market with many diverse competitors than one dominated by a few major players.

Take time to understand the companies that dominate the market, if only to better distinguish yourself from them. Of course, if your company is fortunate enough to control a major share of the market, then you gain the advantage of defining the product or service in the marketplace; you are the proverbial "800-pound gorilla." Even so, you can't be complacent but must plan on committing the resources necessary to preserve or expand your share.

Barriers to entry

In an entrepreneurial company, you might have a new or vastly improved idea to bring to market. That's great, but what keeps new competitors from coming in after you've established a customer base for your new product? In other words, what are the barriers to entry?

Obstacles that stand in the way of a company's entering a given market are called barriers to entry. These barriers apply to your entering a market, as well. What stands in your way of entering a market? Costs, technology, lack of distribution channels? Every company can gain a sense of how best to prepare for future competition by examining the barriers to entry. These include:

- **Investment.** How much money will it take to get on par with competitors? For some industries, the investment required is substantial: Think about what it would take to start up a new, low-cost airline, for example.

- **Government regulations.** In regulated markets like energy and tele-communications, the government can make it difficult to jump-start a new business. Requirements for licenses and permits may raise the investment needed to enter a market. If you want to drive a taxicab in New York, for example, you must purchase a hard-to-acquire "medallion" due to local restrictions on the number of taxis allowed on the streets.

- **Aggressive prices.** Sometimes companies with a major share of a market will sell at a loss—or even give products and services away free—to make it difficult for smaller, younger firms to enter the market. Although illegal in many cases, this can be difficult to prove.

- **Intellectual property (IP).** In some industries, the right to use certain patented devices or processes may keep smaller firms from entering the market—either because they lack the funds to purchase rights to use the patents, or because patent holders refuse to license those rights.

- **Economy of scale.** Larger firms can frequently manufacture products or provide services at a lower cost than smaller businesses can, making it difficult to compete in a market with entrenched competition.

- **Customer loyalty.** Customers who are extremely reluctant to switch from the company that currently serves them present a common barrier to entry.

- **Market saturation.** Entering a market with a large number of players already in place reduces the possibility of gaining a meaningful foothold.

BUILD-YOUR-BUSINESS WORKSHEET

Barriers to Entry

Choose one of the following businesses:

— Work clothes manufacturer

— Socially responsible specialty foods manufacturer

— Software company that produces office automation software

— Financial services company

— Publishing company

With this company in mind, fill in the table below. Indicate how strong the barriers to entry are and, in the final column, how much time it will take new competition to overcome each barrier.

Type of Barrier to Entry	Extent of Effectiveness Factor				How Long Effective
	High	Medium	Low	None	
Patents					
High Start-up Costs					
Substantial Expertise Required					
Engineering, Manufacturing Problems					
Lack of Suppliers or Distributors					
Restrictive Licensing, Regulation					
Market Saturation					
Trademarks					
Aggressive Competitor Pricing					
Economy of Scale					
Customer Loyalty					
Other:					

A Strategic Position Also Defines What You *Don't* Do

As important as helping you determine what to do, a well-defined strategic position is a boon in helping you decide what *not* to do. This saves you a lot of time and money, and also makes you more confident of your business decisions, some of which may not be understood by others.

For example, say you sell gifts. You had been selling to consumers, so local customers were important. But you decide to switch to selling upscale corporate gifts. You stop advertising in the neighborhood and participating in daily deal sites. When your lease expires, you move to a less-convenient location that can't be seen from the street and receives little foot traffic. All this may seem foolish to an outsider. But since you have decided to serve the corporate market, your location matters less.

Your carefully defined strategic position helped you understand what activities were of lower priority. You aren't trying to be all things to all people.

Few barriers to entry last very long, particularly in newer industries. Even patents don't provide nearly as much protection as is generally assumed. Thus, you need to realistically project the period of time by which new competitors will breach those barriers. If your company's competitive position depends on new technology, new manufacturing techniques, or access to new markets, outlining the barriers to entry is essential. This will be one of the first areas judged by potential funding sources.

What Kinds of Strategic Positions Are There?

What makes a company different? Is it the nature of its products or services? The quality or cost? The geographic area or type of customers served? Perhaps the company has proprietary products that customers can't find elsewhere.

Each of the competitive advantages outlined in this chapter offers opportunities but also poses pitfalls. And they may be related: If you're positioning your company on the basis of low price, you'll also need operational efficiencies to reduce costs or else you won't be able to survive against competitors with higher profit margins. Keep in mind that your competition will also use many of these same strategies.

Customer perception factors

This is the "better, faster, cheaper" approach, based on how customers distinguish your company and its products and services from the competition. Some key customer perception factors are:

- **Features.** Specific inherent attributes of the product or service itself.

- **Price.** This factor includes costs other than the actual purchase price, such as installation or additional equipment required.

- **Quality.** Inherent merit of the product or service at the time it's provided.

- **Durability and maintenance.** Quality of the product or service over time; ease of maintenance and service.

- **Image, style, or perceived value.** Added values derived from design features, attractive packaging or presentation, and other intangibles.

- **Customer relationships.** Established customer base and customer loyalty; relationships of sales personnel to customers.

- **Societal impact.** Perception of the company, product, or service relative to issues such as environment, civic involvement, and the like.

- **Convenience.** Ease with which customers can obtain the product or service. This can include the product's ease of use or the business's geography, operating hours, credit policies, and so on.

Concentrating on customer perception factors is the most typical method of attempting to differentiate yourself from the competition. They seem to provide the simplest, most straightforward way to compete. Surprisingly, they may also be the most difficult to achieve and maintain. For instance, competing on the basis of price is often perilous. While it's easy—in the short run—to attract customers on the basis of low price, highly price-sensitive customers are the most fickle, quickly tempted away by the next company offering a lower price. Once you appear to be attracting a significant portion of the market, well-funded established competitors can lower prices (even if they have to take a loss) to compete temporarily until you're no longer able to sustain your losses.

Other perception factors may be harder to "prove" to the market. You may have to spend a lot of money on marketing and advertising to get customers to realize that you offer additional features, more convenience, or higher quality. Once you do, however, you may be able to build a loyal and committed customer base that appreciates the differences between you and your competition.

Internal operational advantages

Another strategy is to gain significant competitive advantages through instituting better internal procedures or operations, giving you substantial benefits—such as higher profit margins—over the competition. Because these advantages are often not seen directly by customers, their significance is often unrealized. Yet many companies have succeeded not by clever market strategies but by running their business better than the competition. For instance, See's Candies' inventory management system results in very fresh candy at its stores, with minimal waste; this results in better-tasting candy and higher profit margins.

Internal operational factors that increase competitiveness include:

- **Financial resources.** Ability of the company to withstand financial setbacks, and to fund product development and improvements.

- **Marketing program and budget.** Amount and effectiveness of advertising and other promotional activities.

- **Economies of scale.** Ability to reduce per-unit costs due to large volume.

- **Operational efficiencies.** Production or delivery methods that reduce costs and time.

- **Product line breadth.** Ability to increase revenues by selling related products; ability for customers to purchase needed items from a single provider.

- **Strategic partnerships.** Relationships with other companies for purposes of development, promotion, or add-on sales.

- **Company morale and personnel.** Motivation, commitment, and productivity of the employees.

Strategic Position Is More than Advertising

Don't be confused: A true strategic position is not the same as an advertising campaign or slogan. Advertising and marketing are means to achieving your strategic position—they help you create the image consistent with your position and get your message to potential customers. Defining a strategic position is about creating a meaningful place for yourself—a position—in the market.

Proprietary products, technology, abilities, or relationships

Another way to gain a competitive advantage is to develop or secure exclusive assets that will be difficult or impossible for competitors to replicate. For manufacturing and technology companies, these may be patents, processes, or copyrights. For others, proprietary assets might include distribution agreements, licenses, strategic partnerships, even hiring certain employees with exceptional talents. The key to deploying this strategy effectively is that you have to identify those aspects of your business where proprietary assets make a real difference, and then you must secure those assets in such a way that your competitors can't easily replicate or circumvent them.

Sales channels

In some instances, you may be able to differentiate your company by the manner in which you reach and sell to customers. For instance, some computer companies, such as Dell, distinguished themselves early on by selling directly to consumers rather than through retail computer outlets. Later, the Internet opened up the opportunity for many other companies to circumvent existing sales channels and sell directly to customers. But using different sales channels as a key strategy doesn't necessarily require a high-tech approach: Tupperware has long used house parties instead of retail outlets to compete against Rubbermaid.

First-mover advantage

"No one's ever done anything like this before." Many entrepreneurs believe their key competitive advantage is that they've developed a new concept—product, service, technology, or online business—before anyone else. They recognize that there's a big advantage in being first; the fear of others beating them to market keeps many entrepreneurs working around the clock.

If you can get your company, product, service, or website established before the competition, you gain what's called the **first-mover advantage**. Being first potentially enables you to capture so many customers that it becomes difficult for a significant portion of the market (in technology terms, the "installed user base") to change.

Being first to a market brings many advantages, including the ability to:

- Capture significant market share before competitors enter the market
- Secure key strategic partners, leaving fewer opportunities for later competitors
- Attract outstanding employees and management
- Capture media attention
- Lock in financing sources, such as venture capitalists

Going after a "first-mover advantage" carries its own risks as well as rewards. In most businesses, there are few truly effective barriers to entry. Will you end up merely serving as the research-and-development arm of copycat companies? There's also the quite real risk that if you're doing something truly new, the market (and financing sources) may not be ready for you. In fact, many second- or third-to-market companies benefit from avoiding the costs of educating the market, conducting extensive research and development, and hiring highly creative people.

If gaining the first-mover advantage is part of your key business strategy, ask yourself, "How defensible is this position? What will I need to make it defensible?" Remember, patents, copyrights, and other proprietary information only go so far. Can you develop strategic alliances or lock in customers, distributors, and financing sources to make it difficult for future competitors to take you on?

With a first-mover strategy, there's also the risk of doing something fast but not well, allowing your inevitable competition to honestly tout itself as a much-improved version. So continually work on improving your products, services, marketing, and operations. Look for ways to leverage being first into being *best*.

Branding

One increasingly important strategy that many companies pursue is intentionally trying to build a brand. If you can become a brand name, customers will develop such a strong relationship with your company that others have difficulty competing.

There are, obviously, many advantages to being a brand name, but it's not easy to achieve. First, it's usually expensive. You must spend a great deal of money on marketing and advertising just to get your name well known. And, though it seems like some brand names develop overnight, especially with online businesses, building a brand is hard to achieve quickly.

Building a truly strong brand is more than merely a matter of securing name recognition. A real brand gives customers trust in your products and services because, over time, you're consistent in quality, price, service, or convenience. This doesn't mean you have to promise the highest quality or the lowest price. It just means being consistent, so the customer can depend on what they'll get from your brand.

If your goal is to build a brand name, you have to look at those factors that you're able to offer and deliver to your customers consistently and repeatedly, making certain you put sufficient company resources into supporting those factors.

Finding your niche

It's often far easier for a company to get and retain a competitive edge by focusing on a specific market segment—or **niche**—rather than trying to win every customer imaginable. A niche, or niche market, however, isn't necessar-

Does McDonald's serve the best burger?

A brand represents consistency. To be a reliable brand, McDonald's doesn't have to promise gourmet food. Rather, its brand depends on giving customers the same experience, the same type and quality of food, and the same cleanliness, at every McDonald's.

Carving out a niche:

- Sets you apart from the mass of competitors
- Gives you a clear focus for your marketing and advertising efforts
- Earns you additional credibility when you're trying to make a sale
- Makes you more memorable and helps you get referrals
- Enables you to charge higher prices than non-specialists

You can choose a niche based on one of two things: your target customer, or your type of product/ service. In other words: who your customers are, or what you do and how you do it.

ily a small market. Rather, choosing a niche means finding something that immediately distinguishes you from your competitors by focusing on something that makes you distinct.

Say you want to turn your knack for design into a fashion business. Telling yourself that everyone needs clothes isn't going to help you design products that stand out in the marketplace. You could choose to target clothes for young women, but that's an incredibly crowded field. On the other hand, choosing to design and sell clothes for a specific niche—let's say plus-size women or, even more specifically, focusing on business attire for plus-size women—allows you to easily differentiate yourself in a smaller but still viable marketplace.

An important thing to note about a niche is that it must be based on objective factors. When asked what makes their business unique, most entrepreneurs will say something like, "We give exceptional customer service," or "We do the best job." Those are subjective criteria. Trying to distinguish yourself based on subjective factors is tough—it takes a long time for customers to recognize that you're actually better than the competition.

But a niche based on objective criteria is immediately understandable—"We create an online accounting application for midsize law firms" or "We manufacture furniture for family-style restaurants"—and clearly sets you apart from your competitors.

Carving out a niche for a new or smaller business gives you an immediate head start. While you trade having a larger total market from which to attract customers, you can more easily (and often more inexpensively) gain visibility and credibility with a more-focused market.

Defining your niche

After you've generated a number of ideas for niche markets, how do you choose the right one for you? First, you'll have to do some research. Judge a potential niche by the following four factors:

- **Sizable:** Your market segment should be big enough to provide you with plenty of customers but not so huge that it will attract too many competitors and be too expensive to reach.

- **Reachable:** How can you let your target market know you exist? Where will you advertise? Look for publications, media outlets, organizations, or events that reach your specific market so you're assured that you can let them know you exist.

- **Self-defining:** Your potential market should have—or feel they have—special needs. After all, that's why they want a specialist!

- **Sustainable:** Select a niche that can support your business over the long haul, one in which you won't quickly deplete the supply of customers. Avoid specialties highly affected by changes in the economy.

CUSTOMER-BASED NICHES: WHO YOUR CUSTOMERS ARE

NICHE	WHO YOUR CUSTOMERS ARE	BENEFITS	CONSIDERATIONS	EXAMPLES
Industry or Business Type	A particular industry or type of business	One of the easiest ways to specialize; familiarity in an industry attracts and reassures potential clients	May require a broader geographic market in order to find enough customers	Website design for hospitals; public relations for plastic surgeons; janitorial service for banks
Demographic Group	Customers defined by age, gender, ethnic group, religion, sexual orientation, income level, etc.	Relatively easy to identify marketing vehicles serving the group	Often helps to belong to the group; group may dislike being singled out; must accept customers outside the group	Children's furniture manufacturer; computer training for seniors; travel operator of group tours for gays
Geographic Area	Customers in a particular geographic area	Easy way to specialize; can be highly successful in remote, underserved locations	May not provide enough of a competitive advantage	A regional airline; a bank serving a local community; a real estate firm specializing in a particular city
Other Specialty	Any group of people that has a common characteristic	Works best if the targeted group has a unique need, served best by a specialist	Group must be large enough to create a demand	Footwear for travelers; frozen entrees for vegetarians; gear for parents of twins and triplets

PRODUCT- OR SERVICE-BASED NICHES: WHAT YOU DO

NICHE	WHAT YOU DO	BENEFITS	CONSIDERATIONS	EXAMPLES
Unique Knowledge	Provide specialized expertise for a particular field or product	For some fields, expertise can be developed on-the-job	Likely to need specialized training, expertise, or understanding	Clinical trials data processing; environmental impact consulting firm; math textbook publisher
Style or Product Mix	Perform work in a distinctive manner or place; create a unique product or product mix	Clear differentiator from competition	Often hard to find distinguishing difference; relatively easy for competitors to enter	Organic-only fast-food chain; on-call auto-glass replacement service; fee-only financial planning

Niche Market Ideas

Use this worksheet to brainstorm possible niche markets to pursue.

Type of Niche	Potential Niche Idea
Industry/Business	
Demographic Group	
Geographic Area	
Other Specialty	
Unique Knowledge	
Style or Product Mix	

Competitive Analysis

Now that you've begun to examine the competition, and you've thought about some of the strategic advantages you would like to exploit or develop, fill out the two competitive analysis worksheets on pages 134–135. These worksheets will help you evaluate your competitive position in terms of both customer preference and internal operational strengths.

The worksheets enable you to assign greater or lesser importance to each competitive factor, depending on the significance of those particular aspects. To complete each worksheet, give each factor listed a maximum possible number of points, ranging from 1 to 10, with 1 being least important to your overall target market and 10 being the most important. Place the maximum number for each factor in the maximum points column.

For instance, on the first worksheet, "Competitive Analysis: Customer Perception Factors," let's say your target market is extremely price sensitive but willing to travel a long way to get a bargain. The purchase price factor might be given a maximum of 10 points and the location factor a maximum of 2.

Keep in mind that you can also allot negative numbers. If, for example, your target market is interested only in items perceived as luxuries, having too low a price may be a liability. If your market is particularly socially conscious, the fact that your competitor conducts tests on animals may be a negative for the social image factor in their evaluation, giving you a competitive edge.

In your analyses, look both at specific competitors—particular companies you compete against—and at the overall type of competition. Once you have finished numbering the factors for your company and competitors, you'll see how this weighting system gives you a better picture of the actual strength of your competitors, as opposed to your own.

Risk

Every business involves risk. Only the most naive and inexperienced entrepreneurs believe their business "just can't fail." Use this section to sit down and think through the various risks facing your new endeavor.

This task might seem daunting. So why shake your enthusiasm? Because risk assessment helps you prepare for and prevent threats to your success. If, for instance, you identify a major risk as the possibility that a well-funded competitor will enter the market, you'll want to take steps to quickly secure key customer contracts or line up significant funding yourself.

What kinds of risk?

It's not just a matter of high risk or low risk. It's also what kinds of risk. Some risks are more tolerable or more important. The key types of risk companies face include:

Competitive Analysis, Customer Perception Factors

Following the directions on page 133, allocate points for each of the factors listed below for both your company and your competitors.

Factor	Maximum Points (1–10)	Your Company	Competitor _____	Competitor _____	Competitor _____	Competitor _____
Product/Service Features						
Purchase Price						
Indirect/Peripheral Costs						
Quality						
Durability/Maintenance						
Image/Style/Design						
Perceived Value						
Brand Recognition						
Customer Relationships						
Location						
Delivery Time						
Convenience of Use						
Credit Policies						
Customer Service						
Social Consciousness						
Other:						
Other:						
Total Points						
Comments:						

Competitive Analysis, Internal Operational Factors

Following the directions on page 133, allocate points for each of the factors listed below for both your company and your competitors.

Factor	Maximum Points (1–10)	Your Company	Competitor _____	Competitor _____	Competitor _____	Competitor _____
Financial Resources						
Marketing Budget/Program						
Technological Competence						
Access to Distribution						
Access to Suppliers						
Economies of Scale						
Operational Efficiencies						
Sales Structure/ Competence						
Product Line Breadth						
Strategic Partnerships						
Company Morale/Personnel						
Certification/Regulation						
Patents/Trademarks						
Ability to Innovate						
Other:						
Other:						
Other:						
Total Points						
Comments:						

- **Market risk.** The risk that the market won't respond to your products or services, because either there is no real market need or the market isn't yet ready. Market risks are very difficult to overcome.

- **Competitive risk.** The risk that the competitive situation will change dramatically, and new competitors will enter the market or established competitors will reposition their products or services to more effectively take you on. You should carefully think through how other competitors might respond to your entering the market and not assume that the competitive environment will remain the same.

- **Technology risk.** The risk that the technology or product design and engineering won't work, or won't work as well as you envision. This may be critically important to your company's success, or it may be irrelevant, depending on the nature of your company, its products or services, its customers, and the like. If your business faces substantial technology risks, what's your ability to quickly and effectively improve the technology?

- **Product risk.** The risk that the product won't materialize, won't be finished in time, or won't work as promised. This is similar to the above, only with non-technology products or services.

- **Execution risk.** The risk that you won't be able to effectively manage the rollout and growth of the company because management isn't sufficiently capable, the time allowed isn't adequate, operations aren't in place, and other reasons. You should be able to demonstrate specific steps you're taking to reduce or eliminate such risks.

- **Capitalization risk.** The risk that you've badly underestimated costs or overestimated income, and you will run out of money. The best way to avoid these risks is to budget realistically and acquire enough funding so you don't run through your cash reserves prematurely. Look for investors who have the ability and inclination to offer additional funds as your company progresses.

- **Global risk.** The risk that, when doing business internationally, you may encounter unanticipated situations that will interrupt or stop your ability to do business, reach your market, or receive supplies.

Balancing risks and opportunities

Once you've outlined your risks, you may feel overwhelmed. But while there are many risks, there are many rewards—otherwise, why would you bother to start an endeavor?

A typical method to illustrate the balance between risks and opportunities is to develop a "SWOT" chart, delineating your company's strengths, weaknesses, opportunities, and threats (thus, "SWOT"). This is a good exercise for quickly sizing up your company's position. Complete the "SWOT" grid on page 137. Be sure to include both internal and external factors, as well as current and potential ones.

BUILD-YOUR-BUSINESS WORKSHEET

SWOT: Strengths/Weaknesses/Opportunities/Threats

In each appropriate box below, list your company's strengths or weaknesses, and the opportunities or threats facing it.

Strengths	Weaknesses

Opportunities	Threats

REAL-WORLD CASE

Social Status: The Rise and Fall of MySpace

challenge

Staying competitive when you're the leader in a rapidly changing market

solution

Stay the course, keep current customers happy, and hope for the best

How does a company that has established clear market dominance keep ahead in a rapidly changing field? When your current customers and business model depend on one model, how do you respond as competitors introduce new business models? It's one of the toughest questions facing entrepreneurial companies, and sometimes even the biggest, most well-funded aren't immune from the challenge.

The rise and fall of the MySpace empire took only six years to play out. Ultimately, the same business strategy that drove it to the top of the social networking world led directly to its failure.

Prior to MySpace, the first social networking site to really prove the power of harnessing individuals' own social circles was Friendster. Launched in 2002, Friendster was based primarily in Asia and was backed by some of the leading venture capital firms in the world. It quickly became a powerhouse, and Google offered to buy it for $30 million in 2003. Friendster turned the offer down.

Meanwhile, MySpace quickly began challenging Friendster. Still a relatively early entrant in the new social networking market space, by 2004 it overtook Friendster, and by 2005 MySpace was considered the world's top social network program. News Corporation acquired MySpace for $580 million that year,[1] expecting it to generate more than $1 billion in annual revenue.[2]

At first, things looked good for MySpace. At the time of its acquisition, MySpace was the fifth-ranked Web domain in terms of page views (putting it in the league of Web giants Yahoo!, Google, and AOL),[3] it had five times the traffic of Facebook,[4] and by 2006 it outranked Google as the most visited website in the United States and had acquired its 100 millionth member.[5] That year, MySpace inked a $900 million advertising deal with Google. It was *the* social network, valued at an astonishing $12 billion in its heyday.[6] The prospects seemed limitless.

MySpace was so powerful that Friendster, based in Kuala Lumpur, increasingly focused its growth in Asia, pulling back on its presence in the United States.

Yet MySpace wasn't watching the competitive and strategic landscape carefully. Because MySpace was easily open to all—anyone could join, and there were few privacy controls—it faced criticism on a number of fronts, including

1. "News Corporation to Acquire Intermix Media, Inc." *News Corporation*. July 18, 2005.
2. "Special Report: How News Corp got lost in MySpace," by Adegoke Yinka. *Reuters.com*. April 7, 2011.
3. "News Corporation to Acquire Intermix Media, Inc."
4. "The Network Effect: Facebook, LinkedIn, Twitter & Tumblr Reach New Heights in May," by Andrew Lipsman. *The ComScore Blog*. June 15, 2011.
5. "MySpace Signs 100 Millionth Member," by Mark Sweeney. The *Guardian*. Aug. 9, 2006.
6. "MySpace loses 10 million users in a month," by Emma Barnett. *Telegraph.co.uk*. March 24, 2011.

online privacy, child safety, censorship, and website performance. MySpace's inability to build an effective spam filter made it seem seedy, driving away members and advertisers.[7]

Meanwhile, the strength of upstart Facebook was growing. Facebook's initial model allowed only those who were connected to a college or university to join. At first, these were only Ivy League universities, giving the social media site an air of exclusivity. Later, members had to have a ".edu" email address, enabling Facebook to capture the highly valuable college market.

By 2009, Facebook had surpassed MySpace's traffic. Meanwhile, MySpace was locked into an advertising revenue deal with Google that limited its flexibility and ability to innovate and compete.[8]

Rather than attempt to address all the technological and cultural Web issues plaguing the MySpace platform, News Corp. chose to focus on generating revenues by increasing its identity as an entertainment-centric Web destination and by forging even closer relationships with the recorded music and movie industries. After all, News Corp. owned many media properties. On a site that already was lagging behind the *social* aspect of the overall social network, this decision to move away from connecting people with people in favor of connecting people with media proved disastrous. At a time when Facebook and Twitter were experiencing meteoric increases in membership, MySpace's membership numbers as well as its traffic dwindled.

Despite numerous rounds of management shakeups between 2008 and 2010, none of the would-be executive saviors of MySpace managed to turn the company around. By the end of 2010, MySpace had no defensible competitive advantage. It had long ago defined its niche as a place for music fans and bands to connect, and had decided to stick with this core competency despite evidence that the social media universe was quickly evolving in another direction altogether. It also ignored complaints from its members that the technology was falling behind, and that the features and user interface were substandard to the newer social networks appearing almost monthly. MySpace management ran the company without adapting sufficiently, or smartly enough, to these two particular challenges.

In 2011, MySpace was sold to Specific Media and Justin Timberlake,[9] where it may be in better hands. Although just a shadow of its former self, it remains one of the top 160 most-visited websites in the world,[10] which gives its new owners a foundation to rethink and perhaps reinvent this once-giant social networking and technology innovator. ■

questions

1. Was it reasonable for Facebook to initially ignore a segment of its market when MySpace was so big and Facebook so small?

2. Friendster turned down a $30 million acquisition offer, and MySpace accepted one for $580 million. Both decisions are considered to have hampered their ability to compete with Facebook. Should they have taken the money? When and how do you know it's time to sell?

3. MySpace later became known as *the* social networking site for music and entertainment connections. Do you think it can build a highly profitable business around this niche?

7. Ibid.
8. "Special Report: How News Corp got lost in MySpace," by Adegoke Yinka. *Reuters.com*.
9. "News Corp. Sells Myspace for a Song," by Jessica Vascallero et al. The *Wall Street Journal*. June 30, 2011.
10. Alexa. Jan. 29, 2012. www.alexa.com.

HELP GOOGLE SURVIVE

Goal:

To learn to think strategically when you're the market leader.

What to Do:

Even market leaders face challenges, and must look over their shoulders at what might be threatening them.

In this exercise, consider the market risks and challenges that Google currently faces. Then build a strategy for staying ahead of the pack.

1. Either alone or in a group, choose one area in which Google currently operates, such as search, social networking, online video, email, or online applications. (There are many more.)

2. Identify the key competitors Google currently faces in the area that you've chosen.

3. Make a list of the competitive challenges Google now faces. Make a list of what challenges might emerge in that area.

4. Make a list of the potential opportunities Google has in that area to improve its competitive position.

CHAPTER 7 Money Management

learning objectives

In this chapter, you'll learn how to:

- Define key financial terms and apply them to a real business

- Understand, analyze, and prepare an income statement, cash flow statement, and balance sheet

- Apply best practices for money management

- Conduct realistic financial projections for an entrepreneurial company

- Determine a company's profit margins and return on investment (ROI)

- Analyze a company's break-even point and determine variable costs

- Bill customers and receive payments

General Financial Terms

You should have a working knowledge of the following key financial terms. You'll need these to produce financial statements, but also to understand money management in your company.

- **Accounts payable.** Obligations owed to others; a list of outstanding bills.

- **Accounts receivable.** Obligations owed to your company by others; a list of outstanding invoices.

- **Accumulated depreciation.** The amount of depreciation a company has already taken in the form of tax deductions; such accumulated depreciation must be accounted for when selling fixed assets.

- **Assets.** Anything the company owns that has a positive monetary value. The two main types of assets are:

  — **Current assets.** Assets that can be converted quickly to cash, with relative ease; these assets are designed to be turned over in the normal course of doing business, such as bank deposits, inventory, and accounts receivable.

  — **Fixed assets (or property, plant, and equipment).** Assets that are the ongoing means of doing business; such assets are generally cumbersome to turn into cash; includes buildings, land, and equipment.

- **Cash.** Immediately available money in the form of currency, checks, credit card deposits (from customers), or bank accounts.

- **Collections.** Income collected from sales made in a previous period.

- **Cost of goods sold (COGS).** Expenses directly associated with producing and making a product or service. Companies differ as to which expenses they attribute to cost of goods, but generally items such as source materials, direct labor, and freight are included. Not included are indirect costs, such as rent, utilities, and other overhead.

- **Cost of sales.** Expenses directly associated with selling a product or service. This typically includes items such as sales commissions, distributor's fees, and so on, but does not generally include more indirect costs such as marketing.

- **Current liabilities.** Any bills, debts, or obligations occurring in the ongoing course of business; any debt due within the next year. Includes accounts payable, accrued payroll expenses, and loans and credit lines with less than one year's maturity date.

- **Debt.** An ongoing obligation of the company, such as a bank loan or line of credit.

- **Depreciation.** The wear and tear on fixed assets; this is a business expense, as equipment and other company property wears down. Not a cash expenditure, but rather a tax deduction.

- **EBITDA.** Stands for "earnings before interest, tax, depreciation, and amortization." In other words, it is the actual profits of a company without being adjusted for taxes or other accounting procedures. It is sometimes used as a measurement of a company's bottom line.

Financial Symbols

The symbols below commonly appear on financial forms:

( )   Numbers appearing in parentheses are negative numbers; they represent losses.

- - -   Single lines represent subtotals.

===   Double lines represent totals.

000s   This indicates that numbers are expressed in thousands.

en·tre·pre·neur·ship key terms

Accrual-basis accounting
Income and expenses are entered in the books at the time of the original commitment, or transaction, to buy or sell, rather than when the money actually changes hands.

Balance sheet
A key financial statement. The balance sheet shows all the company's assets minus all its liabilities. Including equity in the company, the two should balance out.

Break-even point
The point at which a company's sales exceed its costs and it then begins to make a profit.

Cash-basis accounting
Income and expenses are entered in the books at the time money actually is exchanged, rather than when the commitment to buy or sell is made.

Cash flow statement
A key financial statement. The cash flow statement shows how much actual cash went into and out of the company.

Income statement
A key financial statement, also called a P&L (for profit and loss). The income statement shows a summary of the income and expenses of a company.

Profit margin
The amount earned after the cost of goods (gross profit margin) or total operating expenses (net profit margin) are deducted; often expressed in percentage terms.

Variable costs
Costs that change depending on how many sales or products you make. For example, rent is fixed, but cost of goods will vary depending on how many units you produce.

Don't get emotional

Try to view your financial statements in a relatively dispassionate manner. It's difficult, especially when you own your business, to keep emotions from clouding your ability to properly examine your financial reports. If you know it has been a bad month, you may be tempted just to ignore that month's cash flow or income statements. *Don't*.

- **Equity.** Ownership of a company, usually distributed by means of shares of stock or percentage ownership of a company. A person who owns part of a company is said to have an equity interest in the company.

- **Fixed costs.** Ongoing expenses or overhead of a business that occur regardless of the amount of sales. These expenses usually include items such as rent, utilities, salaries, and loan repayments.

- **Gross profit.** Amount of income a company realizes on each sale after accounting for the hard costs of acquiring inventory or raw materials (cost of goods) and before accounting for sales and administrative expenses.

- **Gross sales.** Total sales from all product line categories.

- **Intangible assets.** Aspects of a company that have value not easily interpreted in specific monetary terms or directly convertible to cash; assets such as a popular trademarked name and the goodwill a company has built up over time.

- **Liabilities.** Any outstanding financial obligation or debt of a company.

- **Long-term liabilities.** Loans and other debts that come due in more than a year's time. This year's interest payments on such loans, or debt service, are included in current liabilities.

- **Markup.** The difference between the cost of goods and the price at which they're sold, creating a profit margin for the business.

- **Net cash flow.** Money left over after all disbursements have been deducted from all cash received.

- **Net profit.** Amount of income after deducting all costs of doing business, including administrative overhead and other fixed costs.

- **Net worth.** Value of a company after deducting all liabilities from all assets.

- **Opening cash balance.** Amount of money in the bank at the beginning of the month being evaluated; should be the same as the previous month's ending cash balance.

- **Owner's draw.** Money paid to owner in lieu of, or in addition to, salary, or money otherwise distributed to owners (except for expense reimbursement).

- **Profit.** Amount a company earns after expenses. Can be gross profit or net profit or profit after taxes.

- **Pro forma.** In entrepreneurial companies, financial statements based on projected future performance rather than actual historical data.

- **Reserve.** Money put into accounts for future, unanticipated expenses.

- **Retained earnings.** Net worth amount the company keeps internally for ongoing development of the business rather than distributing to shareholders.

- **Return on investment (ROI).** The total financial gain received in return for the total resources (primarily money) put into a company or activity. Looking at ROI is a good way to compare various investments or scenarios.

- **Revenue.** Total sales of a company before any expenses. Profit refers to the amount a company earns after expenses.

- **Short-term notes payable.** Debts typically due to be paid off within a year. This includes lines-of-credit and other operating credit other than accounts payable.

How to Read and Understand Basic Financial Statements

Money lies at the heart of every business. You may not have gone into business purely to make money, but money is what's going to keep your doors open, and your workers employed. Whether your money is coming in or going out, managing money well is an absolutely critical part of any business.

Good money management is especially important in an entrepreneurial company, in which growth is occurring rapidly, sales may not yet be established, and costs are unpredictable. Every entrepreneur must learn at least the basics of money management if they hope to succeed.

Even if you're not personally responsible for preparing ongoing financial reports, you should have a working understanding of financial statements so that you can better control your company. Such statements provide you with the information you need to make decisions. Many managers mistakenly believe that they are in charge of the big picture, while their bookkeepers and "bean counters" get caught up with mere details. Numbers are *not* just details: They are the vital signs of any business; you must understand your company's numbers so that you can realistically assess its condition.

Income statement

The **income statement** provides a picture of your company's profitability. That's why it's also frequently called either a profit and loss statement (P&L) or an income and expense statement. This form shows how profitable your company is—how much money it has taken in and how much it will make after all expenses are accounted for. But one month's or even one year's profits don't tell your company's whole story. An income statement does not give a total picture of what your company is worth overall (that's where a **balance sheet** comes in), or of how much money it has available (that's where the **cash flow statement** comes in).

Do your homework

Get in the habit of reading your financial statements at least monthly, and make sure you understand what you read. Track items such as sales receipts and expenses daily or weekly. Don't wait for reports to come back from the accountants before knowing your cash position. You will find you have more confidence in your decisions if you comprehend the financial implications of each of your choices.

Sample Form: Income Statement

Year: 2012

	JAN	FEB	MARCH	APRIL	MAY
INCOME					
Gross Sales	$0	$4,000	$4,000	$10,000	$24,000
(Commissions)	0	0	0	0	700
(Returns and allowances)	0	0	0	0	0
Net Sales	0	4,000	4,000	10,000	23,300
(Cost of goods)	0	648	648	1,624	3,892
GROSS PROFIT	0	3,352	3,352	8,376	19,408
EXPENSES— General and Administrative					
Salaries and wages	5,000	7,400	11,400	12,400	15,400
Employee benefits	550	550	1,020	1,020	1,020
Payroll taxes	420	620	1,010	1,010	1,010
Professional services	5,000	500	4,000	400	400
Marketing and advertising	6,400	3,600	8,000	3,000	3,000
Rent	0	0	0	0	0
Equipment rental	500	500	500	500	500
Maintenance	0	0	0	0	0
Depreciation	4,000	0	0	0	0
Insurance	800	0	0	400	0
Telecommunications	200	100	200	200	240
Utilities	500	120	250	420	320
Office supplies	900	250	430	370	250
Postage and shipping	420	160	620	130	900
Travel	110	300	200	300	0
Entertainment	0	0	220	640	390
Interest on loans	0	250	250	250	250
Other: Technology	6,000	0	0	0	0
Other: Furniture	0	0	0	820	0
TOTAL EXPENSES	30,800	14,350	28,100	21,860	23,680
Net income before taxes	(30,800)	(10,998)	(24,748)	(13,484)	(4,272)
Provision for taxes on income	0	0	0	0	0
NET PROFIT	(30,800)	(10,998)	(24,748)	(13,484)	(4,272)

JUNE	JULY	AUG	SEPT	OCT	NOV	DEC	TOTAL
$32,000	$41,000	$56,000	$68,400	$83,600	$100,000	$43,000	$466,000
1,500	1,550	2,470	3,000	3,700	4,400	1,900	$19,220
0	0	0	0	0	0	0	$0
30,500	39,450	53,530	65,400	79,900	95,600	41,100	$446,780
5,190	6,898	9,482	11,382	13,852	16,800	7,324	$77,740
25,310	32,552	44,048	54,018	66,048	78,800	33,776	$369,040
16,800	12,600	19,800	18,200	20,200	22,200	16,600	$178,000
1,020	1,020	1,400	1,400	1,400	1,400	1,400	$13,200
1,010	1,010	1,220	1,220	1,220	1,220	1,220	$12,190
400	400	2,400	400	400	400	400	$15,100
600	3,000	3,500	4,000	500	4,000	500	$40,100
0	0	4,200	4,200	4,200	4,200	4,200	$21,000
500	500	4,000	4,000	4,000	4,000	4,000	$23,500
0	0	240	240	240	240	240	$1,200
0	0	0	0	0	0	0	$4,000
0	400	2,000	700	1,100	700	700	$6,800
260	200	500	400	400	400	400	$3,500
400	350	520	440	420	360	300	$4,400
170	220	2,200	500	500	500	500	$6,790
170	520	120	820	150	600	400	$5,010
50	200	0	300	300	300	300	$2,360
400	150	170	100	100	100	100	$2,370
250	250	250	250	250	250	250	$2,750
6,000	0	0	0	0	0	0	$12,000
0	0	0	0	0	0	0	$820
28,030	20,820	42,520	37,170	35,380	40,870	31,510	$355,090
(2,720)	11,732	1,528	16,848	30,668	37,930	2,266	$13,950
0	0	0	0	0	0	2,092	$2,092
(2,720)	11,732	1,528	16,848	30,668	37,930	174	$11,858

Income Statement

For Year:_____	JAN	FEB	MARCH	APRIL	MAY
INCOME					
Gross Sales					
(Commissions)					
(Returns and allowances)					
Net Sales					
(Cost of goods)					
GROSS PROFIT					
EXPENSES—General and Administrative					
Salaries and wages					
Employee benefits					
Payroll taxes					
Professional services					
Marketing and advertising					
Rent					
Equipment rental					
Maintenance					
Depreciation					
Insurance					
Telecommunications					
Utilities					
Office supplies					
Postage and shipping					
Travel					
Entertainment					
Interest on loans					
Other:					
TOTAL EXPENSES					
Net income before taxes					
Provision for taxes on income					
NET PROFIT					

NOTE: A Microsoft Excel version of this worksheet is available as part of PlanningShop's Business Plan Financials package, available from www.PlanningShop.com.

JUNE	JULY	AUG	SEPT	OCT	NOV	DEC	TOTAL

Once upon a time...

An income statement tells the story of your company's activities. If it's a monthly income statement, it tells the story of your sales and expenses for one month; an annual income statement tells that year's story. Learn to read an income statement, to know a company's story.

A company can be losing money but still be worth a great deal because it owns valuable property, or it can be profitable but still not have enough cash to pay its bills due to cash flow problems. An income statement does not reveal either of these situations.

You read an income statement from top to bottom. The top part of an income statement concentrates on your sales and revenue. You may have a few lines in this section (if you have several business units, locations, or the like) before you get to your total revenue. Then, you start subtracting from your sales. You first subtract the cost of the products or materials it took to make those sales (your COGS—or cost of goods sold). You then subtract the cost of sales, such as sales commissions. Then you subtract your operating and administrative expenses. Finally, you make adjustments to income—such as any funds received from financing (investors or loans). The result is the company's profit (or, possibly, loss).

To prepare an income statement, accumulate detailed information about your sales and expenses. Specific lines on the form should mirror the categories by which you maintain your ongoing accounts. Use the sample income statement on pages 146–147 and the list of financial terms near the beginning of the chapter to guide you as you complete the income statement worksheet on pages 148–149. If necessary, adjust the worksheet to meet your company's needs.

Cash flow statement

If the three most significant things in real estate are "location, location, location," the three most important things in business are "cash, cash, cash." Or, as many small business owners say, "Cash is king." Managing your cash is key to business survival, so your cash flow statement will be your most necessary financial assessment for monitoring how much money you receive and spend. After all, if you can't pay your employees, your bills, or yourself, you're not going to stay in business long. Even profitable firms can—and do—go out of business due to cash flow problems.

A cash flow statement tells you how much money you have on hand to put in the bank at the end of the month (or whatever period the cash flow statement covers) so you can pay your bills. It *doesn't* tell you whether your company will show an overall profit or how many orders you are getting, but instead gives a real-life picture of the money going into and out of your business, typically shown on a monthly basis. Nor does it show you how valuable your company is—since you may own valuable property or patents, but still not be able to pay your bills. That's what a balance sheet does.

In the top part of your cash flow statement, you delineate all the cash actually received during the period covered (whether received as checks, electronic funds transfers, credit card deposits, or in other forms). In the bottom part, you delineate all the cash you've actually put out (once again, whether in the form of checks, ETFs, and the like). At the bottom, you get an ending balance of your cash.

Cash flow statements are important for all companies, but especially for seasonal businesses, those with large inventories, or those that sell much of their merchandise on credit. You must plan for the slow months as well as for the long time lag between paying for materials and actually realizing cash receipts. Maintaining historical cash flow records gives you an idea of what to expect in certain months of the year and helps you plan future cash management. Get in the habit of keeping monthly cash flow accounts.

In preparing your cash flow statement, separate out cash you receive from doing business (sales) and the cash you get from taking out loans or receiving investments (financing). This will give you a better sense of where your money comes from and how much you rely on credit or investors.

Use the sample cash flow statement on pages 152–153 as a guide to complete the cash flow statement worksheet on pages 154–155.

ACCRUAL-BASIS VS. CASH-BASIS ACCOUNTING

Cash flow statements are particularly important for companies that operate on an **accrual-basis accounting** method where income and expenses are booked when the transaction is made rather than when the cash is received. (Corporations and companies with more than $5 million in annual revenue in the United States must operate on an accrual basis.)

In other words, let's say your ski boot company operates on an accrual basis, and you get an order for 1,000 pairs of boots in April. The same month, you order the raw material to manufacture the boots. Both transactions would be booked in the same month on your income statement, but your actual cash flow will be far different. You might pay for the raw materials in May, but not receive payment for the finished boots until October, and only your cash flow statement would show that you had a six-month negative cash balance on that order.

Cash-basis accounting is the easier method, as income and expenses are entered in the books at the time money actually changes hands. Thus, if you receive a $5,000 order in January, but you don't receive payment until March, the $5,000 credit appears as income only on your March statements. If payment is never made, additional accounting entries would later be made to write off the loss. This gives a truer picture of a company's ability to meet its financial obligations than does accrual-basis accounting.

Balance sheet

For those who are new to business, the balance sheet is probably the least understood of the financial forms. In essence, the balance sheet gives a snapshot of the overall financial worth of the company—the value of all its various components and the extent of all its obligations.

The balance sheet accounts for all the company's assets minus all its liabilities. The remaining amount (if any) is figured to be the net worth of the company. The net worth is then distributed either as belonging to the

Cash flow best practices

Cash flow problems occur when cash goes out the door faster than it comes in. This can happen for many reasons. You may be slow billing customers, for example, creating too much delay between the time you have to purchase the materials to make your circuit boards and the time you get paid for those boards. Your job when running your business is to keep an eye not only on the so-called bottom line, but also on the cash flow statement. Here are a number of things you can do to better manage your cash flow:

- Arrange for your payments to suppliers and creditors to align with your payments from customers.

- Keep an adequate cash buffer in the bank at all times.

- Bill customers promptly, and send frequent notifications when an account becomes overdue.

- Give overdue customers the opportunity to make partial payments.

- Give customers discounts for prompt payments.

Sample Form: Cash Flow Statement

Year: 2012

	JAN	FEB	MARCH	APRIL	MAY
CASH RECEIPTS					
Income from Sales					
Cash sales	$0	$4,000	$4,000	$10,000	$24,000
Collections	0	0	0	0	0
Total Cash from Sales	0	4,000	4,000	10,000	24,000
Income from Financing					
Interest income	0	0	0	0	0
Loan proceeds	30,000	0	0	12,000	20,000
Equity capital investments	40,000	0	20,000	0	0
Total Cash from Financing	70,000	0	20,000	12,000	20,000
Other cash receipts	0	0	0	0	0
TOTAL CASH RECEIPTS	70,000	4,000	24,000	22,000	44,000
CASH DISBURSEMENTS					
Expenses					
Inventory	0	648	648	1,624	3,892
Operating expenses	30,800	14,350	28,100	21,860	23,680
Commissions/returns & allowances	0	0	0	0	700
Capital purchases	20,000	0	0	0	0
Loan payments	0	250	250	250	250
Income tax payments	0	0	0	0	0
Investor dividend payments	0	0	0	0	0
Owner's draw	0	0	0	0	0
TOTAL CASH DISBURSEMENTS	50,800	15,248	28,998	23,734	28,522
NET CASH FLOW	19,200	(11,248)	(4,998)	(1,734)	15,478
Opening cash balance	0	19,200	7,952	2,954	1,220
Cash receipts	70,000	4,000	24,000	22,000	44,000
Cash disbursements	(50,800)	(15,248)	(28,998)	(23,734)	(28,522)
ENDING CASH BALANCE	19,200	7,952	2,954	1,220	16,698

JUNE	JULY	AUG	SEPT	OCT	NOV	DEC	TOTAL
$24,000	$31,000	$39,600	$40,000	$61,600	$70,000	$31,000	$339,200
8,000	10,000	16,400	28,400	22,000	30,000	12,000	$126,800
32,000	41,000	56,000	68,400	83,600	100,000	43,000	$466,000
0	0	0	0	0	0	0	$0
0	0	8,000	0	0	0	0	$70,000
0	0	0	0	0	0	0	$60,000
0	0	8,000	0	0	0	0	$130,000
32,000	41,000	64,000	68,400	83,600	100,000	43,000	$596,000
0	0	0	0	0	0	0	0
32,000	41,000	64,000	68,400	83,600	100,000	43,000	$596,000
5,190	6,898	9,482	11,382	13,852	16,800	7,324	$77,740
28,030	20,820	42,520	37,170	35,380	40,870	31,510	$355,090
1,500	1,550	2,470	3,000	3,700	4,400	1,900	$19,220
0	0	0	0	0	0	0	$20,000
250	250	250	250	250	10,250	20,250	$32,750
0	0	0	0	0	0	0	$0
0	0	0	0	0	0	0	$0
0	0	0	0	0	5000	5000	$10,000
34,970	29,518	54,722	51,802	53,182	82,320	70,984	$524,800
(2,970)	11,482	9,278	16,598	30,418	17,680	(27,984)	$72,200
16,698	13,728	25,210	34,488	51,086	81,504	99,184	$0
32,000	41,000	64,000	68,400	83,600	100,000	43,000	$596,000
(34,970)	(29,518)	(54,722)	(51,802)	(53,182)	(82,320)	(70,984)	($524,800)
13,728	25,210	34,488	51,086	81,504	99,184	71,200	

BUILD-YOUR-BUSINESS WORKSHEET

Cash Flow Statement

For Year:_____	JAN	FEB	MARCH	APRIL	MAY
CASH RECEIPTS **Income from Sales**					
Cash sales					
Collections					
Total Cash from Sales					
Income from Financing					
Interest income					
Loan proceeds					
Total Cash from Financing					
Other cash receipts					
TOTAL CASH RECEIPTS					
CASH DISBURSEMENTS **Expenses**					
Inventory					
Operating expenses					
Commissions/returns & allowances					
Capital purchases					
Loan payments					
Income tax payments					
Investor dividend payments					
Owner's draw					
TOTAL CASH DISBURSEMENTS					
NET CASH FLOW					
Opening cash balance					
Cash receipts					
Cash disbursements					
ENDING CASH BALANCE					

! NOTE: A Microsoft Excel version of this worksheet is available as part of PlanningShop's Business Plan Financials package, available from www.PlanningShop.com.

JUNE	JULY	AUG	SEPT	OCT	NOV	DEC	TOTAL

Speed up your financials

To make this process even easier, a Microsoft Excel–based Business Plan Financials package is available for purchase as a supplement to this book. The worksheets are identical to the financial worksheets found in these pages and are in the format expected by potential funders of entrepreneurial companies.

In addition, the Business Plan Financials performs all calculations for you, generates charts, and allows you to "tweak" your numbers to obtain the most accurate financial picture. Once you're satisfied with your numbers, you can print out all your financial forms.

Visit www.PlanningShop.com to purchase and instantly download the Business Plan Financials.

owners of the company—their equity—or as retained earnings for the company to use. These allotments are listed in the liabilities category. Once you do this, the amounts in the assets and liabilities categories are equal: They balance.

Only on the balance sheet can you see the worth of existing property and equipment. Some companies own valuable land or buildings whose worth far exceeds the income of the actual business; other businesses own expensive machinery. Yet other companies may be profitable but heavily in debt.

A balance sheet can be a very frustrating document, especially for an entrepreneurial company. After all, the most valuable things you believe you have—your ideas, your great team, your energy—don't show up on a balance sheet at all. In fact, it's often quite difficult for a small or new company to list on its balance sheet its most important assets—for instance, its intellectual property or the goodwill of its key customers. But if you are seeking bank financing, such as loans or lines of credit, the balance sheet will be one of the key documents lenders look at.

Since much of the information on balance sheets doesn't change very quickly, generally you can prepare balance sheets primarily on a quarterly or annual basis. When completing the balance sheet, you may find you need more help with this form than with any other, especially when trying to figure accumulated depreciation or the worth of inventory. Get help from your accountant, or have your accountant prepare the form. But you must still understand it and vouch for it.

Use the sample balance sheet on page 158 as a guide to complete the balance sheet worksheet on page 159.

Financial Projections: "Bottom Up" vs. "Top Down"

As an entrepreneur, especially if you're just starting out, you may not yet have numbers to actually plug into your financial statements. Nevertheless, in the planning stages of your business, filling out your financials is just as crucial as when your venture is up and running. But it's obviously more challenging when you lack both historical data and experience. If you have no idea how many orders to expect, for example, how will you know how many supplies to order or workers to hire? This is where financial projections come in.

Successful financial projections are achieved by budgeting from the "bottom up," not the "top down." Top-down numbers are enticing to work with because they always come out looking good, yet they're not realistic. Here's how they work: You look at the big picture—the total market size, growth rate, average sales price, and average **profit margins** in your industry. You make what seem to be reasonable assumptions, something like achieving a 10 percent market penetration, or improving margins by 2 percent. Then you fill in your financial statements to make the total come out to the big numbers projected.

For example, say you've invented a new golf club, and you project that you will achieve a 1 percent market penetration within three years. If total annual sales of golf clubs amount to $2 billion, then you'll achieve $20 million in annual sales. With a profit margin of 15 percent, your net profit will be $3 million. Sounds impressive, doesn't it? But it's just not very realistic.

Instead, the best financials are developed from the bottom up. You do the real business-building legwork: Examine different distribution channels, source manufacturers and suppliers, develop a staffing chart, outline your marketing program, and design operations. You plug in numbers from these realistic projections of how much things will cost and then determine how much income you will need to sustain that cost.

So, let's say you're that same golf club manufacturer, and you sensibly build your financials from the bottom up. Here's how it would work:

First, compare distribution channels and then choose one. Let's say you decide to sell through specialty golf retailers and country clubs. This channel has associated costs and impacts on income. You'll need to budget for a sales force to sell to those shops, exhibiting at the annual sporting good trade shows, and advertising in *Golf Retailer* magazine. And you'll only receive 40 percent to 45 percent of the final sales price of each club, since the retailer takes half and the salesperson receives a commission. *Now* you're getting some real numbers to plug into each of the lines of your financial forms.

Reality check

What do you do if, after preparing your financial projections, you realize you won't make money with the business the way you originally envisioned it? You have five options:

1. **Change your business model.** Businesses frequently experiment with business models. In the Internet world, for example, many companies switch from fee-based to advertising-supported models that give away a product or service to users for free in the hopes of building market share. Others, such as the *New York Times,* eventually switched from free to fee-based. When considering your business model, realize that the revenue has to come from somewhere; it's your job to come up with innovative ways to get it.

2. **Change the pricing.** Another possibility is raising the price of your product or service so that you can make a profit on it. Sometimes this just won't be possible. The market may not bear a price hike because competitive products and services are already out there for less, and you can't justify asking for more than they charge. In such cases, think about reducing your expenses (see the next point).

Sales vs. cash

When preparing your financial projections, remember that you often won't receive full payment at the time of an actual sale or transaction. Projecting cash flow solely on the sales made, rather than cash actually received, will leave you seriously short on money.

Some industries, such as manufacturing, have particularly long lag times between orders and payment. A clothing manufacturer, for instance, may make sales many months before payment is due. Even in professional services businesses, retail, construction, and several other types of businesses, you'll find that you establish some credit accounts or do not receive payment until the work is finished, meaning that you have cash expenditures long before you have cash income.

Sample Form: Balance Sheet

For Year Ending: December 31, 2012

ASSETS

Current Assets

Cash	$71,200		
Accounts receivable	34,400		
Inventory	4,200		
Other current assets	1,560		
Total Current Assets		**$111,360**	

Fixed Assets

Land	0		
Facilities	0		
Equipment	20,000		
Computers & telecommunications	0		
Less accumulated depreciation	(4,000)		
Total Fixed Assets		**$16,000**	
Other Assets		0	
TOTAL ASSETS			**$127,360**

LIABILITIES

Current Liabilities

Short-term notes payable	27,350		
Income taxes due	6,100		
Other current liabilities	590		
Total Current Liabilities		**$34,040**	

Long-Term Liabilities

Long-term notes payable	30,000		
Other long-term liabilities	0		
Total Long-Term Liabilities		**$30,000**	

Net Worth

Shareholders' equity	63,320		
Retained earnings	0		
Total Net Worth		**$63,320**	
TOTAL LIABILITIES AND NET WORTH			**$127,360**

BUILD-YOUR-BUSINESS WORKSHEET

Balance Sheet

For Company: _____

For Period: _____ **Ending:** _____ , 20_____

ASSETS

Current Assets

Cash _____

Accounts receivable _____

Inventory _____

Other current assets _____

Total Current Assets _____

Fixed Assets

Land _____

Facilities _____

Equipment _____

Computers & telecommunications _____

(Less accumulated depreciation) _____

Total Fixed Assets _____

Other Assets _____

TOTAL ASSETS ==================

LIABILITIES

Current Liabilities

Short-term notes payable _____

Income taxes due _____

Other current liabilities _____

Total Current Liabilities _____

Long-Term Liabilities

Long-term notes payable _____

Other long-term liabilities _____

Total Long-Term Liabilities _____

Net Worth

Paid-in capital _____

Retained earnings _____

Total Net Worth _____

TOTAL LIABILITIES AND NET WORTH ==================

 NOTE: A Microsoft Excel version of this worksheet is available as part of PlanningShop's Business Plan Financials package, available from www.PlanningShop.com.

3. **Lower your expenses.** The price you charge represents only half the profit equation. The other half is what it costs you to make that product or deliver that service. If you can eliminate certain costs—either costs directly involved in making a product or delivering a service (such as raw materials or gas expenditures) or indirect costs (such as your energy bills or rent)—then you might be able to make a profit without raising the price you charge customers.

4. **Change the product or service.** You may need to alter the specifications of the product or service you had planned on providing so that you can either raise the price or reduce the cost, or both. For example, you may discover that by adding certain premium features to your high-end home entertainment systems, you can charge considerably more for them.

5. **Change your target market.** Sometimes you simply don't make the sales you want and need because you are aiming at the wrong customer base. For example, you may be targeting your new online travel management service at consumers, when you could reap higher profit margins by selling to the corporate market instead.

Measuring Success

In addition to learning how to prepare your key financial statements and to understand what they reveal about your business, you'll want to know how to measure several aspects of your entrepreneurial venture once it's up and running.

Profit margin

One yardstick by which many businesses gauge their success is **profit margin**. It measures what proportion of the money you take in is actual profit, rather than merely covering expenses.

For example, if you sell an item for $100 and your costs are $70, you'd have a gross profit margin of 30 percent, while if someone else's costs were $85, their profit margin would only be 15 percent.

Obviously, the higher the profit margin, the better, because this indicates that proportionally more of what you earn represents profits. Higher profits mean you have more money available for marketing, growth, salaries, and profit for yourself as well as your investors.

Higher profit margins are produced by keeping your prices high and your costs low.

There are generally two types of profit margins referred to:

- **Gross margin.** The total percent of profit, deducting only the cost of goods sold (COGS) or, in some cases, the cost of sales (especially in commission sales). In other words, if you sell a product for $100, but it cost you $50 to acquire that product to sell, your gross margin is 50 percent.

■ **Net margin.** The total percent of profit after deducting all expenses, including overhead. In other words, if you sell a product for $100, and it cost you $50, and all your overhead, marketing, and other expenses cost you $45, you'd have only a 5 percent net profit margin.

You can't compare the profit margins of businesses in different industries or even different markets to determine who's doing "better," because different companies operate under vastly different conditions. For example, a supermarket operating in Manhattan will likely have a radically different profit margin than one in downtown Peoria, Illinois, because the costs of rent, utilities, and staffing are so much higher in New York City, even though the supermarket can charge higher prices.

You calculate your profit margin as follows:

Profit Margin = Net Income (Sales minus all Expenses) / Total Sales

Return on investment (ROI)

Another way that companies measure their profitability is by determining, or projecting, their return on investment (ROI). In short, this is the amount of money earned from the money invested in the company or project. ROI is typically expressed in percentage terms.

As an entrepreneur, you can use the concept of ROI when evaluating different "investments" in new products, marketing campaigns, or expansions of any sort. Say you compare two different sites for opening another restaurant. The first one costs far more, but the potential sales are also far higher. The second costs much less but will generate less revenue. By looking at total ROI, you can evaluate which presents a better use of your money.

ROI is also a particularly important measurement for investors of entrepreneurial companies. If you seek financing for your company, expect investors to quiz you about the expected ROI on their money. They will compare that to the kinds of ROI they can get in other investments. For more on ROI from the point of view of an investor, see pages 183–184.

Break-even analysis and variable costs

Finally, you want to determine how much income you must earn to pay your expenses—at what point you break even. At the **break-even point** you neither make a profit nor lose money; you have only covered the cost of staying in business and making your sales. Your break-even point is important because it shows you how much money you need to make to just keep your doors open.

Most people new to business assume they reach their break-even point when sales equal the amount of fixed expenses: rent, telephone, insurance, and so forth. Fixed expenses are easy to determine, since they remain relatively stable regardless of the amount of sales. But because virtually all sales have some costs associated with them, you must also figure the **variable costs** of sales into your break-even analysis; otherwise you won't have a true picture of your cost of doing business.

Death and... you know what

No one likes to pay taxes. But the good news is that if you're paying them, your business is making money!

You will make some decisions—or alter them—based on tax implications. Some business expenses are fully deductible, others are only partially deductible, others have to be depreciated over a number of years, and yet others are never deductible. You need at least a fair understanding of these issues.

In addition, tax codes are complicated and always changing. Tax laws vary according to the business structure you choose, and business tax laws differ from regulations for individuals. And, of course, tax laws vary from country to country, and every U.S. state and Canadian province has its own tax laws as well. So, find a good accountant to advise you on taxes—what's due when, how various transactions are taxed or expensed, and how you can reduce your tax bill. For more on taxes, see Chapter 16.

CALCULATING YOUR BREAK-EVEN POINT

Your cost of doing business depends, of course, on the type of business you have. In particular, your variable costs may differ substantially, depending on whether you have mostly fixed expenses or whether your costs increase when you make sales.

For example, if you have a manufacturing or retail company, your expenses will go up significantly when you make higher sales, but if yours is a service company or a software or app development company, your variable costs will be far lower—perhaps almost nothing—until it comes time to hire more employees. This is why many tech-development companies are highly profitable.

Look at two scenarios. In one, you make cases for smartphones. In the other, you make apps for smartphones.

If you make smartphone cases, and your fixed expenses (rent, utilities, salaries, and so on) are $120,000 a month, it's not just enough to make $120,000 in sales: You would lose money. You must pay for the raw materials to make the cases, the workers to assemble the cases, the boxes to put the cases in, and the shipping to the retailers. If these costs amount to an average of 30 percent of the cost of each sale, at $120,000 in income, you're still $36,000 in the hole ($120,000 in fixed expenses plus $36,000 in costs of goods).

The total cost of goods keeps rising as your sales rise; unlike your fixed costs, the figure keeps changing and is harder to pin down. But your gross profit margin—the average percentage you earn on each sale after direct costs are deducted—stays basically the same. (As you sell greater amounts, you may be able to increase your profit margin by receiving volume discounts; for the purpose of this exercise; however, you can assume a stable gross profit margin.)

By contrast, if you make apps for smartphones, almost all your expenses would be fixed expenses—your rent, utilities, and salaries for programmers and engineers. Whether you sell one copy of the app or 10,000 copies, your costs remain essentially the same. It's only when you need to add more personnel, such as tech support staff or engineers, or add bandwidth to handle demand that your variable costs rise.

To determine an actual break-even point, you must know your:

- Fixed expenses
- Gross profit margin (average percentage of gross income realized after cost of goods)

Then, to figure the amount of total sales needed to break even, you work the equation:

Fixed Expenses = Total Sales x Gross Profit Margin (GPM)

or, saying the same thing:

Fixed Expenses = Total Sales
    GPM

In the above example of the smartphone case manufacturer, we know:

Fixed expenses = $120,000

Gross profit margin (GPM) = 70% (since cost of goods is 30%)

So, the numbers would look like:

120,000 = Total Sales to Break Even
   .70

Doing the arithmetic, we see that this smartphone case maker must make $171,429 in sales to reach the break-even point.

You can see how a break-even analysis is a vital tool for your internal planning.

Working with an Accountant

As you get your business under way, you'll need the assistance of a good business accountant to help you in most aspects of managing your money. An accountant who understands entrepreneurial business issues can help you decide whether to set up your books on an accrual basis or a cash basis, explain any financial or tax issues you'll face, and assist you in tax planning. You'll avoid a lot of problems by getting things set up the proper way right from the start. And you'll almost certainly lower your taxes, too.

A good accountant can save you more than you pay for one. Some accounting firms can also provide you with bookkeeping or bill-paying services or can recommend a reputable outside bookkeeper. If your business will require lots of invoices, bills, or bookkeeping, you may want to ask about these options, especially if you currently lack the funds to hire an in-house bookkeeper.

Read through this entire chapter before you meet with your accountant, so that you have a more thorough understanding of the issues you need to discuss.

Money-Management Tips

It's not enough to just make a profit; it is certainly possible to be profitable and still not have the cash on hand to pay your bills. Following these money-management tips will help you avoid cash flow problems.

■ **Manage your growth.** You want your business to get bigger, but if you grow too fast you may not be able to sustain it. Growth costs money—you incur many expenses before you see additional income. Managing the expenses associated with growth is particularly challenging in entrepreneurial companies, so plan your growth in a way that you'll have the financial resources to pay for it.

REAL-WORLD RECAP

Money-management tips

- ☐ Manage your growth
- ☐ Review your books regularly
- ☐ Send them your bill
- ☐ Watch your inventory
- ☐ Save

- **Review your books regularly.** When you're running your business, you may not take the time to sit down and look at your financials. Yet you can't manage your money without having the facts. At least once a month, preferably once a week, look at your figures: accounts payable and receivable, expenses, cash flow, and so on.

- **Send them your bill.** Businesspeople, especially consultants and professional service providers, are notoriously slow at sending out their invoices. You may feel uncomfortable asking someone for money, afraid of being challenged on how much you've billed, or far too busy working. Still, the longer you wait to send out your invoices, the greater the chance you won't get paid.

- **Watch your inventory.** If you produce goods, you'll always be tempted to produce more because you get savings based on volume. But inventory can go "bad"—become outdated, unsellable, or time- or weather-worn. Inventory doesn't just apply to finished goods for resale. You may have "inventory" in the form of marketing materials. Keep an eye on your actual use, and make your purchases not only on the basis of price but also on whether you can get small quantities close to when you actually need them.

- **Save.** Every business has income fluctuations. The best way to have cash when you need it is to put some away when you've got it.

How to Get Paid

Sure, you've made the product. Then, thank goodness, you made the sale. But where's the money? It seems obvious, but getting paid is crucial to money management—and to staying in business.

Billing payment terms

Most of your customers won't simply hand over the money they owe you. They'll wait to be "asked." This takes the form of your presenting them with a bill. You have a number of billing options:

- **Standard billing.** This is the most traditional method of billing clients, especially in business-to-business (B2B) dealings. Within a certain period after a product has been delivered or a service rendered, you create a bill that itemizes the product or service purchased and lists the amount and the "terms" of billing (specifically, when the bill is due). Typically this is within 30 days of the bill's date, but it can also be 60 or 90 days or even longer if you're running a special promotion to attract customers.

- **Credit card payments.** This is a highly attractive option, for a number of reasons—most notably, convenience for the customer and immediate payment for you! When a customer uses a credit card, the funds are deposited into your account within 24–48 hours. You pay a small fee for this convenience—about 2 percent of the amount—and in most cases you have to set up a preapproved "merchant account" (or some other method of accepting credit cards, such as PayPal). While credit cards are standard for selling to consumers, even businesses may want to pay you with a credit card.

- **Upfront deposits.** Sometimes you will ask customers to pay upfront some or all of the fees associated with purchasing a product or service, even before the product or service is delivered. You generally would want to do this only with items or services that require you to make a substantial investment in materials you have to purchase or time you need to devote to a client. For instance, it's typical in any construction work to get upfront deposits for the purchase of materials. This reduces the risk that you will perform a lot of work, or accrue a lot of material expense, and then not get paid due to a change of mind on the part of the customer or other unforeseen circumstance.

- **Cash on delivery (COD).** You may well want to collect your price or fee the moment the product changes hands or the service is performed. This has the obvious advantage of improving your cash flow, making your financial situation more predictable, and reducing the risk that customers won't pay on time or at all. Cash on delivery is typical in retail or online sales businesses. The downside is that many customers—especially businesses—tend not to operate this way, and it may deter them from doing business with you

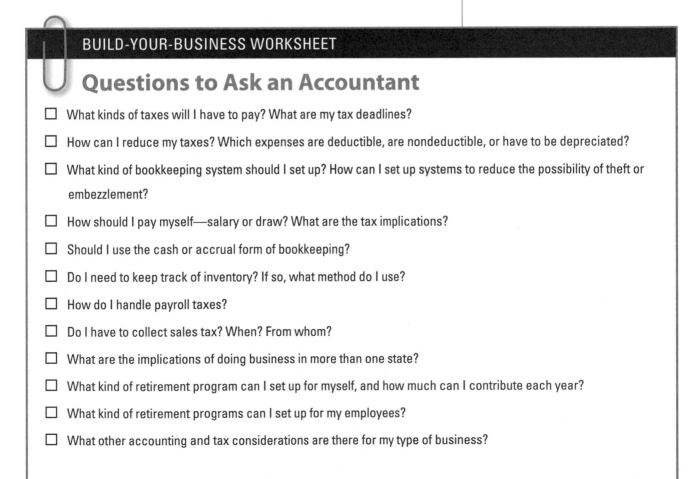

BUILD-YOUR-BUSINESS WORKSHEET

Questions to Ask an Accountant

☐ What kinds of taxes will I have to pay? What are my tax deadlines?

☐ How can I reduce my taxes? Which expenses are deductible, are nondeductible, or have to be depreciated?

☐ What kind of bookkeeping system should I set up? How can I set up systems to reduce the possibility of theft or embezzlement?

☐ How should I pay myself—salary or draw? What are the tax implications?

☐ Should I use the cash or accrual form of bookkeeping?

☐ Do I need to keep track of inventory? If so, what method do I use?

☐ How do I handle payroll taxes?

☐ Do I have to collect sales tax? When? From whom?

☐ What are the implications of doing business in more than one state?

☐ What kind of retirement program can I set up for myself, and how much can I contribute each year?

☐ What kind of retirement programs can I set up for my employees?

☐ What other accounting and tax considerations are there for my type of business?

REAL-WORLD CASE

Heavy Baggage: Debt at Luxury Luggage Maker J. W. Hulme

challenge

After borrowing heavily during boom times, luggage maker J. W. Hulme was in great danger when the economy crashed

solution

Sell a percentage of the company's ownership for a cash infusion to reduce debt, and refinance loans to lower interest rates

J. W. Hulme Co. is a St. Paul, Minnesota–based maker of high-end leather luggage and handbags that has been in business for more than a century. In 2003, Chuck Bidwell and Jennifer Guarino bought the vintage American brand, with big plans for expansion. They wanted to keep manufacturing in America and step up marketing.

To fund their growth, the two owners starting taking on debt—a lot of it.[1] After all, while the economy and the company was growing, debt capital was easily available.

"We took the fast track to growth. We were growing 40 percent a year," Guarino said in an interview with *Upsize Online* magazine. They invested money in designing and manufacturing new lines of products, opening up a retail channel, and reengineering manufacturing operations. Guarino admitted to feeling "uneasy" when Bidwell took on $1.2 million in debt in 2007. $800,000 came from a Small Business Administration (SBA) loan, and $400,000 was in other loans.[2] But she understood Bidwell's desire to expand the company as quickly as possible.

Then came the 2008 crash and the recession that followed. Sales declined. Still, Bidwell and Guarino remained optimistic. Expecting the downturn to pass quickly, they escalated production of new designs. But they made a fatal error: Already overextended on debt, they extended themselves further by ramping up manufacturing without having sufficient funds to pay for it.[3] In the past, their bank had always given them a short-term loan to cover printing of their all-important annual catalogs and sales collateral, and they assumed that this would continue to be the case. They were dead wrong.

Disaster hit all at once, and snowballed. When credit dried up in the marketplace, the bank that had always given them a short-term loan refused to do so. Without sufficient cash in the bank, and with a too-high debt-to-income ratio, they were unable to print their catalog—their most critical method for generating sales. Because of that, sales declined even further. They were unable to pay their suppliers and investors—many of whom were friends or relatives who had provided Bidwell and Guarino with the capital to buy the company in 2003.[4]

---

1. "Restitching a Firm That Nearly Unraveled." Julie Jargon. The *Wall Street Journal*. Aug. 3, 2010.
2. "J.W. Hulme owners work 90-day plan to recapitalize." *Upsize Online*. Q1 2009.
3. "Restitching a Firm."
4. Ibid.

When their overly optimistic sales projections didn't pan out, they were forced to sell off personal assets and scramble for cash to avoid going into bankruptcy.

J. W. Hulme was then forced to lay off staff—a bitter pill to swallow for the two owners, who were proud of owning one of the few American manufacturers of leather goods that had survived the offshoring of the industry. To raise money to pay the bills, Bidwell sold his house, then got an additional $800,000 by selling six vintage Buicks from his beloved car collection. Guarino held onto her house, but struggled to make the mortgage payments. She was also troubled by constant phone calls from relatives worried about the viability of their investments in the firm.[5]

Then the *Wall Street Journal* profiled the cash-flow troubles the firm was having in a front-page article, and, surprisingly, the outlook grew cheerier. Dean Vanech, chief executive of Olympus Capital Investments LLC, bought a 49 percent share in the company for $550,000. Together with the funds from Bidwell's Buicks, J. W. Hulme was able to reduce its debt in half, to about $1 million, and could refinance other bank loans. Bidwell and Guarino then gave other investors additional shares in the company, keeping only a 35 percent stake in the firm for themselves.[6]

Deals starting popping. The blogger Michael Williams, always looking for American-made products to feature on the "American List" on his blog, put J. W. Hulme on the list. Boutique owner Steven Alan read the blog, and began carrying J. W. Hulme bags in his stores located in fashion centers around the world. Upscale department store Barneys featured the bags at an event in its Madison Avenue store, and added a full page of J. W. Hulme products in its 2011 fall catalog.

With 2012 sales projected to reach $2.6 million—a number that is three times J. W. Hulme's 2009 revenues—Bidwell believes the company will finally be profitable. But the owners have learned some hard lessons. The first, according to Guarino, is to be completely transparent with the people financing your business. "We were very frank with our banks," she told *Upsize Online*. Guarino also says she learned that you have more flexibility than you think when up against the wall from a cash-flow perspective. "You have more at your disposal than you think you have. You can negotiate with your vendors—that's cash. You can look at your inventory, and usually find cash."

The biggest lesson, though, remains that the two co-owners of this American manufacturing institution had simply overextended themselves. They let their desire for growth exceed their ability to manage their debt service. Too much debt made them overly vulnerable to economic fluctuations. In the end, they lost controlling interest of their company. They were forced to rely upon extreme—and very personal—measures to pull their company away from the brink. They swear they've learned their lesson. ■

questions

1. Financial management of fast growth is one of the greatest challenges for entrepreneurial companies. What approaches can an entrepreneur take to reduce risks associated with financing growth?

2. With a better economy, J. W. Hulme may again face rapid growth. What steps should the company take to prepare?

3. For an existing company, would you rather give up a majority of ownership to save your company (including the jobs of employees), or close it and walk away?

4. To launch your new company, if you had to give up controlling interest to an investor, would you accept that or walk away?

---

5. "J.W. Hulme owners work 90-day plan."
6. "Restitching a Firm."

RUNNING ON EMPTY

Goal:

Understand ways to better manage your money to avoid getting into a cash flow crisis.

What to Do:

Imagine that you design upscale clothing for men and women. You started out six months ago with $50,000 that you borrowed from friends and family. You've carefully managed your money and, despite having covered expenses for your staff, raw materials, and manufacturing and production costs, you still have half that initial infusion of cash. Several boutiques like your products and have placed some good-sized orders for your first season of clothing. However, your cash flow projections show that you will run out of money in three months. What will you do to keep your business afloat?

1. In this exercise, either working alone or with others, brainstorm on how you will manage to continue to run the business. Choose one or more of the following options:

   a. Look for investors to raise cash.

   b. Based on the fact that you already have made sales, try to secure a loan from a bank or other conventional source of financing.

   c. Borrow more money from friends and family.

   d. Attempt to make more sales and negotiate faster payment terms.

   e. Bargain with your vendors and suppliers for later payments terms.

2. What are the pros and cons of the financing options listed above?

3. Present your final decision to the class. Be prepared to defend it to those who have different recommendations.

CHAPTER

8 Financing Your Business

learning objectives

In this chapter, you'll learn how to:

■ Understand debt financing and equity financing and the differences between the two

■ Determine the various sources of money available to entrepreneurs

■ Conduct research on investors and lenders

■ Recognize what investors and lenders look for in investments

■ Understand what documents potential funders expect to see

■ Evaluate the benefits and challenges of bootstrapping

■ Define how much money will be required for launching and what it's meant for

Looking for Money

You have a great idea for your new business. You've done initial research, worked on your business plan, and identified some talented people you'd like to work with. There's only one problem—you need money to make it all a reality. Where will you get the funds you need to launch your entrepreneurial venture?

Getting the financing you need won't necessarily be easy, yet there are a great many sources of funds for new companies. Some sources may provide financing because they think your idea and business plan are strong; others may finance you because they believe in you (your rich grandmother, for example). But unless you do have that rich grandmother, or money of your own, you'll need to approach the process of raising money as you would any other aspect of starting your business—thoughtfully, with planning, and with the commitment and drive to make it become a reality.

Raising money is a skill that successful entrepreneurs learn; it's part of the start-up and growth process. Although it may be one of the more intimidating aspects of running a business, raising the funds to grow your business—whether from investors, from lenders, or from sales—is a skill you should master. But remember, *not all money is equal*. When you start looking for money for your entrepreneurial venture, you may be tempted to take any type of financing you can arrange. Be careful! The various sources of money seek different types and rates of return on their loans or investments, have varying levels of sophistication and comfort with risk, and provide you with significantly different advantages and disadvantages.

Debt Versus Equity

No surprise here: Everybody who gives you money for your business wants something in return. In particular, they want to make money. They want the money they invest to make money for them, not just for you. How they'll get their money back—and make *more* money—has crucial implications for the management and ownership of your company.

Understanding the differences as well as the advantages and disadvantages of the two types of financing—debt and equity—is crucial as you grow your business.

The right source

When looking for financing, keep in mind that you're going to have an ongoing relationship with your money source. You'll save yourself a lot of time and grief if you seek money from sources that are right for you.

en·tre·pre·neur·ship key terms

Angel investor
A private individual, rather than a professional investment firm, who invests in early-stage entrepreneurial companies.

Bootstrapping
Starting a business with little or no outside financing, generally raising the money necessary through personal savings and sales of products or services.

Collateral
Assets pledged in return for loans.

Crowdfunding
The funding of a business, typically a start-up, by a large group of individuals who each invest small amounts of money online.

Debt financing
Raising funds for a business by borrowing money, often in the form of bank loans or equipment financing.

Debt service
Money being paid on a loan; the amount necessary to keep a loan from going into default.

Dividends
A portion of company profits. Investors may receive dividends, usually quarterly or annually payments, as a return on their investments.

Due diligence
The process that venture capitalists, investment bankers, or others undertake to thoroughly investigate a company before financing; required by law before offering securities for sale.

Equity financing
Raising money for a business, by selling a portion of the company—typically in the form of "shares"—to investors.

Funding rounds
The number of times a company goes to the investment community to seek financing; each funding round is used to reach new stages of company development.

Liquidity event
The point at which investors can pull their money out of a company in which they have invested. This occurs when the company is sold, merges with another company, or begins publicly selling stock.

Return on investment (ROI)
The total financial gain an individual receives in return for putting money in a company. Typically expressed in terms of an annual percentage.

Seed company
A company in the early stages of development, refining its prototype and business concept, hiring initial personnel, locating facilities, and conducting market research.

Term sheet
A nonbinding proposal by an investor outlining the terms on which they will make an investment in a company.

Valuation
The worth, or value, of a company. In the first round of financing a new business, this is usually a negotiated figure with the investors. In subsequent rounds, the valuation is determined by the amount and terms of the investment.

Venture capitalist
A professional individual or firm that invests money in entrepreneurial ventures; typically this is not their own money but money raised by them from other, often institutional, investors.

What kind of money do you want?

As you begin your search for financing, ask yourself these questions:

- Are you willing to give up some amount of ownership of your company?

- Are you willing to have debt that you must repay?

- Are you willing to risk property or other assets?

- How much control of the direction and operation of your company are you willing to relinquish?

- What other help do you want from a funder besides money?

- How fast do you want to grow?

- How big do you want your company to be?

- What do you see as the long-term relationship between you and your funding source?

Keep in mind that you're going to have an ongoing relationship with your money source; make sure it's someone you can live with.

Debt financing

Financing based on the concept of *borrowing* is called **debt financing.** You borrow money from a *lender* who gives you a loan, line of credit, financing for your equipment, and so on. In return, your lender makes money based on the interest they charge you for using their money. Overwhelmingly, you owe the lenders their money back—whether or not your business succeeds.

Debt financing gives you the advantage of retaining complete ownership of your business. You keep control, and you keep all the eventual profits. You borrow a specific amount, and you have to repay only that amount, plus interest, regardless of how profitable your company becomes. The lender doesn't share in the profits or the ownership of the company.

Because lenders do not reap the benefits of substantial profits, they have to reduce risk as much as possible. To do so, they'll likely ask you to secure the loan by pledging your own personal assets as **collateral**. Using debt financing may jeopardize these assets if your business income is insufficient to pay back the loan; and if the business fails, you may still have the debt. This is a major risk, especially for a new entrepreneur.

Debt financing is generally not an option for start-up businesses. Loans from banks and other lending institutions (often referred to as conventional financing) are difficult to secure for new enterprises. Many banks and other lending institutions will only finance businesses that have been operating for more than two or three years, and very small businesses may have difficulty at any time.

In many instances, though, debt financing is a far better choice than equity financing. This is especially true for purchasing expensive fixed assets, such as property or large equipment; for managing short-term cash flow; or for expansion for ongoing, healthy businesses.

Equity financing

Financing based on the concept of *investing* is called **equity financing**. You receive money from an investor who believes your company is likely to succeed. In return, your investor receives equity—or a share of ownership—of the company. The investor makes their money based on your success. Once you succeed, they may receive a share of the profits, and if you sell the company, they get a share of the proceeds. If your company later offers shares of stock to the public—in other words, "goes public"—the investors will eventually be able to sell their shares, typically for substantially more than they invested.

Equity financing allows you to avoid the personal risk of taking on debt. Instead of committing to repay a specific amount of money, you give the investor a piece of the eventual profits and ownership. If your company becomes highly successful, an equity investor may end up receiving many times the amount originally invested. However, if the company fails to produce sufficient profits, these investors may never get their money back.

Thus, equity investors often want to participate in decision-making to ensure that the company operates in a manner that will produce profits. They may take seats on your Board of Directors or even play an active role in management.

In some cases, you may have to give up so much equity that others actually end up with controlling interest in your company. Investors might even be able to remove you from management altogether. Still, a capable investor can bring you sound business advice, useful business contacts, and maybe even links to additional future financing.

Sources of Money for Entrepreneurial Ventures

So where do you go to find the money you need? And what are the obligations and benefits you receive from each source? When choosing a financing source (and you do choose them, just as they choose you), pay close attention to the advantages and disadvantages of each option. If working with an investor, be certain to assess the personal qualities of the individual or the reputation of the venture financing company you use, to determine whether that's a good long-term fit for you.

Ideally, in addition to money, your financing source should also bring you sound business advice, excellent business connections, and the ability to help secure financial support in the future. These qualities are especially important when looking for an angel investor or venture capitalist. Such an investor is likely to play an active part in your company; make certain that it's someone who offers your enterprise other benefits in addition to money.

Venture capitalists

As you search for money, you probably will hear the term **venture capitalist** quite often, but those who use the term may be referring to different entities. True VC firms are among the most sophisticated investors available, typically providing an entrepreneur with more than money. Their knowledge, experience, and connections may prove to be as important to your company as the dollars they bring.

Venture capital firms invest large sums of money pooled from various sources such as pension funds and institutional investors. These private firms are established expressly for the purpose of investing in new and fast-growing companies. Their partners and associates generally have a background in business management or the industries in which they invest.

Typically, venture capital firms invest only in companies they believe can grow to be extremely large: often in the hundreds of millions or even billions of dollars in eventual value. As such, they generally invest large amounts of money at one time to help these companies grow quickly. They're not appropriate vehicles for companies with more modest goals or financial needs.

Equity financing and start-ups

Equity financing is a usual and practical method of funding start-up companies. Most well-known entrepreneurial high-technology firms received equity financing.

The popularity of investing in start-ups—thus the availability of money—goes through cycles. It's far easier to get a new venture funded at a time when the marketplace rewards new entrepreneurial endeavors, particularly through growth, increase in the valuation of the company and its stock, and the ability to take new companies public.

Venture capital firms specialize in particular industries or stages of a company's development. If your company is merely in formation, you need to look for a venture capital firm that invests in early-stage or **seed companies**.

Private or "angel" investors

A frequent source of capital for new or smaller entrepreneurial companies is the private investor, typically referred to as an "angel" investor. Private investors are usually well-to-do individuals, investing their own money and seeking investments that provide more personal satisfaction and the potential of greater financial reward than are offered by conventional investments like stocks and bonds. Private investors can be an excellent source of financing.

Being an angel investor has become more popular over the years, and now there are even organizations and groups of angel investors. These groups help facilitate meetings between entrepreneurs and potential investors. Often, angel investors who are part of an angel network can provide a broader range of assistance (in addition to money) than can a single private investor. Other methods of finding angel investors are through professional financial advisors, accountants, attorneys, and the like, who often know of wealthy individuals seeking investment opportunities.

While some private investors may bring expertise to your business, others may have little to offer besides money. And less-sophisticated investors often have unrealistic expectations regarding the amount and timing of profits. Frequently, they're unfamiliar and uncomfortable with risk, and they may apply pressure for producing profits far earlier than a business can reasonably manage or than is healthy. If you *do* pursue private investors, make certain that the investor understands the nature of your business, and be particularly conservative in your projections of how much profit you will produce, and when.

KEY DIFFERENCES BETWEEN ANGEL INVESTORS AND VENTURE CAPITALISTS

	ANGEL INVESTOR	VENTURE CAPITALIST
Investment Criteria	Growth company	Extremely high-growth company
Source of Investment Dollars	Personal assets	Other people's money; institutional funds
Investment Range	$25,000–$2,000,000	$2,000,000 ı
Expected Return	3–10 times the original investment	5–10 the times original investment
Typical Stage of Investment	Seed, start-up, or early	High-growth start-up and expansion
What They Bring to the Deal	Early funding and hands-on expertise	Large amounts of money, team building, industry-specific strengths
Extent of Due Diligence	Some to significant	Significant to huge amount
Will They Replace Founder as CEO?	Less likely	More likely
Number of Deals	1–3 per year	15–18 per fund per year

Banks

Famed bank robber Willie Sutton, when asked why he robbed banks, supposedly answered, "Because that's where the money is." Banks are, in fact, where a lot of money is, and eventually, as an entrepreneur, you'll probably turn to a bank to help you finance the operations of your growing company.

But just because banks are in the business of lending money, it doesn't mean they're eager to lend money to your new company. Banks are critically concerned about minimizing their risk, and therefore do whatever they can to ensure that the loans they make have a high profitability of being repaid.

Realistically, banks loan money only to companies that have been in business for two or three years and that have proven to be successful.

Banks may lend you money in a number of ways. The two most typical are:

- **Term loan.** A loan for a fixed amount that you pay off over a specific period of time, perhaps many years. This is a good choice for purchasing significant fixed assets, such as real estate or large equipment. Typically, you begin to make payments on the loan within a month or so of taking out the loan.

- **Line of credit.** An amount that you can borrow to use to manage short-term cash flow, such as purchasing inventory or materials to fulfill an order. Generally, the "line" must be paid down to zero at least once a year, and you can borrow any amount up to the total amount of your credit line.

If you do get a bank loan for a new business, you'll almost certainly have to provide a lien against any property you purchase, give a personal guarantee, and often have to put up your own personal assets (such as any real estate you may own) as collateral.

You should be extremely cautious before risking your home, your savings, your college education fund, or any other funds on which your lifestyle depends. However, if the business is incorporated, the company itself may be able to take on the loan debt, thus shielding the owners from personal liability. That's an ideal situation, as only the assets of the business, and not those of the business owners, are at stake. Still, in most new and small companies, professional lenders like banks require a personal guarantee from the owners.

Government agencies

To encourage banks to make loans to smaller businesses, and to reduce their risk, the Small Business Administration (SBA) in the United States and the Canada Small Business Financing Program (CSBFP) in Canada provide guarantees to lenders who make loans to qualified small businesses. These agencies guarantee loans—they do not make them directly.

In the United States, if you're seeking financing, the SBA can provide you with a list of lending institutions active in giving loans to small businesses in your area. Remember, these banks and institutions must approve your

A friend of a friend

Overwhelmingly, the best way to get in front of an investor is to have someone they know introduce you. That can be tough, of course. But it should be part of your fundraising process to identify people who might know funders who would be willing to make an introduction. Once you've been introduced, get to know those funders. Most VCs end up funding companies that were introduced to them by entrepreneurs they've previously funded or otherwise respect.

application, so you must meet bank criteria to qualify. Typically, new businesses have a very hard time qualifying for SBA-guaranteed loans. The SBA guarantee, however, sets interest limits and may make a difference if the lending institution is on the fence about your loan. Expect to provide a personal guarantee for any loan you're granted.

The SBA has many loan programs. The two main ones are:

- a 7(a) loan, which can be used for operating capital and expansion as well as other business expenses

- a 504 loan, which can be used for purchasing fixed assets, such as property

The SBA has created additional loan programs that may be more accessible for new or very small businesses. Its "microloan" program offers very small amounts of money to companies; these are administered through nonprofit and community organizations. Check out the SBA's loan programs at www.SBA.gov.

In Canada, the CSBFP provides loan guarantees only for purchasing and improving land, buildings, equipment, and vehicles. It doesn't guarantee loans for operating capital. Find out more at www.ic.gc.ca/csbfa.

Small business investment companies

Small Business Investment Companies (SBICs) and Specialized Small Business Investment Companies (SSBICs) are private firms that exist to provide both investment financing and long-term loans to small businesses. Some SBICs provide only equity; others rely on debt; and some provide either. Each SBIC has its own policy.

SBICs are licensed by the U.S. Small Business Administration and may receive funds from the government for the purpose of investing in small businesses.

SBICs are good vehicles for financing a small business. However, most of them maintain rigorous evaluation procedures, and you'll have to meet some of the same criteria required when applying for conventional financing or funding from venture capitalists. These days, many of the SBICs only make loans, and they'll seek the same type of collateral and evidence of creditworthiness as banks.

Commercial finance companies

For existing companies that have a hard time getting financing from other sources, commercial finance companies may be a source of last resort. You may be able to borrow money more easily from a commercial finance company, as they're regulated to a lesser degree than banks, but it will cost you more to do so. Moreover, these companies generally make loans to existing businesses with significant collateral—typically collateral that can fairly quickly be converted into money. They will require significant collateral as a condition for making the loan. Given these factors, they're not well suited for start-ups.

Commercial finance companies may be an option for an existing business seeking funds to buy equipment, inventory, or assets highly secured by collateral.

Such finance companies also have their disadvantages. The business collateral they'll expect you to put up will have to be fairly liquid, so they can easily get their money out of those assets if you fail to repay the loan. Because they tend to take on more risk, they charge higher interest rates. Finally, be sure to examine all the terms of the loan carefully.

Friends and family

When you've got a great idea, the people likely to believe in you most are those who know you best. Friends and family frequently help finance new entrepreneurial ventures, whether in the form of investment or loans. Money from friends and family members may be the easiest money to raise—it's unlikely you'll have to go through a bunch of meetings or undergo due diligence from Grandma.

Be careful, though, when financing your business through family or friends. This money may be the easiest to secure, but may cause you to risk personal relationships. By mixing your personal and business affairs, you may find you make both your business and your personal life more difficult. Unsophisticated investors are often nervous about money—they don't understand that it takes time before profits are realized, and view every natural delay or setback with alarm.

If you do take a loan from a personal source, later repay it with the required interest, and subsequently become very successful, the friend or relative may not understand why he or she does not participate in the profits. And, if you're unable to pay back the loan, the relative may never forget and may remind you of your failure at every family occasion for the next 20 years. If you take an investment from a personal source, and your business goes under, your friend or relative may feel that you still owe them money, even though their investment wasn't strictly a loan.

One thing's essential: Put everything in writing! Make all the terms crystal clear. Deal with family and friends the way you would with other funding sources—present them with a business plan, provide detailed information about your venture (including all the risks), and have each document signed.

Crowdfunding: a novel way to raise money

Once again, the Internet has democratized another area—this time, raising funds for start-ups. The concept is called **crowdfunding** and, as the name implies, it's the ability to raise money from a "crowd"—strangers who believe in your idea and are willing to put some of their money into your new business. While venture capitalists invest millions, and angels invest hundreds of thousands of dollars, individuals can "invest" small amounts of money to help you get launched.

Imputed interest

A zero-interest loan from a friend or family member may face what's called "imputed interest" by the U.S. Internal Revenue Service. The IRS will impute interest on a loan and collect taxes from lenders, regardless of whether the lender actually charges interest. All lenders must charge an interest rate that reflects a fair market value. If the IRS views the loan as a gift, the lender must pay taxes on the money if it's more than the maximum allowed by law.

REAL-WORLD RECAP

Sources of funds for entrepreneurial ventures

The many different sources of funds for new businesses include:

- Venture capitalists
- Private or "angel" Investors
- Banks
- Government agencies
- Small business investment companies
- Commercial finance companies
- Friends and family
- Crowdfunding
- Other sources, such as your own assets, credit cards, franchisors or vendors, and strategic partners

Some crowdfunding sites to check out:

- Kickstarter (www.kickstarter.com)
- IndieGoGo (indiegogo.com)
- Angelist (angel.co)
- Crowdfunder (crowdfunder.com)
- Wefunder (wefunder.com)

Using credit cards wisely

Credit card use can make sense in the following situations:

- To pay for expenses that will generate income and improve cash flow, such as inventory, materials, or services needed to complete a job (e.g., lumber in construction, printing in graphic design); or for other short-term manufacturing expenses
- To pay for small items such as office supplies, travel expenses, and meals and entertainment

Depending on which card you choose, other benefits of using credit cards wisely may include:

- Extended warranties on equipment and technology; additional travel insurance and auto rental insurance
- Expenditure tracking and documentation
- Discounts on certain purchases
- Building your credit history

Before the law was changed, only "accredited" persons could invest in entrepreneurial ventures—people with high net worth, who theoretically could afford to lose the money and who were sophisticated investors.

But the Internet has created a way for entrepreneurs, artists, musicians, inventors, and others to reach out, tell their story, and gain support from people who want to back their vision with relatively small amounts (from less than a hundred dollars to thousands). Due to legal limitations, these "investments" were considered "donations," so investors could only get gifts or rewards in return. They could not acquire equity in the new company.

For example, when Eric Migicovsky couldn't raise money from venture capitalists for his new watch concept—the "Pebble," which runs smartphone apps—he used a popular crowdfunding site, Kickstarter, and raised over $10 million from people who received first-generation watches in return for their donation of $99 or more. They could not, at that time, get equity. Migicovsky not only raised more money than he then needed (without giving up equity), he also proved that there was tremendous market interest in the Pebble—so he was able to launch his business with a huge customer base.

Naturally, a whole raft of sites grew up to serve the interest in crowdfunding and provide a platform for connecting those seeking funds for their new projects with those willing to help support the launch of these endeavors. The best of these sites help entrepreneurs stay within the law as new regulations are adopted. Sites also specialize in the types of projects they feature—some focus on the arts, some on technology and science, and so on. If you're considering going the crowdfunding route, look for sites that are a good fit with your type of business or project.

As with other forms of funding, you'll have to be prepared—and do your homework. As "investors" get more sophisticated, they'll want more than just a great video to motivate them to part with their money. They'll want to see that you have a team that can execute, plus a reasonable business plan. And that they'll have a good chance of making their money back—or that at least you'll use the money as intended. Simply because the amounts of cash exchanging hands is smaller, that doesn't mean you won't face some of the same scrutiny you would from established investors.

Other sources of funds

Additional funding sources for starting a new business or expanding an existing one include:

- **Your own assets.** Forget the old saying about using "other people's money." It's better to start or grow a business with your *own* money. If you have sufficient assets, particularly savings or other income that doesn't require you to take on additional debt, you're in the best position. That way, you don't go into debt, and you don't give up equity. If your savings are owned jointly with a spouse or partner, be absolutely certain to get their acceptance and understanding of your plans.

- **Credit cards.** Most entrepreneurs use their own credit cards at some point to help finance their growing business. But be cautious! Credit cards are generally an extremely expensive and risky form of financing. You can incur very high charges and hurt or ruin your personal credit rating if you're even a day or two late on your payments. Credit card debt can also easily get out of hand.

- **Franchisors or vendors.** If you're planning on "buying" a franchise, the franchising company may help you arrange for some financing. It may provide loans itself, or have finance companies it works with. Likewise, some vendors—especially large-equipment vendors—may have financing arrangements. These kinds of loans may be easier to obtain than traditional bank financing, though you may face higher interest rates or less-favorable terms.

- **Strategic partners.** Other businesses that want you to succeed may be willing to help you get under way. If you provide an innovative, highly specialized product or service, a large customer may want your offering, to help them become more competitive. Perhaps it's a company serving the same market that sees your operation as complementary to its own. In some cases, such companies may directly invest in your business or give you loans. At the least, they might be willing to let you use their offices or equipment, or otherwise help offset some of your expenses in return for the benefits you bring them.

The Process of Securing Investors

You can substantially increase your chances of getting funded by investors by first doing your homework *and* legwork. The process of raising investment funds takes time, and it helps if you're realistic, if you understand how the funding process works, and if you know how to make yourself an attractive prospect from the investor's point of view.

Researching investors

A little research can save you a lot of time. If your potential funding targets are established venture capital firms, these institutions are used to answering questions about their funding patterns and have definite procedures and guidelines. Start by visiting their websites. Many VC firms outline exactly what types of companies they fund, cite the criteria for their investments, and include a list of companies they have already funded—their **portfolio** companies. If you can't find what you need on the Internet, don't hesitate to directly contact these professional financing sources for information; they'd much rather answer your questions now than waste their time having to process a business plan in which they have no interest.

With other sources, such as private or angel investors, it may be somewhat harder to get information. If they're members of an angel investing network, they may list the types of companies they're interested in. They are far less

Questions to ask

When researching potential funding sources, these are the questions you want answered:

- Do they fund businesses in your industry?
- At what stage of business development do they provide funding?
- What are the minimum and maximum amounts of funding they consider?
- What are the minimum and maximum potential sizes of the businesses they fund?
- What other criteria do they use to make their funding decisions?
- On what basis do they generally provide funding: equity or debt?
- What other companies in your industry have they funded previously?
- What kinds of information do they require you to submit with your plan? For instance, how many years of financial projections do they want to see?

Why join a networking group?

You can get a great deal of information about funders by joining entrepreneurs' groups in your community or industry. Many larger cities have organizations in which entrepreneurs help one another get started, and members often have first-hand experience with funding sources.

likely to offer specific criteria than venture capitalists. Nevertheless, it's quite businesslike to send a letter of inquiry to ascertain the kinds of investments they're willing to consider before submitting your plan to them.

Make sure your type of business and financial scope fall within the interest areas of your potential recipient. Don't send a plan requesting an investment of $50,000 to a venture capital firm that funds only companies seeking a minimum of $1 million. (Many do.)

If possible, you also want to find out less-tangible information about your funding sources. What is the potential funder really like? When deciding on funding, does the funder tend to place more emphasis on the experience of management, the product or service, or the market potential? Does the funder take a very long time making decisions, or do they respond quickly?

SOURCES OF DEBT FINANCING

	WHAT THEY LOOK FOR	ADVANTAGES	DISADVANTAGES
Banks and Lending Institutions	Ability to repay; collateral; steady current income from business	No dilution of your ownership; no profit-sharing; no obligation for ongoing relationship after repayment; definite preset amount to repay ***Best For:*** Established companies; funding fixed assets, such as property; short-term cash flow management	Difficult to secure for new businesses; must often risk personal assets; financial obligation regardless of business's success ***Worst For:*** Highly risky ventures and new companies lacking assets
Loans from Family or Friends	Your personal character; other personal considerations; likelihood of repayment	Easier to secure than institutional loans; specific amount to repay; no dilution of ownership or profit-sharing ***Best For:*** Companies with no other option; companies with a very secure future	Jeopardizing personal relationships; nervous lenders; unsolicited advice and frequent queries ***Worst For:*** Very risky enterprises; entrepreneurs with difficult family circumstances
Credit Cards, Including Cash Advances	Personal credit score	Relatively easy to secure; immediately available ***Best For:*** Businesses requiring small amounts of money for a limited time; short-term cash-flow management	Very high interest rates; limited amount of money; ties up and risks personal credit ***Worst For:*** Ongoing, long-term financing

Once they've financed a company, how does the funder perform as an ongoing partner? What's the funder's reputation in the industry?

Of course, this information is difficult to glean. The best way to get it is to speak to founders of companies the funder has previously invested in. That also creates a connection that may help you actually get a meeting with the funder. You can also research a funder online through a search engine, or a

SOURCES OF EQUITY FINANCING

	WHAT THEY LOOK FOR	ADVANTAGES	DISADVANTAGES
Venture Capitalists	Businesses in their area of interest; companies with high growth potential; experienced management; new technology	Large sums available; sophisticated investor familiar with industry; expertise, connections, and future funding; understand business setbacks and capital risk **Best For:** Potentially very large companies; sophisticated entrepreneur or industry wizard	Difficult to secure; must have exit possibilities in 3 to 7 years; take substantial equity in company; may oust founders **Worst For:** Small and medium-sized businesses; inexperienced entrepreneurs
Private (Angel) Investors	Good business opportunities with better potential rewards than other investments; appealing concept	Interested in start-ups; easier to secure than professional venture capital; may have industry knowledge or contacts **Best For:** Companies with high growth potential; companies with appealing business concept	May be involved in decision-making without adequate expertise; long-term relationship; may expect profits soon **Worst For:** Companies requiring extremely long development time before profitability or exit; companies with limited growth potential
Investment from Family and Friends	Interest in you and your business concept; chance to make money	Easier to secure than other investors **Best For:** Companies with no other options; entrepreneurs having friends or relatives with significant business or industry expertise	Jeopardizes personal relationships; long-term involvement; unsophisticated, nervous investor; makes friend or relative a decision-maker in your business **Worst For:** Very risky enterprises; companies requiring long development time before profitability

Research Prospective Investors

Fill out this worksheet to help you gather information on potential investors you might consider having invest in your business. Make a copy for each investor you evaluate.

Name of prospective investor: _____

_____

Geographic area they serve: _____

_____

Size of investment they make: _____

_____

_____

Industries they invest in: _____

_____

_____

Portfolio of companies invested in: _____

_____

_____

Any potential referral or reference sources: _____

_____

_____

Formal application procedures, if any: _____

_____

_____

Any comments or evaluations from other entrepreneurs: _____

_____

_____

site like www.thefunded.com. Additionally, if they're particularly receptive to entrepreneurs, you can request an informational interview with the funder.

What makes a business a good investment prospect?

Once you've found an investor, what will make them actually invest in your company? How will you get them to notice you and convince them that yours is a company they don't want to pass up? Remember that investors see a great many deals. They have a number of other, much safer, options for investing their money. So they don't need a specific reason to turn you down. That's why you have to make yourself, your business opportunity, and your business plan *compelling*.

The best way to do that is to be prepared. The stronger your presentation and the better prepared you are, the more an investor will be confident in your ability to build a company.

Use the worksheet on page 189 to help you prepare for some of the really tough questions you'll face.

RETURN ON INVESTMENT (ROI)

You're a good catch if investors believe your business will provide them with a high return on the money they've invested with you—that is, **return on investment**, or ROI. The ROI that investing in your business offers has to be higher—much higher—than what an investor could obtain by putting their money into other, less-risky investments, such as stocks, bonds, or real estate. Investors want to achieve a high return on investments in new ventures because such investing is risky. Some companies fail altogether and bring them zero return. So their other investments have to balance those losses.

ROI is the total amount of money owing to the investor as a result of helping fund your business venture. It's expressed in terms of an annual percentage—that is, the percentage of their investment earned each year of the investment (for example, a 30 percent ROI). This is calculated by dividing the amount of money investors make by the amount they invested, divided by the number of years it took to receive their gains. Investors will closely evaluate your business to determine the rate of ROI they're likely to receive. This helps them compare their potential return against other investments they might make, whether invested in other entrepreneurial companies, or in the stock market, bonds, or bank accounts.

For example, in a highly simplified scenario, let's say an investor has invested $1 million in your company, and received 20 percent ownership of your company in return for that investment. If you sold the company five years later and realized a profit of $10 million on that sale, your investor would be entitled to 20 percent, or $2 million. Their profit would be $1 million—or a 20 percent ROI ($1 million is a 100 percent return, divided by five years).

Generally, venture capitalists and experienced angel investors expect to realize their ROI from your company when you have a **liquidity event**—such

Got competition?

If you're meeting a genuine market need, there are—or will be—other companies who'd like a piece of the action. Investors want to see that you have a thorough understanding of the competition you face, both direct and indirect. Questions they'll ask:

- What differentiates you from the competition?

- What barriers to entry do other companies face in entering your market?

- Who holds patents, trademarks, and/or copyrights?

- What are the start-up costs of similar companies?

- How well funded is your competition?

- Does a successful model for your business already exist? In short, is your idea proven?

What's on a term sheet?

No two term sheets read exactly the same, although they share a basic format. Your term sheet will be drafted to address the specific needs of your company and your investors' situation. At a minimum, your term sheet will include:

- The agreed-upon company valuation and proposed capitalization table (which will show the total amount of securities issued by your company)
- The key financial and legal terms
- The rights of the parties
- All legal obligations of the parties

as selling the company to another company or selling stock on a public stock exchange. Another way investors can receive return on their investment is through receiving a portion of profits, or **dividends**. For example, if your company is highly profitable but continues as an independent company for a long time without going public, you could distribute quarterly or annual dividend payments to investors.

The right market

You may have come up with a great idea, but if the market for what you offer is too small, too hard to reach, or otherwise uninteresting to a funder, you won't find an investor. That's because it takes a substantial-size company to provide sufficient potential financial return to create a worthwhile investment for your angel or VC.

Before sending money your way, investors will examine both your revenue and profit projections and the overall size of your potential market. You'll need to produce research and hard data to prove that your market actually exists—and to demonstrate that it is both substantial and growing.

To prepare a market analysis for potential investors, use the same methods discussed in Chapters 3 (Research) and 5 (Target Market). Investors want to know the answers to the same questions you answered when you first researched your business concept—who is your target market; how big is it; where is it located; what motivates it to buy your product; what are some key trends in your market; and so on.

What information and documents will investors want?

Working with an investor means you no longer run your company alone. Before you enter into this partnership, making sure your business is in order both legally and financially prevents potentially unpleasant surprises. So make sure you have your documents in order.

If the documents checklist on page 185 looks daunting—and even if it doesn't!—consider getting professional assistance to help you sort through the paperwork that you need. Lawyers and accountants can help ensure that your finances and legal matters are in good shape.

A KILLER BUSINESS PLAN

"Send me your business plan." These are likely the first words you'll hear from a prospective investor. A strong business plan is an absolute necessity if you're seeking investor funds. It's the one document that will be used to judge the quality of your idea, your market, and your team. Without an impressive business plan, you won't be able to get past a first conversation.

Your business plan tells the story of your company by presenting your vision for the company's future and explaining how you'll achieve it. The first parts of a business plan an investor will read are the executive summary and the financial statements. Think of these two sections as an ad for the rest of

BUILD-YOUR-BUSINESS WORKSHEET

The Right Documents

Before meeting with an investor, make sure the following documents are in order:

Financials

☐ Forecast income statement, cash flow statement, and balance sheet

☐ Current profit and loss and cash flow statements

☐ List of any major accounts receivable

☐ List of any outstanding loans or major debts/ accounts payable

☐ List of assets

Legal

☐ Corporate structure—that is, incorporation, LLC, or sole proprietorship

☐ Ownership: list of all current shareholders or those with ownership interest

☐ Promised equity, including any to current or former employees

☐ Contracts

☐ Regulatory compliance

Intellectual Property

☐ Intellectual property (IP) protection received to date: patents, trademarks, copyrights

☐ Pending IP filings

☐ Agreements with employees and third parties (including "work for hire" contracts)

☐ Ownership of core technology

☐ Licenses to use others' technology

Employees

☐ Compensation table

☐ Key personnel/functions

☐ Equity awarded/promised

☐ Stock option plan

Advisors

☐ Board of Directors

☐ Advisory Committee

☐ Key outside consultants—attorneys, accountants, other

---

the plan. They need to be concise, compelling, and irresistible to investors. Investors want to see immediately that you have a strong business idea, a large and growing market, and a solid grasp of financials. When they review your entire business plan, they're looking for the "secret sauce"—the key business ingredients no one has but you.

Developing a business plan also helps you think through all the key issues in your business and better prepares you for the probing questioning you'll get from potential funders.

For an in-depth discussion on business plans, see Chapter 4.

Red flag alert: inflated numbers

Most investors will be wary if you predict a market share of more than 1 to 2 percent of a total market for your company's first year. And they won't expect higher than 5 percent in years three through five. Investors look favorably on entrepreneurs who underpromise and overdeliver.

Key issues to negotiate

- Valuation
- Equity division
- Employee (equity option) pool
- Anti-dilution provisions
- Employment contract
- Vesting schedule
- Liquidation preferences
- Control
- Milestones and performance measures

Negotiating the deal

After you find an investor who believes in you and has decided to invest, you'll begin the stressful and complex process of negotiating price and terms.

The most visible thing you'll be negotiating is your company's **valuation,** or what you agree to peg as the worth or value of the total company at the time the investor provides you funding. This will be determined by how much money they give you and what percentage of the company they receive in return. For example, if an investor gave you $1 million and received 10 percent of the company, the valuation of the company would be $10 million.

Be careful not to get stuck on a preconceived idea of your company's worth or the percentage you're willing to give up. Nothing makes an investor less likely to invest in a company than dealing with an entrepreneur they view as irrational and unwilling to compromise. Remember, this is a negotiation. You're almost certainly going to have to give up more than you would like or expect.

Besides valuation, the ownership and control of the company will be the other major factor you'll negotiate. This has great consequence for your personal future involvement in the company. Additional issues you'll negotiate include how the investors will get paid if the company is sold. This will have implications on how much you'll actually make even if the company is successful.

Unless you're dealing with a novice investor, your angel or VC will give you a **term sheet**—a nonbinding document that summarizes all the terms on which the investment will be made.

Over the years, as angel investing has become more sophisticated, term sheets have grown more complex and more detailed. Their increasingly wide range of terms reflects the ever more diverse ways in which investors choose to structure their participation in the investment and the variety of investment securities they opt for, including debt, equity, hybrids, and warrants.

Deal terms are complex—so complex that this book couldn't possibly cover them all. And terms change as investors devise new ways to protect their interests and rights. Moreover, many tax implications go along with issuing securities and establishing a valuation for a company.

You absolutely need an experienced securities attorney on your side. This means your own attorney, not just the investor's lawyer. That's not to say an attorney recommended by your investor can't represent you—adept investors will know experienced lawyers. But make certain you consult with, and pay, an attorney yourself, to review any deal with an eye to protecting you and your interests, not merely the interests of the company or the investor. And you'll need patience and flexibility because the process takes time. You'll want to make sure you protect your rights and interests, but you don't want the angel to decide you're impossible to work with and walk away.

The Process of Securing Lenders

Getting a loan for a new business is always a challenge, often a much more difficult one than finding an investor. After all, investors exist to help start and grow businesses. They're comfortable with the amount of risk that is involved in young companies. In return, they expect high rewards based on taking that risk.

Banks have far different goals and far different purposes. They exist to help companies (and individuals) make large purchases and manage the ups and downs of their cash flow. As a result, they're oriented toward minimizing risk. They make a smaller amount of money (the interest you pay on loans) and do not participate in the rewards if you're successful.

Banks and other professional lenders must minimize risk. They're far less impressed with your great idea than with your personal ability to pay the money back on your loan, whether or not your business succeeds.

Once your entrepreneurial venture has a track record and you're profitable, you'll definitely want a banking relationship. Loans and lines of credit help you manage cash flow and purchase equipment, inventory, and real estate. A great banking relationship can help your business grow. But it's not easy to get when you're starting out.

The three big questions

No matter how much money you want to borrow, no matter who you want to borrow money from, the loan process comes down to answering three main questions.

1. How much money do you need?

This is the very first question any lender will ask you. The answer immediately gives them an idea of whether they're an appropriate fit for your needs. You should have a fairly clear idea of how much you want to borrow before you approach any lender, whether a banker or Grandma.

This is where a business plan comes in. It helps you to understand how much money you need and for what purposes. Bankers are likely to want to see a business plan when they start to do business with you or approve larger loans.

2. What do you need the money for?

Answering this question gives lenders, especially bankers, an idea of the type of loan you need. You'll need—and qualify for—rather different types of loans if you're using your loan proceeds to finance inventory, buy a business vehicle or equipment, purchase real estate, hire new employees, open an additional location, and so on.

Obviously, this question is closely related to the first one. *You* know why you need the money. But you must do your research and articulate your needs clearly before you talk to a banker.

It takes money...

There's an old saying that banks only want to loan money to people who don't need it. That's not true. What *is* true is that banks—and other lenders—loan money to people who are able to pay it back. If you're unable to show the capacity to pay your loan back, you'll have a very hard time getting a loan.

REAL-WORLD RECAP

The three big questions

The loan process comes down to answering three main questions:

1. **How much money do you need?**

2. **What do you need the money for?**

3. **Will you pay it back?**

For example:

- If yours is a start-up, you need to produce a "Sources and Uses of Funds" statement (as well as your total business plan and financials) for lenders as well as investors.

- If you need new vehicles for your business, for example, figure out which models will work best for you, and how much they will cost. Do your homework and present solid, specific information with your loan proposal.

- If you need money to tide you over between paying for large inventory shipments and collecting money from your customers, prepare a spreadsheet with real, historical data, showing examples of the timing and the amounts involved in specific transactions. If possible, make a chart of future needs as well. Show when you must pay for the inventory, when your customers will pay you, how long the time gap will be, and how much money you need to carry you through that time.

3. Will you pay it back?

The majority of the loan application process centers on answering this question. When a banker asks for your credit report, tax returns, financial statements, and other documents, the banker is really trying to determine three things:

- Are you the type of person who pays your debts?

- Will you have the money to pay future debts?

- Do you have other assets to cover your debt in case you aren't able to pay?

Of those factors, lenders focus most on your ability to repay the loan. The main issues they'll look to are your personal credit history, your business's credit history, your business's financial performance, and your personal net worth.

Factors that will also affect your ability to qualify include:

- Length of time you've been in business

- Which lender you apply to

- Previous relationship and history with your lender

- Personal guarantees from you and any other owners of the business to repay the loan

What information and documents will lenders want?

When it comes to making business loans, lenders want to see many of the same company financial statements as investors. The checklist on page 185 outlines these documents. In addition, because lenders often make loans to

BUILD-YOUR-BUSINESS WORKSHEET

Questions Investors Will Ask, and Your Answers

What's the most compelling aspect of your business? _____
_____

Why will people will buy your product/service? _____

What's the size and growth of your market, and how do you know the market is truly that size? _____
_____

What evidence do you have that you'll be able to capture that percentage of market share? _____
_____

Who else is doing this? How do you differ from them? _____
_____

If this is a novel idea, why hasn't it been done before? _____
_____

Where did you come up with your financial projections? How do you know they are realistic? _____
_____

What's going to keep a competitor from stealing your idea? Do you have any intellectual property protection in place?

Can you explain your marketing strategy? What makes you think it will be effective? _____
_____

Can you provide greater detail regarding the production requirements for your product? How about other aspects of

logistics and distribution? _____

What are the potential exits for your company? Have any similar companies been acquired or gone public? How much

have they been acquired for? _____
_____

What in your past has prepared you to be CEO of a company like this? _____
_____

What weaknesses do you currently see in your management team? _____
_____

Can you provide best, worst, and expected case scenarios for future funding needs? _____
_____

Explain the status of your personal lives. What else is going on that will distract you from giving this company your

complete attention? _____

Why do you think I/we would be a good choice of funder for you? _____
_____

BUILD-YOUR-BUSINESS WORKSHEET

Research Prospective Lenders

Fill out this worksheet to help you to gather info on potential lenders. Make a copy for each lender you evaluate.

Name of prospective lending institution: _____

Geographic area they serve: _____

Size of loans they make: _____

Types of loans they make/for what purposes: _____

Industries they typically lend to: _____

What types and age of businesses they lend to: _____

What kind of collateral they require: _____

What kinds of forms and documents you must provide: _____

Where the decisions are made: _____

---

existing businesses (while investors may be investing in new companies), they'll want to see current and historical financial accounts. These include:

- Income statement
- Cash flow
- Balance sheet
- Business tax returns
- Accounts receivable
- Accounts payable

Lenders will also want to review your personal financial statements and personal tax returns. They will ask for this same information from any and all other signatories on the loan and owners of the company.

Dealing with co-recipients

In almost all cases, anyone who owns more than a minimum percentage of the business—typically 10 to 20 percent—will be treated as a co-recipient of the loan. They will have to:

- Provide personal financial statements

- Provide personal tax returns

- Authorize the lender to conduct a credit check and obtain their credit score

- Sign a personal loan guarantee

- Have the loan appear on their future credit reports, including future payment history

Banks and other lenders will look at the credit history of anyone else on the loan, as well as yours, when deciding on whether to make the loan and determining the interest rates to charge.

It's quite possible that anyone who owns a portion of your company may not want to take on financial responsibility by signing a personal guarantee or having their credit record intertwined with your business. If you've given—or sold—stock to key employees, they too may be unwilling to take on the financial obligation of being a cosigner for the loan, and this added burden could affect your working relationship.

Ideally, you considered this fact long before you took on a partner or investor, or gave shares of stock to employees. In any case, sit down with anyone who owns more than 10 to 20 percent of your company and have a frank talk with them *before* you begin the loan process.

If an investor or other shareholder is unwilling to participate fully in the loan process by providing financial statements or signing a guarantee, expect to have to explain this situation to a lender.

The Best Source of All: Raising Money through Revenue

Finally, when looking for money to start or grow your business, never forget the power of making sales. The very best money of all comes from making actual sales to customers.

Think of the benefits: You neither have to give up a piece of your company (as with investors) nor do you take on debt (as with a loan). So, in the process of thinking how you'll get your business off the ground, look seriously at whether there are ways for you to find money through sales—also known as **bootstrapping**.

Bootstrapping

There's a term for growing your business through sales: bootstrapping. Like the name suggests, you pull yourself up by your bootstraps rather than depending on others. Of course, certain types of businesses, such as retail stores, restaurants, and new manufacturing plants, all require significant financing up front, and it's unrealistic to think you could make presales sufficient to fund your start-up expenses.

Still, you *can* start some new businesses less expensively, especially if you're a new entrepreneur. For example, many technology products don't require high start-up costs if a team of technology-wise entrepreneurs starts it together and works for sweat equity (or earning stock through work) until they've established a sufficient customer base. If you develop a new product, you can build a few prototypes and start selling immediately online and at trade shows. Although you'll require some funding even for these initial steps, you take a much smaller risk.

Funding and cash management for growth

Growing through sales is tough when sales are slow, but it's also a challenge when facing very fast growth. And it's tough to finance fast growth from income alone. Typically, you'll spend money faster than it comes in: hiring staff, purchasing materials or inventory, renting facilities, buying equipment.

You may need a lender to help with cash flow, but to seize substantial growth opportunities, it may be time to consider an investor as well.

Raising money through sales is attractive for several reasons:

1. **No investors.** Investors not only take a piece of any future profits, they also have a say in decision-making. That may be a benefit if you have knowledgeable, patient investors, but it can often be a distraction and source of tension.

2. **No monthly loan payments.** If you secure a long-term business loan, you'll have to start making monthly payments right away. That translates to higher overhead and increased stress.

3. **It focuses your attention on your business.** Raising money takes up a lot of time. By growing your business through sales, you can spend your time and energy improving your product or service and finding paying customers.

4. **You learn a lot about your market.** When you or your salesperson hit the pavement to make sales, you get vital, real-life, real-time market information. This is the very best kind of market research. It helps you improve your product or service, refine your pricing, and learn about new opportunities.

If you're fortunate enough to land a big order when your company is still young, you may not have the resources to fill that order. Luckily, this is a better time to approach financing sources. You may find a bank or other lender much more receptive when you have a contract in hand. You may also learn that investors are much more willing to meet with you when you have customers, especially if any of those customers are companies that demonstrate to potential investors your ability to land important deals.

Start-up Costs

One of the first financial challenges an entrepreneurial company faces is figuring out how much money it needs just to get the business up and running.

If you're starting a business with a physical location, whether a retail, manufacturing, or service business, or even one with an office, you'll have costs associated with leases, equipment and furniture purchases, raw material, inventory, and supplies—all before opening your doors. You may have considerable expenses before you see any income, and you need to account for those costs in your financial projections.

Even if you start on a shoestring, you'll still have start-up costs. You'll need some supplies, you'll require a variety of professional services (such as a lawyer and an accountant), and you'll probably want to pay yourself something. Of course, if you work with others to get your idea off the ground, you'll have those costs as well.

As with most financial projections, you may not get your start-up costs right—especially if this is your first business. But do your homework to assess likely costs, be realistic in your projections, and estimate high.

What are your start-up costs? How much will it cost you to make your business operational? Use the worksheet on page 193 to determine your costs to get up and running.

BUILD-YOUR-BUSINESS WORKSHEET

Start-up Costs

List the specific details of your start-up cash requirements. Remember, these are expenses you plan to incur before you launch your business. Post-launch expenditures should be entered in your income statement.

		Cost
Facilities	Land Purchase	
	Building Purchase	
	Initial Rent	
	Deposits (Security/Utilities/etc.)	
	Improvements/Remodeling	
	Other:	
	Other:	
Equipment	Furniture	
	Production Machines/Equipment	
	Computers/Software	
	Cash Registers	
	Telephones/Telecommunications	
	Vehicles	
	Other:	
	Other:	
Materials/Supplies	Office Supplies	
	Stationery/Business Cards	
	Brochures/Pamphlets, Other Descriptive Material	
	Other:	
	Other:	
Fees and Other Costs	Licenses/Permits	
	Trade or Professional Memberships	
	Attorneys	
	Accountants	
	Insurance	
	Marketing/Management Consultants	
	Design/Technical Consultants	
	Advertising/Promotional Activities	
	Other:	
TOTAL		

REAL-WORLD CASE

Tactus Tackles Fund-Raising

Craig Ciesla and Micah Yairi had an incredible idea: What if the flat screen on your iPhone, ATM machine, or car dashboard could suddenly display real, three-dimensional buttons when you wanted them and stay flat when you didn't? Wouldn't that make it easier to type on a smartphone, use electronics if you're blind, or reach a button while you're driving? How cool would that be? Ciesla and Yairi, both PhDs with advanced physics backgrounds, had a way to make this seeming miracle occur: They would be the first to make physical buttons rise from a flat touch screen or panel.

"The concept was solid. The market was huge. Anywhere there's a touchscreen, there could be a need for physical keys. We thought we'd get funding—no problem," said Ciesla. "We were wrong."

They began with a classic case of bootstrapping. While working full-time in other jobs, Ciesla and Yairi toiled nights and weekends at the dining room table or in the garage, working on the core technology and pouring their own money into the business.

"We discussed whether we should have a round of 'Friends and Family' money, but we shied away from that," said Ciesla. "Even if you tell your friends and family that there's a 90 percent chance they'll lose their money, they won't believe you."

"You don't want to damage those relationships," added Yairi. So they started looking for professional investors.

"We put together a business plan and that took a lot of work," he continued. "Based on that, we created PowerPoint presentations, and pitched and pitched and pitched to investors. But we were lucky. We had connections to well-established venture capital firms here in Silicon Valley. One was sufficiently excited about our concept that they helped us craft our VC presentation."

Things were going great; an investment in their company—now called Tactus Technology—from a top-tier venture capital firm was virtually assured.

Yet forces outside their control were at work. This was September 2008. Days before their final presentation to VCs, the investment bank Lehman Brothers declared the biggest bankruptcy in U.S. history. America was now in serious financial crisis.

Venture capital was suddenly paralyzed. A new funding strategy had to be developed for Tactus. The intrepid duo lowered the amount of money they hoped to raise, and targeted angel investors.

To make that work, they decided to trade part of their equity in the company to bring in the appropriate type of people to meet their needs. They would give stock instead of cash, or to supplement it, so that they would need less money. By good fortune, Ciesla and Yairi were introduced to a patent attorney who liked the idea so much that he took equity instead of cash. That allowed Tactus to file critical patents, an important prerequisite before engaging with potential customers.

challenge

Find funding for a killer start-up idea in a volatile economic climate

solution

Alter the funding strategy as necessary and seek out different sources

The new strategy was paying off. In the first week of March 2009, the guys got a "term sheet"—an offer—from an angel investment group excited about the technology. They would get the money they needed to go to the next level.

But once again, timing wasn't on their side. On March 6, the Dow Jones plummeted. The stock market had dropped more than 50 percent in less than 18 months, with no bottom in sight. Private investors overwhelmingly get their investment funds from their stock portfolios, so Ciesla and Yairi's investors vanished overnight.

It took a few weeks to figure out where to go next. "We realized this is something we hugely believed in. We needed more money to protect our intellectual property, to engage with prospective customers, to get a design firm on board to create an improved prototype," said Ciesla. At that point, they turned to friends and family. They also brought on board Nate Saal, a friend and serial entrepreneur, who had founded and sold two prior companies.

In early 2010, they launched an angel investment round and landed their first significant seed investor. The founders now went full-time with Tactus. It was risky to give up full-time jobs, so they told themselves: "We have to raise this amount of money by this date, or we're done."

With an angel round and several patents in place, they started talking to prospective customers. Without getting customer feedback, receiving Series A funding (the first round from VCs) would have been very difficult.

During the bootstrapping phase, the partners put less than $100,000 into their fledgling business. They raised about $200,000 in the friends-and-family round. In the angel round, they raised around $1 million. When they finally got venture funding in 2011, they raised $6 million in their first round.

Stage of company, market focus, size of investment, and level of risk all need to be aligned to find the right VC, they learned. "We spoke with dozens and dozens of venture capitalists. We heard 'no' a lot," said Yairi. "We're a hardware company, and VCs have shifted to a more conservative investing philosophy—investing in software, which can get great returns with less capital outlay. They want established revenues."

"There's tension, figuring out how much to postpone the next phase of raising money," said Saal. "The longer you can stretch funds in your existing stage, the more value you can build, and the more equity you'll keep in the next funding round. How long do you bootstrap? Do you go to friends and family, find an angel investor? Will you do that big round with a VC? Every entity needs to think about the right transition points—and how to maximize value without putting the company at risk."

"Raising funds took longer and required more effort than we expected. It's basically nonstop. It's a constant part of building a company," said founder Ciesla. ∎

questions

1. Craig Ciesla and Micah Yairi eventually turned to friends and family for funding. Should they have done that first? What are the risks with raising money from such individuals?

2. What were the risks and benefits of waiting until they had been granted patents to ask for customer feedback?

3. The partners gave up equity in their company—part of the ownership—to get help they needed. Was this a good idea? Why, or why not?

4. Why do you think Ciesla and Yairi stuck it out, even with such bad luck? What would it take for *you* to be so persistent?

BUILDING A FINANCING STRATEGY FOR YOUR BUILDING BUSINESS

Goal:

Find a way to fund a growing business.

What to Do:

Working either alone or in groups, imagine that you've started a business specializing in finding and selling recycled decorative building materials, primarily for the wholesale construction trade. These are items such as wooden doors, reclaimed hardwood flooring, windows, and such. Your business has taken off, as environmentally conscious homeowners and corporations increasingly seek to incorporate such recycled materials into their homes and buildings, for both quality and cost savings. Your business has been growing very fast—demand has outstripped your ability to source such products, and you have been approached to open locations in additional cities as well as develop an online wholesale marketplace for such goods. You are barely breaking even as you finance your current growth.

So now you need money to finance your growth: to expand your sourcing operations, and potentially to open additional locations and develop an online marketplace. You estimate that you'll need at least $100,000 simply to increase your sourcing, a minimum of $500,000 to add an additional location, and another $1 million to develop a robust marketplace that could become a dominant leader in the field of recycled building materials.

1. Discuss the advantages and drawbacks of each of the following ways to finance your growth, including your sense of the real possibility of securing such financing:

    a. Securing a line of credit from the local bank

    b. Securing a term loan or an SBA loan

    c. Getting loans or investments from friends and family

    d. Finding an angel investor and giving up equity in the company

    e. Finding a venture capitalist and giving up equity in the company

    f. Looking for sourcing of funds—such as grants—to finance "green" businesses

    g. Going public

2. Present your financing strategy to the class. Be prepared to explain why you chose the route you did for financing growth.

CHAPTER 9

Marketing Fundamentals

learning objectives

In this chapter, you'll learn how to:

- Understand the importance of a marketing plan

- Recognize the difference between marketing and sales

- Evaluate why people buy

- Determine how to land those first customers and retain them

- Calculate the average customer lifetime value

- Design the components of a brand

- Define a core message

- Evaluate how much to budget for marketing

- Delineate a pricing strategy

The Importance of a Marketing Plan

You can spend a great deal of money on advertising, promotions, public relations, and other marketing activities and still not be effective. Bad marketing can leave your audience confused about your message and unsure of what you do or sell. Or it may convey the wrong image—you may want to let customers know that you're very competitive on price, but this may actually leave customers thinking your products are cheap and shoddy. You can reach the wrong audience: people who are not prospective customers. Or you can be inconsistent in your marketing reach or audience. Poorly planned marketing wastes money.

That's why you need a complete marketing plan: a thorough program that establishes your goals, message, and target audience, along with the right marketing tactics and vehicles to reach them.

What creates effective marketing?

A successful marketing strategy fulfills the following:

- **Fit to market.** You have to reach the right people with your marketing. No matter how well or how many times you explain why your product or service is the best, if your message doesn't reach the right eyes and ears, your marketing efforts will be in vain. If you sell software programs that help businesses track sales, but you don't reach the key decision maker, your marketing will be ineffective. Although this sounds obvious, many businesses spend money—a lot of it—on marketing without considering who's paying attention.

REAL-WORLD RECAP

Effective marketing

A successful marketing strategy fulfills the following:

- Fit to market
- Effective message
- Repetition

- **Effective message.** The point of marketing is to motivate prospective customers to do something—namely, buy your product or service. It may be to make your **brand** name better known, to create an image around your brand, to let customers know about an offer, or to urge them to take an action. How effectively you express your message is key to whether or not your marketing works.

- **Repetition.** You might be surprised to learn how many times a potential customer needs to be exposed to a company's name and marketing message before it sinks in—typically as many as seven to 10 times or more. This is why you see the same ads and commercials again and again. You have to repeat the same message to the same market over and over and over and over.

Marketing vs. sales

Although the two are often confused, marketing is quite distinct from sales. Effective marketing increases customer awareness of your business and service and also communicates the benefits and advantages of what you offer—your marketing message. It includes activities such as advertising, branding (think of McDonalds, Nike, Coke, and Apple), direct marketing, online marketing, and public relations, as well as numerous other activities, including networking—the meeting of potential customers and referral sources through informal activities, such as joining organizations, attending industry events, or taking people to lunch. In smaller companies, networking may be the major marketing activity.

Return on investment
Without planning, marketing can be a big hole into which you pour cash without getting much of a return. Although it might seem like a great idea to buy a full-page ad in the *New York Times*, the cost could easily outweigh the benefits, based on who your target market is. If you have limited resources—and most younger companies do—you'll have to plan and analyze the best places to put your marketing dollars so they'll reap the greatest reward.

en·tre·pre·neur·ship key terms

Benefits
The ways in which a product or service improves a customer's life or business.

Brand
The complete public identity of a company, product, or service based on all the words, symbols, design, messages, and values connected with it.

Customer acquisition cost
The amount of money it takes, in total, to secure a new customer.

Customer lifetime value (CLV)
The total income to a company, over time, that is likely to be generated by a specific customer.

Customer relationship management (CRM)
A system, using a computer database, for acquiring, communicating with, and keeping track of customers, with the goal of increasing sales, building customer loyalty, and benefiting from the lifetime value of a customer.

Features
The specific attributes of a product or service that distinguish it from competitive products or services.

Influencers
Individuals who, by their use or approval of a product or service, entice others to try it. Influencers are people to whom prospects look for recommendations; they can be key product reviewers, columnists, bloggers, athletes, celebrities, or successful businesspeople.

Tagline
A short, catchy, and memorable group of words, representing a company's message and branding.

Unique selling proposition
A concise description of what you are selling, why customers should buy from you, and what differentiates you from competitors.

Is price king?

Customers don't always choose the lowest price for the same product. In fact, they will often pay more for the exact same item if some of the following factors are in place:

- Reliable seller with a good reputation
- Guarantees
- High level of customer service
- The seller supports a cause the buyer also supports

Some customers will even pay a higher price out of a desire to support local businesses.

Sales, on the other hand, are direct actions you take to secure customer orders. The term "sales" encompasses face-to-face sales (when a salesperson meets with customers to tell them about the company and asks them to commit to buying their product or service), online sales, and cold calling (or telemarketing), which is when a salesperson calls, or calls on, potential customers, pitches the offering, and asks for an order.

Sometimes the line between marketing and sales can be blurred. For example, if you place a coupon in a local paper, is this marketing or sales or some hybrid of the two? Likewise, if you put on a special promotion offering existing customers discounts or rebates if they recommend you to new customers, it can be difficult to separate marketing from sales. For the most part, however, anything that spreads the word about your company, products, or services can be categorized as marketing, whereas anything that directly generates revenue is sales.

Why People Buy

People, businesses, the government, your dog—they all have needs and desires. Without needs and wants, real or imagined, no one would ever buy (or sell) anything. Understanding what motivates customers to buy is an important first step in developing your marketing message and plan. This will help you choose where, when, and whether you want to advertise; what aspects of your competitive position you'll want to highlight in your marketing materials; and even how to price your service.

Benefits vs. features

Customers choose one product over another based on their **benefits** and **features**, and, of course, price. Although the terms "benefits" and "features" are often used interchangeably, their meanings are distinct.

Benefits are the ways in which a product or service improves a customer's life or business. Features are the specific attributes of a product or service that distinguish it from competitive products or services. Take a look at the table below that distinguishes benefits from features.

PRODUCT	FEATURE	BENEFIT
A head of lettuce	Organic	Helps the customer stay healthy by avoiding pesticides
A car	Built-in navigation system	Adds convenience and time savings by helping drivers get to where they need to go
An office chair	Five height settings	Enables business customers to improve employees' comfort, enhance their ergonomic well-being, and boost productivity

The organic cultivation, the navigation system, and the height settings are all features of their respective products. These are factual, and a customer can easily compare the features of your product or service with those of a competitor.

Improved health, convenience, time savings, productivity, and comfort are some of the benefits offered by these products due to their specific features. Some benefits may be less personal and based more on values—for example, a consumer may view organic lettuce as having a better impact on the environment, a benefit valued by many people. Or, if the chair is made in the United States, that may appeal to consumers who prefer to buy American-made products.

Most marketing strategists agree that people are more motivated by benefits than features. It is easier to compare products or services based on features, and that's why marketing material, especially packaging and website descriptions, goes into detail on features. Yet customers are highly motivated by benefits. That's why much of marketing, particularly brand-oriented advertising, focuses on the benefits of the product or service, or the benefit of being associated with a particular brand—even if the "benefit" is to create a certain self-image, such as being hip, fit, youthful, environmentally conscious, and so on.

The "Four Ps"

What messages do you send customers to motivate them to purchase your products or service? Traditionally, marketing experts emphasized the elements known as the "Four Ps" for influencing customers to buy:

- **Product.** The tangible product or service itself.

- **Price.** The cost advantage of buying the product.

- **Place.** The convenience and attributes of the location where the product or service will be acquired.

- **Promotion.** The amount and nature of the marketing activities.

These four elements have been the cornerstone of marketing theory for many years, and it is important to understand them. But because these elements leave a lot out of the marketing picture—especially as customers look for products or services not just to fill an immediate need but also to enhance their overall sense of well-being—you can take a more customer-centric approach to thinking about marketing through the following "Five Fs":

- **Function.** How does the product or service meet customers' concrete needs?

- **Finances.** How will the purchase affect your customers' overall financial situation? This is not just about the price of the product or service, but also about the other savings it will engender and the increased productivity that will result.

- **Freedom.** How conveniently can customers purchase and use the product or service? How will they gain more time and reduce worry in other aspects of their lives?

- **Feelings.** How does the product or service make customers feel about themselves, and how does it affect and relate to their self-image? Do they like and respect the salesperson and the company?

- **Future.** How will customers deal with the product or service and company over time? Will support and service be available? How will the product or service affect their lives in coming years, and will they have an increased sense of security about the future?

Customers, of course, would like to receive benefits in all these areas, and you should be aware of how your product or service fulfills the entire range of their needs. But your primary message must concentrate on one or two of these benefits that can effectively motivate your customers.

Acquire and Retain Customers

Without customers, you don't have a business. The goal of marketing campaigns is to acquire and keep customers. But it's difficult—and expensive—to gain customers. In some industries, the **customer acquisition cost**, the amount of money it takes to get a new customer, may be many hundreds of dollars. So once you have a customer, it's important to keep them.

Attract first-time customers

"If you build it, will they come?"

Just because you've created something new, something better, or something cheaper doesn't mean that customers will flock to your door. It takes a lot of work to make sure customers know about your products and services and then become motivated enough to spend their money with you. One of the first tasks as a marketer is to figure out what it's going to take to get prospective customers (prospects) to become aware of you and your offerings, give you a try, and buy.

For many reasons, customers won't necessarily flock to a new and better offering. Most novice marketers think they're not attracting customers because of the competition, but competition is only part of the reason. The reality is that most of the time, the actual culprit is a lack of awareness of your offerings and insufficient motivation to change.

That means it will take effort to make prospects aware of you as well as incentives for them to try you out.

Given that most customers are set in their ways and don't switch providers easily, what can you do to convince a customer to come to you in the first place? Which marketing tactics can you use to persuade a customer to try you? The following table outlines some successful methods for encouraging customers to both get to know about you and become motivated to try you out.

Whichever approach you use to get first-time buyers to give you a chance, you have to let prospects know about them. You have to effectively get the

Why Customers Buy from You

Why would a customer buy a product or service from you? Pick a product or service that you currently offer, or would like to offer, and use this worksheet to brainstorm about aspects of your company, product, or service that would motivate a customer to choose you rather than a competitor. Then use the right-hand column to make notes about which marketing activities relating to each aspect would enhance your ability to attract customers.

CUSTOMER MOTIVATION ASPECT	WHAT YOU HAVE NOW	WHAT YOU COULD DO TO ENHANCE THIS ASPECT
Awareness		
Features and benefits		
Price		
Brand		
Convenience		
Word-of-mouth		
Affiliation		
Other:		

STRATEGIES TO ATTRACT FIRST-TIME CUSTOMERS

STRATEGY	DESCRIPTION	EXAMPLES	ADVANTAGES	DISADVANTAGES
Introductory Offers	Short-term, deep discounts limited to first-time users; offers for a new product or company	Discount coupons for first oil change; buy one entrée, get one free at new restaurant	Attracts attention; short-term offers can create sense of urgency	May only attract bargain hunters; customers may get accustomed to lower prices
Leaders/Teaser Rates	Exceptionally low prices on a product or service that a company actually loses money on	Supermarkets selling Thanksgiving turkeys at a loss to attract customers who will do all their shopping there	Draws people into your store, to your website, or to your other place of business	Often results in making no money or losing money on the transaction; some laws limit loss leaders and teaser rates
Free Offers	Giving customers your product or service free, often for a limited time	A free month's subscription to an online dating site; free HBO with a cable service subscription	Many customers will try something new for free	Some customers will never buy after the free trial
Sampling	Giving prospects a chance to try your product or service at no charge	Food tastings at a store; a free 30-day trial version of software	Good way to introduce unusual or exceptional products; can be a relatively inexpensive marketing technique	Some customers will go for the freebies and never actually buy
Daily Deal Sites	Extremely attractive offers featured for one day on a website such as Groupon or Living Social	75% off a series of yoga classes; buy one, get one free offer on camping gear	Reaches new user base; good when launching a business or new offering	Can result in little or no profit on customers who redeem the offer; may even result in loss
"Beta" Testing	Asking prospective customers to test products before release or sale to the general public	Often done with technology products but can be applied in a range of industries, such as sporting goods	Testers often become first purchasers (especially when given discounts) and are often influencers	Finding testers can be time consuming
Positive Reviews and Recommendations by Influencers	Asking influencers (people others look to for purchasing advice) to use and review your product or service	Reviews by journalists, celebrities, well-known industry insiders, or peer leaders; usually achieved through PR activities	Influencers can persuade people to buy new products they would otherwise hesitate to try	Can be very difficult to reach influencers (especially celebrities); may result in negative reviews

word out about your product or service—and keep repeating your message. That's where the marketing tactics come in (see Chapter 10). Tactics you'll want to focus on when trying to get first-time customers include:

- Advertising, especially offering discounts and free offers

- Online marketing, particularly reaching out to key bloggers and user review sites

- Direct mailings, including purchasing prospect lists from companies that sell lists they've compiled from various sources (such as magazine subscribers or purchasers of certain products)

- Public relations, aimed specifically at generating positive reviews by **influencers**

- Holding "grand openings" with freebies, to introduce new customers to your store, restaurant, or service and to stimulate publicity

Customer lifetime value (CLV)

An important concept to help you determine how much you can spend in your marketing campaign to acquire a customer is the lifetime value of a customer, also referred to as **customer lifetime value (CLV)**. This is the amount of income you can project that any single customer will bring to your company over the entire time they do business with you. This is important for you to know, so you can better understand how to target customers and figure what you can spend on marketing activities to acquire a customer and still be profitable. Different customers will have different lifetime values, and you can spend more money trying to acquire those customers.

How do you know your customer's lifetime worth in actual dollar figures? The basics involve:

- Estimating the amount of time you expect your customer to continue being a customer is the lifetime of your customer doing business with you

- Determining how much your customer is likely to spend during that period, through all product and service purchases

- Estimating the profit to you from that customer's purchases

- Estimating how much it costs you to acquire that customer and to retain or serve that customer

You need to balance the expected lifetime value of a customer with the costs of attracting and retaining them, to get a sense of how profitable each customer is to you—that's their total customer lifetime value, or CLV.

For instance, if you're a mobile phone service provider, you could estimate a customer's lifetime income to you as shown in the following sample form.

Ask your competitors for work

Believe it or not, competitors can be a source of new business, especially when you're first starting out. If they are very busy or have small clients they can no longer serve profitably, they may be interested in subcontracting or referring work to you.

Sample Form: Estimating Customer Lifetime Value for a Mobile Phone Service Provider

Expected length of time customer will remain signed up with my service (on average):	48 months (4 years)
Expected monthly income per customer:	$80
My estimated costs to service mobile phone account per customer and provide ongoing communication to them:	$20
Estimated profit per month:	$60
Lifetime profit from mobile phone service:	*$2,880 ($60 x 48 months)*
Estimated purchases they'll make of other services (for example, text messaging packages, minute overages):	$800
My estimated costs to provide services:	$200
Profit on other services purchases:	*$600*
Total customer lifetime income:	*$3,480 ($2,880 plus $600)*
Cost to acquire that customer:	$300
Cost to retain and administer that customer's account:	$100
Total customer lifetime value:	*$3,080 ($3,480 minus $300 minus $100)*

Why is it important for you to know the CLV when you're starting on your marketing plan? Because that number gives you an idea of how much you can spend on acquiring and retaining a customer and still be profitable. Using the example above, for instance, if it costs you $3,500 to acquire each customer, you'll never make any money. In reality, you'd want to spend only a fraction of that.

The value of each customer varies, depending on your product and industry, and helps determine how much you can spend on acquiring that customer. For instance, the average life of subscribers to an online dating service may be 10 months, while that of subscribers to a cable service may be 50 months. The dating service charges $30 a month, while cable is $50 a month. However, the cost of providing the dating service is only $2 a member per month, while cable costs $20 a subscriber per month.

In this scenario, the dating service customer is worth $300 in income ($30 x 10 months), with a cost of only $20 to provide service to that member. The cable customer is worth $2,500 ($50 x 50 months) with a cost of $1,000 to provide service. The profit of each online dating service customer is $280, and of each cable customer is $1,500, so you can see that the cable company can afford to spend more money on marketing to acquire new customers.

When you're first starting in business, your customer acquisition costs will be a much higher percentage of the lifetime value of a customer. After all, it costs a lot more to land the first client for your mobile phone service company than the thousandth, because at that point you've already developed your marketing materials, tested your online marketing campaigns, and long ago paid off the graphic designer who designed your ads and website.

Retain customers

Successful marketing involves not just getting customers, but also keeping them. It's estimated that it costs from two to 10 times more to acquire a customer than it does to retain one. For example, it costs far less to send a brochure to a customer who buys from you every year than it does to place TV advertisements to attract new customers. The longer a customer remains with you and continues to buy, the more profitable the relationship. That's why it pays to reward customer loyalty and keep customers with you as long as possible.

What keeps customers coming back? One of the best ways to cultivate happy, loyal, and long-term customers is to consistently give them an excellent product or service at a competitive price. Some companies stay in business for decades with virtually no advertising, customer retention programs, or other special marketing activities—just by doing what they're supposed to do: being a reliable source of a product or service at a fair price and interacting with the customer in a professional manner. This isn't enough for every company, of course (especially new ones), but it *is* a cornerstone of customer retention.

Other factors involved in customer retention include:

- **Good customer service.** Responding to customers' inquiries, showing up/delivering on time, handling complaints and concerns promptly.

- **Competitive prices.** Maintaining fair prices for what the customer is getting and against those the competition is offering.

- **Regular communication.** Staying in touch with customers on an ongoing basis in some way (in addition to bills), perhaps through an email newsletter.

- **Special treatment.** Going the extra mile for a customer with unexpected benefits, such as giving a diner a free dessert for their birthday or washing the customer's car after an oil change.

- **Loyalty and rewards programs.** Organized systems to retain and reward good customers. (See Chapter 10 for more on loyalty programs.)

Subscriptions vs. per-use fees

If you plan to provide a service—especially over the Internet or as a mobile application—you may have the option of choosing whether you want to provide it as a subscription or on a per-use or one-time purchase basis. Subscription models are often considered the "holy grail" of pricing because customers are tied to you on an ongoing basis. A broad range of products and services are offered on a subscription basis, including the obvious, such as publications and telecom, and cloud-based applications. But even products can be sold on a subscription basis—such as the bacon-of-the-month club.

Average Customer Lifetime Value (CLV)

Estimate the average profit your company will make on each customer. Use the appropriate portion of this worksheet, depending on whether you sell a product/service directly or on a subscription basis. If you have different product lines or customer types, make a copy of this worksheet for each one.

TYPE OF CUSTOMER #1 – GENERAL PURCHASES

Product/service purchased: _____

Profit per purchase: _____

Number of purchases per year: _____

Number of years customer will
continue to purchase: _____

Add-on purchases/subscriptions: _____

Profit on add-ons: _____

Total lifetime income: _____

Subtract:

Customer acquisition costs: _____

Customer retention costs: _____

Result—customer lifetime value (CLV): _____

TYPE OF CUSTOMER #2 – MONTHLY SUBSCRIPTION

Product/service subscribed to: _____

Average monthly subscription fee: _____

Profit per month: _____

Number of months customer will
continue to subscribe: _____

Total lifetime income: _____

Subtract:

Customer acquisition costs: _____

Customer retention costs: _____

Result—customer lifetime value (CLV): _____

CRM: customer relationship management

Companies use databases called **customer relationship management (CRM)** programs to manage their interactions with their customers and prospects. Such programs enable salespeople to track prospects and customers, including their response to all marketing and sales activities, as well as to let customer service and other company employees immediately see all communications with and purchases by each customer. Sophisticated CRM programs allow companies to slice and dice their customer lists to figure out which customers are likely to be most profitable, which are most likely to respond to a special offer, which can be retained without special deals, and so on. CRM programs have also permitted businesses to devise sophisticated loyalty and rewards programs.

Many companies at first keep track of customers with just simple contact management programs, their "address books," or even basic spreadsheets. As your business grows, though, you're likely to turn to specialized CRM programs, such as the cloud-based application from salesforce.com. Whatever CRM you choose, the key is to actually use the information, once you've compiled it, to learn more about your customers and prospects.

Brand Identity

Your brand is the totality of the identity of a company, product, or service. Like your personal identity, your business identity is the set of characteristics that allows people to recognize you as a separate, unique entity. It helps people distinguish you from others, remember you, understand what you do, and, often, even develop a certain feeling about you. A brand enables customers to quickly and easily figure out that they're picking up a can of Red Bull, not a can of Monster, or entering a Quizno's for a bite, not a Subway.

Developing a brand consists of defining a company's, service's, or product's:

- **Promise.** A brand promises consistency; customers anticipate experiencing the same thing as the last time they purchased the brand; it doesn't have to be the highest quality or the lowest price, but it should be dependable.

- **Values.** Increasingly, brands stand for a set of values that customers can relate to; because consumers often define themselves by the brand they buy, wear, drink, and so forth, a company with strong values can engender strong customer loyalty.

- **Message.** Your core message is, in essence, your company's "elevator pitch." It concisely sums up what you do, your target market, and your competitive advantage.

- **Identity.** Your brand identity consists of those components—such as your name, logo, colors, packaging, and **tagline**—that make you immediately distinguishable from competitors.

Every cloud has a silver lining

Two of the benefits of cloud-based CRM programs for new entrepreneurs are that you pay as you go and that these applications can grow with you. So when you just start out and only have a short list of contacts, you can subscribe to a plan that suits your needs and your budget. Later, after you've grown, you simply upgrade to a larger plan—without interrupting your access to one of your company's most valuable assets: your contacts. Three popular cloud-based CRM applications to choose from are Salesforce CRM, SugarCRM, and Zoho CRM.

Which comes first? Company name or domain name?

Because a company website is no longer optional—customers usually look for you online first—you'll need to choose a domain name in addition to your company name. Naturally, it's always best to get a domain name that is as close to your business name as possible. Because a domain name is so important, many businesses actually wait to see what domain name they can get before they name their companies!

Your company identity

Once you have created your business identity, your company begins to feel "real"—both to you and to potential customers, suppliers, other businesses, and so on. Your business identity is your brand image and, once established, it represents a precious asset that you must carefully nurture and protect.

To safeguard and strengthen your brand identity, make sure it is:

- **Consistent.** Decide on an appropriate design style, color scheme, and tagline—and then avoid altering them until your business changes significantly or these elements become badly outdated.

- **Reflective.** Your identity should be consistent with and reflect your entire brand: your promise, values, and core message.

- **Protected.** Consult with an attorney and register key elements of your brand with the United States Patent and Trademark Office at www.uspto.gov. If others use, or closely imitate, your name, logo, tagline, or other components, you will need to take action to make sure they "cease and desist." If you don't, you may lose your trademark protection. For more on trademarks, see pages 386–387.

Most important, your brand identity should be used frequently and repeatedly. A brand identity works only if your audience becomes familiar with it. They must see it over and over and over again for it to be effective. Be sure you use your brand identity components:

- On your products, in your packaging, and on any other materials you use to identify your products or services to your customers or clients

- In all your marketing materials, both print (brochures, catalogs, letterhead, business cards, direct mail) and Web (your website, email communications, blogs, and any digital documents you circulate)

- In all your advertising, especially print, Web, and TV ads

Choose your business name

A clever business name can serve as an excellent marketing tool, helping make your company memorable, but if it's too cute, it runs the risk of putting people off. It can be difficult to strike the right balance—which is why coming up with a good name can be frustratingly hard work. Big companies spend tens of thousands of dollars researching names, and sometimes even they fail.

When successful, a name indicates what your business does in a succinct, and perhaps clever, way. It can help you sell your product or service by clearly telling customers what you offer or what problem you solve.

QUALITIES OF A GOOD NAME

A good company name:

- **Communicates the correct information.** Avoid anything in your business name that could substantially confuse potential customers about what you do. Even if you think your name is crystal clear, make sure it is unambiguous and appropriate.

- **Conveys the right feeling.** Choose a name with positive connotations whenever possible: A day spa named Haven or Oasis transmits the sense that customers will escape the stresses in their lives.

- **Won't get outdated quickly.** You're likely to change the scope of your products over time, so be careful not to choose names that are too closely identified with recent trends or that are too limiting. When Twentieth Century Fox Film Studios was founded in 1935 (merging Fox and Twentieth Century studios), the name "Twentieth Century" was associated with the idea of something young and new. Of course, by the end of that century, it no longer seemed fresh, and the company now uses just the name "Fox" for many of its entertainment units.

Elements of your business identity

The four key elements of your business identity are:

- Name
- Logo
- Tagline
- Colors

In addition, you might have other unique, distinguishing elements that make up your identity, such as clever or unusual packaging or product design.

GREAT COMPANY NAMES

NAME	ORIGINS	WHY IT'S GOOD
YouTube	Focuses on the site's origins, which was to allow people to post their homemade videos on the Web for others to see.	The catchy nature of the name perfectly captures the youthful and energetic spirit of the brand.
7-Eleven	Reflects the company's original operating hours, from 7 a.m. until 11 p.m.	Gives critical information on one of the key things that make a convenience store convenient—that it's open at times when other stores aren't.
Nike	Greek goddess of victory.	Appeals to the competitive instincts of the firm's target market of sports enthusiasts.
Amazon	Named after the river, to indicate the tremendous volume potential of online sales.	Has made the firm's presence and high growth rates synonymous with imagining an unstoppable, fiercely competitive force.
Coca-Cola Co.	From the coca leaves and koca nuts of the ingredients making up the flagship drink.	Perfectly describes the ingredients (which were once thought to have medicinal value). The alliteration gives it a pleasant, memorable sound.
Google	A deliberate misspelling of the scientific term googol, the very large number 10 to the 100th, to indicate the huge volume of data the firm would be processing.	Has a friendly, even goofy connotation that makes the very techie notion of a "search engine" accessible to the general public.

Your Company Name

Use this worksheet to list and compare the company names you're considering.

	Name 1	Name 2	Name 3	Name 4
List the business names you've considered thus far.				
Which aspect of the name tells your customers what you do?				
Which aspect of the name tells your customers what they get?				
Which aspect of the name conveys a feeling? What is that feeling?				
Is the name trademarked by another business in your market?				

	Name 1	Name 2	Name 3	Name 4
Are there companies with similar or confusing names?				
Is the name trademarked in a different market category? Which one? By whom? Is there any chance you might one day want to expand your business into that category?				
Who likes the name? Why? Ask your friends, family, and close network.				
Who dislikes the name? Why? Ask your friends, family, and close network.				
What available domain name (Web address) would work well with the name?				
Other comments:				

Good Logos

In general, good logos:

- Are simple
- Are memorable
- Imply something positive
- Are easy to reproduce in both color and black-and-white
- Can be used and repeated everywhere: on products, in advertising, on the Web, and on packaging and marketing materials
- Are not offensive (be careful of international connotations of symbols and colors)
- Are broad enough to keep using as your company grows

- **Is easy to spell and pronounce.** If a name is too hard to spell, it becomes difficult for a potential customer to remember. In addition, people have a harder time remembering names they can't say or spell easily.

- **Is memorable.** If clients or customers have an easy time remembering your name, they're more likely to do business with you again. However, sometimes simple is a better choice than memorable. In fact, a company with a straightforward name like Ergonomic Office Equipment may develop a more successful business than a company with an overly cute name like Got Your Back.

In the end, one of the most important considerations is whether *you* like the name and feel comfortable with it. After all, you're the one who will be seeing and saying it the most. And don't let getting stuck on trying to decide on a name slow down the start of your business. At some point, you need to make a choice and get on with it.

Logos, taglines, and colors

Your company identity consists of more than just your company name. The colors you choose, the typeface you decide on, and the tagline and logo you develop also convey a message to your potential customers. Even your packaging can reinforce your brand identity. Apple spent a good deal of time and money on developing distinct, beautifully designed packaging that conveys a feel even before a customer opens a product.

YOUR LOGO

A logo is an image associated with your company that gives the public another way to remember you. All of us are familiar with logos: the Nike "swoosh," Coca-Cola's distinctive type font, Target's red target. These are not only utterly unique, they actually help define the personality of the company in question.

A good logo conveys something positive about your company. The logo for TiVo, for example—a "smiling" television with antenna protruding out of the top—is quirky and fresh, inviting the world to view it as fun and friendly despite being on the cutting edge of technology.

Because creating your identity is critical to your business success, consider hiring a graphic designer to help you create your logo and other aspects of your company image.

YOUR TAGLINE

Many companies use a motto or tagline either to better explain the nature of the business or to create a feeling about the company or product. For example, "Just Do It" has been Nike's tagline for decades. A tagline helps customers remember what's unique about your business and how you specialize in giving them exactly what they need. Taglines don't have to be catchy to be memorable to your target audience. "Manufacturers of packing materials for technology products," for example, might seem like a boring tagline; still, it could be very effective if what you do is make and sell boxes for computers.

Use your tagline in many places: your stationery, business cards, website, even at the bottom of your invoices and receipts. And, just like your company name, your tagline should be unique. There's even a database you can use (for a fee) to see whether someone else has also thought of that clever slogan you thought so original (www.adslogans.co.uk/).

GREAT TAGLINES

COMPANY	TAGLINE
Salesforce.com	"The end of software"
YouTube	"Broadcast yourself"
Gawker	"Today's gossip is tomorrow's news"
Gizmodo	"The gadget guide. So much in love with shiny new toys, it's unnatural."
Fed Ex	"When it absolutely, positively has to be there overnight"
Nike	"Just do it"
New York Times	"All the news that's fit to print"
M&M's	"Melts in your mouth, not in your hand"
Volkswagen	"Drivers wanted"
Wheaties	"Breakfast of champions"
Avis	"We try harder"
Lay's Potato Chips	"Betcha can't eat just one"

LEVERAGING YOUR COLORS

Most people start businesses without giving colors much thought. Yet everyone will end up using colors to help identify their business. Coming up with a consistent use of color—your color palette—gives you another tool to help customers remember who you are and to convey a sense about your company. Colors are also one of the easiest ways for customers to quickly distinguish you from competitors.

Colors aren't just for printed collateral, packaging, or signs. Businesses often use their colors in their decor and in employee clothing and uniforms as well. In general, anything that projects a consistent brand image should incorporate your colors and logo in some way.

PACKAGING

It's rare that a product doesn't come in some sort of package. Packaging can contribute to a company's identity—Tiffany & Company's blue boxes with white bows, for example. In general, high-end consumer packaging falls on the elaborate end of the scale: Some companies spend almost as much effort on designing the look of the packaging as they do the product.

Do I need a tagline on Day One?

You don't need to have a tagline, and you certainly don't have to choose one before you open your doors. Yet developing a tagline helps you clarify what makes your business special and enables you to sum up your competitive position in just a few words.

Business packaging is more often focused on ensuring that the product survives the shipping process. Packaging of products can thus comprise a substantial proportion of the cost of goods sold.

The most effective packaging reflects a company's identity, including its logo, tagline, and colors. Think of the boxes that Apple's products come in: Seeing a silhouette of an apple with a bite taken out of it, you'd instantly know what the company is without seeing its name!

Core Messaging

What do you want your customers to remember about you? What do you want them to think when they reflect on your products or services? Your core message is where it all comes together. It's a concise summation of what you do, whom your target market is, and what your competitive advantage is. Clearly, you can develop your core message only after you've evaluated those.

Your core message is *not* your tagline (although your tagline may reflect your message). A tagline is an advertising slogan; your core message is a clear definition of your strategic position. Your core message should be based on:

- The nature of your products or services

- The key differentiators between you and your competition

- Your competitive advantages

- Your value proposition

- Your company values

Sometimes this core message is referred to as your **unique selling proposition**. This is a clear summation of:

- What sets you apart from the competition—in other words, your differentiators, what makes you unique

- What you offer the customer—in short, what you are selling

- What's in it for the customer—that is, the proposition

If yours is a large company, selling many different products, you may have a core message for each product line. In a smaller business or in a company with a narrow product line, your company's core message and your product's core message may be the same. For instance, the core message of Planning-Shop (the publisher of this book) is: "We help entrepreneurs succeed by giving them practical, reality-based books and tools." This message is based on:

- **Unique:** a specialty in entrepreneurship (other publishers publish books on a wide range of topics and disciplines) and in being practical and true to life (other publishers may be more theoretical or abstract)

- **Selling:** books and other tools (such as a number of software products)

BUILD-YOUR-BUSINESS WORKSHEET

Create Your Identity

Use the space below to begin developing your corporate identity. You may want to draw pictures as well as use words and phrases to develop the look, feel, and message you want to convey.

Business name
Tagline
Logo
Colors
Distinct product design
Distinct packaging
Decor, employee clothing, or other unique identifying features

When to increase your marketing budget

- During a new product/service/ website launch or introduction
- For a new company launch
- For extremely innovative technology or new approach
- When opening a new location
- When advertising a "sale" or specific event
- In response to a new competitive threat
- When introducing significant new features
- When introducing major price reductions
- If making a material change in company, products, services, or ownership

■ **Proposition:** success. This is the promise PlanningShop makes: "We'll help entrepreneurs succeed."

Message drives marketing

It's imperative that you understand the core message you want to send for your company, product, or service. Without articulating a core message, it's impossible to develop a consistent, meaningful marketing program. You need to keep your core message in mind when you're creating your advertising, website, packaging, and marketing materials (brochures, catalogs) and even your company name. It must permeate every aspect of your marketing, and it must be the foundation of all your marketing activities.

Your core message is what defines your brand. It's what you want customers to remember about you. When you have a strong, clear message, you're much better able to develop a strong brand *and* a strong connection with your customer base.

Your Marketing Budget

As you set out to make your plan, you'll need to know: What's your marketing budget? Most companies have a general sense that they'll have to spend money on marketing, but few companies, especially new, entrepreneurial ones, have any idea of how *much* money they'll need to set aside for their marketing efforts. Unfortunately, there are just no hard and fast rules about how much a company should spend on marketing.

Percentage of sales budget

One method some companies use to come up with a marketing allocation is to set aside a certain percentage of their total sales. According to this method, a company devotes a percentage of its overall sales for all marketing activities (advertising, public relations, brochures, and the like). In other words, if your solar panel manufacturing company had $2 million in sales last year and you set aside 5 percent for marketing this year, your total marketing budget for the year would be $100,000.

Budgeting this way is tempting—after all, it's easy. But it's arbitrary. You may spend way too much or way too little. For instance, certain enormous companies spend only a tiny percentage of their sales on marketing. Costco, the giant discount warehouse company, does virtually no advertising; it's not necessary for its success, and in addition it operates on very slim profit margins. At the other extreme, the online contact management company salesforce.com spent $25.4 million on marketing during its first year in business, with only $5.4 million in sales: 470 percent of its revenues! (That spending has paid off, since its yearly sales are now in the billions.)

In practice, however, the bulk of established companies spend a range of 1 percent to 15 percent of total company sales on annual marketing. That's a wide range: For a $2 million company, that figure could be anywhere from $20,000 to $300,000.

BUILD-YOUR-BUSINESS WORKSHEET

Your Core Message

Use this worksheet to develop the core message, or unique selling proposition, for your company, product, or service.

Unique: What sets you apart from competitors? What are your differentiators?

_____

_____

_____

_____

_____

_____

_____

_____

Selling: What are the specific products or services, benefits, or features you are selling?

_____

_____

_____

_____

_____

_____

_____

_____

Proposition: What is the promise you are making to your customers? What's in it for them?

_____

_____

_____

_____

_____

_____

_____

_____

REAL-WORLD RECAP

How much should you spend?

The following factors help you determine how much to spend on marketing:

- Low profit margins
- High profit margins
- Large or hard-to-reach market
- New business
- Aggressive competition

What factors help you determine how much to spend on marketing?

- **Low profit margins.** Companies that, by the nature of their product or service, make little profit per sale (low gross profit margins) can't afford to spend a high percentage of sales on marketing. Examples of such companies include grocery stores, discount stores, and producers of commodity products (such as raw materials and nonbranded, highly discounted computer hardware). These are typically high-volume businesses. So while their marketing budget as a whole may be huge (imagine the budget for Safeway or Kroger grocery chains), it still represents a minute percentage of their total sales.

- **High profit margins.** By contrast, companies with high profit margins have the ability to dedicate a greater percentage of their overall expenditures to marketing. If you don't have to spend a lot on manufacturing, inventory, or high rent—if you're a software, Web-based, or service company, for instance—you can afford to spend more on marketing. Other examples include purveyors of luxury goods and automobiles.

- **Large or hard-to-reach market.** Certain markets cost more to reach, so you're going to need a bigger marketing budget for these. If the market is very large (such as every new parent in the United States and Canada), your media costs will be high. If your market is diffuse, with many different characteristics (say, all young adults between the ages of 22 and 35), you'll have to try to reach them in many different ways, which is costly. If you're targeting other businesses (B2B) and they're not well aggregated (for instance, not in a specific industry with a trade show or in a specific geographic location), then plan on spending more on marketing to identify and reach these customers.

- **New business.** It costs a lot of money to launch a new company, new product, or new service—more than you'll have to spend, year after year, once your company is up and running. And, of course, your revenues are smaller in the first years, so plan to devote a much bigger percentage of your overall income to marketing in the early years of your new company's product or service.

- **Aggressive competition.** Let's face it, if your competition is spending a lot of money on marketing, there's a good chance you'll have to spend a lot, as well.

Goal-based marketing budget

With a goal-based marketing budget, you do a complete marketing plan, determining your goals and laying out a thoughtful course of action. If your goal is to secure 1,000 new customers, what will it take to acquire them? How much advertising do you need to do? At which trade shows do you need to exhibit? Will you advertise on search engines, and if so, how often?

As you can see, this type of budgeting makes the most sense. It's derived from figuring out what you want to achieve, which marketing vehicles you're going to use and how often, and how much that's all going to cost. Of course, you may have to trim back your marketing budget to meet the realities of your company's financial situation and overall expenditures, but this kind of budgeting is at least based on what it actually takes to accomplish your marketing goals.

Develop your in-house marketing staff budget

When figuring out your marketing budget, you also need to financially account for the time that your own staff will spend on marketing activities.

In most entrepreneurial companies (especially newer ones), staff members often do more than one job. Even if you have one or several full-time marketing employees—such as a marketing director—you'll likely need to call on others in your company to help out with certain marketing activities. For example, you're unlikely to have employees whose sole job it is to staff your trade show booth. Thus, some of the people helping out in your trade show booth today may be assisting you in shipping products tomorrow.

This means that many of the people you list in your in-house staff marketing budget may only spend 10 percent, 5 percent, or even less of their time on actual marketing. That's OK—just indicate what portion of their time they'll spend on marketing activities.

Price Your Products and Services

Figuring out the "right" price to charge for your products or services is often more an art than a science. While setting the right price may be crucial for your long-term success, you may not be able to judge what exactly is the right price until you've experimented with various pricing levels or arrangements.

Setting prices for services—rather than products—is often the most challenging. Even if you do research on what competitors charge, it can be hard to compare quality and even features of the service. Thus, one attorney may charge $100 an hour for drawing up a will, while another charges $400, and the difference may not be their years of experience or even their area of specialty; rather, the price difference may be based more on how much they need to earn, how busy they are, how large a law firm they're in, their reputation, and so on.

But if you're a retailer or a reseller of products or services produced by others, it's often relatively easier to figure out how much to charge. Most industries have generally accepted markups over the cost of goods (for example, 100 percent in department stores; 200 percent for jewelry). You can also ask your suppliers how much other retailers typically mark up their goods. But be careful: There are some laws limiting suppliers from setting the final prices of their goods.

Find a balance

When it comes to budgeting for marketing, be conservative. Consider how much money you know you can afford to spend on marketing, and then ask yourself, "Which other business activities will I have to curtail to spend money on marketing?" Conversely, you should also ask yourself, "What will happen to my income if I *don't* spend sufficient funds on marketing?" There's always a trade-off; that's why it's important to create a marketing plan.

REAL-WORLD RECAP

Your pricing strategy

Be sure to do the following when developing your pricing strategy:

- Do your research
- Test the market
- Try different pricing models
- Offer a range of features and price points for your products or services

If you manufacture or produce goods or services to be sold by others, the reseller will set the final price for the end user. They, in turn, will base their prices, in large part, on what you charge them. If your costs to the reseller are too high, they won't make money and won't purchase from you. That's why it's critical to know what retailers typically sell similar products for and, if possible, what your competitors charge those same resellers.

Of course, when setting prices, you have to cover your costs *and* make a profit. And that's typically how manufacturers and others set prices. This "bottom-up" planning figures your costs for raw materials, labor, overhead, shipping, returns, and so on, and only then sets a reasonable figure for profit.

Your pricing strategy

Although pricing is a complex issue, using the following process when setting prices can help save you time, minimize pain, and get you to your optimal price point.

1. **Do your research.** You need to know what's happening in your market, and with your competitors, before you set your prices. Base prices on the assumption that your customers will comparison shop. If you sell leather lounge chairs wholesale, and most other leather lounge chair manufacturers sell in the $300–$700 wholesale range, you'll have a challenging time charging $2,000 wholesale.

2. **Test the market.** Don't take the existing pricing structure for granted, either. Especially when you're new, you should try to see what prices the market will bear. There might be a reason for you to charge four times as much as your nearest competitor—for example, the grade of leather you offer might be significantly higher, or your workmanship is such that people will gladly pay a premium. Of course, you most likely will need to target a slightly different customer.

3. **Try different pricing models.** Don't just assume that traditional means of pricing your products and services are your only options. For example, the innovative new payroll software you've written might sell better as an online service rather than as a for-purchase product.

4. **Offer a range of features and price points for your products or services.** Product segmentation is a good way to offer customers a range of prices on what are essentially the same products or services. For example, you could offer a base-model, factory-made bicycle for $200 and a hand-made aluminum bicycle for $1,000, but for one made of carbon fiber you might charge as much as $5,000.

Generally, as shown in the chart on the following page, three types of price levels motivate customers. Although some brilliant businesspeople have built great companies knowing how to maintain ultra-low prices or convince customers to pay ultra-premium prices, most businesses need to stick to the normal range.

PRICING LEVELS

PRICE LEVEL	CUSTOMER CHARACTERISTICS	BUSINESSES SUCH CUSTOMERS PATRONIZE	YOUR MARKETING EMPHASIS
Low Prices	Cost-sensitive; less concerned about service, prestige, product/service features, and even quality	Retailers such as Walmart; Internet sites offering rock-bottom prices	You are the "low-cost leader"
High or Premium Prices	Motivated when goods are priced high; question the quality of a lower-priced product or service	Upscale retailers such as Neiman Marcus or Bloomingdale's; small boutiques; high-end electronics retailers such as Bang & Olufsen	The quality and luxurious nature of your products and the elite stature of your current customers
Value Prices	Want the best return for their money; will pay more than a highly cost-conscious customer but expect to receive many benefits in return; won't pay premium prices just for status	Retailers such as Costco, Best Buy, and Target	The many benefits customers receive for a relatively affordable price

True Branding Comes from Within: Dove Beauty

challenge

Find a way to give a commodity product a distinct brand identity and personality

solution

Create a campaign featuring nonmodels to whom real women could relate

Dove is a brand of personal care products owned by the multinational firm Unilever. The products are sold in more than 25 countries, and although the brand has long been well recognized, its products—bar soap, cleansing cream, shampoo, and conditioner—are considered commodities. Dove had decades of marketing history promoting its soap as gentler for skin than ordinary soap, but in an extremely crowded and competitive market, the brand was losing ground. By launching an aggressive and revolutionary advertising campaign featuring "real women" rather than professional models, Dove was able to become the No. 1 cleansing brand and today is growing at more than 25 percent annually.[1]

When a product category is commoditized (meaning it's widely available and interchangeable with the same types of products from other companies), companies find it increasingly difficult to differentiate their products from their competitors' products, and are typically forced to compete on price alone. Given that Dove had always been marketed as a premium product with a higher price tag than competitive products, this created a significant problem for Unilever. One way to fight commoditization is to build a strong brand with a personal identity that transcends a product's actual function. This is what Unilever achieved with Dove, when, in 2004, it launched the Dove Campaign for Real Beauty.

The idea behind the campaign was to reject the unnatural, unattainable image of women typically featured in beauty advertisements. Rather than using waif-thin and seemingly perfect (and mostly Caucasian) professional models to market Dove's beauty products, Dove decided to feature a wide variety of women of different sizes, shapes, and ethnic types. The goal was to connect with the more than 95 percent of women who do not conform to the ideals established by the beauty industry and inspire them to feel comfortable in their own bodies and recognize that, as the powerful Dove slogan said, "true beauty comes from within."

The campaign was first launched in the United Kingdom (parent company Unilever is a British-Dutch company). The women photographed were recruited in a variety of ways. Some were approached on the street; others answered advertisements in local newspapers. Rankin, a noted British portrait and fashion photographer, was chosen as art director because of his worldwide reputation for photographing unconventional models and for bringing out his subjects' personality. As part of the series, Dove paid for billboard ads asking people viewing them to dial a toll-free number and vote on whether the woman on the billboard was "fat" or "fab," with the votes shown in real-time on the board.

---

1. "The Dove Campaign for Real Beauty, A Case Study," by Olivia Falcione and Laura Henderson. *Public Relations Problems and Cases*. March 1, 2009.

The campaign immediately garnered huge press around the world. The "models" in the campaign became celebrities in their own right, and Dove prompted animated discussions—still ongoing—about the unreachable standards set by the beauty industry.

More important, from a sales standpoint, "real women" apparently appreciated the message the Dove campaign was spreading: that beauty comes in all forms. Sales of Dove products for women soared. With the campaign, Dove effectively established a strong brand identity that allowed it to keep its margins high in a fiercely competitive niche.

Finding that its marketing campaign had turned into a social cause worth championing on a larger scale, in 2006 Dove started the Dove Self-Esteem Fund, dedicated to changing the conventional view of beauty for contemporary women from thin, starved-looking models with "perfect" features to women with larger or different-shaped bodies who still feel confident about their looks. To promote the Dove Self-Esteem Fund, Dove produced a series of online short films about women's and girls' self-esteem. These award-winning films included *Daughters,* which was broadcast during SuperBowl XL; *Evolution,* which won two Cannes Lions Grand Prix awards; *Onslaught;* and *Amy.*

The campaign has not lacked controversy. In 2005, Dove introduced a new line of "firming crèmes" that were advertised as reducing fat and cellulite from women's thighs. Although Dove still received kudos for portraying women who wouldn't conventionally be thought beautiful, a media outcry arose about the conflicting message being sent. As one media critic wrote, "Dove's attempts are profoundly limited by a product line that comes with its own underlying philosophy: cellulite is unsightly, women's natural aging process is shameful, and flabby thighs are flawed and must be fixed … oh, so conveniently by Dove's newest lotion."[2]

Yet even these reactions simply proved the point that "no publicity is bad publicity." To say that the campaign has strengthened the brand would be an understatement. Dove has adopted a slogan, "Real women have curves," and uses quotes from its real-world models on its website and in its ads to reinforce the message. Model Shanel Lu says, "I love the thought of being a part of an ad that would potentially touch many young girls to tell them that it is all right to be unique and everyone is beautiful in their own skin." Lindsey Stokes, another Dove model, agreed, saying, "Young girls need to see real women like themselves in print ads or on TV."

Perhaps the biggest sign that Dove's marketing is working is that *other* beauty brands are adopting the "real woman" mantra. Revlon, for example, which for years had only used celebrity models, searched for a nonmodel to be the face of its Age Defying makeup. If imitation is the highest form of flattery, Dove marketers should feel immensely flattered. ■

questions

1. The Dove Real Beauty campaign used a unique message to successfully market its products. But beneath that message was the effective understanding of basic marketing fundamentals. What are those fundamentals?

2. As a result of its Real Beauty marketing campaign, Dove's sales soared and it attracted many new customers. What can the company do to retain these customers?

3. If a brand is a promise, what does the Dove brand promise its customers?

4. What can a company that sells services, rather than commodities, take away from Dove's experience?

2. "Dove's Real Beauty Backlash," by Jennifer Pozner. *Bitch: Feminist Response to Pop Culture.* Issue 30, Fall 2005.

BRUSH UP YOUR MARKETING

Goal:

Create an advertising campaign that will give your commoditized product a distinct identity and personality.

What to Do:

Either working alone or in groups, consider yourself a manufacturer of toothbrushes. Although your products have some special design features that you claim make for more effective brushing, your product category has been almost completely commoditized for many years. You want to figure out a way to differentiate your brand with a distinctive identity and voice.

1. First, create "personas" for different types of consumers you might target. Create at least four different "personas" that specify the following:

    a. Their particular characteristics or niche (for example, Francesca Fashionista; Dan Daddy; Ricky Retired)

    b. Their biggest concern about oral hygiene and toothbrushes (for example, Francesca wants a brilliant white smile; Dan wants toothbrushes his kids will actually use; Ricky wants to avoid high dental bills)

    c. The price sensitivities of each persona

    d. Other likely purchasing considerations for each persona

2. Discuss the types of advertising campaign you'd use to appeal to one or more of your personas—how you would try to position your brand, where and how you might advertise, and so on.

3. Come up with an ad tagline for at least one persona. Create a slogan that would appeal to one or more of your personas.

4. Present your marketing ideas. Be prepared to explain your reasons and why you think your ad campaign will be successful.

CHAPTER

10 Marketing Tactics

learning objectives

In this chapter, you'll learn how to:

- Describe and define the various types of marketing vehicles
- Conduct successful marketing campaigns for print, TV, and radio
- Develop and execute effective online and mobile marketing strategies
- Apply search engine optimization (SEO) and search engine marketing (SEM) to a company's online presence in order to boost search results
- Conduct a compelling social media marketing campaign
- Determine how and when to use daily deal sites
- Develop and execute effective email newsletter campaigns
- Reinforce marketing messages through marketing collateral
- Conduct successful networking through industry associations, trade shows, public relations, and word-of-mouth marketing
- Establish customer loyalty programs that boost sales
- Apply other marketing techniques such as in-store marketing, product placement, and community- and cause-related marketing

Leading marketing tactics

- **Print, radio, and TV advertising**
- **Digital marketing through websites, search, and mobile**
- **Public relations**
- **Marketing collateral materials**
- **Direct mail**
- **Coupons and daily deals**
- **Face-to-face networking**
- **Trade shows**
- **Public speaking**
- **Newsletters**
- **Sampling**
- **Sponsorships**
- **Viral marketing**
- **Product placement**

Which Marketing Vehicles?

Once you have devised an effective marketing message, how will you get that message out and make sure it reaches the right audience? You need to find the right vehicles or tactics to spread it. This means choosing the right places to put your message—the places where the customers you want to reach will see it, hear it, or watch it. Moreover, you want to put your message in those places at a time when potential customers will actually pay attention and then, ideally, take actions that result in sales.

But what forms will your messages take? Ads on a website or a search engine or YouTube? Billboards along a freeway? Commercials on the sports radio station? Coupons in the local newspaper? Perhaps direct mail sent to prospects' homes?

Making the right choices is a challenge. Many entrepreneurs spend a great deal of money experimenting before they find the right marketing vehicles for their businesses. And they won't use just one. Most companies use a number of different vehicles simultaneously.

An almost unlimited range of techniques can be used to market to customers, and an equally wide range of costs is associated with those efforts. Some of these techniques are familiar, such as advertising in print, radio, or TV. Some involve digital marketing—on the Internet or on mobile devices.

Many face-to-face marketing activities, such as exhibiting at trade shows or offering samples, are designed not only to make sales but also to increase word-of-mouth awareness.

Before committing a large sum of money to any one of the marketing options available to entrepreneurial companies like yours, be sure to thoroughly explore your choices.

Print, TV, and Radio Advertising

One of the most long-standing types of marketing is advertising in newspapers, magazines, radio, and TV—in other words, in traditional, what some might think of as "old-fashioned," media. But just because this form of advertising has

en·tre·pre·neur·ship key terms

Call to action
The part of an ad that indicates how you would like the reader, viewer, or listener to respond—what you'd like them to do. "Call now," "Visit our new showroom," and "Try it today" are all examples of calls to action.

Click through
When potential customers searching online click on an ad that appears alongside their search results, they "click through" the ad. Similarly, in email newsletters, click-throughs refer to the links that readers clicked on.

Elevator pitch
A concise summary of a company's service, business, or product idea that can be delivered in a very short time.

Guerilla marketing
No-cost or low-cost marketing strategies, typically involving grassroots and local activities.

Hook
Something that catches the attention or interest of a journalist, reader, listener, viewer, or website visitor. An angle that entices the media to cover your story or prospective customers to pay attention to your ad or story.

Loss leaders
Offering products or services for less than or little more than they actually cost, in order to get customers in the door. The goal of loss leaders is to up-sell customers or encourage them to purchase more profitable products or services.

Marketing collateral
Printed marketing materials used to support a company's marketing efforts. Marketing collateral describes a company, product, or service; these materials include brochures, catalogs, and product information sheets.

Media kit
A collection of materials provided by a media outlet, website, or other location for advertising. The kit gives detailed information about its advertising options, including types of ads, rates, special sections and opportunities, and the number and demographics of its audience. The term also describes the collection of background materials a business provides to the media about the company.

Media outlet
A term used to describe a particular newspaper, magazine, radio or TV station, website, mobile content site, or other press, media, or content option.

Reach
The number of readers, listeners, or viewers served by a media outlet (used mostly for radio and TV).

Search engine marketing (SEM)
Marketing that involves paying for prominent placement on a search engine's results page, based on the keyword used to search.

Search engine optimization (SEO)
Marketing that involves improving your search engine result rankings through a variety of measures, such as strategically placing keywords on your site and encouraging other sites to link to you.

Viral marketing
Marketing approaches that inspire one person to share information with others—spreading the message like a physical virus.

Designing a great print ad

Elements that help make an ad work include:

- A catchy headline that hooks the reader
- A focus on an immediate benefit to the customer
- What makes you unique
- Crisp, concise, compelling copy
- Easy-to-read typeface (font)
- Eye-catching photos or graphics
- A call to action
- A compelling incentive for your customer to act quickly
- Clear, easy-to-find contact info
- White space

been around for a long time doesn't mean it should be dismissed. It has stuck around for a reason: *It works.* This kind of media advertising is effective at reaching both a large mainstream audience (think of the **reach** of a Super Bowl commercial, for example) and a highly targeted selection of consumers (for instance, an ad in a magazine for men who like watches—and yes, such magazines exist).

Traditional media advertising puts your company, product, or service in front of prospective customers while they're reading the news, listening to a talk show, or watching their favorite sports on TV or cable. It can also bring your message to a specific group as they read a magazine or watch a show about their hobby, profession, industry, or special interest.

To advertise effectively in these traditional venues, you need to find out which media attract the attention of your target market—that is, what sections of the newspaper they read, what magazines they subscribe to, what radio stations and programs they listen to, and what channels their TVs are tuned to—and then present your message there as often as your company can afford. To help you figure all of this out, be sure to request **media kits** from the media you're considering advertising with.

Repetition, repetition, repetition

Advertising experts agree: You must advertise frequently—using the same message in the same **media outlet**—for your ad to succeed. While research varies on how many exposures a person must receive before acting on an ad, all the studies are clear: Hearing or seeing something just once doesn't make an impression. Various studies indicate that an ad must be seen or heard at least seven to 10 times before someone will recall it. That's just recall—it takes even longer before someone acts on an ad and answers your **call to action**.

Think of it this way: Say you're at a party where you meet dozens of new people. Even after you've been introduced to all of them, how many names will you remember? Who'll stand out? Chances are, unless a particular person is absolutely fascinating or drop-dead gorgeous, you probably won't remember them. On the other hand, think about the people you see over and over—at your office, at school, or around the neighborhood. You'll soon remember not only their names, but also their faces and personalities and a lot more about them. Repetition leads to remembering.

Advertising works similarly. Media venues are like big parties, and the ads are the guests. If you see or hear an ad only once, you're probably not going to remember much about it—what it said (its message and **hook**), who said it (what company placed it), or what it was trying to sell. But if you see an ad every day or hear it every 10 minutes during your favorite program, you're much more likely to absorb the message (even if you don't like, agree with, or care about it).

Advertising in print

Advertising in print—in newspapers, magazines, or newsletters—is a time-honored method of marketing. Benefits of print advertising include:

- **Shelf life.** A radio or TV ad lasts for a minute or less, and then is gone. A print publication, by contrast, can stay around for days, weeks, even months, offering more opportunities for a customer to see an ad.

- **Pass-along readership.** People share print publications with others, who may also be your target customers. "Pass-along readers" expand an ad's reach and increase your exposure.

- **More specific audience.** In general, it's easier to target your customer using print publications. This is particularly true if you advertise in magazines geared toward readers with special interests (like fashion, yoga, or home improvement) or those with "controlled circulation," which are distributed only to a highly targeted list of readers (such as doctors, executives, or human resources professionals).

Advertising on radio

Like magazines, radio stations cater to specific audience segments—usually in particular geographical areas—and tailor their content to reach them. This makes them ideal for reaching targeted groups in targeted locations. Whether your potential customers are married white-collar workers in your city between the ages of 25 and 45, young Hispanics, or local retirees with second homes, there's likely a radio station where you can find them. Radio stations know exactly who their listeners are (their business depends on it!), and they are eager to share this information with potential advertisers.

Radio offers some distinct advantages over print and TV advertising. The main one is that messages are broadcast to a semicaptive audience, primarily people in cars. When someone is driving, they're less likely to change stations when commercials come on. TV watchers, in contrast, channel surf or wander to the kitchen for a snack during the commercials, or even record shows and skip the commercials entirely on playback. Print has a similar downside: People only peruse the ads that interest them and skip the rest. Other benefits of advertising on radio include the following:

- Radio is typically the last media your customers come into contact with before making a retail purchase, since ads reach them while they're driving—on the way to or in the vicinity of a store.

- Radio is targeted and segmented. Young urban listeners will tune into very different stations than people over 60. Because it caters to well-defined niches, radio is a good medium for reaching a specific target market.

- Radio can be a very effective way to promote a product or service that doesn't require too much description, because listeners already know what it is. Everyone understands what dentists, print shops, and restaurants

Choosing a media outlet

Media kits from the various publications, radio stations, and TV channels you think your target market is interested in will help you determine where to advertise. You can often find an outlet's media kit online: Look for a link on its website with a name like "To Advertise."

Media kits not only list the specifics of their advertising options (such as costs and sizes on a rate card), they also describe the audience demographics, sometimes including detailed information such as percentage of audience by zip code, job title, ethnicity, or particular interests. Your ads will be most effective when you make the right match between what you are promoting and who you're promoting it to. Media kits can assist you in making this match.

"This program is brought to you by..."

In many communities, the local public radio or TV station can be a good, relatively inexpensive choice for reaching a particular segment of the community (say, businesspeople, well-educated, or high-income).

These stations do not accept ads, but they do accept program sponsorships (or "underwriting opportunities"). With a sponsorship, you can get the name of your company, and often the location, website, or other identifying information, mentioned at the time of the program.

Although the nature and content of your "ad" is very limited with a sponsorship, if you fund a popular program over a long period, your business name can become quite familiar to this target audience.

provide. These kinds of businesses can use the radio time to focus on the specific benefits they offer and what distinguishes them from others in their markets.

■ Radio listeners are often fiercely loyal, keeping their dials locked on a particular station, so if you find one that appeals to your target market, it will give you many opportunities to reach them and repeat your message over and over.

■ Since radio broadcasts to a limited geographical range, it's ideal for reaching potential customers if your company relies on business from your local area.

Advertising on TV

People tend to remember TV ads because they tap into two senses—sight and hearing. You can show and tell, reinforcing your brand message on two levels. What's more, your potential customers can hear your message even if they're not in the room with the TV, and can see it even if the volume is off for a moment. A good TV ad campaign can put your product or service on the map for your target audience. TV's other benefits include the following:

■ It enables you to show how a product or service works. You can demonstrate how it will make life easier, or simply better, for your potential customer.

■ TV advertising reaches customers right in their living rooms, bedrooms, and other areas of the home where there's a TV, and where they're usually relaxed. In most cases, they're on their home turf, where they have easy access to a pen and paper to write down contact information if they're interested in what you're selling.

■ Unlike a newspaper ad, your TV ad isn't competing for viewer's attention with several other ads on a page. People only see one TV ad at a time.

■ Appearing on TV gives your business credibility. Being on the medium raises your status because it puts you on the same plane as huge national advertisers (even if you're only paying local rates). That's why many businesses include the phrase "As Seen on TV" in their print ads and other marketing materials.

■ Based on station range and programming, TV ads enable you to target a range of geographic audiences. This runs the gamut from small local populations to larger, more mainstream national audiences. You can also target customers by interest, based on what shows they're watching.

WHERE SHOULD I PLACE MY AD?

After you've decided to advertise on television, you need to figure out where to place your commercial. You can either broadcast (advertise to a large and diverse group of consumers) or narrowcast (focus in on a specific market niche). But remember, you pay for ads based on how many people the ads reach, so you don't want to spend money reaching lots of people who are unlikely to ever become your customers. You want to find the most affordable way to reach the people who have the potential to become your customers.

Monitoring the effectiveness of traditional advertising

Once your ad is up and running, besides comparing your sales figures during an advertising campaign to your sales during periods when you didn't advertise, measuring the results of traditional advertising can be difficult.

You can, though, track a print ad in which you've placed a coupon with a code specific to each publication. When customers present the coupons, you'll know exactly where they found the ads. You can use a similar system with radio and TV ads by asking customers to mention a particular word or phrase to get a discount on a product or service. Informal test campaigns are another option. One month, try an ad in one media outlet; the next month, try a different one. Or test various placements and ad styles (for print publications) or different times of day (for TV or radio) and observe how these changes affect your sales and prospect inquiries.

Media companies will often conduct surveys to see whether viewers, readers, or listeners remember advertising campaigns.

It can be terribly frustrating to not have hard, immediate numbers to determine whether prospects are responding to a traditional advertising campaign. While online, you can get far more data on how many clicks you're getting for an online ad and from what sources. The lack of hard, real-time analytics—or reliable quantitative data on performance as it happens—is one of the main reasons that many companies have turned away from traditional advertising.

Nevertheless, evidence of the effectiveness of traditional advertising is overwhelming. Some of the most successful companies—including technology companies—build brands and launch and sell products by relying heavily on traditional advertising. Apple, for example, built the success of the iPod and iPhone with massive traditional advertising campaigns.

Online Marketing

The online world—connected to the Internet whether on a computer, tablet, or other mobile device—has dramatically changed the field of marketing. Most marketers consider digital marketing approaches essential when trying to make customers aware of their product or service and motivate them to purchase.

Online marketing has remade the world of advertising. Primarily, it's because that's where the people—and the eyeballs—are. Prospective customers can instantly turn to mobile or Web search instead of finding and then paging through print directories such as the Yellow Pages.

But online marketing also offers other benefits. One of the primary benefits is that, in many cases, it can be highly targeted. Ads served up alongside

Banner ads

These types of ads appear on the top, sides, bottom, or elsewhere on the Web pages of companies other than yours. You typically place banner ads on a website with the right "readership" for your product or service. Thus, if you sell tennis rackets, you'd probably want to advertise on www.tennis.com rather than www.baseball.com.

What to put on your website

Your website should contain *at least* the following standard sections:

- Home page
- Overview of products and services
- About the company
- Contact information
- Privacy policy

someone's Facebook page can be geared to that individual's specific demographics, local interests, and past purchases, as an example.

Another highly desirable feature of online marketing is that it provides in-depth analytics in real-time. If you run ads on search engines, you can see exactly how many clicks you're getting and where those clicks are coming from. You can change the wording and immediately see how well those changes perform.

There's no question that a large portion—if not *the* largest portion—of your marketing budget will be spent on online marketing efforts. You have a wide range of digital marketing options to choose from, and you'll almost certainly want to mix your online marketing efforts with traditional advertising and offline, in-person marketing activities as well.

Websites

Every business needs a website. Even if you never sell anything directly online, you still need a website for marketing purposes. Your website serves as the public face of your company. It provides customers and prospects with a way to interact with and learn about your company. And it helps determine whether they'll trust you enough to take the next step and actually do business with you.

Prospects and customers expect to find you online. They want to check out your company's products and services, background, clients or customers, and more. They also want to make sure you're legitimate and learn a bit more about the people behind your organization.

A website:

- Builds your brand

- Provides credibility

- Motivates and encourages prospects to buy

- Provides basic information about your company and business

- Allows you to present detailed information about your products or services

A particularly good website can also give you an edge over your competitors, making you look more professional, established, and capable than others.

WEBSITE ESSENTIALS

Getting a website up and running can be either an easy task, involving just a little time and money, or an enormous undertaking, requiring months of work and many thousands of dollars, perhaps tens of thousands. It all depends on how big and complicated a site you want, how much interactivity you want and need, whether your site must be able to support ecommerce capabilities, and, more important, whether you create a custom site or instead use templates and services that devise turnkey solutions.

Companies providing turnkey solutions for websites often include everything from domain registration to hosting, design templates, a menu of website services (for example, ecommerce or electronic "shopping carts"), standard forms, and, sometimes, customized programming. These make launching a website relatively easy and inexpensive.

Whether you set up an elaborate ecommerce site, or a simple four-page site that merely gives a brief overview of your company and products, remember that your website is first and foremost a marketing vehicle for your company. (There are exceptions, such as when you build an internal website for employees only, but you still need a public-facing website.)

As a marketing vehicle, your website must help establish and extend your brand, create connections with customers and prospects, and assist in telling the story of the benefits of your products and services. Remember, a large percentage of users will access your website on mobile devices, such as smartphones. So make sure your website is mobile friendly or that you develop a mobile version of it.

Of course, you may have many other goals with your website—such as making sales, processing customer service requests, creating community with your customers, and so forth. But such robust websites are not necessary to get your name and message out there. Don't wait until you can have precisely the "perfect" website or have the budget for robust features to get your website up and running.

SEO AND SEM

Build your website, and they will come, right? Not necessarily. For starters, how will people know you even *have* a website and that it contains something they're interested in? Sure, you'll do everything possible offline to direct people to your website—put its address on your business cards, brochures, ads, and so on—but the people in the best position to visit your website immediately are already online. So how do you get them to notice you? One of the best ways is by making sure your site is easy to find via search engines—Google, Yahoo!, and Bing, for example.

For the vast majority of online users, search engines serve as the main gateway to information on the Web. This means that if your website is highly visible in the results that appear when someone types in a keyword or phrase associated with your type of business, there's a decent chance that person will click on over to your website. There are two primary ways to ensure that your website is highly visible on search engines.

SEO: Search engine optimization (SEO) is the process of trying to design your website and the words on it so that it appears naturally in the top results when someone types a keyword into a search engine. With SEO, you don't pay search engines to have your site appear high on results pages. SEO is often referred to as *organic* search.

Let's go over this one more time...

The key to any successful marketing campaign is repetition, repetition, repetition. Remember: It takes multiple exposures for your message to be absorbed by its intended recipients—and even longer to build a brand. This means that you must choose a few tactics that you can employ repeatedly, aimed at the same market, rather than adopt a scattershot approach in which you try one tactic after another on different audiences.

Your Website Checklist

Check off and describe the elements you plan to include on your business website, noting what you want each section to include or say:

☐ Home page: _____

☐ Overview of products/services: _____

☐ About your company: _____

☐ Contact info: _____

☐ Privacy policy: _____

☐ Relevant content: _____

☐ Media/Press section: _____

☐ Testimonials/Awards/Client lists: _____

☐ Newsletter sign-up: _____

☐ Samples/Demos: _____

☐ Catalog: _____

☐ User-generated content: _____

☐ Customer service info and/or forms: _____

☐ FAQs: _____

☐ Site map/Search box: _____

☐ Investor information: _____

☐ Enhanced visuals or sound: _____

☐ Other: _____

SEO is an art *and* a science, based on secret algorithms from the search engines. It's unlikely that you will master it on your own to make your site consistently appear at the top of unpaid search results. Nevertheless, you should understand at least the basics of SEO to ensure that your site shows up, over time.

The first thing you need to do is figure out which words your target customers will most likely use when searching for the types of products or services (or content) you offer. Once you've determined that, repeat those keywords throughout your site—in your content, headlines, page names, and more.

Imagine, for instance, that you own a company that creates and sells educational software parents use to help teach their kids math. There are lots of terms you'd expect searchers to use when looking for products like yours— and these are the terms you'd use when developing your site's content, regardless of whether you were considering SEO: terms such as "software," "educational software," "math software," and even "kids software."

These, though, are all rather broad terms—that is, lots of companies sell math software or educational software. This means your site is unlikely to show up high in natural search results based on those keywords because millions (yes, millions) of other sites are also using them. Instead, you'd be better off focusing on keywords that are more specific to your products—so in the case of that educational software company, something like "kids math software" used over and over would yield better results.

And since these keywords need to be peppered throughout your site if a search engine is to list it high in its results, you need to have SEO in mind right from the start as you develop and update your site.

SEM: By contrast, **search engine marketing (SEM)** refers to the process of paying search engine companies to ensure that your website (or specific pages of it) appears in users' search results—typically either at the top or in a column that appears beside other, nonpaid results. This is also referred to as search engine advertising, paid placement, paid search, or sponsored listings.

Here's how SEM works: Advertisers choose the keywords that they think searchers will most likely use when looking for products, services, and content similar to theirs. Then, when the customer enters into a search engine one of the keywords that advertiser has purchased, a small ad appears either above or near the list of naturally generated search results. Most such ads consist of just simple text, often indistinguishable from the actual search results except for their placement on the page or a faint background color. These ads are quite small—usually just a headline, followed by 10 words or so, plus an inviting link to a website or a page within a website.

SEM has proven to be an extremely effective advertising medium for two primary reasons:

- **Highly qualified prospects.** Searchers are often highly qualified prospects—especially for the most narrowly defined terms. For instance,

Choosing keywords

Critical to success in both search engine optimization and search engine marketing is choosing the best keywords—the ones most likely to be searched on by the largest number of users (who also happen to be the most likely buyers). Here are two tools to help you with the task:

- Wordtracker (www.wordtracker.com). The site offers a free trial.

- Google's Keyword Tool (https://adwords.google.com/select/KeywordToolExternal). You can either enter keywords or have the tool evaluate your site's content and suggest keywords.

if someone types in the term "bike repair San Francisco," there's a good chance they're in Northern California with an immediate need to get their bicycle fixed.

- **Effectiveness of pay per click (PPC).** Another reason that SEM is so popular is that advertisers pay only when a searcher clicks on their ads (called a **click through**). Advertisers do not pay simply for having their ad displayed—and this fact distinguishes PPC advertising from virtually every other type. If you run an ad for your bike repair shop in the newspaper or the Yellow Pages, for example, you'll pay the same amount for that ad no matter how many people actually see it. You may get zero response, but you'll still have to pay. With PPC, you pay only for each click-through to your site that a prospect makes.

Social media marketing

Facebook. Twitter. LinkedIn. YouTube. Blogger. Pinterest. The digital world is a connected world, and is forever expanding. A huge number of people are constantly attached to the Web, their phones, and each other. And as any good marketer will tell you, any time millions of people are connected, a marketing opportunity exists.

Where once social media sites were designed merely to enable individuals to share their interests and opinions, they're now also vehicles for promoting products and services. Many opportunities abound—whether you pay for ads in social media sites or you actively use social media efforts to make your business more visible and create connections to your target market.

One of the first things you need to determine is which social media platforms best suit your target market. Are you trying to reach consumers or businesses? Does a mass-market site (Facebook, Twitter, YouTube), a special interest site (such as Chowhound for food), or a professional networking site (like LinkedIn) suit your offerings? Before launching a social media campaign on a given site, be certain that its audience is truly interested in your offerings.

Once you've identified the most appropriate social media sites, the key to your marketing campaign's success will be providing content that appeals to your target audience. Social media can be a powerful tool for getting a message out fast. If you can capture the attention of an audience with something clever, controversial, or timely, you may be able to generate a powerful **viral marketing** campaign.

Like anything else in your business, social media marketing requires both a strategy and time to execute successfully.

BLOGS

Blogs, short for "Web logs," are frequently updated online journals that can contain text, audio, video, graphics, and photos. From a marketing perspective, blogs work well for businesses in which expertise is valued—for consultants, technology service providers, professional service businesses, and so on.

Whether you create your own blog or regularly contribute to a popular blog in your field, your blogging efforts can greatly enhance your visibility and credibility. If you offer readers something of value (beyond a sales message), it's likely you'll attract people looking for your services or products.

Effective use of blogs can:

- Build name and brand recognition

- Establish you as an expert

- Attract customers and clients

- Create links to your website

- Generate buzz around a new product

- Tap into a committed market

Use social media sites to:

- Spread the word and create buzz about your products or services

- Advertise with campaigns designed to target your specific audience

- Create your own group or community to get feedback from customers

- Build referral sources and networking connections

- Engage more deeply with prospects and customers

- Enhance your credibility by contributing meaningful content to others' sites or posting positive recommendations or reviews

OTHER ONLINE SOCIAL MEDIA MARKETING TACTICS

Creating your own podcast—a radio or TV program that gets downloaded to computers and mobile devices—might be a good option if you have compelling content on the most popular podcast topics: technology, politics, and business. What about a video? While YouTube is the best known of the video-sharing sites, many others are out there, and some of them focus on "how-to" videos, possibly providing a perfect opportunity to showcase your expertise.

Review and community sites give users the opportunity to rate and post comments about the products, services, and companies they use. Examples of these sites are Yelp.com, Angie's List, and Epinions.com. Their comments and reviews can be powerful marketing tools for your business—or they can result in turning prospects away. If your business is consumer oriented, make sure you manage your reputation on such review sites by encouraging satisfied customers to post reviews and by responding to complaints and concerns posted by dissatisfied customers.

CHOOSING A SOCIAL MEDIA MARKETING STRATEGY

With so many interactive online marketing tools to consider, how do you choose the right one for you?

- **Make sure your target market actually participates in these online activities.** Closely follow the LinkedIn groups or Facebook pages, read the blogs, listen to the podcasts, and participate in the community before you decide to spend a great deal of time and money on any particular site.

- **Determine whether you have the time for "unpaid" social media.** Are you willing to develop and maintain an active online presence? If you lack the time, then pay for ads—they can be persistent even when *you* can't.

Don't overdo the deals

Place a cap on the number of deals sold—an absolute must—and start with a small number. Make sure your staff still has time to serve customers paying regular rates and can handle the increased demand.

- **Understand that online activities can come with pitfalls.** Most notably, dissatisfied customers may make unfavorable comments—not all of them even fair or honest—about your products, services, or customer service.

- **Keep experimenting.** Because the Internet is a fast-moving medium, you can quickly adapt marketing strategies to find the approaches that work best for you. And new social networks develop continually.

Daily deals

The prospect of getting a bargain has driven the phenomenal success of daily deal sites such as Groupon, Living Social, and hundreds of others. For some companies, these offers are invaluable business builders. Other companies, which have lost money and attracted only bargain-hunting customers, have rued the day they ever signed up.

A deal site sends an email daily to those who've registered. People interested in your discounted product or service purchase your deal. You typically pay nothing to be included, but the deal site gets a hefty piece of the sale: 30 percent to 50 percent. And typically, you must offer at least a 50 percent discount. So if your business creates custom photo books using images your customers upload to your site, here's what a money breakdown might look like: You offer your $40 leather-bound photo book for $20. With each sale, you get $10; the site gets $10. Those who never redeem the coupon add to your profit margin: Businesses report 5 percent to 40 percent nonredemption rates.

Deals are best offered to launch a new business or get your name out there, for slow or off-season periods to drive new traffic, and to move excess or last season's inventory.

If you're considering offering a daily deal, keep these 10 strategies in mind:

1. Offer services, rather than products. It's generally far less costly since you won't have the cost of goods.

2. To help build a committed customer base, create offers for which customers must come back repeatedly ("your third visit free"; "four manicures for $99"; and the like).

3. Try not to cannibalize existing customers. Craft deals that are more likely to appeal to new customers.

4. Experiment with different offers and several sites to determine what works for you. A more targeted site may be a better fit and less costly than a general, national one.

5. Include your own fine print. Limit redemption to "only one per customer," "not to be combined with other discounts," and other restrictions that make sense to protect you.

6. Avoid sites that require you to deal with them exclusively. Some sites affect your ability to offer deals on other sites; limit your involvement with those.

7. Understand the fees and terms. Make sure you know about all other fees. Some sites charge credit-card processing fees; others may pay you slowly or in long-drawn-out installments.

8. Build your marketing list. Look for sites that give you a list of those who've bought the deal. Some sites give you only an identification number. Others will give you names and email addresses—enabling you to keep marketing to those prospects.

9. Do everything you can to ask for and capture contact information from new customers so you can continue to market beyond the deal or coupon.

10. Negotiate with deal sites. And negotiate hard. There are lots of daily deal sites. Most important, know what works best for you and for your business. Don't let salespeople pressure you.

Keep your expectations realistic. And remember, these sites are more of a marketing tactic than a way to make quick sales. They are a good example of **loss leaders**—offering a product or service at or below cost so as to bring people through your doors.

Email newsletters

Newsletters sent as email offer an extremely effective way to build your business and stay in front of your customers and prospects. They also have the advantage of being fast, easy, and inexpensive to produce.

In an email newsletter, you can include information and tips your customers can use, short articles, business updates, special announcements, or coupons and special offers. For most businesses, avoid filling your newsletter solely with sales information about your products and services—instead, provide recipients with some benefit for opening your email. That way, they're more likely to open the next one you send. If, however, your business strictly sells products, then "news" of discounts, sales, and new products may be all the benefit your customers look for.

Heed a word of caution about all email marketing: Be careful not to abuse it. Send email *only* to those who've signed up to receive email from you or have had some dealings with you (including giving you their business card), otherwise you may be breaking the law. Limit the frequency of your messages; generally once or twice a month is enough for an email newsletter. Try to use a compelling "Subject" line to increase the chance that people will open and read your email. And make sure your mailings are meaningful, valuable, and free of offensive content or language. If not, recipients will soon block your email as spam, and if enough people do that, email filters will block your messages to many larger servers.

Mobile marketing

Mobile devices have transformed the way customers deal with local businesses. How long has it been since you used your smartphone to find a business? To

E-newsletters made easy

Many companies provide easy-to-use, turnkey online email newsletter services to help you create and send email newsletters in a snap. Here's a short list of some:

- AWeber:
  www.aweber.com
- Campaign Monitor:
  www.campaignmonitor.com
- Constant Contact:
  www.constantcontact.com
- Emma:
  www.myemma.com
- JangoMail:
  www.jangomail.com
- MailChimp:
  www.mailchimp.com
- Vertical Response:
  www.verticalresponse.com

reserve a table at a restaurant? To get directions? Likely, not long. Most of us use mobile devices to shop. That's a *lot* of people looking for businesses on their mobile devices. Depending on the type of entrepreneurial venture you launch—mobile marketing is especially well-suited to local businesses that deal with consumers—you'll want to take advantage of mobile marketing.

You don't have to develop a gee-whiz app or use every mobile method available in order to reach the increasing number of people searching for businesses like yours on their mobile devices. You do, however, need a mobile version of your website.

Most of the following mobile marketing techniques are easy, and often free.

- **Get found.** "Claim" your business for free on sites such as Yelp, Bing, Yahoo! Local, Google Places, and Foursquare. When someone in your area looks for a business like yours, you'll show up in the search results.

- **Offer coupons and deals.** Like adding your listing, this is also free and easy to do. You simply add a coupon to the sites listed above. You can also use business-oriented applications especially designed to present coupons to customers based on location, such as Yowza (getyowza.com), CouponSherpa (couponsherpa.com), or DealChicken (dealchicken.com), as well as daily deal sites like Groupon or LivingSocial.

- **Build relationships with customers.** Do this through social media sites such as Facebook or Twitter. More-powerful customer connection programs, like RewardMe, enable customers to receive rewards for coming back to you repeatedly.

- **Display your location, hours, and main products or services.** Make sure your home page has the most critical information in highly readable type—large fonts and dark print on a light or white background—that doesn't require typing or moving away from the home page.

- **Accept payment.** In many mobile service businesses, such as plumbing and contracting, you can accept payment right on your cell phone. Services like Square (squareup.com), Intuit GoPayment (gopayment.com), or PayPal Here (paypal.com) provide credit card swipers that attach to your cell phone. They keep a percentage of every charge processed, but you get paid on the spot.

Marketing Collateral

While you can choose from myriad digital, broadcast, and unique marketing methods, don't forget good old-fashioned print. Words on paper still have surprisingly strong power to get customers to act.

Print marketing materials are the face of your business on paper. Even in a day and age when virtually everyone depends on electronic information, printed materials continue to play an important role in your marketing plans and efforts. You'll give business cards to people you meet at networking events, catalogs to clients during sales calls, and brochures to prospects at trade shows. You may send direct mail marketing pieces to leads, hoping to persuade them to buy what you're selling. In whatever way you use them, print marketing materials help deliver or reinforce your marketing message, attract prospects, and, ultimately, make sales.

Also called **marketing collateral**, print marketing materials include almost any piece of ink-on-paper material you use to promote your business, such as:

- Business cards
- Brochures
- Catalogs
- Flyers
- Postcards
- Sales sheets, product specification sheets, and price lists
- Newsletters
- Direct mail

Networking

People like doing business with people they know. So the more people you know—and the more people who know what business you're in—the more potential customers and referral sources you have. One way to make these contacts is through the process of networking. When you network, you seek out and interact with people gathered for the purpose of building their businesses. Networking usually takes place at a venue such as a meeting, conference, or other event, and involves a *mutually* beneficial exchange of goods and services or information. The best and strongest networks are created by professionals who respect the reciprocal nature of doing business.

If you choose your networking opportunity well, you'll come into contact with people who can help you strengthen your business by:

- Buying what you sell
- Connecting you with others who will buy what you sell
- Providing a product or service you need
- Partnering with you in some aspect of your business venture
- Providing you with useful information about an industry or market

A relatively affordable marketing method, networking generally involves participating in activities such as industry conferences, or groups like a local chamber of commerce or chapter of an industry association. Every community has its share of organizations. Types of groups you can join include:

What a trade show can do for you

At the right trade show, with the right approach, you can:

- Land a big customer
- Launch a new product
- Develop a mailing list of hot leads
- Find a strategic partner
- Enhance relationships with your existing customers
- Learn about new trends and developments in your field
- Find out what your competitors are up to

Consumer shows

Besides real trade shows for industry professionals, in many larger cities there may be "trade shows" that are actually for consumers. These may be food and wine shows, fashion shows, electronics or tech shows, and the like. Assess the cost and worth of such shows on the basis of actual sales you'll likely make, rather than on marketing.

- **Entrepreneurs groups.** You're likely to find lots of entrepreneurs groups, both formal associations and informal get-togethers.

- **Industry associations.** With more than 37,000 industry and professional associations in the United States, you'll likely find a local chapter of interest in your community. Most industry associations hold national or state conferences or conventions, which can be a good venue for networking.

- **Group-specific entrepreneur associations.** You'll find business organizations aimed at minorities, women, religious groups, youth, immigrants, and more.

To find out if there's a group that's right for you in your town, check:

- **Business section of your local newspaper.** Look here for a calendar of meetings or events put on by entrepreneur's groups.

- **Small Business Development Centers (SBDCs).** Go to these to obtain lists of local entrepreneur's groups. (To find an SBDC office in your area, go to www.asbdc-us.org.)

- **Websites of trade associations.** Find an appropriate industry association and join it. Many associations run members-only forums on their websites, and this is the first place to look for a forum that will be useful to you.

- **Yahoo! groups (http://groups.yahoo.com).** Yahoo! hosts all sorts of online groups, with plenty for people with particular interests, plus a fair number of professional groups. Find one that fits your business.

- **Google groups (http://groups.google.com).** You'll find discussion groups here on virtually every topic under the sun. Browse the Groups home page for topic areas that relate to your industry or business specialty.

Trade shows

At trade shows, companies in a particular industry congregate to showcase their latest products, services, and developments. Bookstore buyers can meet publishers at publishing trade shows to discover the hot new authors; supermarket executives and restaurateurs can find new specialty foods at fancy-food shows; and clothing designers can show off their wares to retailers of all sizes. Even dentists can find new dental tools or technology companies can view and try out new tech tools. Trade shows are sponsored by trade associations for specific industries and are generally not open to the public. They usually run for several days and are attended by people from the industry, company representatives, and members of the press.

Not only are key prospects gathered under one roof, they're eager to see what you have to offer. Trade show attendees have an interest in looking at your products or services—that's why they're there. Trade shows are a great way to meet potential new customers and for them to meet you. This is especially helpful if many of your potential customers are located outside your immediate area but will be attending the same show as you. A face-to-face meeting makes doing business a lot more inviting—and the trade show setting makes it easy for you to showcase your product or service and for potential customers to ask you questions about your company.

The type of trade show you choose to attend depends on what you sell and to whom you sell it. Let's say your company makes gourmet salsa. If you aim to sell the salsa directly to as many new customers as possible, your best bet is to exhibit at a broad food show with thousands of attendees and hundreds of exhibitors, like N.A.S.F.T.'s Fancy Food and Confection Shows, taking place every winter and summer. But if you want to position your salsa as a leader in the Hispanic food market, a smaller, more targeted conference might be a better choice—one like the Expo Comida Latina.

Just remember to look before you leap. The best way to determine whether a trade show is a good fit for you and your business is to go first as an attendee, not an exhibitor. You'll discover what the atmosphere is like and who attends and exhibits, plus you'll get a better feel for how business is done at the event. And as an attendee, you'll still be able to take advantage of having many industry contacts gathered in one place. Without being tied to an exhibit, you'll also be able to attend even more meetings and events.

You'll find an extensive listing of trade shows online at TSNN (www.tsnn.com) and Successful Meetings (www.mimegasite.com/mimegasite/index.jsp). The book *Trade Shows Worldwide: An International Directory of Events, Facilities, and Suppliers*, published by Gale Research, is another good resource.

Public relations

The best advertising often comes in the form of free publicity. A story about your business in a trade publication, on local TV, or on a popular website can be more powerful than a paid advertisement. Public relations (PR) involves getting your business or product mentioned to the public—via online as well as print publications—and in media such as television or radio.

A press release is a document that provides the media with detailed information about a particular event, such as the introduction of a new product or service, or a milestone in the development of a company (the thousandth customer, the 25-year anniversary). A press release should include all the info that a media representative needs to write a story about the event, including all the details (dates, names, prices—whatever is relevant). A good press release will also include quotations for the media writer to use. These quotes might come from customers praising the product or service, an industry analyst placing the company or its products or services in a market context, or a representative of the company. Press releases should *always* have contact info that the media can use to get further information about the event.

Product and service reviews are an increasingly important component of a successful PR campaign. A positive review from a trusted source will lead customers to you. In addition to the traditional places where experts review and compare products and services, such as *Consumer Reports* and industry

The who, what, where, when, and why

When designing a press release, remember that most people in the media are overworked. Thus, the easier you make it for them to understand the *who, what, where, when,* and *why* of your product or service, the better your chances of getting publicity.

The most successful press releases have an interesting hook—an aspect of your story that "hooks" readers in, the thing that makes your news compelling. Perhaps you're launching a new line of energy-efficient appliances around Earth Day. Or maybe, near tax time, you're promoting your new online, money-management software that helps people organize their receipts and various bank accounts.

Find an angle for reporters that shows them how your story is timely, amusing, or informative—in other words, don't make them work too hard to cover it.

Trade Shows and Industry Events

Use this worksheet to investigate which trade shows or industry events you should consider attending. Under "Costs" list both the cost to attend or to exhibit and any travel and setup costs expected. Under "Attendees" list as much specific detail as possible about the type of people who attend.

Name of show/event:

Sponsor: _____ Date: _____

Location: _____ Attendees: _____

Costs: _____

Deadlines: _____

Notes: _____

Name of show/event:

Sponsor: _____ Date: _____

Location: _____ Attendees: _____

Costs: _____

Deadlines: _____

Notes: _____

Name of show/event:

Sponsor: _____ Date: _____

Location: _____ Attendees: _____

Costs: _____

Deadlines: _____

Notes: _____

Name of show/event:

Sponsor: _____ Date: _____

Location: _____ Attendees: _____

Costs: _____

Deadlines: _____

Notes: _____

specialty or trade magazines, online review sites like Yelp! and Google Places, where users can submit their own reviews, are very influential, because the ratings on them come from actual users of a product or service. Generally, if other customers say that your new environmentally friendly cat litter is terrific, it's much more credible than if *you* declare this in an advertisement.

Depending on public relations can have its drawbacks, however. Public relations takes time and resources. Your staff—or a PR specialist you hire—will have to write the press releases, make the media contact, call that person, send out products for review, and follow up.

And it can take considerable time for PR to be effective. As well, PR is not controllable. You may get products into reviewers' hands only to be met with negative reviews. Or your efforts could simply be ignored. That's why most well-known companies depend on advertising *plus* public relations to build their brand and sell their products or services.

Your elevator pitch

Before you attend your first networking event or trade show, approach a potential customer or investor, or speak with the press, you'll need to prepare an **elevator pitch**: a concise summary of your service, business, or product idea that can be delivered in one or two brief sentences.

The term "elevator pitch" is based on the premise that sometimes you can only catch an influential or powerful person for a few minutes—let's say in an elevator—and your pitch should be short enough for you to make it in the time it takes an elevator to go up a few floors. Since the typical elevator ride is somewhere in the range of 30 to 60 seconds, you should keep your pitch to 100 to 150 words at most.

An elevator pitch must be succinct, clear, and, perhaps most important, memorable. The person who hears it should be able to remember what you do and what makes you distinct. It should be designed so they could later tell someone else about your company, products, or services.

An elevator pitch is *essential* to marketing. So work on it carefully and practice it until you remember it and can repeat it easily. For more on the elevator pitch, refer to pages 88–90.

Help a Reporter Out

HARO—or Help a Reporter Out—is a service in which reporters can put out an email query of something they're looking to cover. For instance, a technology reporter may be looking for a company developing a new mobile app for the travel industry. If you offer something they're looking for, this can be an excellent way to get your product or service mentioned by a reporter.

Sample Document: Press Release

FOR IMMEDIATE RELEASE

Contact: Rosa Whitten

PlanningShop

Tel: 650-364-9120

Email: Rosa@PlanningShop.com

PlanningShop™

RECORD NUMBER OF BUSINESSES MOVING TO THE CLOUD IN THE COMING YEAR (HEADLINE)

New how-to guide cuts through the hype, helps entrepreneurs succeed in the cloud (SUBHEAD)

(DATELINE) PALO ALTO, CA, APRIL 1, 2012. The "cloud" is hot. Both small and large businesses are moving business applications to Internet-based solutions in record numbers. But how can small businesses and entrepreneurs cut through the hype surrounding the cloud to get the most out of this cutting-edge technology for their businesses? (HOOK)

Recognizing the transformative effect of the cloud on business—and the confusion surrounding cloud computing—Rhonda Abrams, CEO of PlanningShop and best-selling author and syndicated columnist, has recently written *the* book on the cloud for small and medium businesses: *Bringing the Cloud Down to Earth: How to choose, launch, and get the most from cloud solutions for your business.* (WHY, WHAT, WHO, WHEN)

Bringing the Cloud Down to Earth cuts through the clutter and is "jargon-free." It offers a common-sense approach, showing business owners how to boost productivity, work anywhere, easily collaborate with their team, and much more.

Filled with worksheets, checklists, and best practices from companies that have successfully migrated a variety of applications to the cloud, *Bringing the Cloud Down to Earth* enables readers to immediately assess their own needs, evaluate providers, and create a realistic plan for transitioning to the cloud and integrating cloud solutions with on-premise applications. (MORE DETAILS)

"The cloud represents a huge transformation for business. In many ways, it's as game-changing as the Internet itself," says Abrams. "It will change the way entrepreneurs run their businesses, and if they want to stay competitive, they need to understand the cloud." (QUOTE FROM COMPANY EXECUTIVE)

John Jantsch, author of *Duct Tape Marketing* and *The Referral Engine*, has this to say about *Bringing the Cloud Down to Earth*: "No matter how you refer to it, working in the Cloud is a fundamental business practice these days, and Abrams has done a terrific job of making this sometimes confusing subject relevant and practical for businesses of all shapes and sizes." (QUOTE FROM REPUTABLE SOURCE)

About Rhonda Abrams: (BACKGROUND INFO)

Rhonda Abrams is recognized as one of America's leading experts on helping entrepreneurs grow successful companies. Her weekly column in *USA Today* is the most widely circulated column on entrepreneurship in the U.S. She is the author of more than 15 books, including the best-selling business plan guide in America, *Successful Business Plan.*

An image of the book cover is available at the following link: www.planningshop.com/about/media.asp. (ADDITIONAL RESOURCES)

EDITORS: If you would like more information about this topic or to schedule an interview with Rhonda Abrams, please contact Rosa Whitten at 650-364-9120 or Rosa@PlanningShop.com. (CONTACT INFORMATION)

BUILD-YOUR-BUSINESS WORKSHEET

What's the Hook?

Use this worksheet to brainstorm possible hooks for your press release.

Identify potential hooks for your PR story:_____
_____
_____

Holiday, special month, or season: _____
_____
_____

Local angle on national trend: _____
_____
_____

Surveys, statistics: _____
_____
_____

Lists or tips: _____
_____
_____

Innovation: _____
_____
_____

Awards, recognition: _____
_____
_____

Other: _____
_____
_____

Write several versions of one sentence that ties the hook to your company, product, or service:
_____
_____
_____
_____
_____

Offsite events

You can generate word-of-mouth by participating in an event that will attract your target market. For example, a job placement service could sponsor a job fair, which would entitle it to place its logo on the main entrance banner and receive a public thank-you from fair organizers on the fair's website. This public acknowledgment not only increases the placement service's exposure, but also enhances its image among job seekers and businesses looking to hire.

REAL-WORLD RECAP

Word-of-mouth marketing tactics

- Referral programs
- Public testimonials
- Online review sites
- Onsite events
- Blogs
- Offsite events

Word-of-mouth marketing

Perhaps the most effective type of marketing is what's known as "word-of-mouth" marketing—sometimes referred to as WOM. Word-of-mouth marketing is exactly what it sounds like: finding ways to spread the word about your business from one person to another (from one person's "mouth" to another). With WOM, your goal is to generate buzz about your product or service that will spread naturally and ignite interest in your offerings.

Word-of-mouth marketing is powerful because people trust what their friends, associates, and family members tell them. Think about it—if your buddy tells you how cool a new mobile app is, or your girlfriend tells you about how much money her accountant has saved her, you're far more likely to download the app or call the accountant than if you had merely read a story or heard a commercial about those offerings.

Many companies that have been in business for many years will tell you they don't do any marketing—they just rely on word-of-mouth from their many satisfied customers. But "word-of-mouth" is a bit of a misnomer. It implies that the buzz about an offering just happens spontaneously. Nothing could be further from the truth. Customers forget you after a time, even if they're satisfied with your business and services. You must constantly think of ways to encourage them to remember you and then spread the word. This takes planning and time.

The following tactics are effective methods of generating word of mouth.

- **Referral programs.** You want your best customers to tell their friends and family about you, so ask them to do just that—and then reward them when they do. Create a program that provides incentives for your customers to tell others about you. Offer them discounts on products or services if they send you friends or colleagues.

- **Public testimonials.** Kudos from satisfied customers make a big impact. Put testimonials on your website and in your marketing materials. If you participate in a professional network and have done work for any of its members, ask them to give a testimonial to the group through an announcement at an event or over the network's group email (often called email list-serves).

- **Online review sites.** Positive reviews on sites such as Yelp.com, Angie's List, Google Places, and Yahoo! Local can be powerful marketing tools for your business. Although you have no control over what reviewers post about you, you can claim your business page on these sites and add information about your company.

- **Onsite events.** Host an event at your business that brings potential customers in and gets them talking about your business. A service business could hold a grand opening with wine and cheese and offer discounts on services; a retail business could hold hourly drawings for prizes.

- **Blogs.** If you have a product or service that would interest readers of a particular blog, contact the blogger, send a free sample, and ask them to mention it on the blog if they like it. A recommendation will be much more powerful coming from a trusted blogger.

Customer Loyalty Programs

It pays to take care of your best customers, those who purchase frequently or are highly profitable. Good customers want to feel valued by a business, and companies want to ensure that the best customers keep coming back. Customer loyalty programs are designed to do exactly that.

Tech tools for loyalty programs

The best loyalty programs enable you to capture your customers' contact information so you can continue marketing to them. Many tech tools—including mobile apps, CRM programs, and other databases—are designed especially for managing or leveraging loyalty programs.

TYPES OF LOYALTY PROGRAMS

TYPE OF PROGRAM	DESCRIPTION	BENEFITS	EXAMPLE
Memberships or Clubs	Discounts or rewards for people who agree to sign up to be a member of your club or be associated with you.	Works well with customers who are regularly targeted by competitors' marketing campaigns.	Supermarket "clubs" that offer customers discounts and special deals in return for enabling the store to track their purchases and market to them.
Free Reward after Multiple Purchases	Enticing customers to keep coming back to you by offering them something free after they make a certain number of purchases.	Motivates customers to return; possibility of capturing customer information so as to continue marketing to them.	A spa that offers a free treatment after a customer's 10th appointment.
Buy-Ahead Discounts	A significant discount or freebie for buying multiple products or services in advance.	Generates advance income for a company; especially good if customers would otherwise stop purchasing.	A 12-month membership in a gym for the price of only 10 months when customers pay up front.
Upgrades or Special Services	A special treatment or better product offered at no extra charge.	Fulfills the desire of customers to see themselves as valued.	A hotel room upgrade in recognition of numerous visits.
Discounts after Purchase	Discounts given as a reward after purchase, which can be used in the future.	Encourages additional purchases and thanks customers.	A clothing company that provides customers, after a purchase, with a discount coupon for their next purchase.

The most obvious example of these programs is airline frequent flyer programs. But even a fully punched rewards card for a local coffee shop, with which a customer can get a free cup of coffee, is a loyalty program. Large or small, these programs keep customers attached to you, and they all have some basic attributes in common:

- The customer gets a reward—discount, freebie, upgrade, or special service—for being a regular or big customer.

- They provide a way to keep track of customers' purchases.

- Often, to join the program, customers provide the company with their contact information, which enables the business to keep marketing to them and communicating with them.

From time to time, you must evaluate the cost of your loyalty program. Are you giving free products or services to customers who would have been buying from you anyway? Are your rewards eroding away your profit margins to an untenable extent? Be sure to examine how much you spend on rewards you give to customers versus the CLV (customer lifetime value) of those customers.

Other Marketing Techniques

The term "marketing" covers a huge range of techniques—virtually any method to get your name, brand, or message in front of customers and prospects. Marketing techniques are continually evolving. After all, it takes more and more effort and creativity to capture attention in an increasingly distracted world.

The table on the following page examines a number of marketing techniques. Some are traditional and mundane, such as signs. And some would be considered **guerilla marketing**—inexpensive, grassroots activities that get your name, message, and brand in front of customers. These tactics tend to be deployed close to the customer; they show up where the customers are, and manage to get your name noticed without being offensive. They subtly or overtly grab customers' attention and impel them to buy.

OTHER MARKETING TECHNIQUES

TACTIC	DESCRIPTION	BENEFITS	EXAMPLES
In-Store Marketing	Marketing aimed at catching a shopper's eye (or ear), drawing them to a product, and convincing them to put that product in their cart.	Customers in the store are ready to make purchases.	Fixtures; signage; endcap displays; point-of-sale displays; in-store radio; shopping cart ads; video displays; window displays.
Sampling	Giving away your product or service for free to prospects to entice them to buy it.	Customers are more likely to buy a product if they try it and like it.	Handing out samples at the supermarket or warehouse store; free, limited-time use of online services or software; first time free.
Advertising Specialties	Items you give away to customers and prospects, imprinted with your name, logo, or message.	Perceived as gifts rather than ads; recipients are much less likely to throw away a "gift," making your ad persistent.	Often inexpensive (toys, knickknacks, office supplies); sometimes relatively expensive (leather portfolios, electronic devices, carry-on suitcases).
Signs	Fixed signs, movable signs, banners, posters, and other physical announcements.	Often relatively inexpensive; remain in place for long periods; generally, you invest in them only once.	A sign placed over the front door of your store; posters displayed on campuses; neon billboards in New York City's Times Square.
Product Placement	Companies paying to have their products shown in movies, on TV, and in magazines; placing your product with highly regarded individuals.	Can be done low-cost by placing products in well-respected venues or with influencers who help drive others' choices.	Members of a high-tech industry association who see their chairperson using your new handheld device.
Transit Advertising	Ads placed where people are stuck in transit—sitting in a taxi, waiting for a bus, standing in line at an airport terminal, or driving at a crawl in rush hour traffic.	Can reach a very large audience that, in most cases, can't escape.	Airport and airline ads targeting executives or tourists; ads for local restaurants in or on taxis, trains, subways, and buses.
Community-Related Marketing	A for-profit business advertises that its business practices are consistent with certain values, that it gives part of its proceeds or some other benefit to a nonprofit organization, or that it's committed to a social cause.	When presented with similar products at similar prices, customers often choose the one they can feel good about purchasing; choosing a product or company that reflects their values can trump even price considerations.	A company that produces a natural food energy bar enjoyed by hikers gives part of its proceeds to an organization that protects the environment; a chain of coffee shops promotes the fact that it uses only fair-trade and sustainably farmed coffee beans.
Cause-Related Marketing	A for-profit business associating itself with local community nonprofit organizations.	Positively associates your company with an event or group that consumers value.	Sponsoring a Little League team (and sewing your company name on its uniforms); a natural food energy bar company donating products to an environmental group's fundraising hike.

Marketing Vehicles Comparison Chart

Now that you've considered the large number of marketing vehicles available to you, use this worksheet to narrow down all the choices to the ones that best suit your business.

QUESTION	PRINT MEDIA Newspapers, magazines, phone book	BROADCAST MEDIA Radio, TV	ONLINE Website, SEO and SEM, daily deals, mobile marketing	SOCIAL MEDIA MARKETING Blogs, Facebook, Twitter, LinkedIn, YouTube
What market do they reach?				
How big is their reach?				
What percentage of their market is my target market?				
What is the cost per thousand (CPM) reached?				
What frequency will I need to be effective?				
What is the reasonable immediate response I can expect?				
How expensive is the ad to prepare?				
What are this vehicle's advantages?				
What are this vehicle's disadvantages?				
Other:				

MARKETING COLLATERAL Brochures, fliers, direct mail	NETWORKING, TRADE SHOWS, PUBLIC RELATIONS	SIGNAGE Vehicles, buildings, billboards	OTHER In-store marketing, advertising specialties, product placement

REAL-WORLD CASE

If You Blend It, Will They Come? Blendtec's Viral Videos

challenge

With a limited advertising budget, get the word out about a commodity product

solution

Create a series of videos appropriate for the YouTube audience

When you have a small marketing budget, you have to be creative. Sometimes that involves looking at your product or service in an off-beat way.

In November 2006, George Wright had just been hired as marketing director at Blendtec, a leading maker of blenders, mixers, and kitchen mills. Walking through the plant one day, he heard a strange grinding sound. He followed it to find the company's president and CEO, Tom Dickson, putting 2x2 pieces of wood in a blender and chopping them up. It turned out that this was Dickson's idea of quality assurance (QA): He'd randomly check out the chopping and blending power of appliances by grinding up the hardest things he could find around the manufacturing plant.

Wright was intrigued. And then he was struck with a brilliant idea. He went out and, after spending less than $100 on supplies—a white lab coat, marbles, a garden rake, a McDonalds Extra Value Meal, a rotisserie chicken, a can of Coke, and a few other things—he shot a series of short videos with a small handheld video camera that showed Dickson blending these items in the workers' break room. Wright's goal was to promote a fun, even wacky pseudoscientific scenario that might catch the attention of consumers, staring Dickson as the mad inventor/scientist, while at the same time demonstrating the quality of Blendtec products.[1]

Founded in 1975 by Dickson, Blendtec had always been at the leading edge of innovation for designing and manufacturing mixing, blending, and milling products for both home and commercial use. Until Wright's arrival, Blendtec had done no advertising, apart from placing staid print ads in trade publications. Wright was eager to try out word-of-mouth marketing. He posted the videos on YouTube under the title "Will It Blend?" He didn't have to wait long. Within five days, the videos had accumulated more than six million YouTube views.

Realizing he had a viral hit on his hands, Wright immediately began promoting the videos via the firm's Web page, Twitter, and Facebook.

---

1. "Corporate Social Media Case Study: Blendtec," DemingHill.com.

He also created the company's own YouTube channel, which quickly found more than 200,000 free subscribers eager for the *next* video.

To make the experience more interactive and "sticky," the "Will It Blend?" show began blending crazier objects under a large subtitle that warned "Do Not Do This at Home." Wright also encouraged fans to email their requests for objects to be blended—and used the opportunity to ramp up the entertainment value of the show. Never taking themselves too seriously, Wright and Dickson filmed one segment in which they pretended they were going to try and blend a crowbar—the single most requested object from fans. However, right before flipping the switch, a crew member's cell phone was scripted to go off. Mocking a temper tantrum, Dickson then collected the cell phones of everyone in the room and blended them up instead.

Wright was also quick to notice which segments resonated most with his growing fan base, and pushed them to the limit. The most popular segments of "Will It Blend?" involved Dickson blending Apple products, including an iPhone, an iPhone 3G, an iPhone 4, and even a much larger iPad. These created such a stir that Blendtec set up contests on its website, www.blendtec.com, to give away the shredded products, an entire Apple product (a new copy of whichever one had been blended), and a new Blendtec blender.

The offbeat approach fit the nature and audience of YouTube, making the videos a huge hit. The video with Dickson blending an iPhone got more than 10 million views. Blendtec's retail sales increased more than *700 percent*, and the videos have been featured on major mainstream media outlets like *The Today Show, The Tonight Show, The History Channel,* the *Wall Street Journal,* and others—enabling Blendtec to get far greater reach with limited marketing dollars.[2]

Of course, few companies are ever fortunate to have the success that Blendtec achieved, with a bit of creativity. And getting a video to successfully go viral takes a good deal of luck. Still, the first step in a viral marketing campaign is to look at what might engage your target customers, and be willing to take a very fresh, even whimsical, look at your product or service. ■

questions

1. What other low-budget marketing strategies could Blendtec have implemented?

2. Watch two or three Blendtec "Will It Blend?" videos. How does the company reinforce its brand through these videos?

3. Although Blendtec's one-of-a-kind marketing campaign can't be duplicated, what lessons could you take away from its experience?

4. Do you think some products or services are completely unsuitable for an offbeat marketing approach? If so, which ones, and why?

2. "BlendTec Will It Blend? Viral Video Case Study," by Christian Briggs, Jan. 2009, *SocialLens.com.*

CLEANING UP, BIG TIME

Goal:

Create a series of videos to post on YouTube in the hopes they'll go viral.

What To Do:

Either working alone or with others, imagine that you run an ecofriendly ("green") diaper service: You drop off clean cloth diapers to families and pick up dirty ones to launder. When you first opened your business, you were the first diaper service in the area to make a commitment to sustainable laundry methods. Now all your competitors claim to be green as well. You want to launch a video campaign on YouTube with the hope that it'll "go viral."

1. First, discuss what makes a video go viral. What causes you to forward one video to your friends, and not another? What type of viral video is likely to appeal most to your target audience: the parents of very young children?

2. Come up with an idea for a *series* of videos that you could use in an ongoing campaign. Sketch out four specific videos for the series. Be extremely detailed in your descriptions.

3. Present your video concepts to the class. Be prepared to explain why you think they have the potential to go viral.

CHAPTER

11 Sales and Distribution

learning objectives

In this chapter, you'll learn how to:

- Understand the importance of sales

- Determine how to structure and compensate a sales team

- Describe the various types of sales channels and their advantages and disadvantages

- Analyze different retailers and choose which ones to pursue

- Identify and evaluate potential distributors

- Outline effective sales operations and procedures

- Identify potential customers, or "leads," and recognize their likelihood of becoming buyers

- Determine sales goals, outline productivity levels, and choose appropriate sales methods

- Create effective sales bids and proposals

- Deploy successful sales techniques

- Demonstrate how to close the deal

Sales Are the Heart of Business

If your marketing strategy is successful, soon potential customers will be interested in your products or services. Now, you just have to make the actual sale.

Any action you take that involves making direct contact with people with the goal of placing an order or securing a client falls under the category of **sales**. Sales are critical for your business—indeed, everything in your business must be geared toward sales if you want to be able to have the money to stay in business. Obviously, the quality of your product or service is important, but your ability to sell is every bit as critical. History is filled with failed companies that made outstanding products or services but simply couldn't make the sales.

Some entrepreneurs view the prospect of making a sales call with the same fear and loathing as a tax audit. After all, your talent lies in your ability to make mouth-watering apple tarts, create compelling logos, or build software, not in trying to convince people to part with their hard-earned cash. Sorry: That's no excuse. If you can't picture yourself in the role of salesperson, it's essential that you get someone on your team who can.

As you grow, you'll likely have staff members whose primary or sole responsibility is to make sales. Selecting, managing, and motivating your sales team will be an ongoing task of you and your executive team, because the quality and performance of your sales force has a significant impact on your long-term success.

Keep in mind that you, as the entrepreneur, are also going to be, at some point and in some way, the "salesperson" for your company. If yours is a very small company, you almost certainly will be involved in making many, if not most, sales calls. But even in a very large corporation, key executives get called upon to meet with customers and prospects. And when you're raising money to fund your business, you will certainly be "selling" your business to investors and lenders.

So learn to get comfortable with sales, because they lie at the heart of every business.

Sales Staff

In one sense, everyone at your company is involved with sales. Whether it's the person who answers the phone, thus giving the first impression of your company to customers, or the shipping clerk who makes sure an order is correct—every potential interaction affects future sales.

en·tre·pre·neur·ship key terms

Brick and mortar
A traditional business such as a retail store, service business, or bank that operates out of a physical building, as opposed to online.

Bricks and clicks
A business that has both a physical location and an online presence, such as a clothing manufacturer that sells its clothes in its own stores as well as online.

Channel
An avenue through which a company sells its products or services (such as through distributors, retailers, or online).

Cold call
Making a sales call on a prospect who has not yet expressed any interest in your product or service or contacted you.

Distribution chain
The series of intermediaries that exists between a business that creates a product or service, and the final end-user, each of which passes the product or service on to the next business to distribute or sell until it is sold to the end-user.

Lead
The name or contact information of a person or business that is a potential customer; a "hot lead" is one who has expressed some interest in buying or has contacted the

company; a "cold" lead is one that has not yet expressed any interest in buying.

Sales
(1) The process of contacting and communicating with prospects with the intention of securing an order or purchase; (2) also referred to as "revenue" or "income," sales is the total amount of money made from the products or services sold.

Sales cycle
The stages customers go through when deciding to buy a product or service: the time it takes between first contact with a prospect and the closing of a deal.

Sales pipeline
The total group of prospects who are in any stage of the sales cycle, from first identification as a lead, to initial contact, to all sales calls or communications, through negotiations, to purchase. Companies want to keep their pipelines full so they always have potential customers.

Wholesaler
An intermediary between the producer or manufacturer of a product or service and the retailer or other merchandiser who will actually sell that product or service to the end-user. Wholesalers have the responsibility for making the sales to retailers, collecting payment, and (typically) fulfilling orders.

Yet at the heart of your sales force are those members of your staff who have the specific responsibility for contacting prospects, telling your story to potential customers, convincing them to buy, negotiating prices and terms, and staying in touch with customers for future sales. These are the people who come in direct contact with your prospects and who most immediately determine whether your product or service is actually purchased. These key staff members are your sales team, and you must carefully plan how you make the best use of their skills and time.

Great salespeople are extremely valuable. But they're not easy to find and keep. Sales can be very tough on a person's ego—there's usually lots of rejection, after all—so, as the company leader, your job will be to manage your sales team to keep them motivated and energized. And, of course, it's also your task to design the team's structure.

You have many options to choose from when planning the structure of your sales team. How you structure that team is directly related to your business model and, of course, to which products or services you're selling.

Sales activities can be conducted on your business's premises, or online, or at other businesses (such as retailers and in public locations), or even by calling on customers at their places of business or homes.

- **Inside sales force.** These employees remain on the company's premises to secure sales and take orders. The types of inside sales personnel include:

  — **Floor salespeople.** Salespeople who interact with customers who come to a place of business to shop and make purchases, particularly useful in retail environments; examples would be car salespeople, department store salespeople, and so on.

  — **Account or territory reps.** Individuals responsible for making sales to a specific set of customers or geographic area, typically used for business-to-business sales.

  — **In-bound telephone sales.** Staff handling calls from customers or prospects coming in to place orders or make inquiries, whether from catalog, online, direct mail, advertising, or other sales efforts.

  — **Online "chat" personnel.** These are similar to in-bound telephone sales reps, taking inquiries and orders from those connecting online; these can be through either text or voice.

  — **Out-bound telephone sales.** Often referred to as "telemarketers," these are salespeople on the phone reaching out to prospects.

- **Outside sales force.** These are salespeople who visit customers' locations to call on prospects or who solicit orders in locations other than a company's place of business. They can be making appointments; doing **cold calls;** staffing booths, kiosks, or tables set up in well-trafficked areas; attending to trade shows, and so on. These can be company employees who work away from company premises most or all of the time, or they can be independent contractors (see below).

- **Sales reps.** These are independent contractors who take on the responsibility of doing outside sales for one or more companies—often in the same field. For example, an apparel sales rep might handle a number of clothing manufacturers' lines and call on apparel store buyers, or an independent sales rep might work for only one apparel company or distributor. Cost is the primary advantage of this approach, as you might be able to secure the services of a well-connected sales rep without having to pay benefits or other expenses that come with having someone on payroll. The best sales representatives are in demand, and you'll have to convince them that you are worth taking on as a client.

- **Outsourced sales force/telesales service.** Another option is to make use of the myriad third-party sales/telesales services that exist. These are outside companies with their own sales staff that make sales calls on your behalf. This can be a costly choice, though a highly effective one, depending on the quality of the service in question.

Your company may have a mix of different types of sales personnel. For example, you may have account reps who handle your corporate customers, a telemarketing or online sales team that handles consumer business, and even outside sales reps working with some of your other sales **channels**.

Sales force compensation and training

The best salespeople are motivated to make money. They're more likely to do a better job for you when they feel there's a financial reward for making a sale or increasing the size of an order. Moreover, you want to align your interest—which is to procure more orders—with their self-interest, which is to make more money.

That's why a compensation package for your sales team should be designed to achieve the maximum results for your bottom line. Typically, that means that many sales personnel receive compensation that's based, at least in part, on commission—receiving a percentage of the actual sales they make.

Depending on their responsibilities, you'll either pay a flat salary, commission only, or, as is often common, a base salary plus commission, as outlined below. It's often believed that basing at least a portion of a salesperson's compensation on the amount of sales will provide an incentive for them to work harder and close deals.

- **Straight salary.** Sales personnel receive a salary—either monthly or hourly—and their compensation is not related to the number or amount of sales they make.

- **Straight commission.** Sales personnel receive no salary. Their total compensation is based on the amount of sales they make. The commission must be fairly high to make this viable.

Stay within the law

Remember, with most salespeople, you still have to meet federal and state laws on minimum wage—with one major exception. Outside sales personnel can be exempt from minimum wage and overtime laws when working on commission, as long as they are truly outside sales and not making calls from a fixed place (whether your business or their home).

Spiffs

One tactic that's often used in sales—although sometimes questionably—is to give salespeople a "spiff," or a special bonus or commission for selling a specific product or service. Some manufacturers do this to encourage retail salespeople to make a special effort to present and showcase their product to customers; business owners frequently do this to incentivize salespeople to move excess or profitable merchandise. For example, many companies offer a "spiff"—extra money—to salespeople who sell customers extended warranty policies when buying electronics or appliances, as these are highly profitable.

■ **Salary plus commission.** Sales personnel receive a base salary but they also receive commissions (or other bonuses) for making sales. The commissions serve as an incentive, while the base salary provides an ongoing wage (and may keep the employer within the minimum wage laws). Occasionally, the base will be a "draw" against commission—meaning the salesperson is guaranteed a certain amount each pay period, assuming they'll earn that much in commission. This gives them stable earnings, but if they consistently fail to meet their base, they're likely candidates for being fired.

Keep in mind that the lower (or lack of) base salary you offer, the higher percentage commission you'll have to pay (or the higher ticket price on the products or services you sell). After all, salespeople want to make a decent living. You have to determine—and always run the numbers—what balance of base or commission is right for your business.

With most sales personnel, it's also standard practice to set quotas, meaning to require a minimum number or dollar value of sales made within a certain period, as well as to provide bonuses or other incentives for meeting quota. Quotas are often based on the previous year's (or other time period) sales, plus an amount expected of growth. Setting numerical targets can be highly motivating to salespeople—many of whom like to reach for specific goals (and who can be quite competitive with other salespeople as well).

In figuring out your compensation structure, you'll have to consider issues such as these: What commission percentage will you provide? Will you give bonuses for reaching certain goals? Will you use other incentives, such as awards, gifts, or vacations? Will district managers or other supervisors receive commissions on their staff's sales?

Sales Channels

A **sales channel** is simply the means by which a product or service gets sold to the end-user. For instance, if you manufacture landscaping tools, you could sell directly—by opening your own stores or by selling directly to users online—and then you'd be in the retail channel. Or, your staff could sell to retailers, such as gardening stores and nurseries, who in turn sell to end-users. In other words, you would be a wholesaler, and your sales would come through their retail operations. Or you could engage an independent sale rep to call on those retail stores. Or you could use a distributor who sells to landscaping companies, gardening stores, and at trade shows for the landscaping trade—in other words, using an intermediary.

Which sales channels you'll use is a key component of figuring out your business model—what type of business you're actually in, how much you can charge for your products or services, and how much money you'll make.

Channels are important precisely because businesses often can't handle all aspects of getting products or services into customers' hands on their own. In many cases, they simply don't have the personnel or financial resources to do it. They need to devote their time, effort, and capital to their core business,

COMMISSION-BASED COMPENSATION PACKAGES

	DESCRIPTION	ADVANTAGES	DISADVANTAGES
Commission-Only	The salesperson only earns income on sales they actually make. You can only use this arrangement with salespeople who qualify as independent contractors.	You, as the employer, have less up-front risk.	Because the employee takes the greatest risk in this type of arrangement, the commissions are the highest—which means a lower profit margin for you.
Base plus Commission	The salesperson earns a base salary—typically lower than a full-time, noncommissioned employee—and supplements their earnings with commissions. Inside salespeople must get a base salary to bring them up to at least minimum wage.	This arrangement offers the employee a certain level of security but can still motivate them to make sales. As an employer, you reduce the amount you'd have to pay a salary-only worker and ideally increase sales at the same time.	Unlike commission-only and draw-against-commission arrangements, you have to pay a salary to your employee, regardless of the number of sales they make.
Draw against Commission	The salesperson receives funds up-front against future commissions—before they've actually made sales. This type of arrangement may only be legal with someone who qualifies as an independent contractor.	If the salesperson does not earn back their advance, they often have to pay it back to the employer. This arrangement provides more stability for the salesperson and less risk for the employer than a base-plus-commission situation.	If the salesperson underperforms, such an arrangement can lead to very uncomfortable and awkward situations.

whether it's making landscaping tools, manufacturing computers, or creating works of art or movies.

Often, a series of intermediaries exists between an entrepreneur and the end-user, each of which passes the product or service onto the next person or organization until it finally reaches the end-user, and each of which has different responsibilities and costs. This is called the **distribution chain**.

Sticking with the example of the landscaping tool, for example, if you had a tool that would be priced at $100 retail, you could sell direct to end-users, charging that full amount (or offering some discounts) at your own stores—either physical or virtual. But you'd have the cost of your retail store, or website, plus the costs of marketing and attracting customers yourself, fulfilling their orders, maintaining inventory, paying your sales personnel, and so on.

Sales Force

List below the type of sales force you use, and how many salespeople you have in each category.

Inside sales force: _____

Floor reps: _____

Account reps: _____

Inbound telephone sales: _____

Online chat: _____

Outbound telemarketers: _____

Outside sales force (employee): _____

Outside sales representatives, agents (nonemployee): _____

Outside telemarketing services: _____

Other: _____

_____

How do you divide responsibilities (e.g., by product line, territory, customer type)? _____

_____

_____

Do sales personnel have additional responsibilities as well as sales? _____

What commissions do you pay sales personnel? _____

Do commissions vary by product line or goals achieved?_____

What other incentives or bonuses do you provide? _____

_____

For which expenses do you reimburse sales personnel (e.g., travel, entertainment)? _____

_____

What expenses must sales personnel pay for themselves? _____

Who supervises sales personnel?_____

Do they receive commissions or bonuses based on performances of people they supervise? __ Yes __ No

Who trains sales personnel?_____

How often is training provided?_____

What kind of training is provided?_____

_____

Which other employees are involved in generating sales?_____

_____

By contrast, if you sold wholesale to retailers, you wouldn't have all that overhead, but you'd only be able to charge retailers about $50, because the retailer would need to add a substantial markup to cover its costs of marketing and retailing. And you'd still have the cost of marketing to the retail stores yourself—hiring salespeople, exhibiting at trade shows, and the like.

You could transfer most of those responsibilities to a distributor—who'd maintain the sales force to call on retailers and perhaps also fulfill orders. That would reduce your overhead and headaches, but you might only get $35 or so, as the distributor would take a commission on the wholesale price at which they sell your tools to retailers.

As you can see, there's a trade-off between how much you can charge, how many layers are between you and the end-user, and how much responsibility (and cost) you have for making sales directly.

Types of channels

You will have your choice of a range of channels. These choices include:

- **Selling direct.** This is where you directly "touch" the customer by selling a product or delivering a service, either yourself or through a sales force, mail order, the telephone, or over the Internet. When using a direct sales channel, nothing stands between you and the people who buy your product or service for their own use.

- **Using an agent.** An agent is an individual who sells directly to others, usually end-users, on your behalf. For example, agents are typically used in the financial services and insurance industries. Chances are good, for instance, that you buy your insurance from an agent, who in turn represents one or more insurance companies. Yet agents are also common in a wide range of industries, including the arts. Agents typically mark up products to higher prices than consumers would pay if they were purchasing directly from the company.

- **Brick and mortar retailers.** These are businesses that sell products or services directly to the end-user from a fixed location, like a store. The business model here is straightforward: The retailer buys the product (or service) from the producer, or from a wholesaler or distributor, and then sells it to the end-user. A **brick and mortar** retailer is responsible for maintaining and merchandising inventory, advertising and attracting customers, convincing end-users to make a purchase, and collecting payment.

- **Online sales.** Otherwise known as **bricks and clicks**. Many businesses sell directly to end-users from their own or others' websites. They can sell merchandise they have produced themselves or that has been made by others. Online retailers may take actual possession of inventory and do fulfillment, or they may have "drop ship" arrangements with manufacturers or distributors, so they don't have the responsibility and cost of owning inventory. Online retailing isn't mutually exclusive with other channels. Many manufacturers or wholesalers have websites where retailers can go to

Channel conflict

When two (or more) channels conflict with each other—in other words, sell to the same customers but perhaps at very different prices—you have channel conflict. The Internet created a great deal of channel conflict, as many companies that sold goods or services through retailers, direct sales forces, or agents began selling direct to consumers over the Web.

For example, think of athletic shoes. Once, they were almost exclusively sold by retailers, often specialty athletic shoe retailers. But when shoe manufacturers realized they could sell directly from their own websites, they started offering the same shoes, naturally at lower prices. Soon, they began to also sell their shoes to online discount shoe retailers. The manufacturer's long-time "customers"—athletic shoe stores—felt betrayed because of this channel conflict.

In general, but not always, businesses must be careful to protect their channel partners from these kinds of conflicts, because if your partners are unhappy, they may not be your partners long.

REAL-WORLD RECAP

Types of sales channels

- Selling direct
- Using an agent
- Brick and mortar retailers
- Online sales
- Licensing
- Wholesalers and distributors

purchase large lots of goods, or where, in fact, consumers can buy products directly from the manufacturer. Many businesses use a combination of both brick-and-mortar and online sales channels.

- **Licensing.** Under a licensing agreement, you grant someone else the right to sell something whose intellectual property rights you own. For instance, you may have great designs for T-shirts, which you make and sell in the United States, and decide that you'd like to expand your market globally. By licensing your T-shirt designs to international clothing manufacturers, you could expand your reach and income with little investment. Perhaps you've developed a software program that can be embedded in a number of other programs or in hardware—you could license your software to be included by other producers. Photographers license images to be sold as art or for use in textiles, while engineering firms license their designs or specifications to other businesses, even competitors.

- **Wholesalers and distributors.** Rather than having to reach and serve customers yourself, using a wholesaler or distributor saves you the need and cost of building a large sales force and fulfilling orders, especially small ones. Wholesalers and distributors sell to others, typically to those who, in turn, sell to end-users (such as retailers). Wholesalers and distributors are often dismissed as the classic "middleman"—the person (or business) that stands between you and your end-user. Yet they serve a valuable function. Many large retailers—think "big-box stores"—simply won't deal with small suppliers; they use distributors to reduce the number of vendors they have to interact with. For your part, you may not be able, or willing, to deal with all the fulfillment requirements of your many retailers, let alone have the wherewithal to sell to them. Distributors and wholesalers take a percentage of the sales price, but they save you the cost and hassle of finding and servicing retail customers yourself.

CHANNELS FOR SERVICE BUSINESSES

Distribution channels are used for services as well as products. The same definition applies: The channel is the means by which you deliver your service to end-users. For example, those in some aspects of the hospitality industry—such as hotels, tour guides, adventure tour providers, and vacation home rental businesses—often sell their services through a variety of outlets, including travel agents, tour packagers, airlines, and online reservations systems. Although you can go directly to a hotel to book a room for a vacation, many people prefer to go through an alternate channel—often an online travel site—to do their travel planning.

Retailers

If you plan to sell your products through retailers, your choice of which ones is critical. The retailer must attract a sufficient number of customers, promote and merchandise your products, and pay you in a timely fashion.

ADVANTAGES AND DISADVANTAGES OF VARIOUS CHANNELS

CHANNEL TYPE	ADVANTAGES	DISADVANTAGES
Direct	You keep more of your money because there's no middleman involved. You know who your customers are and "own" them, so you can contact them for future sales or get direct feedback from them on how to improve your products or services. You're in a position to sell the customer additional products and services.	You're entirely responsible for reaching and servicing the customer. You have to do the marketing, make the sale, and provide post-sale support. You're also responsible for billing and bad debts.
Agent	Agents go out and market your goods or services, so you have more time to spend on your creative and business endeavors. They negotiate for you, often getting you a better deal than you could get for yourself. They handle contracts and other business and legal details, and provide you with advice and guidance.	They take a percentage of your income— usually 15% or 20%. Because it's usually an exclusive relationship, if they underperform, you're precluded from going elsewhere. Their reputation in the industry is your reputation, so if you have a less-than-good one, your creative and business endeavors will suffer.
Bricks and Mortar Retailers	Retailers deal with customers. They maintain the retail space and are responsible for its costs, merchandising, marketing, and customer service. They purchase your goods, usually on a nonreturnable basis. If you have a good retailer, they can sell your products into markets you wouldn't have been able to enter on your own.	You sell to them at a deep discount, typically 50%, and they often also demand good payment terms (such as 90 days). They can be extremely demanding, and they own the customer. You have no quality control over the environment. If you're dependent on just a few retailers, their economic well-being can make or break your company.
Licensing	An additional revenue stream with little or no up-front expense on your part. Licensors allow you to extend your brand to other product lines.	Quality control is always a concern. You run the risk of diluting your brand or hurting your brand image if your licensing partners have different ideas or quality standards than you do. The potential for intellectual property theft is greater.
Online Sales	A low-overhead way to reach and service customers. You gain worldwide reach. You're in direct touch with the customer, and can try to sell to them again. You can track your customers' preferences and behaviors precisely.	Can be difficult to service customers from all over the world. Can eat up time responding to queries and requests for help. You must build and maintain a marketing-oriented website. You must fulfill orders yourself.
Wholesalers and Distributors	Distributors act as your sales force and can be a highly efficient way to reach a large market. They perform billing and collections and handle paperwork. Frequently, they manage warehousing and storage as well. They service the demands of large accounts. They give you the ability to concentrate on aspects of your business other than selling and distribution.	They take a percentage of your sales income, and they own the customer relationship. If they represent too many companies, your products or services might not be well represented.

Ideally, you'll choose retailers (and they'll choose you) that reflect well on your brand. You may want to be associated with high-end department stores, for instance, or with boutiques or cutting-edge stores. But remember, there's much more to your relationship with your retailer than image. You want to make certain they're good buyers—knowing what will sell well in their store and in what quantity—and also good payers, paying you on time. You also need to know that their demands of you as a supplier are reasonable.

Don't be overly entranced by big or well-known retailers. Major retailers often have costly requirements about how you must package and ship merchandise, and then they usually make payments very late. Many are also notoriously tough negotiators when it comes to price. You may think that the deal you finally closed with that well-known big-box retailer is a dream come true, yet once you discover how thin your profit margin will be, coupled with the retailer's strict requirements on everything from how you label your boxes to which shipping company you use, you may end up feeling that all the effort and expense of fulfilling this huge order simply isn't worth it.

Be cautious, too, of overly large first orders. Large orders can place huge demands on your resources, often requiring you to invest significant sums to fulfill those orders. What happens if your goods don't sell well? The retailer will drop you, and you'll be stuck. So, whenever possible, consider "testing" in large retailers before accepting huge orders.

If you sell directly to retailers (instead of using a distributor to reach them), be sure you understand all the terms of your arrangement. Who pays shipping? Will returns be permitted, and under what circumstances? What discount will they be given? How long will they have to make payments?

Agents, distributors, and wholesalers

In the business world, whether you're buying or selling, you'll likely need a "middleman"—a person or company that puts buyers and sellers together. While middlemen (better called "intermediaries") may be much maligned, in reality they serve extremely valuable functions.

With the advent of the Internet, the business world was supposed to become "disintermediated," that is, we were supposed to be able to get rid of the middleman. After all, manufacturers can sell directly to end-users, without the need for all those people in the middle   wholesalers, distributors, retailers, and others. Theoretically, this should make everything less expensive because fewer hands take a cut, and make a profit, at each step.

Yet while this disintermediation has occurred in a few instances (buying a Dell computer directly from Dell, for example), most manufacturers don't want to be bothered with selling goods on a "one-off" basis, then having to deal with fulfilling small orders and all those pesky customers with their endless questions and complaints. And buyers don't want to wade through dozens—even hundreds or thousands—of choices.

No, we need intermediaries: wholesalers, distributors, and independent sales representatives. They serve as the marketing and sales-and-service arm for manufacturers.

In turn, intermediaries also serve buyers as "editors" (selecting the best choices from myriad options) and provide individualized service and order fulfillment, especially for smaller customers.

Distributors

Few decisions directly affect your business and your finances as much as the selection of a distributor. To a large extent, they control whether your products have a fair chance to ever reach potential customers. If your distributor can't get your products into retail stores, you won't be able to make sales.

Your distributor's financial practices—how long they take to pay you and how often, how they report sales, and what percentages they charge—in large part determine your cash flow and profits. And, of course, you want to make certain your distributor is both honest and stable.

If you're just starting out, you may feel lucky to get *any* distributor to represent your product, because good distributors are in demand by many manufacturers. Nevertheless, be selective!

"Shop" for distributors, and never choose solely on the basis of how much (what percentage) they'll charge for their services. Compare at least a few distributors. If possible, meet with a representative face-to-face. Always ask for references, and check with some of the other manufacturers they represent. Have their other clients been satisfied? Have they encountered problems?

To find a list of potential distributors, contact your industry trade association. Well-respected and known distributors are likely to be active in trade associations, and many associations maintain lists of distributors.

When entering into a distribution agreement, you should absolutely get a legally binding contract, spelling out all the various aspects of your arrangement. Hire an attorney knowledgeable about distribution agreements to review your contract—even if the distributor says it's their "standard" contract. Some of the issues to include in your agreement are covered in the worksheet "Distribution Considerations."

Sales Operations and Procedures

Since sales lie at the heart of any business, you need to plan how you'll efficiently and effectively achieve your sales objectives. As you begin to make sales calls and presentations, you need to first identify the procedures you'll use to identify and reach potential customers, keep track of prospects and customers, track progress and retrieve sales information, and delineate the level of results you expect from your sales force.

Reliable distribution is a must

You'll almost certainly use other parties to bring your product to market—distributors, wholesalers, retailers. These intermediaries provide a variety of assistance in getting your product or service to customers, including their:

- **Sales efforts and sales team**
- **Reputation and relationships with customers or retailers**
- **Expertise in understanding the market**
- **Advertising and marketing efforts**
- **Additional services to you, such as warehousing and shipping**
- **Extra services to customers, such as shipping, installation, and product training or support**

Plan Your Distribution Needs

Answer the questions below to help you evaluate your current distribution needs.

How is your product or service to be sold to the consumer? _____

_____

_____

_____

Is there a wholesaler or distributor between you and the consumer? __Yes __No

If so, how many such companies do you use? _____

What are those companies' key qualifications and advantages? _____

_____

_____

_____

What are their drawbacks?_____

_____

_____

_____

If you use only one or two distributors, how secure are they? _____

_____

_____

_____

What is their reputation among consumers? _____

_____

_____

_____

What kinds of payments or commissions do these distributors receive? _____

_____

_____

_____

What kinds of alternative distribution methods are available? _____

_____

_____

_____

Distribution Considerations

When you enter into a distribution contract, negotiate the following considerations. Be certain to have all agreements reviewed by a competent, experienced attorney.

	Distributor 1	Distributor 2	Distributor 3
Distributor Name and Contact Information			
Is the agreement exclusive or nonexclusive? What is the length of the terms, and how can either party terminate the agreement?			
What percentage do they charge? When and how often do they pay you, and what holdbacks from your payments, if any, do they make?			
What other services do they offer, and at what fees? What are the total fees you and the distributor are responsible for?			
Who is responsible for nonpayment by their customers?			
What minimum performance guarantees do they offer?			
What marketing efforts do they guarantee? What charges for marketing efforts do you incur, or which sales materials are you responsible for?			
How are damaged goods handled or paid for?			

Sales operations have become increasingly sophisticated over the years, even in start-up and entrepreneurial companies. CRM—or customer relationship management—programs make it easy for companies to keep track of prospects, identify which sales vehicles and messages are working, and monitor the success of individual salespeople.

As you plan your sales procedures, you must consider several aspects of your operations.

Lead generation

The first step in making a sale is to identify potential customers—or **leads**. A good lead is a person or company that has the potential to become a buyer. In other words, they have the need or interest in your product or service, have the financial ability to purchase, and are someone you can reach with your message.

"Hot leads" are prospects with the best chance of converting to a sale; typically, they've expressed some interest in your offering already and are clearly in the purchasing mind-set. For example, a hot lead is someone responding to a direct mail piece or who's registered to get a download of a trial version of your software or who's stopped by your booth at a trade show. If you're selling cars, a hot lead might be the person who walks onto your lot and says, "Hi, my car's broken down, can't be fixed, and I have no way to get to work." That person will buy a car soon! Hot leads clearly are highly desirable.

"Qualified leads," by contrast, are prospects who've clearly got the interest and wherewithal to purchase what you're selling. For example, if you're selling software, the IT manager of a company that obviously needs your software might be a qualified lead. If you're selling new BMWs and a prospect comes in driving a used BMW, they're probably qualified to buy a new one (not guaranteed, of course), although they may not necessarily be ready to buy—in other words, they may not be "hot."

"Cold" leads are those names and contact information you get from other sources. These may or may not have a strong interest or need for your product or service, nor are they necessarily qualified to purchase. However, cold leads often do convert to paying customers, and therefore much of selling involves reaching out to cold leads. It's possible to buy lists—such as subscribers to magazines, purchasers of related products, past attendees of trade shows—as a source of cold leads. For instance, if you sell SUVs, you can purchase a list of new mothers or pregnant women from a local hospital (and yes, they do sell such lists!), on the assumption that growing families need larger cars.

When you reach out to cold leads—either in person or on the phone—it's referred to as a **cold call**. Cold calling can be tough, but most experienced salespeople have done it at some point, especially since much of sales is really a "numbers game."

Sales cycle and pipeline

In many fields, customers don't make an immediate purchase. Sure, you may walk into a grocery store to buy milk, or a department store to buy a shirt, but the bigger the purchase, the more likely you are to take your time making a decision. The same is especially true when selling to businesses.

The length of time it takes, and the stages in making a decision, is referred to as the **sales cycle**. For example, in making a purchase of a new car, the sales cycle may involve a first-time visit to the car dealership, then a test drive, a follow-up visit, price negotiation, and later the final purchase. The average decision-making time for a car buy might be a few weeks. In selling to large corporations, the sales cycle may take many months or even years.

Since it takes some time to convert many prospects to an actual sale, you need to keep track of your **sales pipeline**—or prospects anywhere along the sales cycle. A CRM program can help you keep an eye on your sales pipeline, so prospects don't get overlooked.

Goals and productivity levels

How will you know that your sales force is doing an adequate, even a good, job? How will you determine their compensation? As part of your sales procedures, you'll need to establish specific, measurable objectives for each salesperson and for the total sales force; you'll have to realistically assess the number of sales possible for each sales representative, given the nature of their assigned territory, product line, or customer base. To adequately compensate sales personnel, you may want to set sales quotas, based on your realistic assessments.

Of course, in a new company, goals and quotas are notoriously difficult to set accurately. You won't yet know how long it should take to secure a sale or what level is realistic for each salesperson. That's where tracking can help you. Compiling accurate data on the number of contacts being made by each salesperson, their conversion rate, the time of average sales cycle, and so on, will help you—over time—learn how to set meaningful and achievable, yet suitably motivating, goals and objectives.

Bids and proposals

In many businesses, bids or proposals are a large part of the sales process. Whether it be bidding on putting in a new deck on a consumer's home, equipping a new production plant for a company, designing a software system for a corporation, or performing many other services, your bid or proposal may determine whether you'll get the job.

Bids and proposals can be tremendously challenging to develop—especially for newer companies. You want to make sure you're profitable, yet you want to get the job, and that often means being very competitive on price. Often, you may not know all the variables that may affect your costs.

While your salespeople may be involved in the bidding/proposal process, you'll likely want to make certain to get input from those who will actually perform

The long and short of sales cycles

The term "sales cycle" refers to the timing or stages customers go through when deciding to buy a product or service. They must recognize a need for a product or service and then begin investigating possible ways to fill that need. In the final stage, the customer actually purchases the product or service. Different types of products and services, and different types of customers, have different sales cycles, ranging from very short (hours or days) to months or even years.

the service and buy the materials and labor. Salespeople naturally want to put in winning bids, but they may not understand the true nature of your costs.

Consult with others in your industry for "usual and normal" fees for your type of products or services, although these can be difficult to ascertain.

YOUR FORMAL PROPOSAL TO THE CLIENT

A proposal is a document, typically used in professional services, that lays out exactly what you'll deliver to a client and what it will cost. The proposal should include the following components:

- **Background or statement of need (for professional services).** Explain why the client is coming to you, show that you understand the reasons the work is being undertaken, and outline the needs.

- **Scope of work or deliverables.** Outline exactly what work you'll do for the client and what "deliverables"—such as reports, designs, and materials—you'll provide. This should be fairly detailed.

- **Description of company.** Provide a short description of your company so that the client knows why you're well suited for the work. Even if the client has already decided to use you, this section reinforces that decision.

- **Delivery date, timeline, and due dates.** Detail the due dates for the various stages of the project or the final completion date; indicate if any known contingencies may change the timing.

- **Delivery terms.** If you're selling a physical product and there are details relating to its delivery (such as who pays freight), spell out the conditions under which the delivery must be paid and so forth.

- **Fees, price, and payment terms.** Clearly list the fees for the project. If you're charging by the hour, list both your hourly fee and the estimated total for the project. If you're charging by the project, list an hourly fee if the client adds additional work. Describe who's responsible for which expenses—for instance, who pays for travel or out-of-pocket costs. List any payment terms, when the payment is due, and any late charges for late payments.

- **After-sales support or tech support.** If any, list them here.

- **Returns policy, warranties, and guarantee.** If applicable, include them.

- **Acceptance and date.** Include a line for each party to sign and date.

Sales Contact Methods

How will you actually get in touch with your prospects and leads and also generate new leads? Your marketing vehicles are your primary methods for attracting prospects and customers to you. But it's also worthwhile to identify which procedures you'll use most frequently for actually making contact with your prospects and delivering your sales pitch. The chart on page 278 outlines some of the most common methods of reaching prospects and their advantages and disadvantages.

BUILD-YOUR-BUSINESS WORKSHEET

Creating a Proposal

Background/statement of need: _____

_____

_____

_____

_____

Scope of work/description of work to be provided/deliverables: _____

_____

_____

Bio of provider/description of company: _____

_____

_____

Delivery date/timeline/due dates: _____

_____

_____

Delivery terms (if any):_____

_____

_____

Fees/price: _____

_____

_____

After-sales support/tech support: _____

_____

_____

Returns policy/warranties/satisfaction guarantee: _____

_____

_____

Acceptance/date: _____

_____

_____

_____

_____

Use the worksheet "Sales Procedures and Operations" to outline the process and productivity levels you expect in your sales efforts.

Making the Sale

Now that you've assembled your sales team, determined your sales channels, and outlined your sales procedures, it's time to hit the pavement (or the "virtual pavement").

Successful sales techniques

Selling is a craft, not an art. It's a skill that can be learned. Here are a few keys to successful sales techniques.

SALES CONTACT METHODS

SALES VEHICLE	PROS	CONS
Meeting in Person	Personal, builds relationships. Can listen to customers' needs and address their concerns directly, on the spot. May be able to do in well-trafficked locations, such as malls—or can be at prospects' homes or businesses.	Time consuming and expensive. Customers resist setting up one-on-one sales meetings. Must be prepared for a lot of rejection—in person.
Phone Calls	Reach customers directly. You can make your sales pitch without involving an intermediary. Much less expensive than calling on prospects in person. If carefully targeted, can be effective.	Time consuming. Telemarketing and telesales have bad reputations. Many people won't listen to sales pitches when called. Others have put their names on "do not call" lists.
Direct Mail Solicitations	Reaches many potential customers, very efficiently. A good way to communicate sales and discounts.	Much of it is ignored. Can be expensive. Response rates are very low. Bad for the environment (in terms of trash).
Mail Order Catalogs	Often stick around for a long time. For some companies, customers look forward to receiving catalogs.	Can be expensive to print and mail. Bad for the environment.
Email	Inexpensive. If targets are carefully selected and have "opted in" to your list, your emails are welcomed and can be a good way to communicate new products or services and promotions.	The vast majority is ignored. Spam filters prevent most such email from being seen by targets (exceptions are established customers who opt in for such contact). If classified as a spammer, you could be prosecuted.
Online or Mobile Sales	Very efficient and appealing for the customer. Provides excellent data analytics on what's working. Offers can be changed quickly.	Must have effective online merchandising and robust sales technology. Must maintain and update website and drive traffic to it, which can be expensive.

Sales Procedures and Operations

On this worksheet, outline the procedures and productivity levels you expect in your sales efforts.

Customer Identification

How do you identify potential customers? _____

Do you use cold calling? _____

What prospect lists, if any, do you purchase? _____

What other methods do you use to determine customer interest? _____

Do you capture the contact information of your website visitors? _____

Customer Contact

How do you contact customers? Email? Phone calls? _____

Who contacts potential customers? _____

How many times is a potential customer contacted before they're discarded from the list? _____

When are potential customers contacted? _____

How long does each contact take? _____

How frequently are current customers contacted for follow-on sales? _____

Who contacts current customers? _____

Sales Productivity

What are your sales goals? Specify volume and revenues expected within a certain time frame. _____

What percentage of your revenues will come from online sales? _____

What percentage of your website visitors do you project will convert to purchasing customers? _____

How many times, on average, must a potential customer be contacted before securing: An appointment?___   A sale?___

What percentage of potential customers agree to an appointment or demonstration? _____

What percentage of those agreeing to an appointment or demonstration subsequently purchase? _____

How many calls will each salesperson be expected to make, and in what time period? _____

Who handles phone, mail, email, and online orders? _____

Who ensures that orders are filled promptly and accurately? _____

Does this information get reported to the salesperson? __ Yes __ No How? _____

Who checks credit? _____

Other sales procedures: _____

_____

_____

The Do Not Call List

Through the National Do Not Call Registry, consumers can request that they not be called by telemarketers or telesales personnel. Once consumers are on the Do Not Call list, telemarketers are prohibited from calling them.

There are, however, some exceptions. If telemarketers or telesellers have an established business relationship with a consumer, they can call them for up to 18 months after the consumer's last purchase, delivery, or payment—even if the consumer is on the National Do Not Call Registry.

In addition, a company may call a consumer for up to three months after that consumer makes an inquiry or submits an application to the company. Or if a consumer has given a company written permission, the company may call them. If you engage in telemarketing, you must honor the Do Not Call Registry scrupulously. Fines can be steep! For further information, go to www.telemarketing.donotcall.gov.

- **Listen.** No skill is more important to making a sale than listening. A great salesperson hears what customers want—their concerns and priorities. When calling on a customer, it's tempting to immediately launch into a sales pitch, especially if you're nervous. But by listening, you can better understand how your products or services meet the customer's needs and desires. If a potential customer for your property management service is concerned primarily about safety, don't keep going on about how great your gardening is. Don't just tell the customer what you think they'll be interested in; don't stick to your standard sales patter. Better yet, find out what their concerns actually are and address them.

- **Ask questions.** You can't listen to a customer unless you get them talking. Ask relevant questions to draw them out. "What are you especially worried about for your property? What's the first thing you check when you come for a visit? What's your chief concern about entrusting your property to such a service?"

- **Tell them what they get, not what you do.** This is a common mistake. You work with your product or service every day, so it's natural to focus on details of your work. Yet customers don't want to know the ins and outs of your business; they want to know how you'll meet their needs. So don't bore your potential customer with excruciating details of how you manufacture the widgets by hand. Tell them what the widgets do—and focus on their benefits rather than their features.

- **Appreciate the benefits of your product or service.** Genuine enthusiasm is contagious. If you truly believe you're offering the customer something worthwhile, you'll be a more effective salesperson. On the other hand, if you don't believe in your product or service, you shouldn't be selling it.

- **Provide a clear benefit for the purchaser.** Success has two sides. True, your goal is to profitably exchange your product or service for money. Yet if you fail to satisfy the customer by meeting their wants or needs, you're only halfway to a successful sale. That's why an important part of any sales call is to look at both sides: talk, and also listen so that you can learn what the customer's really looking for and what's important to them.

- **Don't oversell.** It's tempting to land a sale by telling customers everything they want to hear, but that's almost certain to lead to their being dissatisfied or disappointed. One way to avoid this is to actually underpromise and overdeliver, thus making customers delighted with what you've sold them and extraordinarily pleased with its value.

- **Close the deal.** It's not enough to make a convincing argument on behalf of your services or product. You must turn that pitch into an actual sale by asking or directing the customer to buy the product or service you're trying to sell. In person, this can be uncomfortable, but your potential customer is waiting for you to say, "Can I ring up this sale right now?" or "Let's discuss the terms of the contract." If you don't practice asking for the money, you'll walk out of many sales calls wondering what happened.

Many a sale has been lost because the salesperson omitted to take this very basic but important step. Even on the Web, you must close the deal and direct customers to make the purchase. That's why you see so many "Buy Now!" buttons on websites, to help persuade dithering consumers to say "yes" to the deal.

■ **Be profitable.** Make sure that after you add up everything it costs you to produce and deliver a product or service, including your sales expenses, you actually make money. Thus, as you negotiate price—and you'll usually have to do some negotiating—be sure you earn a profit.

Limit choices

How much will you offer customers when you make a sales pitch? Typically, salespeople often think that giving customers a lot to choose from will lead to higher sales. Not necessarily. It seems counterintuitive, but often giving customers fewer choices may lead to closing the deal.

Studies of consumers' buying behavior have demonstrated that limiting the number of their options can be a far better sales technique. In one experiment, researchers set up tables at a supermarket where customers could sample jams. On some occasions, there were 24 different flavors of jam available for tasting. Other times, only six flavors were offered. The result? Far fewer people actually bought jam when they had been presented with 24 flavors. Those with a more limited choice were far more likely to make a purchase.

Many large companies have learned that too many choices are counterproductive; some have made fortunes in the process. When Steve Jobs returned to run Apple, one of the first things he did was drastically reduce the variety of computers that the company made. At the time, Apple had dozens of product lines. Jobs came in and slashed Apple's products to just four, then made sure each was exceptional.

Customers with too many options experience "choice overload." When confronted with all those choices, they have trouble making decisions—which means they're less likely to buy—and feel less satisfied when they finally do.

Many companies think three choices are about right. If you look at many services, for example, you'll typically see three options: the equivalent of an economy, a regular, and a deluxe version (these may have fancier names—premium, professional, expert; silver, gold, platinum, and so on). Three works well, because many people naturally gravitate toward the cheapest choice, and others to the most expensive.

Talking about price

Finding the right time and method to talk about price can be tricky, especially if you offer products or services with a broad span of possible price points. Professional services—such as consulting, legal, engineering, architectural, and the like—can be particularly difficult to discuss from this perspective, because their cost depends on the size and demands of a particular job.

Up-selling and cross-selling

You should always look out for opportunities to make more money from each sale. Two ways are to up-sell (selling a pricier and more function-rich version of a product or service) and to cross-sell (selling complementary products or services).

Say you just booked a series of 10 hour-long massages for a new client, to be fulfilled over a 10-week period. You might want to up-sell that package by convincing the customer to extend the standard hour to a more expensive 90-minute massage. Or you could cross-sell by offering body lotions and relaxation tapes to complement the massages.

The sales pitch

At some point, you'll need to make an actual sales pitch—that is, directly ask a prospect to buy your product or service. A sales pitch has three distinct parts:

- Your pitch (describing your products or services, company, customer benefits, and competitive advantage—based on what you've learned from listening to the customer first)

- The customer's concerns and objections

- Your rejoinder, or reply, to those concerns and objections

After you've been in business for a while, you'll have heard the objections or concerns that keep most prospects from making the decision to buy. Work on responding to those, so you'll sound confident should they arise in the course of a sales call. It's generally best to anticipate objections and respond to them before they're raised. That way, you can address whatever shortcomings or problems the prospect may be thinking about but doesn't want to mention out loud.

The three critical skills for discussing price are:

- **Getting the timing right of mentioning price.** The timing of mentioning a price to a potential client depends on a lot of factors, such as how your pricing stacks up against competitors' pricing and whether it will cause "sticker shock" in your prospect. General rules of thumb are to lead with your price if it's much lower than the competition and will be a pleasant surprise, and to wait until after you have described all the benefits of your product or service if your price is the same as that of your competitors or higher.

  The one hard and fast rule you must follow is to provide the estimate and get the customer to agree to a price before starting actual work. This might seem obvious, but you'd be surprised how many fledgling entrepreneurs are so eager to get business that they omit this most important step! Even if you charge by the hour, give an approximate estimate of how many hours you think a job will take and have clients sign an estimate or letter of agreement. If the scope of the job changes—for example, if a client has engaged your product design company to create the design for a new product and later realizes they also need a design for its packaging—make sure to provide a new estimate, and have the client sign off on it.

- **Estimating price accurately.** Key to your ultimate success—whether you'll actually make money from your work—is being able to accurately predict how much work is involved, and the costs, when you're making bids or proposals for work. This is a skill you'll improve over time. It's almost inevitable that you will make mistakes at first, which is why it's a good idea to build in a healthy buffer when providing an estimate—whatever you can get away with, while still remaining competitive. The best way to learn how to estimate accurately is to keep track of your time and expenses, so that you can see—over time—how much any job truly costs you.

- **Negotiating to fit customers' budgets.** An essential skill in setting prices is negotiating. Often, customers have unrealistic ideas of what they can get for their money. Rather than walking away without a sale, attempt to work with them. Ask the customer what their budget is—most of the time they'll tell you—and instead of just saying, "I can't do the job for that amount," let them know what you *can* provide, within their budget. This might involve cutting back on volume or eliminating certain features. In effect, you're making a counter offer, letting them know how much you can provide for the money they're willing to pay.

  For example, if a homeowner wants to add a room and their budget's only $5,000, instead of saying, "That can't be done," you can say something like this: "For that amount of money, we could add a deck or change some windows. It would cost at least $30,000 to add even a small room." By laying out a range of choices, you help them learn about costs; you can still make the sale; and everyone can leave the negotiating table happy.

Closing the sale

A "closing" occurs when you come to an agreement about the price, scope, and other terms of the sale. The sales cycle has been completed, and you can now move into the next phase—actually performing the work or delivering the product. The closing is essential because no matter how good your sales pitch is, or how proficient you become at estimating a project's scope and price, if you can't get the customer to actually agree to the purchase, you haven't been successful. Several elements characterize an effective closing:

■ **The customer agrees to the sale.** This is the primary requirement of a closing: that both you and the customer come to an agreement about the exchange of goods or services for money.

■ **You arrange a time to deliver the goods or start the project.** Make sure you're very clear about when the customer will actually receive the products, or when you'll begin providing the service. If your customer is not situated locally, specify when you'll ship your product and by what method—that is, courier, next-day air, postal service, or other.

■ **You establish how the goods or services will be paid for—and when.** Payment terms are almost as critical as the actual price you charge. Will the customer pay in cash, by check, by credit card, or on account? If the latter, how much time do they have before they must pay? Thirty days, 60, 90? Will you charge interest? All this must be clearly spelled out.

■ **You formalize the agreement with a written document.** Although many successful entrepreneurs believe this step is optional and prefer to rely on "handshake" agreements, it's always best to have things in writing. Whether it's your proposal or another kind of contract, document every key aspect of the agreed-upon deal. Don't leave anything ambiguous or up to chance. It's always best to be meticulously clear about everything related to your sales agreement.

Reinforcing the purchasing decision

One of the smartest things you can do after the sale is to reassure customers that they've made the right decision. "Buyers' remorse" is often a typical response, so head this off by sending them a follow-up email congratulating them on their choice of products or commending them for choosing your service. Include quotes from previous customers or other accolades you've received for your goods or services. All of this is every bit as important as providing compelling evidence before the sale that you were the right choice.

Ask whether you can include them on future mailings announcing specials, promotions, or new developments at your firm. And keep checking back with them regularly. If you deliver a quality good or service and, without being too aggressive, follow up with communications that keep your name in front of them, chances are good that customers will return time and time again and will even spread the good news about your company to others.

In the end, the best way to make future sales is to keep a current customer very happy.

Do your homework

As with so much else in business, research can be the key to success. Before approaching potential clients, gather as much information as you can about them. Research them on a search engine, go to their website, and do everything you can to learn as much about their businesses and needs as possible before giving them your sales pitch.

REAL-WORLD CASE

Runaway Success: Rent the Runway

Launched in 2009, Rent the Runway (RTR) allows women to do what men have been doing for decades: rent expensive outfits for special occasions. Rather than paying $500 and up to buy a dress, and much more than that when they add in shoes, jewelry, a handbag, and accessories, women simply go online and pick a designer outfit of their choice from thousands of options. They pay only about 10 percent of the cost of the dress. They receive it via an express shipping service, and when they're done, simply drop it in the mail using a provided box and prepaid postage. No need to clean or iron it. If they need shoes or accessories to match that special dress, no problem: For minimal cost, they can rent those too.

RTR was the brainchild of cofounders Jennifer Hyman and Jennifer Fleiss, who met as classmates at the Harvard Business School and quickly bonded. During a break from school, Hyman visited her sister in New York, who had a closet full of clothes and "nothing to wear." Hyman's sister would have loved to buy a Calvin Klein or Proenza Schouler but couldn't afford the price. When Hyman returned to business school and told Fleiss of her sister's dilemma, the two—being budding MBAs—had a brainstorm: Why not rent out these types of dresses? Because they would rent out the same dress over and over, they could profitably purchase expensive clothes and rent them for a fraction of the price. Rent the Runway was born.[1]

RTR adopted a direct-to-consumer sales model. Through its website, it rents out "event" outfits, valued between $300 and $2,000 retail, for rates ranging from $30 to $200. Accessories cost extra. For customers uncertain of their size, RTR offers to ship two sizes for the price of one. If anyone needs advice choosing, RTR stylists are even available by phone. Customers can purchase insurance inexpensively if they want to guard against something happening to a dress.[2]

Rent the Runway's first sales target was young professional women in large cities—like Hyman's sister, the original inspiration for the concept. The two founders figured this market segment had many occasions to dress up. Their marketing plan emphasized public relations; they were profiled in the *New York Times*, the *Wall Street Journal*, *Forbes*, and even fashion magazines. They had no a sales force.

But Hyman and Fleiss soon noticed they were attracting a group of buyers they hadn't foreseen: college women.

"College aged women…are already renting for all of the occasions in their lives, whether it is sorority recruitment, date functions, 21st birthdays, tailgating parties, spring break, or graduation," said Hyman, in an interview.[3]

---

1. "A Netflix Model for Haute Couture," by Jenna Wortham. *New York Times,* Nov. 8, 2009.
2. www.renttherunway.com.
3. "Calling All College Fashionistas! Rent the Runway Kicks Off College Rep Program." Highland Capital Partners.

Like many smart entrepreneurs, the two founders recognized that if a segment of customers was finding them on their own—not as a result of a marketing effort—the likelihood was, that with a meaningful effort, they could significantly grow sales in that segment. So they strategized on how to increase visibility and orders among this niche even more.[4]

Yet the two founders didn't have the money to hire a sales team. Instead, one option they examined was the use of college "brand ambassadors." Many companies were already targeting the college market by engaging students as on-campus brand representatives. Companies such as Red Bull, Gatorade, Foursquare, and many others engage students to put on events on their campus, sponsor campus activities, and get the word out to their peers. This form of marketing costs the company relatively little—students are paid primarily in product, resume-building recognition, and perhaps a small stipend.

Hyman and Fleiss decided this concept would work for RTR, too. They hired "Runway Reps"—college women who would increase RTR's presence on their campuses. At the same time, these women would also gain the opportunity to make some money while increasing their entrepreneurial skills.

In August 2010, RTR kicked off its program with 30 universities in the United States. It hired two to three reps per campus, whose job was to throw parties to showcase the kind of clothes RTR rents, and to set up fashion shows featuring women from their universities wearing RTR dresses. The reps also use social media and personal interactions to evangelize the brand.

Runway Reps represent the blending of a marketing and a sales effort. Runway Reps aren't salespeople in the traditional sense—they don't receive commissions based on how many women from their colleges end up using the RTR service. And they're not a multilevel marketing program—Runway Reps aren't rewarded by soliciting others to become reps as well.

Overall, they do more than just raise brand recognition for the company. Runway Reps may earn credits they can apply for their own RTR rentals, can compete for cash prizes and recognition, and often directly encourage their fellow students to use RTR's services and give students discount coupons to encourage them to make purchases (all typical sales personnel functions).

This kind of sales/marketing approach is often viewed as a win-win situation: The students get to do something they like and increase their skills and experience, while the company acquires a very inexpensive sales force.

Seizing on the ripe college market and the growing influence of low-cost, on-campus ambassadors has proven to be an excellent driver of profitable sales for Rent the Runway. The company became profitable before the end of its second year of business, and even managed to convince premier venture capital firms to invest in it, raising more than $30 million in venture financing. By 2012 it had aggressively expanded its on-campus ambassador program to more than 150 schools. ■

questions

1. What types of data make it possible for a company to notice when an unexpected customer segment is starting to make purchases?

2. Rent the Runway Reps aren't compensated directly for making sales, as are most salespeople. Do you think giving them commissions or salaries would increase the number of sales RTR makes? Why, or why not? How would that affect their overall profitability?

3. How do you feel about the concept of "brand ambassadors" on college campuses? Should colleges allow students to be on campus evangelizing other students for off-campus, commercial businesses?

---

4. Ibid.

MAKING A LIST— NAUGHTY OR NICE?

Goal:

Imagine that you're launching a new company selling veterinarian equipment. You've developed an innovative exam table that holds dogs and cats steady while keeping them comfortable during vet examinations. This is something many vets would find very beneficial, but the table costs more than traditional vet exam tables. You're planning a marketing campaign—buying ads in publications for vets—and exhibiting at trade shows, but your sales team will also contact vets directly. Your problem: how to get the contact info of vets—meaning good leads.

What to Do:

A number of list brokers sell contact info for veterinarians: names, addresses, phone numbers, size of practice, and, in some cases, email addresses.

1. You're considering buying a list. Answer the following questions:

    a. If you do buy a list, how will you contact the people listed on it?

    b. How do you feel about cold calling these leads?

    c. How do you feel about sending these leads unsolicited direct mail pieces?

    d. How do you feel about sending these contacts unsolicited emails? Do you consider this "spam"?

2. Do you think cold calls are worth the extra time and trouble they take? In which types of businesses do cold calls make the most sense?

3. What kinds of precautions must you take when contacting names on a purchased list? What kind of precautions should you take? (HINT: Think opt-in.)

4. If you don't purchase lists, what other methods could you use to generate leads for your salespeople to approach vets?

5. Which types of companies benefit from buying a customer list? Which types of companies, if any, would not benefit from buying a customer list? Do purchased lists work better for some industries than others?

6. Compose a model script for a personal cold call for vets' names on the lists. If you work with others, take turns role playing—one person plays the salesperson making a sales call, and others take on the role of prospects.

12 Management and Leadership

learning objectives

In this chapter, you'll learn how to:

- Evaluate the skills of the current members of the management team

- Identify the skills lacking on the team in order to ascertain what outside talent is required

- Determine which company positions the founders will fill

- Assemble a Board of Directors and an Advisory Committee

- Determine which types of consultants and specialists are needed

- Define a management structure

- Demonstrate effective leadership

- Establish and nurture a corporate culture

Your People Determine Your Success

Good ideas may be the foundation of an entrepreneurial venture, yet people are at the heart of its success. One of the first things that investors look at when deciding whether to fund an entrepreneurial company is the management team. Who are the founders and what are their capabilities? Who are the people in key positions and what kind of experience do they have? What kind of team have the founders already put together or or what kind do they plan to form as they grow their company?

That's why most entrepreneurs must give serious thought to the kinds of people they'll need on their team. They have to consider which roles need to be filled, and when. Some of these key team members will be employees; some may be consultants. And a few key members of your team may be your advisors and board members.

All companies—including new, entrepreneurial ones—also need to develop a management structure and leadership style that motivates employees. Even the best people can only do their best work in a system that encourages, recognizes, and rewards achievement. If you can create such an atmosphere, you can give yourself a true competitive edge.

In planning your management, focus on three main areas: 1) the roles you need filled on your team; 2) the people who'll fill those roles; and 3) your management structure and leadership style. Together, these represent the core of your management plan.

Your Management Team

Who are the people most important to your company's future? Who are the people determining the strategies you will pursue? Who makes final decisions? Which members of your management team decide on the products or services you will sell and the prices you will charge? Who will head up your marketing or sales efforts?

As you assemble your company's management, the first layer of your management team will consist of founders, key employees and **principals**, a **Board of Directors**, an **Advisory Committee**, and consultants and specialists.

Founders

Usually, the most important person in an entrepreneurial business is the founder or founders, especially in a start-up.

In the early days of a start-up, the founders are absolutely critical to a company's success. Without outside funding, an entrepreneurial start-up rarely has the money to hire outside, professional leadership. So it falls to the founders to create the business plan, develop a prototype, make initial sales, and begin to build a team. It is the founders' drive, intelligence, connections, persistence, and ideas that will play the largest part in launching a company.

If the company needs to raise outside funds, the founder or founders will be the ones who will be examined by potential investors or lenders. Potential investors want to see if they inspire confidence in their ideas, and have experience, stability, and maturity. Potential lenders, by contrast, want to see if they have the credit history and personal financial ability to pay back loans.

Roles for Founders

Typical roles for founders in entrepreneurial companies include:

- President and/or Chief Executive Officer (CEO)
- Chief Operating Officer (COO)
- Chief Marketing Officer (CMO)
- Chief Technology Officer (CTO)
- Director of Business Development

en·tre·pre·neur·ship key terms

Advisory Committee
A nonofficial group of advisors; has no legal authority or obligation.

Board of Directors
The members of the governing body of an incorporated company. They have legal responsibility for the company.

Corporate culture
The atmosphere of a company. Corporate culture is made up of the aggregate attitudes, experiences, beliefs, and values of all employees at a business.

Directors and Officers Insurance
Insurance that protects individuals sitting on the Board of Directors from being sued if a company does something wrong.

Lines of authority
The formal structure of a company that outlines how decisions will be made, employees will be supervised, and job functions and responsibilities will be allocated.

Open-book management
A management style in which a company discloses information, especially financial information such as income statements and balance sheets, to all employees.

Principals
The high-level employees in your company who balance and expand the talents of the company founders. Principals include the Vice President, Technical Director, Marketing Director, and so on.

Evaluating your management team

When considering hiring the key players for your team, ask yourself the following questions:

- Do they possess the skills necessary for their specific jobs?

- Do they have a record of success?

- Have their business setbacks given them insights that will help them in their current roles?

- Do their personalities make them effective members of the team?

- If they have supervisory responsibility, are they able to direct and motivate employees effectively?

- Taken as a whole, does your team incorporate the full range of expertise and management skills you require?

In start-ups, the founders usually serve as the top managers and exercise day-to-day control over affairs. They set strategic direction, build and manage a team, and typically make sales and negotiate prices and deals.

For this reason, when figuring out your management team, take a good, honest look at the talents and skills of the founders, even if one of them is you yourself. Clearly recognize what skill sets and talents are lacking in your founders. That enables you to identify the skills and talents you need to find by hiring others and makes it more likely that you'll realistically focus on finding outside talent to complete your core team.

When examining the founders, decide on which positions they are capable of holding in the company, and for how long.

Often, a founder may serve as both President and CEO (Chief Executive Officer) until significant funds are raised or the company grows substantially. Occasionally, either the founders themselves or, more typically, major investors will bring in others to serve in top positions as the company gets larger—moving the founders to other positions, such as in technology development or marketing.

But if the founders remain active in the leadership of the business—which is highly likely—it's important to identify which roles they are truly best suited for.

Key employees and principals

Early in your venture, you'll realize you need to attract individuals with other capabilities to balance and expand the founders' talents and skills. These key employees—or principals—will play major roles in your company.

What responsibilities are you likely to need addressed first in your new venture, and what kinds of roles and responsibilities usually handle such responsibilities? Naturally, staffing requirements vary, depending on the nature of the products and services you sell. In general, most companies need to address the functional areas outlined in the table on the following page.

As you put together a plan for your management team, consider the entire range of functions you'll need handled by key personnel. Of course, in the early days, one person—perhaps a founder—will handle a number of these roles. As you grow, you'll want people who will specialize in handling key responsibilities.

Be careful not to offer high-level titles to inexperienced personnel early in your business. If, say, you offer a friend who's helping you write code for your new mobile app the role of "Chief Technology Officer," you may find it difficult to take that title away as your business grows and as you need to hire someone else with greater management experience, or perhaps someone who has previously led engineering teams.

RESPONSIBILITIES AND ROLES OF KEY EMPLOYEES

RESPONSIBILITY	ROLES
Overall management and strategy	President and CEO (Chief Executive Officer), Vice President, Product Manager
Planning and execution of day-to-day operations and functions of the business	Chief Operating Officer, Production Manager, Plant Manager, Technical Director
Marketing and sales	Chief Marketing Officer, Business Development Director, Director of Sales, Marketing Director, PR (Public Relations) Director, Director of Communications
Product development, especially of technology products; management of technology systems	Chief Technology Officer, Director of Engineering, MIS (Management Information Systems) Director, IT Director, R&D (Research and Development) Director
Financial management	Chief Financial Officer (CFO), Controller, Accountant/Bookkeeper
Hiring and managing staff, ensuring adherence to labor laws, dealing with personnel issues	HR Director/Personnel Director, Training Director, Office Manager

Board of Directors

Once a business is incorporated, the law requires it to have a Board of Directors, typically needing to meet at least once a year. In very small corporations, the directors are usually just the principals running the company. The board then serves little more than a legal function.

In larger companies, however, the board often includes members outside of management. Most frequently, these board members are people who have invested money in the company. Venture capitalists typically require board seats as a condition of their investment. A lead investor will often serve as Chairman of the Board.

Members of the Board of Directors have a fiduciary duty to protect the interests of the shareholders of the company—not to protect employees or even founders (except to the extent that they are shareholders). They control decisions of the company, often overruling the founders and other key personnel.

Obviously, investors serve on boards to protect their money; they want to exercise some control over the management and direction of the company they've invested in. But management should not view these investor/directors only as "Big Brothers," watching their every move. They often bring valuable insight and judgment to the company and contribute to its overall viability and success.

Key Management

List which of the following key responsibilities and roles you'll need for your venture, indicating the desired skills and experience for those roles. Taken as a whole, does your team incorporate the full range of expertise and management skills you require?

Responsibility: Overall management and strategy

Roles (indicate which ones to be filled and by whom, if known):

President/Chief Executive Officer:_____

Vice President(s): _____

Product Manager(s): _____

Other: _____

Actual or desired experience, education, skills: _____

Responsibility: Planning and execution of day-to-day operations and functions of the business

Roles (indicate which ones to be filled and by whom, if known):

Chief Operating Officer:_____

Production Manager(s): _____

Plant Manager(s): _____

Technical Director(s): _____

Other: _____

Actual or desired experience, education, skills: _____

Responsibility: Marketing and sales

Roles (indicate which ones to be filled and by whom, if known): _____

Chief Marketing Officer: _____

Business Development Director:_____

Director of Sales:_____

Marketing Director:_____

PR (Public Relations) Director: _____

Director of Communications:_____

Other: _____

Actual or desired experience, education, skills: _____

Responsibility: Product development, management of technology systems

Roles (indicate which ones to be filled and by whom, if known):

Chief Technology Officer : _____

Director of Engineering: _____

MIS (Management Information Systems) Director:_____

IT Director: _____

R&D (Research and Development) Director:_____

Other: _____

Actual or desired experience, education, skills: _____

Responsibility: Financial management

Roles (indicate which ones to be filled and by whom, if known):

Chief Financial Officer (CFO):_____

Controller: _____

Accountant/Bookkeeper: _____

Other: _____

Actual or desired experience, education, skills: _____

Responsibility: Hiring and managing staff, ensuring adherence to labor laws, dealing with personnel issues

Roles (indicate which ones to be filled and by whom, if known):

HR Director/Personnel Director: _____

Training Director:_____

Office Manager: _____

Other: _____

Actual or desired experience, education, skills: _____

Types of consultants and specialists

Consultants and specialists you might use, in addition to attorneys and accountants, include:

- **MANAGEMENT CONSULTANTS:** To help you plan your business, develop strategies, solve particular problems, and improve management techniques.

- **MARKETING CONSULTANTS:** To design ways to position your company in the market, oversee the creation of advertising and promotional materials, and structure your sales strategy.

- **DESIGNERS:** To add perceived value and improve your company's image through the talents of people with skills in graphic design, product design, packaging design, website design, or interior design.

- **INDUSTRY SPECIALISTS:** To contribute special knowledge or specific technical skills to your company. Experts offer consultation on, for example, kitchen design for restaurants, production line design for manufacturing companies, and merchandising for retail stores.

- **TECHNOLOGY SPECIALISTS:** To help you identify your technology needs and solutions, and to set up your database, website, communications systems, and the like.

As you form your Board of Directors, you might also want to include members who bring specific business expertise, such as financial acumen or industry knowledge. Such directors typically receive compensation for their service on the board.

Remember, though, that the Board of Directors has legal responsibility for the corporation. It has the final decision-making authority for who serves in key management positions, such as the President and the Chief Executive Officer (though those roles can be combined in one person). The board may remove even a founder from running their own company. Directors can be sued if a company does something wrong, and it's typical that, in larger companies, individuals will require a company to purchase insurance (**Directors and Officers Insurance**) to cover them before they'll accept a board seat. So be extremely careful about whom you ask to be on your board—it is not something to be offered or accepted lightly. Thus, outsiders should be chosen after much thought.

Advisory Committee

You may identify a number of individuals whose ongoing judgment and advice you want for your company, but whom, for legal or other considerations, you don't want on your Board of Directors. One way of using their services, other than hiring them, is to institute an informal Advisory Committee. Such a committee can also be helpful to a proprietorship or partnership that does not have a Board of Directors.

An Advisory Committee is an informal group with no legal authority, no legal liability, and no set rules about how many people must be involved. In fact, it never even has to meet; your Advisory Committee can simply consist of a few people who've agreed to let you turn to them for advice now and then.

The point of having advisors is to seek advice—so look for people whose advice you'd like to have and whose wisdom you trust. Ideally, you'll find experienced and balanced individuals. Good potential Advisory Committee members are seasoned entrepreneurs, individuals with experience in your industry, or people with substantial contacts to prospective customers or funders.

One of the best things about asking people to serve on your Advisory Committee is that they then have a sense of involvement in and commitment to your company. They may initiate conversations with you, make introductions to useful contacts, and give you helpful guidance.

Consultants and specialists

Most companies use outside providers to perform certain tasks. These outside consultants and specialists can contribute valuable expertise and experience to younger, smaller companies. It's not necessary that every function—even relatively critical ones—be handled by people you employ on your staff.

Consultants can bring young and growing businesses the specific expertise of highly qualified individuals without the expense of full-time employees. Specialists with particular skills can help fill the gaps in your management team. For instance, you might not yet be able to hire a full-time Marketing Director, but you could use the assistance of a marketing consultant.

Even as you grow, you'll most likely continue to use some consultants to bring additional expertise and capabilities to your company. It's typical for even the largest companies to use outside law firms, accounting firms, public relations agencies, research firms, and more.

The use of consultants can also enhance the image you present in your business plan if you're looking for funding. Being represented by a respected law firm in town, or having your accounts prepared by one of the major accounting firms, adds credibility to your company.

It's important, though, to understand the difference between independent contractors and employees as far as the law is concerned. Chapter 16 discusses these legal issues in depth.

Management Structure

How will you actually run your company? How will decisions be made? What are the **lines of authority**? In other words, how will you structure the management of your company? A company's organization and management style act as powerful, invisible forces shaping both the daily working atmosphere and the future of the company.

In a new or very small business, there's usually not much formal organizational structure. It's typically easy for everyone to communicate frequently, and it's pretty clear who's in charge—the founder or founders.

Yet as a company grows, it becomes necessary to have some kind of management structure to provide accountability and enable communication. Entrepreneurs are usually impatient with these kinds of management considerations—they simply want to focus on making the product or service and securing sales. But without an organizational structure, it's easy for vital jobs to fall between the cracks or for tensions to arise. Indeed, a frequent source of conflict in partnerships is the failure to delineate areas of responsibility and decision-making.

An organizational structure, ideally, makes it easier to get things done efficiently. Overstructured companies, of course, do just the opposite—they burden people with unnecessary bureaucracy. So you'll want to keep lines of authority and communication clear but uncomplicated.

The first place to begin is with the formal structure—the "official" lines of authority. Who will have responsibility for which functions? How will employees be supervised, and by whom? How will you ensure ongoing communication—both from the top down (from supervisors to their employees)

Flat Management

Many entrepreneurs use a "flat" organizational structure in which everyone interacts as peers (though with differences in responsibilities and salaries) and teams are empowered to make decisions in their area of responsibilities. While the most important decisions are still made by the senior management, there are few layers of authority.

Open-door management

When considering your leadership style, consider how accessible you are to those who work with you. Some leaders are only comfortable with an authoritarian style, in which decisions are made at the top and passed down through the ranks. The trend in business, though, has been toward a more open and relaxed management style, with lots of communication that encourages innovative thinking and initiative among all employees.

and from the bottom up (from those doing the work to provide insight and suggestions to decision-makers)?

Some questions to ask when thinking through your management structure:

- Should responsibilities be allocated by functional area (e.g., marketing, finance, product development), by product line, by geographic area, or by some other method?

- Which functions will each manager have responsibility over? How much independent decision-making authority will each be given?

- Which employees will each manager supervise?

- How will you communicate between function areas or key management?

- Perhaps the quickest and clearest way to communicate your management structure is through a graphic organizational flow chart as on page 297.

Leadership

Leading your team is perhaps the most important task for any entrepreneur. An entrepreneur who is an effective leader of people has a far greater chance of building a successful company than someone who is technically brilliant but unable to motivate and manage others. Indeed, you have a far better chance of staying at the helm of your company as it grows if you can become an effective leader. So it's important to develop your capabilities in such skills as communication, motivation, team building, and the like.

Being a boss is a skill you have to learn—and relearn. Just like any other business skill, perfecting it takes practice, thought, and input from others. If you want employees who are productive and motivated, you'll have to learn to be a good and fair leader. At the most fundamental level, you'll have to examine your own attitude toward those who work for you. Are they valuable and valued members of a team, each worthy of respect? Or are they interchangeable resources, easily replaced if you can find someone cheaper or more malleable?

Keep in mind that your attitude toward your employees shapes their attitude toward you and their jobs. When managers trust and empower employees to think about how to solve problems—not merely to carry out specific tasks as specifically instructed—they give those employees the potential to unleash impressive amounts of creativity and energy. And, not incidentally, you'll retain the people you've spent a lot of time and money hiring.

Effective leaders do the following:

- **Set standards.** Clearly state expectations, and be consistent. Develop and distribute clear policies. Even a young company should have a basic employee manual outlining benefits, holidays, sick leave, and such. Let employees know on what basis they will be judged, then stick to that. The best way to set standards is to set an example for others. Employees resent being held to higher standards than the boss.

BUILD-YOUR-BUSINESS WORKSHEET

Your Management Structure

Using the example below as a guide, draw your own management structure.

FLOW CHART EXAMPLE

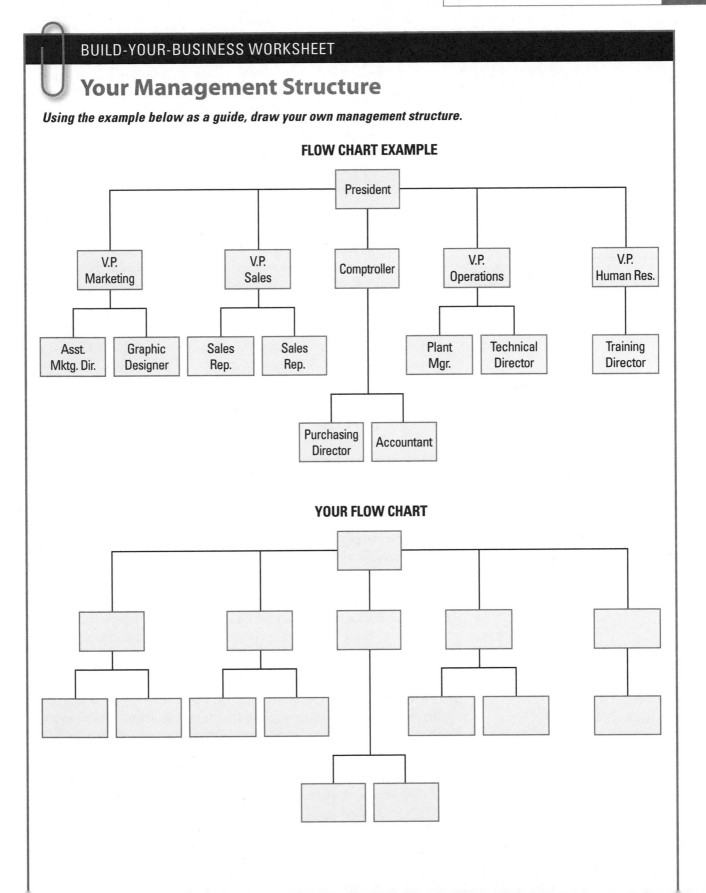

YOUR FLOW CHART

Do as I do

Your team will only be as honest and ethical as you are. If you cheat customers, your employees are far more likely to cheat you. If you do not gossip or lie, *they'll* be less likely to gossip or lie. You set the standard. No matter how idealistic your company's formal code of conduct, what really matters is your behavior.

REAL-WORLD RECAP

Leadership 101

Effective leaders do the following:

- Set standards
- Act fairly
- Choose the right people
- Pay fairly
- Train
- Communicate
- Empower employees
- Respect
- Provide feedback
- Acknowledge contributions
- Reward

- **Act fairly.** Make certain that your standards are reasonable and fair and that the goals you set are actually reachable. Don't change the rules constantly—one of the worst things you can do is to want things done one way today and another way tomorrow. Be careful not to play favorites with employees, and never use benefits to manipulate them.

- **Choose the right people.** If an employee is smart and capable, they'll help your business grow. Hire for attitude and adaptability rather than merely for skills. Look for the ability to learn quickly, common sense, good work habits, and a willingness to take on any task.

- **Pay fairly.** A good leader attracts good people. Yet you can't hire the right people if you do not have a fair salary and benefits package. Expect to have higher turnover, see higher absenteeism, and spend more time and energy on personnel problems if you fail to provide fair and competitive compensation.

- **Train.** Good leaders provide employees with the knowledge and tools for them to do their jobs successfully, which often entails training. In an entrepreneurial business, employees should be able to pitch in on many jobs, so they need training beyond specific tasks. Therefore, educate your workers about your whole business, and emphasize problem-solving.

- **Communicate.** Perhaps the biggest mistake companies make is failing to share information. Employees feel included and empowered when they know what's going on. Listening is also a part of communicating. Many managers forget to use one of their most important resources— their employees' minds. Enlist their suggestions and set goals together. Have problem-solving sessions where employees help devise solutions to company problems.

- **Empower employees.** The best leaders create effective employees by giving them the authority to act independently and make certain decisions. Most employees will learn how to do their jobs better than you can teach them. Enable them to use their brains, not just their backs.

- **Respect.** Recognize the unique skills and talents of each person who works with you. Demonstrate to them that you believe they are capable of doing their jobs, even if it takes some time for them to learn. People generally live up to the trust—or mistrust—that others show them.

- **Provide feedback.** You can't expect employees to improve if they don't receive regular, constructive feedback. Employees are better able to meet your needs if management lets them know when they do well and how they could have done better. Make sure they hear specific suggestions, not just a litany of complaints.

- **Acknowledge contributions.** One of the least productive things an employer can say is, "I don't need to thank employees; they get paid!" We all need to be thanked and recognized. Find opportunities to thank people, both individuals and the staff as a whole.

■ **Reward.** A successful entrepreneurial company will grow rapidly, and your team plays a huge part in that success. As you grow, and your income grows, make certain that employees feel that they share—monetarily—in that success. This may be through bonuses, profit sharing, or stock options. You want your team to feel they are building something together and are benefiting from it.

As a business founder, you really have *two* jobs: leader and manager. Your challenge is balancing how to give employees the responsibility and authority they crave while maintaining standards and guarding the organization against problem employees.

MANAGER VS. LEADER: THE BOSS WEARS BOTH HATS

A MANAGER	A LEADER
Tells employees what needs to be done	Sets high-level goals and strategy; establishes clear standards and values
Trains employees (or arranges for training) in how to do their jobs well	Keeps the business on track to reach those goals
Monitors/measures success on a daily procedural or process level	Monitors/measures success at the financial or organizational level
Helps prevent things from going wrong	Helps things go right
Fixes problems when they do occur	Empowers others to take action to fix problems

Your Corporate Culture: What Do You Stand For?

Management structure and leadership style are two major components of what's often referred to as **corporate culture**. In other words, what's the atmosphere in a company? How formal or informal is it? How much flexibility and authority do employees have? Can they have a good work/life balance?

At its most basic level, a corporate culture is made up of the aggregate attitudes, experiences, beliefs, and values of all employees at a business. A corporate culture can be one in which employees work very hard but also play hard. Or it could be one in which individual workers possess a great deal of autonomy—to the point where they don't need to come into the office except for meetings or other special occasions. Some businesses attempt to formalize their corporate cultures by writing down their corporate "values"; in other cases, the culture is simply the spirit that infuses the organization more spontaneously.

Social responsibility

Your commitment to social responsibility is also a part of your corporate culture. Are your business practices socially responsible? Do you take steps to be environmentally conscious? Some companies, even young ones, allow employees to devote a certain amount of paid time for volunteering. Others match employee contributions to their favorite charities (up to a certain amount). And some companies support their own favorite causes or charities. (For more on social responsibility, see Chapter 17.)

Leadership Traits

Use this worksheet to consider your leadership style and the skills you might need to acquire to become the kind of leader you admire.

Management trait you admire *or* find unhelpful: *"I want to…"* or *"I don't want to…"*	How it translates into a specific action to take/*not* take: *"Do's"* and *"Don'ts"*	Skills you need to enhance to achieve this management trait:

Much of the reputation you will earn as a company comes from your corporate culture, so it's worthwhile considering what kind of corporate culture you hope to establish in your entrepreneurial venture. You probably already have a vision of the kind of company you yourself want to work in: one where everyone enjoys coming to work, works hard and shows dedication, is treated with respect, maybe even has a little fun.

When many people think of a company's "culture," they think first of things such as how formal or informal its work environment is. Are employees clad in jeans and T-shirts? Or do they wear uniforms or business clothes, such as dresses and shirts with ties? Do you bring in pizza on Fridays? Do employees have to clock in and clock out?

Your company's corporate culture is less about these superficial things than it is about what you and your business stand for—your business values. How will you treat your employees? How will you show them respect? How will you interact with your community and the world in general? What code of ethical conduct will you adhere to when doing business?

Many companies make it clear that they are truly committed to valuing families, guaranteeing that employees only have to work late or on weekends in true emergencies and that parents can take care of sick children when necessary.

Will you have all the answers to these questions about your company's culture when you launch your business? Of course not. Expect your culture to evolve over time. After all, if you want a dog-friendly workplace and a terrific candidate for your VP of sales is allergic to pets, you'll have some decisions to make. But, if you at least have a framework in mind from the outset, you can begin to sculpt a culture that fits you, your business, and your values.

Remember, in the long run, how you and your managers treat your employees may be the most important thing you do, other than how you treat your own family. If you treat employees with respect, pay them fairly, and create an environment in which they can grow, you not only improve your business, you also make a positive impact on your community—and the world.

Having a great company culture:

1. **BOOSTS EMPLOYEE LOYALTY:** Employees who fit well with your culture are likely to be extremely loyal and satisfied, reducing employee turnover.

2. **HELPS RECRUITING EFFORTS:** If you create a company with integrity, respect for all, and a fun atmosphere, you'll have candidates lining up at your door.

3. **ATTRACTS CUSTOMERS:** If your business's culture resonates with your customers—and if you consistently deliver on your commitments to them—they're going to be more inclined to do business with you.

4. **DRIVES DECISION-MAKING:** If you've cultivated a business culture that is committed to integrity and honesty, then you already have a framework for making decisions.

5. **ESTABLISHES A POSITIVE REPUTATION:** You may not realize it, but the word gets out—to customers, vendors, fellow business owners—about how you run your business. When you're seen as a fair and decent employer, as well as a good businessperson, your reputation is enhanced in your community.

REAL-WORLD CASE

The Art of Corporate Culture: The Sky Factory's Five Principles

Perhaps only an artist would want to create a company in which the company itself is as much a work of art as the products it produces. About building a company, Bill Witherspoon, painter and founder of The Sky Factory, told *Inc. Magazine* that "both painting and company-building start with a blank canvas. In a painting you create beauty with the addition of each brush stroke. In a company you create it with the addition of each talented, engaged person and with each thoughtful act."[1] He decided to apply artistic principles to building and managing a company.

Witherspoon's vision was truly *about* visions. Noticing that most workers today are enclosed in esthetically unappealing closed rooms—or, if they have windows, the windows look out on less-than-inspiring streets or industrial areas—he decided to create and market "virtual windows." What's a virtual window? Exactly what it sounds like. Using high-resolution backlit images, acrylic tiles, and daylight-quality lighting, The Sky Factory opens up vistas of mountains, oceans, forests, or any other beautiful scenes you can imagine—by projecting virtual windows on walls (or skylights on ceilings). In the process, he's enchanted architectural designers, art publications, Feng shui enthusiasts, naturalists, interior designers, and technologists. Judging by the coverage in the mainstream press, including *Inc.,* the *New York Times,* and the *Wall Street Journal,* he's succeeded in building a beautiful company as well.

The Sky Factory's customers are typically businesses that operate in industrial urban environments, in buildings with little or no natural light and—if they even have windows—no stunning views. Using a mixture of technology, video, and animation, The Sky Factory turns such drab spaces into inspiring work areas in which employees look out onto tranquil lakes, leafy forests, or snow-capped mountains. Best of all, the virtual views are dynamic: The wind blows ripples onto the lakes, the forest trees sway with the breeze, snow falls on the mountain tops. The Sky Factory achieves all this while also bathing the room in natural light that's perfectly aligned with the scene being viewed out the virtual window. You might think that such beauty could be distracting. Yet studies have shown that productivity actually goes up, not down, when employees have such pleasing scenes to rest their eyes on.

As innovative as The Sky Factory's products are, its management philosophy is even more forward-looking. Its secret sauce for building a beautiful—and highly profitable—company? Five cultural principles: transparency, flat-hive management, consensus, service, and performance.

challenge

Encourage workers to help build a company, not just take home a paycheck

solution

Nurture a collaborative culture in which all workers participate in decision-making

---

1. "How to Build a Beautiful Company," *Inc.com.* June 8, 2010.

Transparency means that, with the sole exception of private personal matters and compensation, there are no secrets in the company. From Witherspoon down to the part-time administrative assistant, everyone possesses as much knowledge as anyone else. For example, all financials for the company—sales, costs, profits—are disclosed to the entire company at weekly team meetings so that everyone understands the business's financial stability.

"Flat-hive" management means that all workers are considered equals. Flat management starts with the principle that there are no managers and supervisors, and there are only owners. Witherspoon explained that "My first decision was to give people the opportunity to purchase discounted ownership, and 100 percent of employees have participated. The responsibility for revenue and profit belongs to everyone." To that end, self-motivated employees participate in multiple job-teams, each charged with a different function within the company. Because Witherspoon is wise enough to know that meetings of workgroups can easily deteriorate if no one is in charge, each one has a facilitator—but the facilitator responsibility circulates among members of the group. All employees get their turn at facilitating. The goal: Each employee learns how to do everything within the company.

The core value of "consensus" means that all business decisions are made by agreement arrived at both by small teams and—for larger decisions—by the entire company as a whole.

Service is the single most important value, because it brings everything together. Witherspoon says it's core to both the employee and customer communities. But he distinguishes between two attitudes that businesses can bring to service. The most common attitude is that the business does something for the customer—and then expects a return. For example, most organizations that care about customer service do so because they hope to receive, in return, customer loyalty and higher revenues per sale. By contrast, Witherspoon subscribes to the *other* idea of service—the selfless kind. "I do something for you without thought of a return. I help you spontaneously and without thinking about it."

Finally, performing well is applying all the other four concepts to the ultimate goal of superb results. And performance, to folks at The Sky Factory, means a great deal more than financial performance. It means delivering quality products, and having pride of ownership in everything each employee does.

Witherspoon makes clear how creating that service experience for both its customers and workers matters: "That appreciation of what we are doing is what keeps great people here, and great people will ensure that The Sky Factory endures. After all, that's what great art does. Endures." ■

questions

1. Many successful companies practice **open-book management**, disclosing financial information to all employees. What are the potential benefits of this disclosure?

2. Why would some companies *not* want employees to have access to all information in a company, including financial information?

3. How do you think owning a piece of a company through profit sharing or stock options affects employees' attitudes?

4. Besides open-book management and profit sharing, how else could The Sky Factory motivate employees?

GROWING UP WITHOUT FALLING APART

Goal:

To weigh the advantages and disadvantages of different management styles.

What to Do:

Imagine that you head a company that creates innovative, high-quality toys and games. You have 25 highly motivated employees, most of whom you hired yourself. You've built the company with an open-book management style—every Friday at lunch, you all meet and go over what's happening at the company and, while final decisions rest with you, you ask all employees for their input on major decisions and almost always act on their choices. Employees work in teams to devise new toys and have a great deal of independence in which toys they create. In your profit-sharing program, each employee gets an equal share of a portion of the company's profits.

The good news: Your company's products are so popular that you can't keep up with demand. To expand, you must hire many more workers. However, attempting to manage by consensus is already difficult. The conference room during team meetings is already full.

You attribute much of your company's success in creating innovative toys to your management style, which nurtures employees' independence and sense of ownership. Yet you recognize that with a growing workforce, you face many more challenges in the way you manage.

Revise your management strategy in ways that will take into account a growing workforce but still maintain your company's creativity. Ponder the following points:

1. You won't know—or have much of a personal relationship with—some of the employees as the company grows. How can you make sure each one is capable of making decisions that are good for your company?

2. Many of your employees, in your still-small company, perform a number of tasks. As the company grows, the roles become increasingly specialized. How will people in specialized roles, such as product engineers or shipping clerks, be able to make decisions that benefit the entire company?

3. Your profit sharing is now based on company-wide performance, and already, some people are disgruntled that they work harder but receive a similar share of the profits as others.

4. A few of your company superstars love the existing, consensus-driven, ownership culture and have stayed at the company because of it, even though they could command higher salaries elsewhere. They will threaten to leave if the culture changes too much.

5. Consider ways to adapt your management style to keep your workforce motivated, creative, and feeling a sense of ownership as your company grows. What would you change about your current management? What would you keep the same? Why?

CHAPTER

13 Human Resources Issues

learning objectives

In this chapter, you'll learn how to:

- Understand the basic differences in employee status

- Define basic human resource laws

- Determine employee compensation and research pay rates

- Design a benefits package

- Find and attract excellent job candidates

- Conduct interviews with potential candidates

- Evaluate prospective employees and choose a candidate

- Identify the best methods for retaining employees

- Determine when it's time to let employees go

Bringing Others on Board

Entrepreneurs can't do it all themselves. It's impossible to build a company of any size and worth unless you can build an excellent team. If you want to grow your business, you'll have to bring others on board. You'll need to know how to find, hire, motivate, reward, and retain both employees and any independent contractors your company may use.

That means it's important to spend time learning how to select the right people, put them in the appropriate positions, make the most of their talents, and keep them motivated to do a great job for you. Part of your necessary skill set is also becoming familiar with the most fundamental labor laws and requirements.

As your company grows, you'll get help with all these. Eventually, you'll have a Human Resources ("HR") or personnel department or staff to help manage employee issues. They'll help you recruit and screen job applicants, manage benefits and personnel issues, and ensure that you follow applicable laws.

Still, as an entrepreneur, *you* are the ultimate leader of your team. If you select the right people and learn the basic skills of how to be a boss, you'll be on your way to greater satisfaction and a successful, healthy business.

Employee Status

One key HR issue with which every entrepreneur must become familiar is the concept of employee status. This may seem arcane, yet an employee's status determines both their rights under the law and how you must treat them in terms of pay, working conditions, and other labor laws.

The three most important types of employees—in the eyes of the law—are **exempt employees**, **non-exempt employees**, and **independent contractors**.

In broad strokes, the distinction among these types of employees is as follows:

- Exempt employees are covered by fewer labor laws, but employers are still responsible for their share of payroll taxes. Exempt employees are managers who must be paid a minimum amount per month. They are paid on a salaried basis.

- Non-exempt employees are covered by all labor laws, and employers are responsible for their share of payroll taxes (such as Social Security, Medicare, and unemployment). They are paid on an hourly basis.

- Independent contractors are individuals who perform certain tasks or handle projects for a company on an outsource basis. They are not covered by labor laws, and the employer is not responsible for payroll taxes.

Of course, many companies would prefer to classify workers as independent contractors so they don't have to pay payroll taxes. Or, they would like to treat some employees as managers so they aren't responsible for overtime. Some workers, too, would rather be classified as independent contractors because they won't have payroll taxes deducted from each paycheck, and many of their business expenses are tax deductible.

However, you are limited in making these choices. While classifying workers as independent contractors or managers may benefit you financially, employment laws restrict those choices even if both you and the worker agree to such classification. It's critical, therefore, to understand the basic outline of what makes a worker an employee—exempt or non-exempt—and under what circumstances you can classify one as an independent contractor.

en·tre·pre·neur·ship key terms

Americans with Disabilities Act (ADA)
Prohibits discrimination against the disabled by any business with 15 employees or more.

Equal Pay Act (EPA)
Requires all businesses to provide equal pay and compensation to both men and women for work that is equivalent.

Exempt employees
Employees covered by fewer labor laws than non-exempt employees. Employers are still responsible for their share of payroll taxes. Exempt employees must be managers who receive a certain minimum pay per month.

Fair Labor Standards Act (FLSA)
The primary federal employment law that covers workers in the United States.

Independent contractors
Individuals who perform certain tasks or handle projects for a company on an outsource basis. They are not covered by labor laws, nor is the employer responsible for payroll taxes.

Non-exempt employees
These workers are covered by all labor laws, and employers are responsible for their share of payroll taxes (such as Social Security, Medicare, and unemployment).

Occupational Safety and Health Act (OSHA)
Varies by industry and protects workers from unsafe conditions such as exposure to chemicals, fire hazards, and the mishandling of heavy machinery.

Help wanted, but what type?

- **FULL-TIME EMPLOYEES:** People on payroll for 30–40 hours per week. Paid on an hourly or salaried basis.

- **PART-TIME EMPLOYEES:** People on payroll from a few hours to 25 or 30 hours per week (state laws vary as to what constitutes part-time). Usually paid on an hourly basis.

- **TEMPORARY OR SEASONAL EMPLOYEES:** People who work for a short period, either part-time or full-time, often to handle a temporary increase in workload for seasonal work (such as Christmas holidays or summertime) or to fill in for absent workers (such as those on maternity leave). Temps may be put on payroll, treated as independent contractors (if their work meets IRS criteria), or hired through a temporary staffing agency and treated as employees of that agency (thus "leased" from the agency).

- **INDEPENDENT CONTRACTORS:** Individuals, not on your payroll, who perform tasks, work on projects, or consult with you. Conditions must meet IRS criteria.

- **INTERNS:** Students or entry-level individuals eager to learn about your industry. They can be unpaid if they receive school credit.

Criteria for employee vs. independent contractor

Few areas of tax law are murkier than—or can get a business in as much trouble as—the laws relating to classifying workers as independent contractors. In the United States, the Internal Revenue Service (IRS) and federal and state labor agencies aggressively pursue companies that intentionally (or unintentionally) classify someone as an independent contractor yet treat that worker as an employee. The IRS has gone after huge corporations as well as small mom-and-pop businesses and, once they find a violation, they're likely to go back through many past years of your taxes. So be careful.

The IRS and other government agencies prefer employers to classify their workers as employees. Why? Federal, state, and city governments want to make certain that anyone doing the work of an employee gets treated as such. Employees are entitled to many legal protections, including rules regarding overtime and unemployment. And the government wants to protect as many workers as possible.

Also, because employers are legally responsible to withhold tax money from employees' salaries, government agencies can depend on receiving tax payments. Independent contractors, by contrast, invoice employers and receive paychecks from which no deductions have been withheld. They manage their own tax payments and can be less reliable about submitting their taxes.

The IRS once maintained a set of specific rules governing independent contractor status, but, responding to businesses' legitimate need for greater flexibility in hiring independent contractors, the IRS has since broadened the rules. But this means that its unclear guidelines sometimes make it quite difficult for businesses to classify independent contractors.

Nevertheless, the main issue the IRS uses to determine employee status is who *controls* the worker. The more control you have over the worker—such as when, where, and how they work—the more likely the worker is your employee and not an independent contractor. The nature of the work they do for you does not alone determine their status.

The IRS looks at three areas:

1. **Behavioral.** Does the worker control how they do the work? The IRS reviews issues such as who determines the employee's work hours and location, who controls the order or sequence of that employee's work processes, and who owns the tools or equipment the worker uses to get the job done.

2. **Type of relationship.** How permanent is the relationship of worker to employer? Is the work performed a critical, regular part of the employer's business? Does a written contract exist? Is the worker responsible for their own benefits?

EMPLOYEE VS. INDEPENDENT CONTRACTOR: THE RIGHT CLASSIFICATION

EMPLOYEES...	INDEPENDENT CONTRACTORS...
Do not run their own businesses	Are independent businesspeople, especially if they are incorporated
Work in your office and use equipment you provide	Choose their work location and provide their own equipment, tools, and materials
Work hours specified by you	Set their own hours
Work per your instructions and may receive training from you	Decide how to perform their services, and in what order, and usually receive no training
Are paid for their labor regardless of business performance	Can earn a profit or suffer a loss (in their own business), depending on the quality and quantity of services they provide
Work for you on a continuing basis	May manage multiple clients or customers and typically work for you on an as-needed project basis
Receive employee benefits	Are responsible for their own benefits
Are usually paid by unit of time (hourly, monthly)	Are usually paid a flat rate by project but can be paid hourly
Can quit or be fired at any time	Can be terminated or leave, according to the terms of their agreement with you

3. **Financial.** Does the worker have a significant investment? Do they own their own tools? Do they make their services available to others and work for outside businesses?

Because its rules are somewhat fuzzy, the IRS does provide some protections for businesses that make mistakes in treating employees as independent contractors—as long as those mistakes were made in good faith. They'll investigate whether a business relied on the advice of an attorney or accountant, followed industry practice, and acted consistently.

But—and this is critical—there's absolutely no protection for a company that doesn't file the necessary tax forms for independent contractors. Each year, you must file a form (Form 1099-MISC, *Miscellaneous Income*) with the IRS, reporting payments to independent contractors over a certain dollar amount. If you fail to file 1099s and the IRS later challenges you on the classification of your independent contractors, you're in very hot water indeed.

Review the "Right Classification" table above for the criteria the IRS uses to evaluate control of a worker and therefore how they are classified.

Do your homework!

Remember, you can run into danger by misclassifying an employee as an independent contractor, and never the other way around. The IRS won't tell you that you "should have" classified an employee as an independent contractor.

If you're unsure of employee status, fill out IRS Form SS-8, *Determination of Worker Status for Purposes of Federal Employment Taxes and Income Tax Withholding*. It's available on the IRS website (www.irs.gov). If you still have questions, speak with an accountant or attorney.

**FLSA:
Fair Labor Standards Act**

The main federal law governing labor laws is the Fair Labor Standards Act (FLSA), first enacted in 1938, and revised and broadened regularly.

The FLSA has seven main aspects that you need to know about and comply with: which employees are covered by the FLSA; minimum wage; overtime pay; child labor; equal pay for equal work; posting requirements; and record-keeping requirements. To learn more, go to www.dol.gov/whd/flsa/.

Criteria for "exempt" vs. "non-exempt" employees

Once you've classified a worker as an employee rather than an independent contractor, you also have to determine whether—in the eyes of the law—they are *exempt* or *non-exempt* from labor laws, such as minimum wage and overtime (the **Fair Labor Standards Act [FLSA]** in the United States, or provincial laws in Canada).

What, you might ask, is the purpose of having two different types of employees—exempt and non-exempt?

The government wants to protect wage earners, especially those who perform routine tasks for the lowest wages, to make certain they are paid fairly and are not overworked without additional pay. But the government also wants to leave companies flexibility in how they deal with other types of workers—such as managers and executives.

For instance, it would be downright silly to require a corporation paying a CEO hundreds of thousands of dollars to also pay her overtime. However, it's just unfair to allow that same corporation to force a shipping clerk to work 70 hours a week for a mere $100.

To distinguish between types of employees, the U.S. government considers some employees "exempt" from federal labor laws and others "non-exempt."

- **Non-exempt:** These employees are covered by all labor laws. They are paid on an hourly basis. You must pay them at least the minimum wage (both federal and state), and they must receive overtime pay of 1.5 times their regular pay when they work more than 40 hours in a week.

- **Exempt:** Certain employees are exempt from both minimum wage and overtime pay rules. They must be bona fide executive, administrative, professional, or outside sales personnel. Job titles do not determine status—the nature of the work does. They must be paid on a salaried (versus hourly) basis and make at least $455 per week.

Basic U.S. Labor and Human Resource Laws

Once you start working with others, you also must understand the basic rules that apply to you as an employer. The government, rightly, wants to protect workers from unfair treatment, making sure they are paid fairly and work in safe conditions. You, too, as a good employer, will want to ensure that you treat your employees well and act within the law.

At the beginning of your entrepreneurial venture, definitely consult with your attorney to make sure you follow applicable laws. Once you have an HR director or department (or a consultant), it will be their job to help keep you within the law.

Even with others' help, from the very beginning of your business you—as an entrepreneur—should understand the most fundamental labor laws and requirements. Don't let the idea of laws governing employment scare you. Just become familiar with the basics, and you'll almost certainly stay out of trouble.

Most entrepreneurs quickly find themselves sufficiently knowledgeable about these regulations to know when they might be getting into an area covered by the law, at which point they realize they'd better ask a lawyer or seek more guidance. The major areas of employment law that you'll need to know about are as follows.

- **Minimum wage.** In the United States, you'll be subject to both federal and state minimum wage laws. With few exceptions, you must pay employees at least this amount. (As of 2010, the U.S. minimum wage was $7.25 per hour.) If workers are paid on a piecemeal basis, the amount must still equal the hourly minimum wage. State laws vary on how you must pay workers who earn tips or work on commission sales, but they still must make at least the minimum wage on an hourly basis.

- **Overtime, working hours, meal and other breaks.** In the United States, non-exempt workers must be paid 1.5 times their regular rate after 40 hours of work in any one week. You aren't required by federal law to provide lunch breaks or other meal breaks. However, if an employee works and eats lunch at their desk, they must be paid for that time. Short breaks—bathroom and coffee breaks—are considered part of the regular workday and must be paid. Exempt employees are not covered by overtime rules. Note, however, that many states require paid lunch or rest breaks, so check your state's laws.

- **Training and other paid time.** You are not required to give employees training, but if training *is* required, they must be paid for the time they spend in training. Any time traveling while on the job (such as between work sites during the day) or waiting time on the job must be paid.

- **Time off, required leaves.** The Family and Medical Leave Act (FMLA) requires employers to provide up to 12 weeks *unpaid* leave because of their own or a family member's serious health condition, or because of the birth or adoption of a child.

- **Equal opportunity/discrimination.** The law prohibits *any form* of employment discrimination based on age, sex, religion, race, color, national origin, or disability. The rules are sweeping. You can't discriminate in hiring, advertising, pay, benefits, promotions, or layoffs. You can't create a hostile atmosphere, and it is your job as an employer to make certain that no employees create a hostile atmosphere for other employees because of their inclusion in any of those covered classes. Moreover, you must make "reasonable accommodation" for an employee's religious practices.

REAL-WORLD RECAP

Familiarize yourself with the following major areas of employment law:

- Minimum wage
- Overtime, working hours, meal and other breaks
- Training and other paid time
- Time off, required leaves
- Equal opportunity/discrimination
- Equal pay for equal work
- Hiring the disabled
- Child labor laws
- Eligibility to work
- Workplace safety and health
- Posters and record-keeping

- **Equal pay for equal work.** The **Equal Pay Act (EPA)** requires all businesses to provide equal pay and compensation for work that is equivalent for both men and women. It doesn't matter whether the jobs have different titles; if the work is substantially the same, you must pay the same wages.

- **Hiring the disabled.** The **Americans with Disabilities Act (ADA)** prohibits discrimination against the disabled by any business with 15 employees or more. The term "disability" is broadly defined—it covers anyone with any kind of physical or mental disability or disease. However, the person must meet normal job requirements and perform normal job functions, though you may be required to make "reasonable accommodation" to permit disabled employees to do their job.

- **Child labor laws.** In almost all cases, the minimum age for nonfarm employment is 16, but no one under 18 can work in hazardous conditions. Teenagers age 14 or 15 may be able to work in certain occupations, outside of school hours and when the work hours are limited.

- **Eligibility to work.** In the United States, you can only hire American citizens or noncitizens who have the right to work in this country. By federal law, every U.S. employer is responsible for verifying an employee's right to work here.

- **Workplace safety and health.** The **Occupational Safety and Health Act (OSHA)** protects workers from unsafe conditions. While OSHA regulations vary by industry, they cover such things as exposure to chemicals, fire safety, and working with heavy machinery.

- **Posters and record-keeping.** The U.S. government requires you to keep records relating to every employee, ensuring that you comply with the law. You are also required to post notices of employees' rights where employees can see them. You can purchase premade posters summarizing or quoting all the laws for about $25.

Employee Compensation and Incentives

One aspect of having employees that most entrepreneurs like you grapple with is compensation: "What's the right amount to pay?" you might wonder. "Should I offer a salary, an hourly wage, or a commission?" "How do I get a great employee at a salary I can afford?" Before you make these decisions and determine an appropriate wage for your new employee, you first need a clear job description of the position you're filling. That way, you can begin by comparing what other companies in your industry and in your area pay to hire similar workers. That job description will serve as the basis of the research you'll do to find out prevailing wages.

As you set about figuring out the right amount to pay an employee, you, of course, also have to figure out what you and your business can afford. What you'll end up paying your new employee will depend on a number of factors, including:

- What the prevailing wages are for that type of job in your industry, in your locale

- How difficult it is to find someone, given the labor market's current condition

- How attractive your work environment or opportunity is

- How experienced the candidate is

- How important that person or that position is to your company's success

- How soon you need someone

- What your cash flow and budget can realistically handle

As you set your pay scale, your goal is not to figure out how little you can pay but rather what you *should* pay. You want to pay enough to attract good, reliable employees who will stay with you and add to the value of your company. To do that, you must be competitive, both in salary and in benefits.

Compensation packages

When looking at what to pay an employee, you and the prospective employee will consider the entire compensation "package." Employees will want to know about their wages, of course—whether paid hourly or on salary. Still, you can sweeten the deal with other incentives—whether in the form of cash or benefits.

Types of compensation you can offer include:

- **Salary.** Amount of money paid annually to a manager or executive, regardless of company or personal performance.

- **Hourly wage.** Amount of money paid for each hour worked by an employee, regardless of company or personal performance.

- **Bonuses.** Additional cash given, usually at the end of the company's fiscal year, based on company or personal performance.

- **Commissions.** Cash paid, based on a percentage of sales made.

- **Profit sharing.** Cash distributed to all eligible employees, based on the company's annual profit.

- **Equity.** Stock in the company, which gives the employee a direct financial stake in the overall performance of the business.

For more info

Although the laws are many (and some quite complex), the federal government has a number of websites that provide more information.

Start with www.sba.gov—the government's entry-point website for business. Also check the U.S. Department of Labor's website (www.dol.gov). Use the search term "state labor offices" to find links to your state's site. For answers to your questions about employment laws, contact your state's labor department.

And remember, it's always a great idea to seek advice from an attorney familiar with labor laws in your state.

- **Stock options.** Ability to buy stock at a future date at a currently set price; if the worth of the company goes up, these options can be exercised, giving the employee a financial gain.

- **Tips.** In some industries, employees can also receive tips—or a share of tips—left by customers.

- **Overtime.** Some employees appreciate and look forward to receiving occasional overtime pay—at 1.5 times their normal hourly wage; others may resent having to work overtime.

Researching comparable pay rates

When trying to figure out what to pay employees, begin by doing research on comparable pay rates. If you pay too little, you won't be able to attract excellent candidates. And, of course, since you're a growing company, every dollar counts, so you don't want to overpay employees, either.

As you conduct research on comparable pay scales, keep in mind that you want to look for comparable pay based on the following:

- **Job duties.** Try to compare pay based on actual job duties, rather than simply job titles, because different companies may give different titles to people who perform the same or highly similar functions. Comparable pay scales for entry-level and low-level jobs may be fairly easy to find; "comps" on executive or managerial pay may be more difficult to learn.

- **Location.** Pay varies dramatically based on location. Pay scales in larger cities, in cities along the U.S. coasts, and in economically healthy areas tend to be much higher than those in smaller communities or in the middle of the country.

- **Industry.** Some industries pay very well, while others are notorious for underpaying. Technology, science, and health care tend to pay well (especially for specialists, engineers, and skilled workers). Education, publishing, retail, and food service tend to pay less competitively.

- **Business size.** Generally, small companies can't afford to pay as well as larger corporations. This is not always true, however.

It helps to research comparable pay by checking with industry associations, other business owners, career websites, online salary websites, and the U.S. Bureau of Labor Statistics (www.bls.gov/oes).

Employee Benefits

Good benefits are crucial to making your place of employment more attractive than others. Many of the best workers will only accept a job where they receive certain types of benefits—such as health care, paid vacation, and paid sick leave. To be competitive with other employers, you must offer a "package" of benefits.

The most widely offered, and desired, employee benefits are as follows:

- **Health care.** In the United States, companies that offer excellent medical and dental benefits have always been particularly attractive to job seekers, especially ones with families. Federal law is changing regarding business health care requirements. To attract the best people to work in your business, expect to offer a competitive package of health care benefits.

- **Vacation.** Although not required by U.S. law, offering paid vacation is a necessity to retain the best workers. Generally, begin with two weeks' paid vacation for most workers (executives may get more), and increase paid vacation as job tenure rises.

- **Sick leave or personal leave.** This too is not required by federal law in the United States, though there is a national movement to get states and the federal government to mandate paid sick days. Most employees, especially hourly workers, can't afford to lose income, so if you do not offer any paid sick days, they will have to show up for work even when ill, possibly infecting other employees and customers (and perhaps prolonging their illness). That's probably why 73 percent of all full-time workers in the United States receive some paid sick leave. Many companies also offer personal leave days—or lump them with sick days—so an employee can take care of personal or family affairs.

- **Retirement contributions.** Setting up some kind of retirement program in which you, as an employer, contribute an amount to an employee's retirement is typically valued by employees, especially those who are prudent enough to look ahead. The most popular program for employers is a "401(k)" plan to which both the employee and employer contribute a small percentage of the employee's income each month.

Finding Excellent Employees

Simply put, the future of your company depends on the quality of your employees. Yet it's a challenge to find and retain outstanding workers, since competition is always stiff for the best employees.

First things first, though. You'll want to determine what, exactly, you need employees to do. Start by clarifying on the worksheet "Employee Needs," the tasks and responsibilities you require them to handle. That will set the foundation for the job descriptions you'll develop and will also help you identify which candidates can best perform those duties.

Writing a powerful job description

The key to successful hiring is to have a very clear definition of the position you're filling. Job descriptions spell out the critical duties, roles, and responsibilities of a specific job. After candidates read a well-crafted job description, they should know precisely what the position involves. This clarity should help them figure out whether the job suits their skills, background,

May I pay my employee in cash?

Yes, you may pay an employee in cash. But, no, you may not pay cash to evade taxes. You must be able to produce a paper trail that shows the amounts you paid, along with the withholdings and deductions. This can be a tricky area, so talk to your accountant or payroll service to make sure you're staying well within the law. It's a *much* better idea to pay by check or direct deposit.

and interests. A well-crafted job description helps you attract the candidates you want and weed out the ones you don't.

Developing your job description is time well spent, because you'll use it to:

- Clarify and define exactly what tasks you need your employee to handle and what experience, skills, and traits you'd like them to have

- Write an effective help wanted ad

- Evaluate job performance against duties and expectations once the employee has started

- Update and redefine the role as the employee gains skills or your needs change

Consider the following criteria when writing a job description:

- **Skill sets desired.** Envision the daily tasks and activities your new hire will have to perform. What are the must-have skills? What would be nice to have?

- **Past experience needed.** Which critical aspects of the job would benefit from specific past work experience? Are you looking for a particular educational background, or for someone with specialized training? Do they need prior industry knowledge or experience performing certain job functions?

- **Personal characteristics desired.** Which personal traits, if any, are critical to the job? Do you need an outgoing and friendly employee for a customer service job? Or creative traits for a marketing position? It's OK to include personal traits on a job description if they're key to finding a good fit, but avoid potential legal problems by focusing on qualities needed to do the job well, not factors like age or gender.

- **Where you'll compromise.** Know if you'd be willing to provide on-the-job training for a candidate with the right personality and less experience. Make sure your job description emphasizes the things that are the most important to you.

- **Tasks you'll want help with in the future.** As your business grows and attracts more customers, what duties will you want this employee to perform? Forecast for your reasonable immediate future growth, and plan well ahead.

Ingredients of a strong job description

You want more from your job description than just a basic list of roles and duties. An effective job description defines:

- Job title

- Work hours and location. Is the position full-time or part-time? If part-time, which specific hours/days?

Employee Needs

Use this worksheet to identify the tasks you need to accomplish to run your business; how much time each will take; the skills, education, and experience you're looking for; and how much you'll pay for this work. Use the information to help you write a job description and craft a "help wanted" ad.

Tasks to Accomplish	Hours per Week	Skills, Education, and Experience Required	Pay Rate

Remember the taxes

When budgeting for employees, be sure to figure in the cost of payroll taxes and benefits. Budget roughly an extra 15 percent to cover taxes. If you offer a generous package of benefits, your employee costs— including benefits and taxes— could increase by as much as 30 percent, significantly affecting your cash flow.

- Job duties and responsibilities

- Vital contributions this person is expected to make to the company

- Skills, educational background, work experience, or certifications required and/or desired

- Personal characteristics required and/or desired

- Compensation (specify salary, hourly, base + commission, etc.)

- Reporting relationships and how you expect the employee to work with you and/or coworkers

Complete the "Write a Job Description" worksheet on page 319 to outline what you need and want for each position you have to fill.

Advertising your job opening

Once you've developed a compelling job description, you'll want to turn that into a help wanted ad and get the word out to appropriate job seekers. Your goal is to attract many qualified, good candidates and to find the best fit for you.

One of the easiest places to start is through those closest to you—people you know who may know qualified applicants. You can send out a simple email, and post notices on your favorite social networking sites, such as Facebook. Word-of-mouth can often be the best way to find candidates who come with personal recommendations.

Other places to advertise your job opening:

- Your company website

- Career websites

- Craigslist/local media sites

- LinkedIn/other social media sites

- Industry-specific sites and industry association media

- College career centers

- Unemployment offices

- Classified ad in the business section of your newspaper

- Sign in your window

BUILD-YOUR-BUSINESS WORKSHEET

Write a Job Description

Job title: _____

Reports to: _____

Hours/location: _____

Job duties and responsibilities: _____

1. _____

2. _____

3. _____

4. _____

5. _____

6. _____

7. _____

8. _____

Vital contributions and outcomes of the position: _____

Required qualifications of candidate (specific skills, education, years of experience, certifications, etc.): _____

_____

Other desired skills, including personal characteristics: _____

Salary/hourly wage, benefits, other compensation: _____

TIPS TO SPOT GOOD AND BAD RESUMES

GOOD SIGNS IN A RESUME	WARNING SIGNS IN A RESUME
Past on-the-job experience that meets your needs	Little or no past job experience (unless entry-level job)
Completed education or training, especially if related to your job needs	Failure to complete degrees, education, or schooling
History of continually increasing job responsibilities and titles	History showing lack of promotions or of progressing job improvements
Stable employment history; continually employed; stays at jobs for reasonable periods	History of moving from job to job quickly; gaps in employment history
Personalized cover letter or email showing they've read job description; detailing how they meet your needs	No cover letter, or a "blanket" response indicating little knowledge of your job needs
Any special skills, experience, or accomplishments that make them unique	Typos and general sloppiness in resume, cover letter, or application

Reviewing resumes for winners

With the word out about your job, ideally you'll attract lots of applicants. When the resumes start coming in, keep your job description handy. Look for candidates who clearly meet your requirements. Don't simply be swayed by the fact that an applicant went to your college or engages in your favorite sport.

Evaluate applicants by:

- Their resume or application: how well their background meets your requirements

- Their cover letter, email, or other communication: what it tells you about how professional they are in their approach, their fit and enthusiasm for the job, and other impressions you have of them

- Any referrals from people you know whose judgment you trust

- Any other indicators that make them a likely prospect

Conducting in-person interviews that click

If you're fortunate, you'll get a highly qualified pool of applicants. Once you've reviewed resumes, you'll want to select a few of the best candidates for in-person interviews. Here are some interview best practices to consider when planning how you'll spend your face-to-face time.

- **Plan questions ahead of time.** Take a few minutes before the first interview to make a list of things you need to know about candidates and their backgrounds.

■ **Ask open-ended questions.** Avoid questions that can be answered with a simple yes or no. Also avoid leading questions with an obvious right answer. You want to ask open-ended, thought-provoking questions that begin with *what, when, where, how,* or *why.* Those questions require the candidate to relay more information and provide insight into who they are.

■ **Set the tone.** Start with a firm handshake and a friendly smile. Polite, just-getting-to-know-you chatter for the first couple of minutes can break the ice and put you both at ease.

■ **Tell the candidate what to expect.** Explain the process and the expected length of the interview—then stick to them. Let the candidate know that you'll take notes during the interview (jot down what they say, not your opinions, at this stage).

■ **Plan what you'll say about your company.** The best candidates may have more than one job interview, so tell potential candidates not just about the job they'll be doing, but also about the upside of working at your company.

■ **Review your benefits.** Many applicants are particularly motivated by benefits, especially health insurance. If you offer these benefits, make sure to tell applicants.

■ **Don't make promises you can't keep.** Never make any promises about job security, salary increases, or career advancement. Those can get you in legal trouble later.

■ **Remember to listen.** During interviews, don't do all the talking. It's appropriate to explain the job, but most of the time the candidate should be talking, not you.

■ **Know what you can't ask.** Be careful! Some questions are illegal. You can't, for example, ask about a candidate's plans for having a child, marital status, religion, or age. But it's perfectly legal to ask about hobbies, interests, and long-term goals.

■ **Put them to the test.** Get a feel for "hands-on" ability by asking candidates to apply their knowledge to a realistic scenario. Ask a potential office manager how they would improve a particular process. Have a candidate for a marketing position suggest improvements, on the spot, to a page on your website or to some of your marketing materials.

■ **Leave time for questions.** At the end of the interview, always ask if the applicant has any questions for you. See how they think, and find out what's important to them. Expect the best candidates to ask you meaningful questions about the job. Questions about your products and services show an interest in how your business operates. It's reasonable that they'll inquire about salaries and wages. But if the only questions are about vacation, work hours, and money, then they may not be seriously evaluating whether the duties of the job are a good fit for them. By letting the candidate pose some of the final questions, you can get insights that lead you closer to filling your open job position.

Ask good, probing questions

Choosing a set of questions that you'll ask each interviewee gives you a solid basis for comparison at the end:

■ **SELF-APPRAISAL QUESTIONS:** Find out how candidates perceive themselves by asking how they would describe their ability to complete specific tasks. To find out even more, ask the candidate about someone else's opinion, such as "What would your previous manager say about how you...?"

■ **SITUATION-BASED QUESTIONS:** Think of a real-world situation that your new employee will be in, then ask a "what-if" question about it. You want to hear how they would apply past experience in their new job.

■ **STRENGTH AND WEAKNESSES QUESTIONS:** Ask your candidate directly what they think their strengths and weaknesses are. Follow up with questions on how they developed that strength, or how they plan to overcome their weakness.

QUESTIONS YOU LEGALLY CAN AND CAN'T ASK A JOB CANDIDATE

NO	YES
What is your maiden name? Do you go by Ms. or Mrs.?	What is your name?
What is your date of birth? How old are you?	Are you over the age of 18?
When did you graduate from high school? College?	Did you graduate from high school? College?
Are you an American citizen? Where were you born? What is your nationality?	Are you eligible to work in the United States?
What language did you speak growing up?	Do you speak any languages other than English that could prove useful in this position?
Are you married? Do you plan on having children? Do you have children? Have you arranged for child care?	Do you have any conflicts with the company work schedule?
Which religious holidays do you observe?	Can you occasionally work on holidays and weekends?
Do you have a disability? Do you suffer from any chronic illnesses? Do you take any prescription medications?	Can you perform [physical tasks relevant to the job description] with reasonable accommodation to any of your particular needs?
Have you ever been arrested?	Have you ever been convicted of a felony?
Are you a member of the Army Reserve?	Do you have military experience?

Selecting from among candidates

With luck and thorough preparation, you'll have several excellent candidates for your job opening. How will you choose among them? Even after interviewing, you may have to decide between candidates. Here are a few tips on how to pick from among them.

■ **Hire for attitude, train for skills.** Don't get hung up looking for specific skills, such as knowledge of a particular computer program. If you find a smart and willing person, you can send them to a class. There are exceptions, of course—if you need someone to fly a plane, you need an experienced pilot—but most skills can be taught.

■ **Hire the unusual.** Increase your applicant pool by expanding your vision of a typical employee. Do you typically hire young people? Try recruiting retirees. Have you considered actively seeking people with disabilities? Sometimes the best employees don't look like the ones you already have.

■ **Check references.** Even if you have no reason to doubt an applicant's honesty, you can learn a lot by checking references. Use reference checks not only as a way to confirm employment but also as a way to learn how to work more effectively with your new employee. Questions you can ask former employers include the following: "What kind of training, either for skills or for attitude, would you suggest to make the applicant an even better employee?" "What job duties required you to give the applicant more direction than others?" "What duties did the candidate particularly enjoy or do well?"

■ **Act fast.** Good applicants don't stick around long. If you see someone you really like, be prepared to decide and make an offer. But never hire just because you have a job to fill. It's better to keep a position open than to be stuck with the wrong person.

DIVERSITY

A diverse staff provides various perspectives and can help your company succeed. It can also help you avoid costly mistakes, such as when the MGM Grand in Las Vegas had to completely redesign its main entrance—which had customers walking through the mouth of a gargantuan lion—when they learned that the reason Asians weren't going to their hotel was that walking through a lion's mouth was considered very bad luck.

Embracing diversity may be a smart strategy for improving the bottom line. Here's what a new company can and cannot do:

1. **Don't discriminate:** in hiring, buying, or serving customers. (And discrimination is illegal.)

2. **Take a hard look at yourself:** Many entrepreneurs are more isolated in their interactions and worldview than is good for business.

3. **Reach out:** Seek a broader range of job applicants, suppliers, customers, and marketing vehicles. Join organizations serving diverse target markets.

Making the job offer

Once you have decided on a candidate, you must check them out more thoroughly before offering them the job. In some cases, you may have to negotiate pay and other benefits.

Here's what a typical process entails:

1. Decide on top candidate.

2. Perform reference checks.

3. Call or meet with candidate and make offer.

4. Negotiate salary and benefits (if necessary).

5. Get candidate's signature for drug and background screening (if necessary and permissible).

6. Conduct any other background screens (if necessary).

7. Send a formal offer letter (see sample offer letter on page 325).

Step outside your comfort zone

People tend to hire people who are similar to themselves. That means you may not give adequate consideration to those who are less similar to you. So check yourself: Are you fairly and honestly evaluating candidates who differ from you in background, age, race, gender, and national origin?

The very best businesses harness the talents of diverse people with diverse personalities. They bring fresh perspectives to the job—and possibly help you reach other types of customers as well.

Negotiating well

Many—if not most—job applicants may try to negotiate on salary or wages. After all, they're going to test the waters to see whether they can possibly make more money, especially if you've waited until they're the final candidate (and they know it!) before you bring up the subject of pay scale. If you've already discussed salary during the in-person interview, they may be reluctant to mention the issue again, or they may ask about raises.

If your salary or wages are considerably lower than other prevailing wages, expect every qualified candidate to negotiate. If you want good people, you'll have to change your pay scale.

When negotiating on salary or wages, ask the candidate what salary they need to accept the job. Make them give you a specific number—especially as you've already offered a salary to them. Then you can see how far apart you are and whether there's room in the middle you can both live with. Remember, if a candidate is very unhappy about the salary but takes the job anyway, they're likely to start hunting for another job as soon as they can, and you'll be faced with the entire hiring process again.

Other approaches to consider as part of a negotiating process:

- Increased benefits
- Future raises
- Training or advancement

Be sure to to call attention to any other benefits you offer—especially ones they're unlikely to find with other employers. All of these make your job offer more competitive.

Retaining Employees

Once you've hired great employees, make sure you treat them well. If they're that good, others will want them, too! Here are some tips on getting good employees to stay, once you've got them on board.

- **Recognize achievement.** Everyone wants to be appreciated. When employees do a good job, let them know you noticed. Say "thank you"— often. Find ways to recognize employees who do their jobs well on a day-to-day basis as well as those who accomplish something unusual or significant on your behalf.

- **Reward hard work.** As important as it is for employees to receive verbal recognition for their contributions, it's also great for them to get tangible rewards. This doesn't always have to be a major salary increase or bonus; sometimes just an unexpected treat can go a long way.

Sample Document: Offer Letter

_____ [Date]

Dear _____,

On behalf of XYZ Marketing, Inc., I'm pleased to offer you a position as Office Coordinator. In this role, your salary will be _____ per pay period, which is equivalent to a rate of _____ per year. You will report directly to me. Your first day of work will be _____. Work hours are from 8:30 a.m. to 5 p.m.

The offer described above is contingent upon the results of your reference check, background check, and credit check. Please sign and return an authorization to conduct a credit check that accompanies this letter.

A summary of your benefits is enclosed with this letter. If you have any questions, please don't hesitate to contact me.

On your first day, you will be asked to complete a Form I-9 in compliance with the Immigration Reform and Control Act. As part of this compliance, you must present us with documents that identify you and indicate you are eligible to work in the United States. This must be done within three days of hire.

You will need to complete and submit the benefits enrollment forms within 30 days of your date of hire. If you have any questions regarding the I-9 or benefits information, please contact me and I'll be happy to walk you through the process.

I look forward to working with you and to the contributions you will make to XYZ Marketing, as well as the opportunity to provide you with professional growth. Please indicate your acceptance of our offer by signing below and returning one copy of the letter, with your original signature, to me no later than [date].

Sincerely,

_____ [Your name and signature]

I accept/decline (please circle one) XYZ Marketing's offer of employment. I understand that my employment with XYZ Marketing, Inc. is considered "at-will," meaning that either the company or I may terminate this employment relationship at any time without cause or notice.

_____ [Employee name and signature]

- **Give salary increases.** Your employees know what other people in similar jobs earn. They know the salaries you're giving to new employees and what their coworkers make. Don't wait for an employee to become dissatisfied with their pay and ask for a raise; they may just leave instead.

- **Be realistic in your expectations.** It's human nature to focus on what an employee is missing rather than what an employee offers. Let's face it, though: No one is perfect. So appreciate employees for what they bring to your organization.

- **Create a "blame-free" atmosphere.** Your very best employees want to be able to use their judgment and their brains. They'll thrive in an environment where they know they can make decisions and take reasonable chances without getting berated if something goes wrong.

- **Share information and success.** Employees feel a stronger sense of ownership when they understand the company's overall goals and strategy. So share information. Also, look for ways that employees can benefit financially from the company's long-term financial success, whether in the form of bonuses, profit sharing, or even an equity interest in the business.

- **Enable employees to grow.** After a while, the best employees get bored doing the same job. If the only way they can grow is by leaving, they will. Instead, invest in your employees. Help them take classes, learn new skills, and take on new responsibilities.

Even in a new company, a written set of personnel policies helps create a sense of security and fairness for employees. It reduces confusion, confrontation, and potentially even litigation.

The contents of your official policies reflect, in part, your company culture and the values your company holds. The way you treat employees, customers, and vendors; the standards you set for quality; the behaviors you expect or will tolerate in the workplace; and your benefits—all should reflect your company values.

Your personnel policies should cover issues such as:

- Benefits
- Paid time off: sick leave, vacation, holidays, personal time off
- Work hours, overtime, time cards
- Safety
- Employees' personal conduct on the job
- Customer service
- Use of company property
- Reimbursement and expenses

- Confidentiality and security
- Ethics
- Performance reviews

As your company grows, these policies will evolve. In a small company, with a motivated staff, you may be able to keep personnel policies brief. But as you grow larger, you'll find you need to spell out your policies in greater detail.

Letting Employees Go

As you start your entrepreneurial business, you're hardly thinking about getting rid of employees—you just want to find great people to help you build your company.

Unfortunately, the time may come when you have to let an employee go. This is never a pleasant task, and it's one that is difficult to get used to, no matter the circumstances that prompt the necessary departure.

Due to the uncertain income of new, entrepreneurial companies, layoffs can be an unfortunate fact of life. Your company may be growing, and you may staff up to meet demand, only to find that the orders suddenly slow or you lose a major client. At the point where you can no longer afford to have an employee (or employees) on payroll because of financial considerations, you may have to lay off some of your staff. That's particularly hard, because these employees may have been doing a great job for you, and you hate to lose them. That's why you might try to keep them on payroll as long as you can.

The most difficult situation is when you have to fire an underperforming employee. Obviously, you will have to fire employees who are not performing their jobs in ways that meet your performance standards, who engage in illegal or unethical behavior, or who endanger other employees. For legal reasons, you should keep written records that document the performance-related issues you've encountered with problem employees and show that you gave them the opportunity to correct those issues before terminating them.

Whether laying off or firing employees, it's important to do this as humanely and decently as possible, and to give terminated employees severance pay to help them support themselves until they get another job (unless, of course, they've done something illegal or unethical). Some companies will give employees a one- or two-week notice, but most will ask the terminated employee to leave immediately, even if they pay them for that notice-time. It's never a good idea to have a laid-off, fired, or disgruntled employee remain on the job.

Before laying off or firing any employee, it's always best to consult an attorney. You need to make sure you handle the process in such a way as to avoid litigation for wrongful termination or any other reason.

Hiring During Rapid Growth: Microsoft and the Lure of "Permatemps"

challenge

Staff up to meet market demand when the duration of that demand is unknown

solution

Rather than take on permanent employees, hire a large number of temporary employees to work onsite indefinitely

Let's say you have a rapidly growing entrepreneurial business. You need more workers, and you require them to work in your office every business day, during business hours. You want them to do specific work in the manner in which you want it done. But you're not sure exactly how long you'll require their services. Six months? A year? Two years? Who knows? Because of this, you'd prefer not making the arrangement permanent.

That's exactly the situation that the computer software giant Microsoft found itself in, back in the 1990s. The company was experiencing a massive growth spurt. As in any company facing a need for many more skilled workers, management had to decide whether it made sense to add full-time employees to payroll or find another solution until it had a better idea of whether the growth—and income—would be sustained long-term.

Microsoft decided against expanding its employee base. Instead, it took a then-popular route for entrepreneurial firms in volatile markets. Instead of adding workers to its permanent payroll, Microsoft hired independent contractors. Some of them were hired through personnel agencies supplying temporary workers, while others worked on individual contract. In this way, Microsoft was able to find an army of educated, experienced workers, but didn't have to provide them with the costly protections and benefits of employees. This saved Microsoft significant sums of money and gave managers greater flexibility in dealing with their workers.

Although theoretically hired "temporarily," some of these contractors worked for Microsoft for years—becoming so-called "permatemps." A permatemp is exactly what it sounds like: a permanent temporary worker. If that sounds like a contradiction, it is.

Moreover, these independent contractors and "permatemps" worked side-by-side with regular Microsoft employees. They did the same jobs, possessed the same experience and credentials, and were held to the same quality standards. They worked at

Microsoft offices on Microsoft's schedule and on Microsoft's equipment. But they were *not* receiving the same benefits—such as health insurance, paid vacation and sick days, or the ability to participate in retirement plans. Most egregiously (at least to the contractors), they were not part of the Microsoft Employee Stock Purchase plan at a time when Microsoft stock was soaring into the stratosphere. Contractors watched coworkers get rich while they took home hourly-wage paychecks for doing the same work.

These independent contractors/permatemps got increasingly unhappy. And, in 1993, they filed a class action lawsuit against Microsoft. *Vizcaino v. Microsoft* demanded that the Microsoft temp workers receive the same benefits they would have received if they'd been properly classified as employees.

After many years, Microsoft settled the case for $97 million. It's estimated that between 8,000 and 12,000 workers qualified for an award under the settlement. And after *Vizcaino* was settled, the IRS issued a ruling that Microsoft, in addition to paying its employees for lost wages, benefits, and stock-buying opportunities, also owed millions of dollars in unpaid payroll taxes. Adding up the costs of the settlement and untold millions more in legal fees and IRS fees and penalties, Microsoft was significantly the loser.

Moreover, *Vizcaino* changed the employment landscape forever. The Ninth Circuit Court of Appeals held that even though most of these temporary workers were "employees" of a temporary staffing agency that "leased" them to Microsoft, they were also, legally, the employees of Microsoft. In short, they were actually entitled to the same protections and benefits as other employees. The fallout from the ruling is that even if a company uses a temporary employee from a staffing agency, under certain conditions that temporary worker may be deemed to be an employee of the client company—and not a permatemp.

As a result, to avoid falling into a similar hole, many companies put highly restrictive policies in place when hiring independent contractors or temporary workers. Many companies will limit a temporary worker to no more than six months to a year of contract work, thus ensuring that they're not viewed as company employees in the eyes of the law and the IRS. ∎

questions

1. In what other ways could an entrepreneurial company acquire the workers it needs when it doesn't know whether its income will be steady?

2. What do you think Microsoft could have done differently (if anything) that would have kept it from getting into this situation?

3. Do you agree with Microsoft's position or the temporary workers' position? Do you think the court was right?

4. Can you think of any companies that handle their need for temporary workers better?

Plan ahead as you continue to grow

No matter what you do to keep employees content, some good ones will want to move on. Be supportive and respect their personal goals that you may not be able to satisfy. Make it clear that you have an "open door" policy that would welcome them, should they someday want to return. Stay in touch with them; invite them to holiday parties or summer picnics. That way, they'll be more likely to return—or to send other potential great employees your way.

AND THE JOB GOES TO...

Goal:

Decide how you will prioritize skills and attitude or personality when you hire employees.

What to Do:

Your growing business needs someone to help you with marketing. You want this person to help you focus on the right target market, independently create a marketing plan, and then oversee the development of marketing materials, a website, and a social media strategy. Obviously, marketing is critical to your company's success.

You have two apparently capable candidates for this position. Both seem bright and hard-working. You must choose either:

1. A person with only two years of marketing experience and who wants a full-time job. By hiring them full-time, you will have their full attention, be able to direct their workflow, and require them to be in the office every day at the times you set. But you will have a long-term commitment to their salary and will have to pay taxes and benefits.

2. OR a person with 10 years of marketing experience who only wants to work as a contractor. By hiring them, you will get more experience, greater capabilities, and less training time; only pay them for the hours they actually work; and not be responsible for taxes or benefits. However, their hourly pay will be considerably higher, they will have other clients demanding their attention, and they may not always be available at times you need them.

Which candidate should you choose and why?

CHAPTER

14 OPERATIONS

learning objectives

In this chapter, you'll learn how to:

- Determine needs for facilities

- Analyze the options for producing a particular product or service

- Locate and evaluate suppliers of raw materials, finished products, and other materials necessary to conduct operations

- Evaluate processes for order fulfillment and customer service

- Understand insurance needs

- Develop a disaster recovery and business continuity plan

- Evaluate your company's carbon footprint and determine how to reduce it

How Will You Run Your Business?

Entrepreneurial ventures often are launched and funded based on a great idea or a terrific management team, yet they rise and fall—make profits or lose money—based on their operations. How will you actually produce and deliver your product or service? How will you make sure you have the right goods at the right time—and not too many goods, or the wrong ones? How will you ship, store, and manage your **inventory**? If you run a service business, how will you make certain that your service providers are in the right place at the right time with the right materials to do their jobs?

The term "operations" covers the entire infrastructure, equipment, processes, and procedures that enable you to produce and deliver your product or service in a way that lets you run a profitable business. Operations are vital because, without them, nothing gets done: You don't have an office or manufacturing plant, much less one with electricity, running water, and networking capabilities. You don't have the machinery to make your products, or a warehousing facility to store them, or a trucking fleet to get them to market.

Operations may seem dull—after all, how many people are excited about lowering the number of steps necessary in a manufacturing process, or shaving a day off the time it takes to ship a product? Yet it's exactly these types of issues that often give a company a competitive advantage or create continuing profit margins.

Moreover, operations today also includes making sure a company functions in ways that protect the environment, lessen waste, and lower energy consumption. These decisions can have important consequences far beyond the reach of any one company.

Operations encompasses the entire spectrum of management, planning, and execution of the making, sourcing, and shipping of a company's products or services, as well as delivery and support to customers.

Facilities

One of the first operational issues you'll deal with is where you will work. You may launch your start-up at your dining room table or in your parents' garage, but, with luck and hard work, you'll soon outgrow that option. As you expand, you'll have to find some place for you and your employees to work, produce, and sell your goods or services. Even if the site of your business doesn't seem critical, keep in mind that your choice of facilities and neighborhood *will* have an impact on how you and your employees feel about coming to work. A pleasant building in a safe neighborhood with nearby parking and friendly neighbors can make work more enjoyable. It can even help you recruit quality employees.

en·tre·pre·neur·ship key terms

Contract manufacturing
A type of outsourcing specifically relating to production of goods. Generally, a company provides the design specifications for its product to a third party that then manufactures that product to specifications. Contract manufacturers typically specialize in manufacturing a certain kind of good for many different companies that "make" a product.

FIFO
Short for "first in, first out," FIFO is a method of valuing and recording inventory. The oldest unit the company produced (for a manufacturing company) or received (for a reseller) is the first one sold, meaning the older inventory goes out the door first.

Inventory
Goods kept by a company to be sold or to be used in the making of its products. These can be in the form of finished merchandise available for sale, whether made in-house or purchased from others; raw materials needed to produce goods for sale; or other physical goods to support the company's production and sale of its goods or services.

Just-in-time inventory
A way of reducing inventory (and the cash that's tied up in it) to the absolute minimum by receiving goods for sale or manufacture as close as possible to the time they're needed.

LIFO
Short for "last in, first out," LIFO is a method of valuing and recording inventory. The most recent unit the company produced (for a manufacturing company) or received (for a reseller) is the first one sold, meaning the newer inventory goes out the door first.

Offshoring
Having some of a company's operations, manufacturing, or other functions performed in another country, either by using foreign vendors or by transferring operations to that country.

Outsourcing
Using an outside company or vendor to perform some functions of your business, such as manufacturing, IT, human resource management, or public relations.

Raw materials
The unfinished goods or basic physical components, either natural or man-made, that will go into the making or manufacturing of finished goods for sale. These goods could be completely untreated (for example, eggs supplied to a bakery) or could have been previously manufactured to a certain level but are not yet finished to the point of sale (for instance, the manufactured glass supplied to a smartphone manufacturer).

Supply chain management
The process of planning, implementing, and controlling the operations of the entire life cycle of a product as efficiently as possible. Supply chain management spans all movement and storage of raw materials, work-in-process inventory, and finished goods from point of origin to point of consumption.

Is "hoteling" really a verb?

The trend in office space arrangement is to provide ever smaller personal spaces for employees. Where once a manager might have enjoyed a private office with a window, and later a cubicle, these days office arrangements often have open-space arrangements with few, if any, dividers. One trend is toward "hoteling" in which personnel—who often work on the road or at home—no longer have their own space at all, but "check in" to communal spaces when they're in the office.

First, though, you must prioritize your needs. How you rank them depends on what kind of business you're in—retail, manufacturing, service, or another type of industry—and on your specific business activities. You also must figure out approximately how much space you require and what your budget can handle. Most of all, your needs will be matched to how you'll use the facilities.

- **Office and administrative.** Virtually all businesses need at least some office space. Many businesses *only* need office space, in the form of professional, sales, or administrative offices. On the other hand, if the main purpose of your business is retail or manufacturing, your "office" may represent only a small portion of your total site.

- **Retail.** Location, location, location. One of the most important considerations for a brick-and-mortar retail business is the choice of location. Do you want to be in a mall? On a popular pedestrian street? In a particular neighborhood? If your business is easily seen by passers-by (in a mall or on a well-trafficked street), you can save considerably on marketing and advertising costs. These locations typically charge higher rent, but paying more to get a more visible and accessible space may be well worth it. Customers also have to be able to get to your store easily. If they have easy access—by walking, driving, or taking public transportation—you already have a competitive advantage over businesses that are harder to reach or find.

- **Manufacturing.** What do you make? Toys? Computer peripherals? Packaged organic vegetables? The nature of your product will dictate the kind of facilities you require. Your production facilities can also have a direct impact on your profitability. Are they set up to save on energy use and costs? Can you design efficient production processes? Are you near your customers or shipping facilities? How much does it cost to have waste removed? Understand all costs and benefits as you choose your space. Also consider whether you need your own facilities or whether **contract manufacturing** facilities (such as industrial kitchens) are available. Such facilities give you the flexibility to start up without investing large sums of capital.

- **Warehouse and storage.** Some facilities are used primarily for storage. In these situations, you have many of the same concerns as manufacturing—shipping, docks, utilities, safety, access, security, and proximity to distributors. Be particularly cautious of environmental and zoning considerations that may affect the products or materials you can store. Depending on the nature of what you store, consider factors such as humidity and temperature.

- **Virtual.** Perhaps you're one of the lucky few who can run a business from any location because of technology. In that case, your chief concerns will revolve around whether the facility in question can support the technologies you need. For example, is it already wired for high-speed Internet access, and can it handle the bandwidth you need? Likewise, will you have sufficient power and a reliable source of electricity to support a computer-intensive operation? If you have special equipment, can the facilities handle the energy requirements? Are there security issues you need to address in your choice of facilities? In addition, how vulnerable are your facilities to emergency situations such as earthquakes, fire, flood, or hurricanes?

If all these basic requirements have been met, then you have the luxury to consider issues related to cost, convenience, and comfort. You can even locate outside a metropolitan area, where leases cost much less, or in places that wouldn't be suitable for either retail or manufacturing.

If you're a retailer or service provider, you'll be concerned about the neighborhood or business district you operate in. What other businesses are nearby? What kinds of automobile or foot traffic do you need to be successful? Will you depend on "drop-ins," or expect that people will make a special effort to come see you? The chart below shows examples of how business needs relate to choice of location.

REAL-WORLD RECAP

Facilities needs

How will you use your facilities?

- ☐ Office and administrative
- ☐ Retail
- ☐ Manufacturing
- ☐ Warehouse and storage
- ☐ Virtual

LOCATION, LOCATION, LOCATION

TYPE OF BUSINESS	BUSINESS NEEDS	BEST LOCATION
Seafood restaurant chain	Populated areas; vacation crowds	Seaside tourist towns
Women's clothing manufacturer	Facilities with capacity for a large number of employees and industrial equipment; shipping and receiving areas	Industrial area close to transportation for easy shipping and receiving of products and supplies, and a short commute for employees
B2B IT services	Close proximity to a business center	Street visibility not required, but close proximity to customer sites is important
Telecommunications company	Highly skilled workforce	Facilities with the right technology infrastructure; well-educated, metropolitan population
Green construction for commercial market	Skilled workforce; close proximity to business centers	Larger cities and metropolitan areas

Manufacturing a Product

If you plan to produce and sell a product, you have to decide whether you'll build it all yourself or use the services of a contract manufacturer to build it to your specifications, assemble it from standard components or from components made to your order, or purchase it outright from another manufacturer. If you choose the latter, you must further decide whether to "brand it" with your name and logo before selling it to others. Telephones, computers, and many appliances are often marketed in this fashion. You'd be surprised to learn how many brand-name goods are actually made by just one or two manufacturers.

Your vendor's problem is *your* problem

Pay attention to how socially responsible your vendors are. Their practices reflect on your business, as well as weigh on your conscience. Does your supplier conform to "green" environmental practices or does it pollute? Of increasing concern is whether vendors maintain ethical and fair labor practices—especially in developing countries where labor laws are less stringent than in developed ones.

Design your production process

Your production process will vary dramatically, depending on the nature of your product. The process of creating hand-made crafts differs vastly from that of manufacturing high-tech electronics. Whatever the product, you need a "process"—a plan for how you'll handle your product or service from the time an order is placed until it's delivered to the customer.

Even if you "produce" a service rather than a tangible product, you'll benefit by considering the process by which you prepare and carry out that service.

Questions regarding the design of your production process include:

- What **raw materials** or inventory do you need? How will you get them? Where will you store them?

- What are the steps for turning those materials into finished goods?

- What labor does each step require?

- How will you ensure quality control?

- How will you ship your products or goods? Which shipping providers will you use?

- How will you pack your products? What materials will you need for packing? Where will you store those materials? Where will you do the packing? How will you prevent theft or loss?

- What kind of electricity, gas, water, or other utilities do you need as part of your process?

Some of the many things to consider, whether you build, assemble, or buy a product, are:

- **Materials.** What kind of materials do you—or your supplier—need to make the product? Will you start with raw goods or existing components? For instance, if you're making mountain bike frames, you'll need to decide whether you're going to set up a manufacturing facility to work with the actual raw metal, or whether you'll send the design to a contract manufacturer and merely assemble the frames yourself. If you intend to use existing components, are there standard sizes and dimensions you should employ in your design, to keep your costs down? For example, manufacturing super-rugged laptops will be infinitely cheaper if you conform to the dimensions of existing mobile disk drives, network cards, and other components rather than designing your own from scratch.

- **Sources.** Who will provide the materials and services you need? It's a good idea to have more than one source, especially for critical supplies or services, as it increases the likelihood of cost competition and makes you less reliant on one vendor and, thus, more vulnerable if something happens to them.

- **Reliability.** A product's reliability has to do not only with the quality of its components, or of the product itself, but also with the suppliers of your materials. Will they ship orders to you on time? Will they carry enough inventory for you to meet your customer commitments? Look into the quality of the customer service your suppliers provide: Are they good communicators? Can they respond quickly to changes in your requirements? These are the sorts of things that can make or break a fledgling business that depends on outside suppliers.

- **Cost comparisons and evaluations.** Naturally, price considerations come into play throughout the manufacturing process. Still, you might not necessarily want to go with the lowest-cost supplier. The quality of its materials might be substandard. Or its reliability (see above) might be a worrisome issue. Worse, it might not be financially stable and could leave you in the lurch right when you need to deliver to a key customer. Choosing the right supplier thus means evaluating candidates across a broad range of dimensions, including quality, service, reliability, and financial stability. A good way to think about it is that you're not just looking for low *cost* but good *value*.

- **Equipment needed.** Depending on which aspects of manufacturing, assembling, or shipping you plan to handle yourself, you'll need to consider what equipment you need to get the product out the door and into distributors' or customers' hands. These requirements vary significantly, depending on the nature of your business. The term "equipment" could range from simple computers for your mobile app development firm, to woodworking tools for building custom pine furniture you sell over the Internet, to commercial-grade kitchen appliances to run your catering business, to industrial equipment to manufacture electronic components.

- **Contract manufacturing.** In many industries, contract manufacturers can produce goods to other companies' precise specifications. Using the services of a contract manufacturer means you can usually get to market sooner, and at lower cost, because you need not bear significant upfront expenses such as building a manufacturing plant and finding and training workers. Moreover, you often can tap into the expertise of a company that has manufactured similar goods for many years. For example, with over 200,000 employees, Flextronics is one of the world's leading contract manufacturers. It manufactures electronics for many well-known brands, yet is virtually unknown to consumers. Contract manufacturers exist in many industries.

Best practices in manufacturing

Manufacturing techniques have dramatically improved over the years, the better to drive waste and inefficiencies—and therefore excessive costs—out of the process. Two of the chief advances in this area are "lean manufacturing" and "just-in-time" inventory management.

Version 1.0

One concept that has taken hold in the development of certain products is the "Minimal Viable Product." The idea is to quickly get a product to market, and later make improvements based on the experience of actual customers. Google's product development mantra, for instance, is "Experiment, Expedite, Iterate." In other words, the company tries a lot of new things, moves quickly rather than getting stuck, and refines and improves along the way.

Clearly you don't want a minimally viable product for a medical device or automobile. But in some categories, such as online services, mobile apps, and personal electronics, consumers are willing—even eager—to pay for version 1.0.

REAL-WORLD RECAP

Operations considerations

- ☐ Materials
- ☐ Sources
- ☐ Reliability
- ☐ Cost comparisons and evaluations
- ☐ Equipment needed
- ☐ Contract manufacturing

■ **Lean manufacturing.** This is a management philosophy that focuses on eliminating waste to cut costs and, ultimately, deliver more value to customers. Lean manufacturing is based largely on concepts identified by the automobile manufacturer Toyota. That company outlined "seven wastes" that stand in the way of an optimal manufacturing process: overproduction, waiting, transporting, inappropriate processing, excess inventory, unnecessary motion, and defects.

■ **Just-in-time manufacturing.** This strategy schedules the production of goods as close as possible to the time a sale is made—ideally, after an order is received. By manufacturing your products "just in time" so you can deliver them to customers when needed, you trim expenses by not sitting on substantial inventory and thereby reducing the possibility of excess inventory. One method to accomplish just-in-time manufacturing is building-to-order. Much of the growth of computer-maker Dell came about because it was able to assemble computers to order quickly, thus providing customers with a custom product while at the same time reducing the stock of unsold computers. Be aware that just-in-time manufacturing requires close coordination with suppliers, distributors, and customers.

Quality management: ISO 9001

Poor quality can be costly—not only in the form of faulty goods you have to discard, but also in the form of lost customers. In an increasingly global world, if you want to sell your goods internationally, you'll likely want to follow procedures to get your products or processes certified as meeting international quality standards. These measures are set by the International Organization for Standardization (ISO) and have been adopted by more than 90 countries worldwide. To find out more about such procedures, check the ISO website at www.iso.org.

Large purchasers may require you to adhere to ISO standards, especially being certified as meeting standard ISO 9001 for quality. Such certifications ensure that the products they purchase are of good quality, environmentally sound, interchangeable, and the like, depending on which certification they require. In addition, to be sold in most countries, many products require ISO certification. These include, not surprisingly, electronics such as semiconducting materials, printed circuits, and boards; aircraft and space vehicles; and food and agricultural products. There are many ISO standards, including those for office paper, bobbins for yarn and thread, and the size designation of clothing. As well, there are environmental standards (ISO 14000) and social responsibility standards (ISO 26000).

Even if you produce products that may not require ISO certification, new customers will certainly feel more at ease working with you if they know that you adhere to worldwide standards.

Outsourcing and offshoring

Luckily, you don't have to do everything yourself. One way to reduce the cost of producing a product is by **outsourcing** it—hiring and paying another company or vendor to provide a business function or service for you, or to manufacture your product or component product.

For example, a company may outsource the manufacturing of its products to another company, or may outsource its technical support service to a separate company. Technically, using any independent contractor to accomplish a key business function, such as managing your company's public relations or human resource functions, is also considered outsourcing. You can outsource to companies in your own country or internationally.

One primary reason for outsourcing is to *save money*. By hiring another business that specializes in a certain aspect of operations—say, manufacturing, distribution, or even customer service—you reduce the size of your permanent staff and drive your fixed costs down.

Another reason to outsource is *focus*. By contracting out noncore functions, you can concentrate on the aspects about your business that matter the most, rather than those that are peripheral. This particularly benefits newer companies, in which growth and change happen quickly.

Typically, a company only outsources "noncore competencies," that is, the functions that don't distinguish it from competitors, while keeping its key competitive advantages in-house. For instance, a company may keep all the design functions of a new electronic device in-house but outsource its manufacturing. After all, you want to maintain control over those elements of your business that give you a competitive advantage over time.

A third reason for outsourcing is *capability*. You can also outsource functions that another company might do more proficiently and efficiently than you can do. For example, a new company may not be proficient in human resource and benefits issues, while there are outsourced providers who stay up-to-date on changing labor laws and practices.

Outsourcing may also enable a new company to get to market faster. A contract manufacturer likely already has the equipment, processes, and staff in place to produce your product. Acquiring all those yourself would take far longer, meaning a much longer time before you could begin to make sales—and bring in money.

When you offshore functions, you move key business functions to another country. Either an outside vendor located in that country performs your operations, or you actually set up your company's operations there. **Offshoring** is often done to reduce costs, since labor in many countries abroad costs less, though offshoring may also be done to get closer to suppliers or customers. Setting up an independent subsidiary of your own company in another country to both lower costs and reduce taxes also constitutes offshoring.

Shipping your product

You'll also have to consider how you'll ship your product to your customer, whether that customer is the actual end user or a retailer or distributor that sells to end users. Shipping costs include not only the price of transportation but also any fees for storing or warehousing the product between the time it's made and when it's shipped, plus all handling costs. Some products also have to be put into an inventory system, be insured, or require special packaging or handling—all of which can add to shipping costs.

Many companies have learned the hard way that offshoring typically generates hidden expenses that may reduce anticipated savings. Some companies that offshore key services—such as software development—have found that they must spend significantly more of their onshore staff time developing clear project descriptions and requirements and that projects are not completed as quickly.

Many legal and ethical issues arise when a company begins to offshore aspects of its operations. For a more in-depth discussion of these topics, see Chapter 18.

Producing a Service

If you're performing a service rather than producing a tangible product, you have many similar issues to address as in producing a product, plus other unique ones. Clearly, you still must determine your needs for appropriate facilities, supplies and materials, equipment, and so forth. However, some factors are particularly important in service businesses.

- **Labor.** In many service businesses, your "product" is delivered by a human being. Whether you provide legal services to corporations or child care for parents, people are responsible for "producing" what you sell. Therefore, labor is an even more important component of service businesses than of manufacturing companies. So one of the first things to consider when planning a service business is whether you can continually have access to the number and quality of people you'll need to run your business. Is there a sufficient supply of trained people in the geographic area you serve? Can you hire them affordably? What kind of training will you need to provide? Supervision? Security? Labor-intensive businesses always present unique challenges.

- **Consistent quality.** Quality is one of the critical factors determining whether people will buy your service—and return for more. Yet in a service business, with the likelihood that many different people deliver the service, one of the greatest challenges is maintaining consistent quality. To do so, you'll need to develop clear quality standards and guidelines for the delivery of your service. Training is a vital component, so you'll need to regularly and continually train your employees. Even if your service business doesn't depend entirely on individuals—perhaps you have an online service, for example—developing and maintaining clear quality standards is an essential component of your long-term success.

- **Materials and equipment.** Many service businesses require substantial upfront investment. For instance, an airport shuttle service entails the purchase or lease of a fleet of vans; a graphic design firm might need powerful computers with high-resolution color monitors, special software, and high-quality printers and copiers. Other service businesses might leverage unique supplies or equipment to produce fine-quality services, such as a carpet cleaning service with proprietary cleaning fluids or supplies. Consider what equipment and supplies you'll need for your service business and whether you'll have regular access to these as you grow your company.

- **"Production."** Just as when making a product, you must plan how you will "produce" and deliver your service. This entails figuring out the exact nature of the service, the quality and qualities of the service you'll provide, the method of delivering the service, how you'll ensure consistency, and so on. Thinking of your service as a product helps you plan and price every component. For example, if you start a catering company, a lot more than merely the cost of food goes into planning. You'll want to plan how and where the food will be prepared, how it will be transported and kept safe in transit, where it will be heated or reheated, what containers you'll use, how you'll acquire and train staff, and on and on. You'd be advised to develop standard flow charts that can be filled in for each booking, outlining every step and supply item needed.

- **Growth.** Another consideration with a service business is whether you'll be able to grow the business enough to achieve your long-term financial objectives. For example, expanding a service business beyond a specific geographic area can be difficult, because you must reach and serve your customers in person. Or, your ability to attract and train capable staff to follow you to another city may be limited. As you plan your service company, consider ways in which you can grow even after you become successful.

Research and Development

In business as in life, one thing is certain—change. Your target market is forever changing: developing new tastes, being swayed to use the hottest product. Technology changes, affecting the way you make, sell, and deliver your products or services. Prices change, suppliers change, and competitors change. A company that stands still will almost certainly fail in the long run. You must not only keep on top of new developments that are going to affect your business but must continually evaluate how you can improve your offerings and your operations. That's where research and development—or R&D—comes in.

Some companies need relatively large R&D components because they deal with constantly evolving technology or rapidly changing consumer preferences. Yet even companies that sell traditional products (chocolate chip cookies, say) need to develop new products based on changing customer preferences (such as gluten-free cookies), new technology (perhaps creative ways to make, package, or deliver cookies), or other developments.

Your research and development activities may range from running a complete department staffed with researchers experimenting with new products and new equipment, to merely subscribing to certain publications and attending conferences. Regardless of the extent of such activities, research and development must be a priority in any business.

Select suppliers that understand your needs

Usually, competitive supply sources exist, giving you a number of choices and enabling you to negotiate better prices. Still, don't make your decisions based on price alone, for you may find the price right but the delivery time and quality problematic. Select suppliers with which you can communicate well; make certain they understand your specifications and can consistently meet your standards.

Examine the ways you plan to stay aware of developments likely to change your company's products, services, and practices. Make certain that key employees are likewise involved in research and development activities.

Supply Chain Management

Almost every business has goods or materials coming into the company and finished products or services going out. The companies you rely on to provide you with incoming goods are essential to the continuing operation of your business. They constitute your "supply chain," and how you manage that chain is called **supply chain management**.

Because most businesses will experience difficulties with their suppliers at some point, try not to be dependent on just one; your financial future will be too vulnerable if it fails you. Work to develop excellent relationships with your suppliers; you'll want them to feel that you are in a partnership together so that they will try to do everything possible to meet your needs. Be responsive to their needs, as well; work out payment plans and communication methods to reduce pressures on them.

Finding suppliers

If you're new to business, where do you find the supplies you need to make your operations run smoothly?

- **Word-of-mouth.** The best way to find a supplier is the old-fashioned way—asking for a recommendation from someone who's knowledgeable. If you don't know anyone in the same industry, ask others in related industries (for instance, ask a printer for the names of graphic designers, or vice versa) or those who might have a similar need (such as for shipping services or customized signs).

- **Trade associations.** Excellent sources for locating suppliers are trade associations. Besides holding annual or regional conventions as well as trade shows where suppliers exhibit their products and services, many associations publish supplier directories, both in print and online. (See Chapter 3, for information on finding and using these sources.)

- **ThomasNet.** Consult ThomasNet, the ultimate resource for locating suppliers and vendors. Its website features a free, searchable database of products manufactured in the United States. You'll find this site particularly useful for hard-to-find industrial products. Go to www.thomasnet.com.

- **Tradekey B2B directory.** Tradekey is one of the world's largest online marketplaces for importers and exporters. It connects worldwide wholesale buyers with importers and exporters, distributors, and agents in more than 220 countries. Go to www.tradekey.com.

- **B2B Yellow Pages.** You can find suppliers in more than 70 industries that offer products, services, and information for your business through the

B2B Yellow Pages. A special section on "B2B Shopping" helps you find the best products, prices, and shopping comparisons for business supplies and more. Go to www.b2byellowpages.com.

- **eBay Business and Industrial.** Most people think of eBay for consumers, but the site also has a section for industrial supplies and products sold in large lots. Go to http://business.shop.ebay.com.

- **Yahoo! B2B Directory.** Most online directories maintain separate categories for business-related topics. Yahoo, one of the oldest directories, has an extensive list. You can find it at http://dir.yahoo.com/. Click on "Business & Economy" and then look for "Business to Business."

Inventory management

Many businesses overlook the vital contribution that careful inventory management makes to a company's profitability. How much money you've got tied up in supplies or finished product sitting in your warehouse makes a direct impact on your bottom line. Every box of raw material is not simply taking up space; it's money sitting around, losing value.

Of course, if you don't have sufficient inventory, you occasionally can't make sales. Every business dreads the possibility of receiving lucrative orders it can't fill due to inadequate supplies. And sometimes you don't only lose sales; you lose a customer. This is the risk in maintaining too low an inventory.

The answer is to develop inventory management systems that substantially increase the flow of information from the sales point to the production and purchasing teams. Information can reduce the amount of guesswork that goes into maintaining inventory. You'll know how sales are going, even on a daily basis.

METHODS OF INVENTORY MANAGEMENT

One of the approaches to inventory management is **just-in-time inventory** control. This concept emphasizes keeping inventory stocked only to the levels needed to produce or sell goods "just in time" for delivery, usually in response to orders in-hand. Such a system significantly reduces the amount of money you have invested in inventory sitting idle in warehouses, at your store, or on factory floors. This may somewhat increase the costs of such goods, and it depends highly on adequate communication systems and good supplier relationships.

In devising your inventory control and communication procedures, you'll want to devise a management information system (MIS). Usually such a system focuses on the computerized maintenance and communication of information, such as order and stock levels, reorder dates, historical tracking of sales, and so forth. A computer consultant can help you select and adapt an MIS for your company.

LIFO or FIFO?

You'll also need to discuss how you want to value and record your inventory. Two commonly used methods are **LIFO** (last in, first out) and **FIFO** (first in, first out). These are basic methods of valuing your remaining stock that can have significant tax implications, so you should reach this decision in consultation with your accountant.

Supplier Comparison Chart

	Supplier 1	Supplier 2	Supplier 3
Name of Supplier			
Sales Rep and Contact Info			
Range of Services/ Products Offered			
Direct Costs			
Additional Costs			
Payment Terms			
Order Turnaround Time			
Shipping Costs			
Other Maintenance/ Support			
Other:			

BUILD-YOUR-BUSINESS WORKSHEET

Determine Your Supply Needs

Answer the questions below to help you evaluate your current supply needs.

Who is responsible for your purchasing decisions? _____
_____

What are the key goods or materials necessary? _____
_____

What are the average costs of these goods? _____
_____

List your sources of key goods or materials: _____
_____

List any alternative sources of these supplies: _____
_____

Are any goods available from only one or two suppliers? ☐ Yes ☐ No

If so, how reliable or secure are these suppliers? _____
_____

Can your suppliers provide you with "on demand" or short-notice goods? ☐ Yes ☐ No

If so, what additional costs will you incur? _____
_____

Will your suppliers negotiate no- or low-minimum order contracts? ☐ Yes ☐ No

What kind of credit terms will your suppliers offer? _____
_____

What are your average credit costs? _____
_____

Which key factors determined your choice of suppliers? _____
_____

Other supplier issues: _____
_____
_____
_____
_____
_____
_____

BUILD-YOUR-BUSINESS WORKSHEET

Inventory Control

Complete this worksheet to assess your inventory control procedures.

Who is responsible for inventory control?_____
_____
_____

What is the minimum level of inventory necessary to be maintained at all times? _____
_____
_____

What is the minimum amount of time necessary to get materials from suppliers? _____
_____
_____

What is the minimum amount of time necessary to produce goods to order?_____
_____
_____

What is the minimum amount of time necessary to ship goods?_____
_____
_____

How is information about sales translated to the production and purchasing departments? _____
_____
_____

What management information systems does your company use? _____
_____
_____

What steps do you take to reduce theft of inventory? _____
_____
_____

What other inventory control steps do you take? _____
_____
_____
_____
_____

Order Fulfillment and Customer Service

Remember, your work isn't finished when you produce a product or secure an order from a customer. You still need to make sure your customer receives the product ordered, in good condition, and in a timely fashion. You need to know that you've satisfied your customer.

Surprisingly, many companies pay relatively little attention to order fulfillment and customer service, since they don't seem pressing concerns or sources of increased profit margin. However, order fulfillment is part of any current sale, and customer service is part of any future sale.

Customers are constantly demanding better and better service. They expect to get what they want, when they want it, and to be treated graciously and fairly in the process. Many companies are renowned for their customer service and have built entire marketing strategies around it.

Some companies assume they're doing just fine by way of customer service because they don't receive many complaints. But you can't judge how well you're serving your customers merely by the number of complaints you receive; the unhappy customer who doesn't complain is almost certainly a lost customer. At least, a customer who complains gives you a chance to make the problem right.

So, it's your job to make certain that customers have little reason for complaints. Training all employees—from the shipping clerk to the sales representative—in customer service can pay off handsomely for you, in customer retention and referrals. Build sufficient flexibility into your policies so that you can easily handle unusual or difficult requests. Empower employees to make certain decisions on the spot (such as accepting returns) instead of requiring each customer request to be approved by a manager. Make it easy for your customers to let you know what they want, by soliciting customer suggestions and feedback.

Examine your order fulfillment process. Often, orders are not communicated clearly or quickly to the processing department, and valuable time is lost due to inadequate internal communication. Assess the methods by which you prepare goods for shipping and deliver goods to customers. If you hire outside companies to ship or deliver your product directly to the customer, make certain they can deliver on emergency or rush-time schedules, or line up other shippers for such deliveries.

Look at the kinds of services you provide customers after sale. Good customer service emphasizes developing an ongoing relationship with your customers, so you'll need return, repair, service, and warranty policies that reassure customers of your continued interest in them—even after you have their money.

Three key elements to superb customer service

- Be honest in all your dealings. Honesty is not only the right thing, it also directly affects your ability to make sales, retain customers, and (ultimately) stay in business. In an age when any customer can rate your company on online user-review sites, you must treat each and every customer with care, respect, and honesty.

- Promise only what you can deliver. This has a direct impact on customer satisfaction and how you'll be rated. It's much better to underpromise and overdeliver than to oversell and overhype and then disappoint your customers.

- Follow through with commitments. If you say you're going to do something, do it. Period. If you promise to be on call to customers 24/7 to fix any problems that arise with your cloud-based inventory management application that they subscribe to, make sure you do exactly that.

Performance bonds

In some cases, a contractor may be required to post a performance bond—a type of insurance—that protects clients against losses in case the contractor fails to complete a project or performs unsatisfactorily. This occurs most typically in property construction, where a contractor's bond will reimburse the client in case the contractor goes bankrupt before the project is completed or the project has significant flaws.

Insurance

One of the more frustrating tasks you'll encounter when running a business is purchasing insurance. After all, you can't "see" what you're getting, and yet you often will be required to have it or will want it to protect your business and your employees. If this is your first business, you'll be absolutely overwhelmed by the various types of insurance you may need, want, or be offered.

Insurance is a way to protect the value of property, life, or one's person against loss or harm arising in specified contingencies, such as fire, accident, death, disablement, or the like. Figuring out your insurance coverage will be daunting—guaranteed! So you'll need a good insurance agent, or, better yet, two or three. Ideally, you'll find an agent who understands business insurance for companies of your size and industry. It's best if they're a broker who can offer you policies from a number of different companies rather than just representing one company's products.

To find a good insurance agent, ask for referrals from other business owners or from service providers. Check with your industry trade association as well. Many trade associations offer lower-cost insurance specifically for the needs of companies in your industry. But always do your research: Just because a policy comes from a trade association doesn't necessarily mean it's best for you.

Consider these three dimensions and types of insurance:

- **Incentive.** Insurance you purchase because your workers (including you yourself) desire it—such as medical, dental, and life insurance.

- **Protection.** Insurance you purchase to protect your business from the unexpected—liability, accident, fire, theft, and business interruption.

- **Legal necessity.** Insurance that others—perhaps your landlord—require (such as fire or liability) or that's required by state law (for example, workers' compensation).

Types of insurance

You need insurance. End of story. As tempting as it may be to go without it—especially in the early, cash-strapped days of your entrepreneurial venture—you *must* have it. Some types of insurance are required by law or by a landlord (typically, they'll require fire and liability insurance as a condition of a lease), or even by a customer (especially large corporate customers, who may demand that you have liability and other insurance). Other types of insurance (like fire or business continuity insurance) are optional but vital to protect your investment, should something go wrong.

- **Workers' compensation insurance.** All employers are required by law to maintain workers' compensation insurance. This provides workers who are injured on the job with some financial payment and protects the business in case of lawsuits due to serious employee accident or death. Although some states allow companies to be self-insured, these companies frequently must prove they have the financial resources to make payments to workers and cover themselves in case of an incident.

- **Business insurance.** Often called "business liability insurance," business insurance provides protection for your routine daily operations. The exact type of insurance you'll need depends on your business type. There is insurance to protect against customers who get hurt on your premises or any harm done by product defects, as well as insurance to protect you if a customer sues because a service is perceived to be of an inferior quality.

- **Malpractice insurance.** Typically, professional service providers (such as physicians and attorneys) purchase malpractice insurance to pay for lawsuits and any financial awards in case a patient or client sues based on a belief they were harmed because the provider performed the job in a negligent fashion.

- **Health insurance.** Medical, dental, and vision are typically included in health insurance plans. Although these days fewer companies pay 100 percent of health insurance for employees, providing such insurance benefits helps attract top-notch workers to your organization.

- **Business continuance insurance.** Business continuance (sometimes referred to as "business continuity") is insurance that covers any losses from situations that prevent your business from operating. These can include natural disasters like hurricanes, flooding, earthquakes, and fire.

When shopping around for these various kinds of insurance, make sure you're comfortable with the financial stability and reputation of the company providing your coverage. The last thing you want is to pay expensive premiums over an extended period, only to have the insurer be unable or unwilling to pay up in the event that you suffer a loss.

Emergency Preparedness and Disaster Recovery

Bad things happen even to good companies. Sooner or later, your company will face a significant problem. It could be a natural disaster—flood, fire, earthquake—or it could be something more mundane such as a burglary, power interruption, slowdown from a supplier, or a product failure. As you develop your internal operational procedures, include contingency planning to help you anticipate and prepare for the unexpected.

Of prime importance is to make sure you have proper procedures in place to protect your workers and yourself. Devise a disaster plan to ensure the safety and well-being of employees, and plan a method for you to communicate with employees during emergencies. You may want to have other emergency preparedness training or fire drills, especially if you work in any kind of production facility or with hazardous materials.

Next, make sure you develop procedures to safeguard your records and data in case of emergency. Without your data, you will have a very hard time getting your company back up and running, and an even harder time collecting on insurance or any government assistance. So safeguarding procedures should include regular backup and storage of data offsite. An easy, inexpensive approach is to use an online data backup company, or use cloud-based data storage, so that you copy your records daily over the Internet.

Next, look at those things that are absolutely critical for your specific business, and find ways to make certain they are protected or able to continue even after an emergency. Remember, a disaster elsewhere can be a disaster for you if your critical vendors become unavailable (say a tornado wipes out a factory). Develop a list of suppliers in other parts of the country, or even the world, for backup.

Remember to also examine your business insurance. In addition to insurance to cover loss of physical equipment, records, and inventory, you might want business interruption insurance.

Emergencies also come in the form of personal disasters—illnesses and accidents—so examine your procedures to pay bills, deposit checks, and run payroll if key personnel become unavailable.

"Green" Your Operations

As a new company, you have the opportunity to plan your operations from scratch. By making sure your operations are "green"—or designed to minimize negative effects on the environment—you'll not only help the planet, you'll also save money in the long run, and often in the short run, too.

Some choices—like installing solar panels on the roof of your facilities, or retrofitting a leased building to make it more energy efficient—may come with higher price tags than conventional choices at first, but these improvements eventually pay for themselves.

The fact is that every company can save money (and help save the planet) by taking a few easy steps. Reducing waste of any kind is one of the most important. Waste squanders your resources as well as the earth's. Think of any kind of waste as money you've spent on something you didn't use productively. In your production process, look for ways to eliminate waste of all kinds—whether raw materials, energy, or equipment. Use recycled and reclaimed materials if possible, buy supplies that arrive with less packaging, and choose more energy-efficient equipment. If you use water as part of your manufacturing process, find ways to use less, or recycle it to water your landscaping. All these steps are smart, money-saving measures, and they reduce your environmental impact.

Your green efforts don't have to end when the production process does. Do you use the most efficient methods to ship? Can you cut down on your product's packaging? Can you reduce the weight of your product or shipping materials? If so, you'll save money on shipping and use less energy.

For some facilities—especially manufacturing plants, but even stores and warehouses—energy consumption is a large expense. If you fall into this category, consider hiring a third-party energy auditor to both analyze your consumption and help you increase your use of renewable energy sources. Perhaps you're air conditioning a large room that you use infrequently, or generating a lot of heat during your production process. Putting heating and cooling on timers, controlling when machinery and equipment comes on and off in your manufacturing plant, and capturing waste heat, for example, combined with the use of renewable energy sources, can increase your energy efficiency and improve your bottom line.

If you have an office, one of the easiest things to do is turn off all electronic devices and utilities overnight and on weekends. Your printers, monitors, and copiers are all on "standby" mode, meaning they still consume a bit of energy. Also, look for ecofriendly supplies and raw materials. Encourage employees to use less paper and recycle what they do use. Get a water filter for your office's kitchen faucet rather than buying plastic water bottles. When you need office furniture, don't buy new; instead, find one of the many companies out there that offer refurbished furniture, and help keep desks, chairs, and cubicles out of landfills—and more money in your bank account. These are just a few of the countless options you can implement in your office to reduce your carbon footprint while improving your cash flow.

Encourage employees to walk, bike, or take public transportation to work if possible. Promote—or enable—carpooling or vanpooling. The social networking company Facebook originally gave employees an extra $600 a month if they lived within one mile of work and walked or biked. If yours is the type of business that lends itself well to telecommuting, allow your employees to work from home a few days each week. One of the biggest sources of energy consumption is that consumed in getting employees to work.

By making a substantial commitment to ecofriendly operations, you can stand out from your competitors while carving a niche in the market. Some limo and taxi services only use hybrids, for example. That gives those companies a clear distinction from the dozens of regular limo and taxi services. Many customers make choices based on a preference for environmentally sensitive products or services, and this can give you a competitive advantage.

Other Operational Issues

A variety of other operational concerns will face your company, depending on the size and nature of your business. Some of these topics might include protecting the safety of your workers (see Chapter 13), exporting goods (see Chapter 18), or dealing with governmental regulations. Other resources for some of these topics are also listed in Chapter 20.

REAL-WORLD RECAP

Go green; save green

Just some of the ways you can "go green" and save money are:

- Choose renewable energy if possible
- Eliminate waste of any kind
- Use recycled and reclaimed materials
- Buy supplies with less packaging
- Choose energy-efficient equipment
- If you use water in your manufacturing process, find ways to use less
- Ship efficiently; try to reduce the weight of your packaging
- Arrange for an energy audit
- Turn your equipment completely off at night
- Purchase ecofriendly supplies and raw materials
- Buy refurbished furniture
- Encourage employees to carpool, walk, or bike to work; permit them to telecommute
- Install a water filter in the company kitchen

REAL-WORLD CASE

If the Shoe Fits (and Even if It Doesn't): Customer Service at Zappos

challenge

Grow an online retail business with very high shipping costs, yet remain profitable

solution

Create extreme customer loyalty and streamline operations to achieve efficiencies

One day in 1999, at the height of the dot-com boom, Nick Swinmurn went shopping for shoes in San Francisco. Despite spending hours going from store to store, he couldn't find the shoes he wanted. After returning home empty-handed, Swinmurn tried shopping online but found himself defeated there as well. Online stores of every type were springing up, but none was devoted to a huge selection of shoes. Swinmurn saw a market opportunity from his personal need and knew that the investment environment at that time made substantial growth possible.

Although potential investors were initially skeptical that anyone would buy online something as individual and difficult-to-fit as a pair of shoes, Swinmurn had research showing that 5 percent of shoes were already being sold through mail-order catalogs, and that shoes were a huge market. He received a $500,000 investment, and he and his investors—one of whom, Tony Hsieh, would later become co-CEO—changed the name of the company from shoesite.com to Zappos—reminiscent of the Spanish word for shoes, "zapatos."

Swinmurn's original idea was to offer the absolute best selection in shoes. Selection would be the company's competitive advantage. But when Zappos couldn't get a number of shoe brands to participate, the company realized it had to differentiate, based on customer service. From the beginning Zappos offered free shipping. When someone ordered ground shipping, Zappos sent it overnight instead, amazing the recipient. The company also offered free *return* shipping—and accepted returns up to a year after purchase. The goal was to surprise and wow customers…and to get them talking about Zappos.

Yet all this was costly. Shipping is extremely expensive, and two-way shipping significantly reduces profit margins. Zappos believed in delivering purchases *quickly,* which is also expensive. One way Zappos reduced its cost was to use "drop-shipping." In other words, the manufacturers (or their distributors) sent orders directly to the customers from their own warehouses rather than from Zappos'. The advantage, of course, was that Zappos could maintain far lower inventory levels—thereby reducing costs. But it also had far less control over the customers' experience. Shipments would come from different sources; they could be slow, lost, or just plain wrong.

So in 2002, Zappos built its own centralized distribution warehouse next to a UPS facility in Kentucky. That meant that orders could often be shipped out the same day they were received. And the next year, the company discontinued the practice altogether of drop-shipping from other companies.

Zappos also realized it needed to make sure its customer service representatives were well trained, highly customer motivated, and passionate about the company. The company instituted above-industry salaries, extensive training, and lots of extra perks for employees. New Zappos hires are put through a five-week training course (extraordinarily long by industry standards) to ensure that they are fully immersed in corporate culture, customer service, and distribution skills. Then, at the end of their training, they're offered $2,000 to leave. Anyone not completely enamored of the company is encouraged to take the money and go. Few do. (In 2011 *Forbes* ranked Zappos 15th on its list of the 100 best companies to work for.)

Another way that Zappos differed from the industry was in how it treated call center workers. Unlike in other call centers, calls to Zappos are not timed, nor do the call center workers have to meet minimum sales goals. In the end, all of this paid off. With lower turnover—the company's call center turnover is under 7 percent, compared to 150 percent industrywide—Zappos saves considerable dollars in recruiting, hiring, and training costs.

Another way Zappos keeps costs down is by eliminating errors. Employees are rewarded when spotting potential mistakes in shipping or warehousing. Without the need to correct costly mistakes after the fact, operational expenses are also kept in line.

Zappos considers customer service an *investment*, not a cost center. Although returns amount to approximately 35 percent of overall revenues, 75 percent of orders come from repeat customers, who typically buy, on average, 2½ times within a year, spending more each time.

By depending on happy customers to spread news of the company through word-of-mouth marketing, Zappos also keeps its advertising budget low. A full 43 percent of new customers come from word of mouth.

Zappos was first profitable in 2006, and since then has had an unbroken record of profitability. It was acquired by Amazon in 2009 (a short 10 years after its founding) for about $1.2 billion, and is operated as a wholly owned subsidiary. ∎

questions

1. The great customer service at Zappos increases costs—free, same-day shipping; extensive employee training; and so on. Do you think the company can reduce costs in other areas of operations to help offset these costs? If so, how?

2. By offshoring its customer call center, even if Zappos offers wages and perks much higher than the going rate, it would stand to save substantial amounts of money. Do you think Zappos should consider this? Why or why not?

3. In what other ways do you think Zappos can affordably enhance its customer service?

TURN THE TABLES ON COSTS

Goal:

Calculate ways to improve operational efficiencies without sacrificing quality.

What to Do:

Imagine that you're a U.S. maker of oak tables and chairs. Your company has been in business for more than 100 years, and is one of the few American table and chair manufacturers left in business—most other furniture manufacturing has gone overseas. You only produce a limited line of designs and have small-run rates to ensure the high quality for which your company has been known since its inception. True, you charge a premium price for your high-quality goods, but now your costs are rising to the point where you have to make operational changes to save money if you're to stay in business. You want to do this without compromising on quality.

1. Either working alone or with others, examine all aspects of operations to determine where you might be able to reduce costs.

2. Without knowing all the specifics of this company, consider where there might be inefficiencies or where you might be able to implement cost-saving measures in each of these areas:

   a. Use of technology for customer data management and order taking

   b. Shipping

   c. Inventory management

   d. Customer service

   e. Production and manufacturing

   f. Supply chain management

   g. Personnel management

   h. Billing and collections

3. Come up with other strategies for streamlining operations, if you can think of any, that will enable you to continue offering high-quality, American-made furniture at a reasonable price point.

CHAPTER

15 TECHNOLOGY

learning objectives

In this chapter, you'll learn how to:

- Determine technology needs

- Evaluate the best technology options for particular business needs

- Understand the difference between on-premise and cloud computing

- Distinguish between security and privacy concerns

- Establish solid technology policies and procedures

- Manage mobility

- Practice good data management skills

Technology Is the Backbone of Your Business

Every company is a technology company. Even if you're not in the business of making or selling technology, technology is essential to your success. This is as true as if you're building mobile apps for the iPhone as if you're selling shoes or manufacturing chocolate. Technology makes you efficient—if you doubt this, try to imagine your work life without your phone or your laptop!

Technology does everything from improving personal productivity by automating formerly time-consuming and tedious manual tasks, to helping customers find you through your website or social media, to enabling you to deliver products and services to buyers anywhere in the world. It helps you stay on top of your finances and get your bills paid. It keeps your customer lists in order and maintains communications with them. It helps you make sure you have the inventory you need, when and where you need it. It aids you in meeting customers' after-sales support needs. In short: Technology is an integral part of every entrepreneur's planning and every company's operations.

Once, technology was largely treated as an afterthought: Entrepreneurs would plan their business, put their business processes in place, and only then figure out how to automate them. No longer. Now, thinking of how technology will help you run and manage key corporate functions is an essential part of your upfront business planning. Technology not only automates routine tasks—its wise use also gives you a competitive edge. Technology is an *investment* that, if you do it well, gives you a robust return.

Here are some of the many ways technology benefits you:

- **Saving money.** Technology automates many processes previously done by hand, by humans, and more slowly. Integrated data technology reduces double or triple entry of data. This can give you tighter control over your finances. **Analytics** gives you information to more accurately evaluate specific efforts, such as marketing campaigns, and to adjust or eliminate unprofitable ones. A well-thought-out technology implementation can significantly reduce your operating costs.

■ **Saving time.** With the proper systems, the day-to-day productivity of your individual workers can be higher and your overall organization can be tighter, saving time and costs. For an entrepreneur, embracing technology can often speed time to market, meaning sales can be made more quickly.

■ **Improving quality.** Automation can dramatically reduce errors and defects, whether you make products, provide services, or manage data.

en·tre·pre·neur·ship key terms

Analytics
The quantifiable evaluation of data, providing greater insight into the performance of key business functions, especially those managed digitally. For example, website analytics show how many visitors have come to a website, where they've clicked, how long they've stayed, and so on. Other analytics provide feedback, often in real-time, of such things as customer response to online offers, sales performance by geographic region, and the results of marketing campaigns.

Application
A digital program running on an electronic device that enables a user to perform a specific task or tasks. Examples of business applications include word processing, email, and spreadsheets.

Cloud computing
Frequently referred to simply as "the cloud," a way of delivering computing power and applications over the Internet as a service rather than a product that the end-user purchases and maintains in-house. Software, memory, and storage space are all shared and provided to computers, smartphones, and other devices as a utility (much like the way electricity is provided). "Cloud computing" is a broad term, entailing both infrastructure (such as computing power) and applications (such as email, file sharing, and accounting).

Integration
Enabling different applications, whether on-premise or in the cloud, to communicate with each other and work together. In general, the more an application is integrated with other related applications, the more productive users and employees will be. For example, integrated sales and accounting programs eliminate or reduce the need for the double entry of data.

On-premise software
Software that is purchased (or licensed) by the end-user, whether a business or consumer, and installed on their own hardware, then managed and maintained in-house. Traditionally, virtually all software was on-premise, but this changed as cloud computing and SaaS became popular.

SaaS
The acronym for Software as a Service, which is software that is delivered over the Internet as a service, frequently on a subscription basis, as opposed to software that a company purchases and owns, runs on its own hardware, and supports and maintains in-house. These are typically business and personal applications.

Scalability
When used in relation to technology, the ability of a system (usually hardware and applications) to grow in power or capacity as needed. Scalable systems enable entrepreneurs to efficiently continue to support their rapidly expanding businesses.

Server
A powerful computer that provides computing power or other resources (storage space, software applications, and email, for example) to users who have desktop computers, laptops, tablets, or smartphones connected via a network.

Service level agreement (SLA)
A term frequently used in service industries—particularly in the IT field. An SLA delineates in the contract the degree and quality of the service. Thus, a website hosting company might guarantee 99.9 percent uptime in an SLA, or a tech support SLA might promise customers 24/7 service and ensure that all phone calls are returned within one hour.

Analytics and customer feedback enable you to quickly improve your offerings and continually boost quality.

- **Increasing capabilities.** Technology, especially many cloud-based services, provides entrepreneurs—even start-ups—with powerful capabilities that were once available only to large corporations. Automation allows you to offer a greater range of products or services far more rapidly, as well as to shorten time-to-market of new offerings.

- **Enhancing customer loyalty.** Technology provides a vast range of methods to stay in touch with, track, provide service to, and make sales to customers. Technology enables personalization and customization at low cost. All of which enable you to increase customer loyalty and satisfaction.

BUSINESS FUNCTIONS AND EXAMPLE TECHNOLOGIES

FUNCTION	TECHNOLOGIES	WHAT IT DOES
Communications and Collaboration	Voice technologies, email, audio and video conferencing, collaboration tools, file sharing	Allows you to communicate with employees, customers, and partners in the office or remotely
Office Productivity	Word processing, spreadsheets, databases, presentation programs	Enables you to complete routine office tasks, such as preparing documents and reports
Marketing	Website, customer relationship management (CRM) programs, email and email newsletter programs, social media	Enables you to communicate directly with customers and find and reach prospects
Sales	Order entry software, point-of-sale applications, sales/contact manager applications, online checkout and shopping cart programs; mobile payment applications	Ensures efficient and accurate sales processing and reporting; supports and enables your sales team
Finance	Spreadsheets, accounting software, tax software, invoicing and billing	Tracks, organizes, analyzes, and optimizes financial data
Operations	Management information, inventory management, shipping management programs, manufacturing systems, asset management	Aids the efficient management of day-to-day operations and enables management to have detailed information
HR	Payroll, benefits, time tracking, employee scheduling, other HR applications	Maintains accurate and detailed records of all aspects of the company relating to employees and personnel
Customer Service	Customer contact applications, website "chat" functions, telephony systems, voice response systems	Cost-efficient methods enable customers to interact with the company and receive personalized customer service

Choose the Right Technology

The number and variety of technology solutions available to start and run your business can be overwhelming. With dozens—even hundreds—of categories of software **applications**, each supporting a different part of your business, how do you choose among this embarrassment of technology riches?

Your first step in developing a technology plan for your new company is to identify which business functions you need to perform. It's easy to get entranced by some cool new app or the latest device, yet you want to make sure you spend your tech money and use your time to achieve important business objectives. Moreover, once you've chosen certain applications—such as your accounting programs or data storage solutions—changing is often difficult, time-consuming, or costly. So your technology choices, just as with every aspect of your business, deserve careful planning.

Use the worksheet "Identifying Your Technology Needs" to identify the technologies you might use to meet your core business needs. For example, your core need may be a website with the ability to make sales.

Hardware, software, and applications

Once you have a good sense of what your organization needs, you can start looking at specific solutions to determine which ones you'll implement in your business.

Technology is generally divided into two categories: hardware and software. Hardware refers to physical equipment and includes all the devices: computers, tablets, printers, production equipment, and the like. Software refers to the applications that power the hardware and make it functional, whether the software is embedded in the equipment itself (often referred to as "firmware," since it's fixed), is installed separately, or is accessed over the Internet (from the "cloud"). Much of what once was thought of as "software" that came on a floppy disc or a CD is now thought of more broadly as "applications."

A smartphone is a good example of a seemingly simple piece of technology that includes all the above categories. The phone itself is hardware. Alone, it can't do anything. But it comes embedded with an operating system and other programs that enable the physical device to make and receive calls, snap pictures, play music, and much, much more. In addition, you can access "apps" to enable additional functionalities on your phone, such as playing games and mapping your route. If your phone can access the Internet, you can log on to capabilities in the cloud—software stored on the computers of cloud-based providers—to perform other functions, such as retrieving your email or sharing large documents.

As you plan for your technology needs, you'll consider your hardware and software or application requirements. Of course, you'll always want to make certain that your software and applications are compatible with your hardware.

There's an app for that

Good news: There are systems for virtually every business function. Need a way to process payroll from your smartphone? You'll find an application that manages every part of that—from pulling data from employee time-tracking, to deducting personnel taxes, adding bonuses, and sending reports to the IRS—all with a few clicks, whether you're at your desk or on the road.

Need a way to manage your inventory and track what's in stock in the warehouse? The market offers more inventory management packages than you could possibly imagine, each with its own blend of functionality and features. Which one you choose depends upon your needs.

Identifying Your Technology Needs

Complete this worksheet to identify the business needs you have in each functional area of your business and the key capabilities any tech solutions must include. As you do your research, list the specific tech solution that can meet those needs.

Functional Area	Business Needs	Key Functionality Requirements	Potential Tech Solutions
Marketing (e.g., website, email newsletter, database management)			
Sales (e.g., customer relationship management, order tracking, bidding and proposals)			
Finance (e.g., accounting, tax)			
HR (e.g., payroll, benefits management, time tracking)			
Customer Service (e.g., order tracking, website chat, tech support)			
Project Management (e.g., collaboration tools, file sharing, calendaring, videoconferencing)			
Business Intelligence (e.g., management information systems, analytics)			
Operations (e.g., inventory management, energy management, quality control checks)			
Administration (e.g., scheduling, reporting, presentation, document sharing)			
Industry-specific needs:			
Other:			

Expect to be bewildered—and frustrated—as you sort out all your tech needs. Indeed, some young businesses, especially those without an information technology (IT) guru on staff, prefer to engage the ongoing services of a tech consultant.

Some basic criteria for judging technology products

Evaluate all technology based on a few high-level capabilities:

- **Ease of use.** How quickly and easily employees can learn to use a system is critical. Not only does a well-designed user interface help get your team up and running much more efficiently, it also can require less training—and less money on training budgets—as well as less downtime. And if a system proves easy to use, employees will actually *use* it!

- **Ease of management.** How easy is the system to manage and maintain? This category includes such things as how often you'll have to upgrade your users to new versions of the application, how frequently you'll need to apply software patches for "bugs," and whether the system requires a lot of hands-on maintenance simply to keep it operational. Can you manage the system from a central location, or must you have access to each user's machine to do any work on the application?

These issues affect the overall cost of the system as well. With cloud-based applications, the cloud application provider handles many of these management and maintenance issues. But whether you choose **on-premise software** or cloud-based, some application vendors, in addition to the license fees, charge annual maintenance fees to cover these things. In many cases, the maintenance fees are mandatory.

- **Integration.** Since you'll almost certainly run multiple applications from multiple vendors in your company, you need to understand if—and how—they work together. Some applications come with interfaces (called application programming interfaces, or APIs) that allow them to be easily hooked to other systems. Others have an "open" architecture, meaning that they'll easily integrate with solutions from certain other vendors. With **integration**, you can avoid having to enter the same information multiple times. For example, customer information could flow from the first contact with the customer to the final billing without your having to rekey in all that data.

The ease with which your applications integrate usually depends upon how well they adhere to industry standards. The less "proprietary" the application, the less you'll risk being locked into a particular vendor. Always check that you have an "exit strategy" so you can get your data out of a particular system without requiring custom programming.

Think lean

In every aspect of your business, but especially in technology, attempt to be a "lean start-up." Buy only the tech you need, when you need it, and look for ways to minimize costs. Cloud-based applications make it possible for entrepreneurs to launch businesses with relatively little tech investment. Because the software applications are hosted on cloud-based providers' computers, it's possible to access powerful solutions with very simple devices.

- **Scalability.** Can your application grow with you? As a new company, you'll likely add staff quickly and unpredictably, expand your customer base, or even change the products or services you sell. So keep scalability and flexibility in mind as you firm up your tech choices. At what point will you likely run into capacity or performance issues because you've added too many users or too much data to the system? Can you add or subtract users as needed? Must you buy more capacity than you need now to ensure a sufficient amount later (that's costly for a start-up company)? **Scalability** enables your system to grow in power or capacity as you need it to.

- **Mobility.** Can your employees, contractors, and partners access the applications they need from remote or mobile locations? Or is the data and functionality locked at a fixed location? In general, with business more and more being done remotely—often globally—you want the ability to securely access both data and functionality from off-premises.

- **Vendor support.** What's the quality of the support that the vendor provides? What's the "uptime" the vendor of business applications promises in its **service level agreements (SLA)**? What time is its tech support available, and where is it located? Precisely because you'll be so dependent upon technology to run your business, having a vendor that's able to provide you sufficient support when you need it is critical.

- **Cost.** Naturally, one of the factors you'll consider when making tech choices is how much the solution will cost. Remember, cost is more than merely the initial price. Consider the "total cost of ownership"— meaning the expenses of the technology, including initial purchase price, subscription costs, upgrades, maintenance, training, and the cost of any downtime or lost productivity if you happen to choose inferior products. Often, the initial cost may be lower, but the overall cost of ownership higher (as is sometimes the case with cloud-based solutions). However, in a new business, you may be willing to make such a trade-off to keep your start-up costs as low as possible.

Leverage the vast stores of knowledge on the Internet

With so many choices, each product claiming to offer you the best of the best, how on earth do you decide?

The good news is that you have access to numerous review sites that evaluate the various strengths and weaknesses of individual solutions. You can read in-depth reviews from both professionals and users that will guide you in making the best decision for your business. Such reviews will generally tell you which features are critical in a particular solution, and how the various options measure up in terms of these features.

These features will understandably vary, depending upon the type of solution you're considering. Take CRM software—considered by many to be a must-have for successfully managing the customer relationship through the entire life cycle of your sales, marketing, and support efforts. You'd want to make sure the application contains the ability to report on sales for particular sales reps or certain types of accounts. When evaluating time-tracking applications, you'd want to see how easy it is to generate and access reports on each employee's sales results, arrival times, or overtime work. Leverage the information available to help you decide.

Generally, you'll want to narrow your selection down to two or perhaps three finalists for serious consideration in any category. Then use a trial version of your final choices and give the people who'll actually use them a chance to express their opinions. The last thing you want is to accrue a lot of "shelf-ware"—technology that you bought because you thought it was a good idea, but no one uses it so it just sits on the shelf.

Consider industry-specific applications

Your business is special. You operate in a particular industry, and the demands of that industry mean you're likely to have special needs. Of course, many technology solutions can be used by any type of business—such as word processing or spreadsheets. But chances are good that, at some point, you'll need or want an application specifically designed to meet the needs of your type of business in your industry. After all, running a restaurant is much different from manufacturing medical equipment or designing office buildings. Not surprisingly, you can find systems—both hardware and software—that address many of the unique functionalities you need in your particular industry.

When searching for industry-specific systems, ask the following questions:

■ **How much experience does the vendor have in your industry?** Is this system truly tailored to your industry, or is it just a generic system that someone slapped some light features on in an attempt to make sales? Always investigate the roots of the vendor. How long has it been serving your industry? Does it have former industry workers on staff? Does it really seem to "get" your particular needs and challenges?

■ **Can you speak to current and past customers with businesses like yours?** Always talk to businesses in your industry that currently use the system—and preferably have done so for a decent length of time. Ask them how well it meets their needs, whether it's missing any key functionality, and whether everything works as advertised. Also, ask for the names of customers who no longer use the system. It can be enlightening to find out why they stopped using it.

■ **How customizable is it to meet your particular needs?** Even systems that have been calculated to support businesses in your industry may need to be tweaked to fit your unique requirements. Always find out how much freedom you have to customize a system so that it supports your processes, policies, and procedures. And ask how easy it is to do that customization. Some systems may be customizable, but only at great trouble and expense.

Plan for mobility

Long gone are the days when employees worked only at a desktop computer hard-wired to a company's network. Today, employees need to be mobile—whether taking their laptop to the conference room or working over their smartphone around the globe. Your customers are mobile, too. They'll visit your website from their tablets and shop from their smartphones. Make sure your company is designed for mobility—whether with cloud-based apps for your employees or mobile apps for your customers.

REAL-WORLD RECAP

Industry-specific systems

Evaluate industry-specific tech solutions on the following basis:

- How much experience does the vendor have in your industry?
- Can you speak to references in businesses like yours?
- How customizable is the system to meet your particular needs?
- Does it integrate with off-the-shelf applications for general use?
- How financially stable is the vendor?
- How portable is your data?

Why businesses love the cloud

- Get additional computing power and high-quality services
- Get up and running quickly
- Get more predictable costs
- Access the application and data from anywhere
- Pay only for what you need, as you go
- Eliminate disruptive software upgrades
- Keep data more secure
- Expand capabilities without investing in infrastructure
- Transform capital expenses to operational expenses

- **Does it integrate with off-the-shelf applications for general use?** Just because you want an industry-specific production system for your citrus processing plant, doesn't mean that you won't also want to use some other technology. You want to be able to integrate the production system into your inventory management system, your accounting program, your shipping application, and so on.

- **How financially stable is the vendor, and what does its future look like?** One of the biggest challenges with industry-specific systems is that many providers one day close up shop or go out of business. Because companies that create industry-specific solutions often serve small markets, they may not be viable in the long run. You don't want to be stuck with a system with no future support or upgrades.

- **How portable is your data?** If something happens to the vendor or you want to make a switch, can you easily get your data out of its program? Make sure you don't suffer from "vendor lock-in" because you've gone the industry-specific route.

On-Premise or in the Cloud?

One of your first—and biggest—decisions when shopping for technology is whether to install and manage it on your own premises or to choose an offering "in the cloud."

Ah, the cloud. At its most basic level, **cloud computing** offers you resources—applications, file storage and sharing, and processing power—that you access over the Internet. You can use these resources even though they don't reside on hardware (computers or **servers**) on your premises—whether your office, plant, warehouse, or home.

The most common types of cloud solutions used by most businesses are known as **SaaS**, or Software-as-a-Service. These provide actual applications, such as accounting programs, rather than merely data storage or processing power, that you access remotely. You use your computer, smartphone, or tablet, or indeed any "smart" device, to tap into those resources over the Internet.

The opposite of cloud-based computing resources is on-premise resources. With on-premise computing resources (software applications, data storage, email, and the like) you, or someone within your organization, or an outside consultant you hire, will choose, maintain, upgrade, and integrate your technology solutions. You may have the ability to customize applications and technology configurations for your particular needs. You pay for the solutions up front but then only have to pay for upgrades and maintenance—there are no ongoing fees. You have a lot of control over your technology, though that can pose a big challenge, and often an expensive one, especially if you lack IT staff.

That's where the cloud comes in. Cloud service providers maintain, upgrade, manage, and sometimes even integrate your computing needs and business applications. You typically pay a monthly subscription per user. You access the application over the Internet, rather than from on-premise computers or servers. You can "turn on" and "turn off" resources, as needed, by adding or dropping the number of users. You gain flexibility, scalability, and powerful business functions without the infrastructure and its costs. However, you may have less flexibility and choice. You may be able to slightly configure a cloud solution for your needs, but by design it won't be fully customizable. Plus, you have the ongoing monthly cost. Over the lifetime of a cloud solution, the cost could easily be higher than the direct costs of an on-premise solution.

One example of the costs and benefits of the cloud versus on-premise solutions is data backup. It's essential to back up critical business data, offsite, to protect against damage, destruction, theft, and the like. After all, if a fire destroyed your business, you'd need to be able to retrieve copies of your important files from a place untouched by the blaze. Even if a file is merely corrupted, you want to have a secure copy.

With an on-premise data backup solution, you either have to physically make copies of your data and regularly take those copies to an offsite location, or have to transfer the data over a secure Internet connection to data storage servers that you maintain in a remote location. You may be able to rent that storage space on others' servers, but you still have to maintain the operating systems as well as to continually arrange, monitor, and manage the backup program. The good news is that the data is in your complete control, including the level of security safeguards you put in place. If you have highly secretive or sensitive data, or you're uncomfortable with the level of security that cloud solution providers promise, this may be a choice you want to make.

By contrast, with a cloud-based backup service, for a monthly or annual fee, any files you designate are regularly and automatically copied and sent over the Internet (typically encrypted for security) to the providers' storage servers. Once you set up the system, there's typically little that you have to do to maintain or monitor the backups. It happens automatically. If a file gets corrupted for any reason, you just log on to the cloud service and download a fresh (accurate) copy. And if you're hit with a flood or fire, all your data is immediately available, wherever you may be. The backup solution provider maintains security—often at a level that you yourself may not be able to provide. But the costs can add up, especially if you have huge amounts of data.

Is software dead?

Start-ups are among the most enthusiastic users of cloud-based solutions. Many of them are altogether bypassing traditional on-premise software. Even for such typical on-premise applications such as word processing and spreadsheet programs, numerous new businesses turn to cloud-based SaaS solutions such as Google Docs.

It makes sense. After all, start-ups are strapped for cash. Using cloud-based solutions, they don't have the large capital expenses of buying expensive software or powerful hardware. They don't need to buy more than they require, anticipating growth. They can add more capacity—or subtract it—as needed. And if a particular SaaS solution turns out to be wrong, they can quickly change.

Comparing the Cost of a Cloud Solution to an On-Premise Solution

Fill out the worksheet below to examine the costs of cloud and on-premise applications.

Costs	Cloud Application 1	On-Premise Application 1	Cloud Application 2	On-Premise Application 2
Application Purchase Price				
Software Upgrades				
Operating System Upgrades				
Configuration/Implementation Services				
Hardware Requirements				
Software Maintenance, IT, and Support				
Contract Management Services				
Security Systems and Procedures				
Miscellaneous Transition/ Migration				
Training Users				
Other:				

Security and Privacy: You Need Both

In any business, security and privacy are both *critical*. You need to protect your physical technology assets—your hardware—and equally, if not more importantly, you need to protect your data and other virtual assets. Your data network can be vulnerable to those who intentionally want to access valuable information, such as Social Security numbers, credit cards, bank accounts, your company data, and so on. It can be the target of random data vandals and viruses. It also needs to be secure in the sense that it's maintained appropriately so that your data is not corrupted and is there when you want it.

Your servers need to be in secured (locked) rooms to which only authorized people have access. Losing a laptop can unfortunately be the same as losing data and access to sensitive systems. If an employee hasn't password-protected the laptop or has stored passwords in the browser, then anyone in possession of the laptop can rummage through your business information.

Security is one of the main reasons many growing businesses choose the cloud. When all your physical (servers) and virtual (data) resources are in the cloud being managed by a third party, the problem is taken off your hands. Of course, you still need to choose your cloud vendor carefully—for the security will only be as good as the vendor makes it. So when you choose your cloud solution provider, ask how it ensures that your data is secure, both virtually and physically, and also research how professional reviewers rate its security.

Ensuring that data is *private* is also critical. Privacy is different from security. Privacy is about limiting access to certain data to appropriate people. For instance, you need to make certain that personally identifiable information (PII) of employees, customers, and partners isn't accessible by anyone except those who absolutely need access to it for business reasons. Only authorized employees should have access to payroll records, health insurance records, or other personal data. Privacy not only includes personal information but company data as well, such as making certain that employees in one division can't access data from another or that once employees leave, they no longer have access to company files and can't take company information with them. For that reason, you need to have a privacy policy in place that dictates very specifically what information each member of your organization has access to.

Various levels of access will apply. For example, managers will need access to more aspects of a system than regular employees. HR workers will have special permission to go into the records of employees under specific circumstances. Many government regulations dictate the privacy of data, so be careful with your information.

What makes a good password?

Unfortunately, it's relatively easy to figure out passwords—either through automated "password cracking" programs or by a brilliant hacker who knows enough about an individual user's personal information to make a good guess. To prevent that from happening, share these password "best practices" with your employees:

- Don't use real words, names, or proper nouns. These types of passwords are the most easily cracked by automated programs.

- Create passwords of at least six characters or numbers in length. If possible, create even longer ones—more than eight characters or numbers is ideal.

- Use at least two numbers. Positioning the numbers at the beginning of the password strengthens it.

- Never use a string of sequential numbers or letters. All-too-common passwords made up of 1-2-3-4 or a-b-c-d are easily broken.

- Never use a personal number associated with you. This means no phone numbers, Social Security numbers, license plate numbers, birthdates, and the like.

REAL-WORLD RECAP

Technology policies

- Security policies
- Privacy policies
- Email policies
- Web-surfing policies
- Personal use of company equipment
- Company access to employees' accounts
- Treatment of departing employees' data and technology

Establish sensible technology policies

Early in your company's existence, you should begin to develop policies that spell out precisely how employees are permitted to use the technologies and data entrusted to them to do their jobs. These policies will evolve and expand as your business grows, but they should touch upon a number of key points:

- **Security policies.** This should include everything from good password practices, to who has access to the physical computer room, to what kind of devices can connect to the corporate network. Employees enamored with the smartphones, tablets, and other gadgets that they've bought for their own use want to use them for work—either by bringing them into the office, or using them at home or while on the road. This raises security issues. Many people don't practice rigid security policies in their homes; what happens if an employee brings in a malicious virus on a personal laptop that wreaks havoc with the corporate network? What if they lose a laptop or transfer sensitive data to personal files? Think through all aspects of employee behavior that could have a negative impact on overall security.

- **Privacy policies.** This includes which employees have access to which data, what steps will be taken to ensure that private information is completely protected, the destruction of unnecessary private data (such as that from unhired job applicants), and the extra security measures required around data protected by industry or government regulations.

- **Email policies.** Email is a significant source of viruses, corruption of data, and phishing (phony attempts to get sensitive data). It's important to train all employees on good email "hygiene." You may also want to adopt policies covering what kind of email employees can send—such as personal email from their work account. In many industries (for example, ones that deal with legal or government documents), you'll want clear policies about the retention and deletion of emails.

- **Web-surfing policies.** Establish policies about the appropriate use of the Internet during work hours, both in terms of time spent and in terms of what content can be accessed. You may want to block certain kinds of content (for example, pornography or live TV feeds), or certain sites from being accessible over the corporate network.

- **Personal use of company equipment.** Many companies issue laptops to employees, especially those who work on the road or from home. Some companies have strict policies that such laptops are for business use only—but that may be unrealistic, especially for those who travel. However, the equipment belongs to the company, and you'll want to make clear which personal uses are allowed and which ones are not.

Your Technology Policies

Use this worksheet to brainstorm your company's technology policies.

Key Issues	Concerns	Suggested Policy
Security Policies		
Privacy Policies		
Email Policies		
Web-Surfing Policies		
Personal Use of Company Equipment		
Company Access to Employee Accounts		
Treatment of Departing Employees		
Other:		

REAL-WORLD RECAP

Three ways to leverage your data

- Be able to find it
- Analyze it
- Understand it, then apply what you've learned to your business decisions

Manage Data Effectively

Your company's information will be one of your chief assets. Guard it and use it wisely. In addition to security and privacy concerns, consider three aspects of leveraging your precious data to get the most value from it:

- **Be able to find it.** Corporate data is stored in many places—in disparate databases, in different applications, and especially on individuals' computer desktops. It's a fact that we spend a lot of time gathering and storing data—but then often have trouble getting it out again. You can address this issue in several ways. First, you can install an "enterprise search" application that does for your internal data what Google has done for the Web (in fact, Google has an enterprise search product that it sells to businesses): By searching through every place in your company where data has been stored—including networked PCs—enterprise search allows you to find the data you need, when you need it. A second solution is to integrate data from various systems into a central repository. Note that this is a difficult and expensive option to pursue, and hard to implement without doing quite a bit of custom programming.

- **Analyze it.** You should also deploy sophisticated, computer-based analysis techniques—called analytics—to examine your data. Can you discover any patterns in your sales by geography? What will your financial situation look like 12 months ahead if costs keep rising at the current rate? Does demand for your product or service drop when you raise prices? All these are questions that you can answer by deploying analytics applications on your corporate data.

- **Understand it, then apply what you've learned to your business decisions.** Successfully analyzing something doesn't always mean you know how to interpret it to make business decisions. Frequently, the output from analytics programs is so highly mathematical and technical that few people can understand it. Having some sort of way to parse the results and create reports that make sense from a business perspective is also key to fully leveraging your data stores. Some analytics programs offer "dashboards" that allow you to query the analyses, using plain business language, and get graphical results back that are easy to digest.

Technology for Technology Companies

If you're in the business of creating or managing technology, your own tech needs will be greater than other companies'. Although all companies will want to include technology in their planning, the growth and success of your business depends upon your being technologically sophisticated.

If you develop cutting-edge technology tools, you'll likely employ, and need to employ, technically sophisticated engineers, marketers, and salespeople. In general, you'll want to layer an extra level of technical savvy on top of your employees' other skills.

The technology they use to do their jobs may be quite varied, too. Although administrative assistants and finance professionals might have the same type of devices as their peers in other companies, engineers and designers and marketers may require more powerful and sophisticated workstations and applications. Technology companies tend to go beyond using the leading-edge technologies to "bleeding-edge" ones—in other words, the tech that the earliest of early adopters use. Sometimes this is risky—but then they also typically have more technically sophisticated people on staff, who can work through any challenges they face.

Even if you're developing relatively simple technology—perhaps new mobile apps, for example—you will most likely need to purchase a range of devices to test your application on. In your budgeting for a tech company, plan for larger tech expenditures in all aspects of your business. Organizationally, tech companies look different from other firms because they have technology development and testing departments where the products are designed, tested, and, if required, manufactured. These technologists are distinct from those in the IT department, which is the unit responsible for supporting the basic technology infrastructure for the firm. As your firm grows, you're likely to have a chief technology officer (CTO) who is in charge of development, as well as a chief information office (CIO) who is in charge of the IT department. Despite both departments' revolving around technology, these are distinct groups, with quite different and particular roles.

Change is Constant

Technology is always evolving, always changing. Generally, technology creates more-powerful and versatile tools in ever smaller and less expensive packages. Breathtakingly innovative breakthroughs with the power to transform entire industries occur year after year. Keep an eye on what's new in technology. Pay attention to how technology is used by your competitors as well as by leading companies in other industries. Staying ahead on technology typically gives start-up entrepreneurs a significant competitive edge.

Get IT help

Although dealing with technology has become much easier for businesses over the years, tech decisions and planning can still be overwhelming, especially for entrepreneurs who are not techies themselves. Expect to need the services of technology specialists, either by hiring them in-house or by using competent consultants. Just as most businesses need outside accounting and legal advice, you're likely to need technology expertise on a regular basis.

REAL-WORLD CASE

Prescription for Success: Cloud-Based Nurse Management

Managing one's own health care can be a nightmare. ISYS was established to help individuals on workers' compensation navigate the often-complex task of walking through the maze of physicians, insurance, and medications. Founded in 1997, ISYS employs nurses in California, Nevada, and Arizona to coordinate doctor appointments for patients, attend the appointments, and accompany the patients to any physical therapy or other outpatient services. They provide their professional opinions of the quality of care the patient receives, and in general collaborate closely with health care providers and insurance companies alike to help injured employees return to health and work as soon as possible.

Until 2008, ISYS used a standalone, on-premise, PC-based application called CaseTracker to record the hours that field nurses worked and the tasks they completed. Nurses would keep track of what they did and how long it took, using any method that suited them, such as jotting down information in a traditional paper notebook. They would then type this into a Microsoft Word document and email it to the ISYS home office. There, administrative staff would enter the data into the system, using the Case-Tracker software. From CaseTracker, ISYS could then calculate what each customer owed for services that ISYS workers had performed.

Yet the work didn't end there—the customer still required an invoice. To generate that, an ISYS administrator would print out a CaseTracker report that itemized the charges, and then once again manually enter the data, this time into the on-premise accounting application, QuickBooks. Only then could an invoice be generated.

Data was entered at least three times: first by the nurse and then by the administrative assistant into CaseTracker and QuickBooks. If a customer ever had a question about an invoice, ISYS would have to first consult QuickBooks, then look up the details of the account activity in Case-Tracker—or, in some cases, call or email the field nurse for details. All this was very time-consuming and prone to errors.

"We were rapidly expanding, which was a positive thing, but the process for invoicing customers was cumbersome and costly because it required so much personnel time," said Diane Campos, general manager of managed care services at ISYS. "We needed to make a change."

At the end of 2008, Campos approached a CRM company called salesforce.com with a list of questions. Could its cloud-based customer relationship management application meet the needs of ISYS? Even though the ISYS invoicing process didn't fit into the traditional sales, marketing, or customer service category that Salesforce CRM was designed for, Campos hoped it could be customized to meet her needs.

challenge

Manual and repetitive handling of data entry and billing, increasing both costs and errors

solution

Moving to a cloud-based application and enabling the integration of data across both cloud and on-premise applications

"We definitely wanted a Web application that was flexible enough to capture our nurses' time and activities and track by customer account," she said. "Salesforce.com listened to us describe our dream application, and said we could easily build a customized application that would precisely meet our requirements."

So far, so good. Still, Campos wanted to push the envelope further by integrating the salesforce.com application into QuickBooks, thus automating the invoicing process from start to finish. That's when Campos heard about integrating applications—enabling one application to "talk to" and share data with another. ISYS accomplished that with Dell Boomi. "Knowing that an integration tool existed that could do what we wanted was a big plus," she said.

Salesforce.com referred Campos to a strategic consulting partner that provided programming and program management services to build the application as well as Boomi integration links. The project was successfully completed in 2009. This was a fairly customized solution, relatively early on in cloud integration development, and, thus, fairly expensive. However, it has transformed ISYS' work flow, dramatically cut operational costs, and reduced errors.

Although ISYS didn't do a formal ROI, Campos said, "We estimate that we have saved what it would have cost to hire another fulltime person and another halftime person. Given that an administrator would be paid $35,000 or $40,000, plus benefits, that's a substantial annual savings."

Today, ISYS nurses in the field use smartphones to log on to salesforce.com from wherever they're working, right as they deliver services, and enter their hours and activity logs directly into ISYS' system. That data is received by the ISYS home office instantaneously. The nurses love it, as it saves them considerable time and trouble, and lets them focus on their main jobs—caring for patients—rather than on paperwork.

Integrating the entire process end-to-end eliminated the human errors that inevitably occur in repetitive manual processes. And the application has proven highly reliable: In the two years since deploying the application, ISYS has had zero downtime.

Campos is especially appreciative of the analytics and reporting capabilities of the application. "Our management team uses the dashboard to check on such things as how many new case referrals we've received in a given day, week, or month," she said. "They can then drill down and see which nurses were assigned to each referral, and how many hours each of them worked."

Information like this can help ISYS understand whether it needs to hire more nurses for a particular city or geographic region, or whether certain nurses are being stretched too thin with too many cases. "It would have been very difficult to calculate these things using our old manual system," Campos said. ◼

questions

1. ISYS nurses enter personal, health-related data from the field, often with smartphones. What types of security and privacy issues do you think this raises? How could ISYS address those issues?

2. To gain a future benefit (saving time and money while reducing errors), ISYS had to make a very expensive investment. When would such an upfront investment *not* have been advisable?

3. Do you know of any business situation you've encountered that could benefit from a cloud-based solution? From an integrated solution? Describe the current problems you see and the expected benefits.

HIGH TECH, HIGH TOUCH

Goal:

Decide when to automate processes, and when to add a human touch.

What to Do:

Imagine you're opening a luxury hotel. You want it to be cutting edge in terms of technology, but you still want to treat guests with a personal touch. For example, you could automate room service ordering. Guests could order online, or with their smartphones, or through the TVs in their rooms. Then staff could deliver the meals on antique-looking carts, serving guests on fine china with crystal, linens, and fresh flowers. Or you could use technology to track your guests' entertainment and spa or workout center preferences. When they again stay at your hotel, you could present them with customized offers, again through email, their phones, or the room TVs.

Your biggest challenge will be balancing technology with a personal touch. For example, you could auto-

mate the entire check-in process, and even eliminate the door attendant. But fully automating these procedures would take away from the warm atmosphere you want to create.

1. Working alone or in groups, brainstorm a list of customer service processes and other related procedures that a hotel typically performs.

2. Which processes will you automate? Which will you choose to conduct with a human touch?

3. For the processes you'll keep "hands-on," can you use technology to improve their efficiency?

4. For the processes you'll automate, how can you add a personal touch to them?

5. What processes would actually cost less money to automate but would compromise your goal of a "high-touch" business?

6. Pick two or three of your ideas to present to the class. Be prepared to explain the relative costs and benefits of implementing these processes.

CHAPTER

16 LEGAL ISSUES

learning objectives

In this chapter, you'll learn how to:

- Evaluate the various company legal structures and select one

- Determine whether to take on a partner

- Establish and evaluate partnership terms and draw up partnership agreements

- Understand the various forms of intellectual property (IP) and how to obtain IP rights

- Analyze and create simple written contracts and agreements

- Determine which licenses, permits, certifications, and ID numbers are necessary

- Establish a basic understanding of taxes

Company Legal Structure

Taking care of your company's legal health is like taking care of your personal health: An ounce of prevention is better than a pound of cure. Time after time, entrepreneurs end up in legal battles costing thousands of dollars that could have been avoided with a $300 trip to an attorney.

When starting a business, one of the first questions you need to answer is what legal form your business will take. This may sound like a question that shouldn't be important to a lot of businesses—especially when they're just starting out. Who needs to pay hundreds of dollars in corporation or legal fees to a government agency simply to acquire a certain kind of legal structure?

Choosing a legal form affects how much you pay in taxes, who can invest in your company, and most important, your own personal financial security. Three things to keep in mind when choosing a legal form are:

- **Liability.** Legally, corporations and other corporate forms (see the following section on legal structures) are considered individual entities. As such, the corporation—not individual shareholders—is responsible for the actions of the business. In other words, if something goes very wrong and the company is sued, only the assets of the corporation are at stake, not the owners' personal assets. (There are some exceptions to this rule, but generally, your personal liability is greatly limited.)

  Obviously, having liability limited to the company's assets is quite desirable, since it means your personal assets—your home, investments, and savings—can't be seized if your company has a legal judgment against it.

- **Double taxation.** No one likes paying taxes, and you certainly don't want to pay taxes twice—once on income for the business and then again when that income is distributed as profits to you. Instead, look for a legal form that allows for the profits of the company to pass through to the owners, without having to pay corporate taxes first.

- **Ownership.** Some legal forms of business limit the number or type of people who can invest in your company. If you're seeking a large number of investors or international investors, find a corporate structure (for instance, a C corporation) that permits such stockholders.

REAL-WORLD RECAP

Three things to remember when choosing a legal form

- ☐ Liability
- ☐ Double taxation
- ☐ Ownership

en·tre·pre·neur·ship key terms

Buy-sell agreement
This spells out the terms by which one partner can buy the other out. In the event of a dispute, the departure of a principal, or differing goals, a buy-sell agreement can enable the company to survive.

Copyright
Legal protection covering any type of work that is "fixed" and "tangible" from others who would copy, imitate, or steal that work.

DBA
"Doing business as" (DBA or d/b/a) is a legal term that means the business name differs from the legal name of its owner(s), whether they are human or corporate.

Fictitious business name
A business name that differs from the legal name of the owner(s).

Intellectual property (IP)
Unlike physical or real property, refers to creations arising from the human intellect and inventiveness, such as inventions, designs, artistic works, software, names, and music. IP is typically intangible and has value in commerce.

Nexus
A presence in a particular state. A company has a nexus once it reaches a certain threshold for business activity in that state. At that point, it must pay income taxes and must collect and remit sales taxes to the state.

Nondisclosure agreement (NDA)
Protects a company's ideas. By signing an NDA, a person promises not to disclose any of the confidential information they learn during their dealings with another company.

Pass-through taxation
Allows the income or loss generated by the business to be reflected on the personal income tax return of the owners, eliminating the possibility of double taxation.

Patent
A government-issued protection of an invention, protecting the inventor from having others copy or sell imitations of the invention for an extended period.

Quarterlies
Tax estimates paid every three months, generally based on the previous year's earnings.

Trade secret
A formula, practice, process, design, instrument, pattern, or compilation of information used by a business to obtain an advantage over competitors.

Trademark (or Service mark)
A word, phrase, symbol, or design (or a combination of these) that identifies and distinguishes the maker of a product (or service) from makers of other, similar, products (or services).

TYPES OF LEGAL FORMS OF U.S. BUSINESS ORGANIZATIONS

LEGAL FORM	WHAT IS IT?	ADVANTAGES
Sole Proprietorship	An unincorporated business owned by one person. If you don't set up a legal structure, and no one else owns any part of your business, you have a sole proprietorship.	Simple. No legal forms or costs to establish. No double taxation.
General Partnership	A business with more than one owner. All partners actively participate in the business.	You have the time and talents of more than one person. No double taxation.
Limited Partnership	A business with an owner or owners who manage the business (general partners) and other partners who do not (limited partners).	Protects the personal assets of limited partners, who aren't responsible for the debts and obligations of the business. Limits investors' financial exposure.
Limited Liability Company (LLC) or Limited Liability Partnership (LLP)	A popular legal form that provides much of the protection of incorporating with most of the simplicity of a sole proprietorship. LLPs are LLCs for certain professional practices.	Protects personal assets against most business losses. No double taxation. Relatively simple, inexpensive to establish and maintain. Can distribute profits and losses disproportionately.
"C" Corporation	A corporation is a legal entity, separate from its owners. Major investors often want companies to be C corporations.	Protects owners' personal assets against corporate losses and obligations. Can issue stock. Unlimited number of stockholders. Costs of benefits for employees and owners are deductible.
"S" Corporation	A type of corporation that allows pass-through taxation instead of double taxation. S corporations are less popular since the introduction of LLCs.	The personal liability protection of a corporation with the pass-through taxation treatment of a sole proprietorship.
"B" Corporation	A type of corporation, allowed for in a few states, that is organized for the public benefit as well as for the benefit of the shareholders.	Gives directors of a company more legal protection and responsibility for making decisions motivated by achieving a public good rather than merely maximizing profits.
Not-for-Profit, "501(c)(3)" Organization	An organization, agency, institution, charity, or company with charitable, educational, or other public benefit goals, that has been certified as tax exempt by the IRS.	No federal income taxes; usually exempt from state and local taxes. Donations are tax deductible. Has members and Board of Directors rather than shareholders.

DISADVANTAGES	TAX TREATMENT	WATCH OUT FOR
The business owner, and possibly their spouse, has unlimited personal liability for the debts, obligations, and judgments against the company.	Pass-through profits and losses. The business owner can deduct losses against other personal income.	In community property states, spouses may be liable for business debts as well as having an ownership interest in the company.
Each partner can enter into contracts and incur debts for which all partners are responsible and have unlimited personal liability.	Pass-through profits and losses to the partners who pay tax at their individual rates. Partnership pays no taxes but must file a Form 1065.	If in business with others, you have a partnership whether you draw up documents or not, and partners have a share of the business and other rights.
Limited partners cannot participate in running the company. General partners are all liable for the company's obligations.	Limited partners can deduct "passive" losses against "passive income" only, and the amount they can invest is capped.	If a limited partner participates in any way in the management of the company, they can lose their liability protection.
Each owner can enter into contracts and incur debts for the entire LLC. Must file Articles of Organization with your state; often requires annual state fees.	Pass-through profits and losses to each owner. LLCs pay no taxes but must file a Form 1065.	Can be cumbersome converting from an LLC to a C corporation in order to accept VC financing or to be acquired by a large corporation in return for stock.
Double taxation. Must file articles of incorporation with your state. Annual state fees. Requires record-keeping, annual meetings, and a Board of Directors in most states if more than one stockholder.	Double taxation: Corporation and shareholders each pay tax on income. However, if the corporation keeps significant cash reserves, this can have lower tax consequences than pass-through taxation.	Securities rules affect how you sell stock and to whom. Use a lawyer to help you determine whether to set up a C corporation.
Disadvantages over an LLC include limits on number and residency of stockholders, proportionate distribution of profits and losses, and more record keeping.	Pass-through taxation, but profits and losses must be allocated at same percentage as ownership.	Ask your lawyer if there is any benefit in choosing an S corporation over an LLC or C corporation in your specific situation.
Limited number of states allow this option.	Same tax treatment as other corporations.	Requires an annual "benefit report," detailing which public benefits the company has achieved, that meets independent, third-party standards.
Must not be operated for the financial benefit of any individuals; no profits distributed to individuals. Must meet IRS requirements.	Tax exempt.	May not engage in any political activity. Typically must raise money through contributions and grants. Board of Directors can oust founders or restrict salaries.

BUILD-YOUR-BUSINESS WORKSHEET

Your Legal Structure

LEGAL FORM

What is the legal form of your company currently?

☐ Sole proprietorship

☐ Partnership

☐ Subchapter S corporation

☐ C corporation

☐ Other, describe:_____

☐ Limited liability company

☐ B corporation

☐ Not-for-profit corporation

☐ No legal entity/status

What is the intended legal form if different from above?

☐ Sole proprietorship

☐ Partnership

☐ Subchapter S corporation

☐ C corporation

☐ Other, describe:_____

☐ Limited liability company

☐ B corporation

☐ Not-for-profit corporation

☐ No legal entity/status

OWNERSHIP

If a sole proprietor or partnership, list the owners: _____

_____

_____

If incorporated, how many shares of stock have been issued?_____

_____

_____

Who owns the stock and in what amounts? _____

_____

_____

In which state(s), province(s), country(s), etc. are you legally incorporated or registered to do business? List dates and specifics: _____

_____

_____

Have you secured written agreements between/with:

☐ Principals, partners

☐ Suppliers

☐ Investors

☐ Key employees/management

☐ Customers

☐ Strategic partners

Dealing with Partners

Nothing affects your day-to-day work life more than the people you work with. Yes, work can be satisfying when you have challenging tasks, play with cool technology, or make lots of money. But whether or not you feel like getting out of bed in the morning can be greatly influenced by whom you're going to work with that day.

Deciding whether to have a partner

If you're going to take on a partner, carefully consider why you want or need one. As you start your business, you may feel uncertain about being on your own, but that feeling of uncertainty may pass quickly. A partner will be around for a long, long time. Remember, partners own a piece of the business. Even if you bring in someone with only a minority interest as a partner, your future is tied to them.

The best way to take on a partner is with clear-cut definitions of responsibilities and authority. It's nice to believe you will make every decision together, but that's not realistic. Who, in the end, gets to call the shots? And be careful about going into business with a friend—often both the business and the friendship suffer.

Make certain your partnership expectations are realistic. Are they willing to work as hard as you? Do they bring the same level of talent or skill (although perhaps in a different area) as you? Do they have the same long-term view of where they want to be? Partnerships can be terrific, but when things go wrong between the partners, it can often mean the demise of the whole company.

Partnership agreements: How to protect yourself

If you intend to go into business with other people, even a spouse or a friend, formalize your arrangement with a written partnership agreement. If you already work with a partner, you still need to do this! If one partner doesn't want to do this, that's a big red flag. Take the time to work out as many details as you can. Be certain to include a way to buy each other (or the other's heirs) out of the business. A messy "divorce" from a business partner is as difficult as a messy marital divorce—with potentially greater financial consequences. Drawing up an agreement, often called a **buy-sell agreement**, now will help avoid difficulties if you later decide to go your separate ways.

And here's something to keep in mind: In the eyes of the law, you don't need a written agreement to have a partnership. If, over a beer, you and a friend decide to start selling your own special salsa at a street fair, you make up a batch, and you start selling some salsa to friends, you may have become partners. Your friend may acquire rights to your salsa recipe, and you may each be responsible for all bills and obligations. So be very clear about the nature of the relationship *before* you begin working with anyone.

Getting to know you...

Spend time getting to know the business skills, attitudes, and aspirations of any potential partners—even if you've been friends or acquaintances for years. Find out whether their goals, work style, and values fit yours. You have more leeway, legally, to ask questions of potential partners than of employees.

Of course, make certain your potential partner is honest, but also examine their personal attitudes, how they handle stress, how much money they need and how soon, family or other demands on their time, and any other issues that may affect your working relationship.

Discussing Partnership Terms

Work with one or more other students and determine with your "partners" the terms of your partnership. If you are launching a new business with partners, after completing this exercise, meet with a lawyer to draw up a formal partnership agreement.

Ownership Division Who owns what percent?	
Goals How big a company do you want to have? Where do you see the company being in five years? What personal goals of yours will affect how much time you have to spend with the company?	
Jobs/Responsibilities What jobs and responsibilities does each partner have? Can partners work for any other company or do any other work on the side?	
Decisions How will general business decisions be made? What decisions does each partner have final authority on? Who has the final authority for decisions for the company as a whole?	
Communication How will you communicate regularly? How will you resolve serious disputes?	
Exit strategy and dissolution agreement What happens if one partner wants to leave the business or move? What if one partner wants to sell the company? What happens if a partner dies or becomes disabled?	
Other issues:	

You'll also want to discuss with your lawyer what legal form your partnership should take. A simple partnership does not provide protection for your personal assets or your partner's. Instead, consider incorporating or becoming a limited liability company (LLC) or a limited liability partnership (LLP).

Protecting Your Intellectual Property (IP)

One of the most important legal considerations for an entrepreneur is the concept of **intellectual property,** or "IP."

Every company has certain intangible assets that are, or can be, extremely valuable. Most of them come under the heading of IP—assets that have value because of the knowledge, recognition, and inventiveness they consist of. Some businesses, such as software companies, publishers, inventors, consultants, and so on, only have products composed of intellectual property.

It's easy to understand and place a value on physical property. We know how much a running shoe or a mobile phone may cost. But what's the value of the Nike "swoosh"? The design of an iPhone? The content of a Beatles song? We all recognize that these things possess a value far beyond simply the physical property, because of the value of the ideas or the brand recognition behind them: in other words, the intellectual property underlying the "swoosh," the iPhone design and interface, or the Beatles' timeless music and lyrics.

Entrepreneurial companies quickly acquire intellectual property beyond their physical property, and you'll want to protect that IP. If you design and manufacture furniture, you'll want to protect its design and not merely the wood that you use to make it. If you develop a luxury resort, you'll want to protect its brand name, not just the buildings. If you devise ways to manufacture products cheaper and faster, you'll want to find ways to protect those processes.

While protecting intellectual property is always a challenge—it is, after all, intangible—there are several methods to protect a company's IP.

Copyrights

If you're creating works that others might want to copy—content (such as text, books, articles, or blogposts), music, art, software, illustrations, videos, apps (such as mobile phone or Internet-based applications)—you'll want to protect what you've created. This is where copyright law comes in. **Copyrights** cover any type of work that is "fixed" and "tangible" even if it's only computer code, words spoken on an audiotape, or images "fixed" in a movie.

Copyrights do *not* cover ideas, no matter how unique—only the particular fixed expression of those ideas. For instance, you can't copyright your idea for the story of a boy who goes to a school for wizards, but you *can* copyright your novel telling the story of that boy. Once you have received a copyright, you retain the rights to that creation, and no one else can make a movie about your hero without your permission. You also can't copyright "facts." So

Buy-sell agreements

Sooner or later, it's likely that one or more partner will leave a partnership due to personal reasons, disagreements, or death or disability. A buy-sell (or buyout) agreement spells out, in advance, how the company will be valued and how the departing partner, or their heirs, will be paid (for example, over time or with the proceeds of an insurance policy). A buy-sell agreement should also cover what happens if a partner becomes divorced, since part of their ownership interest could become the property of their ex-spouse.

It's highly advisable to put a buy-sell agreement in place as soon as a partnership is formed. It's more difficult to discuss these issues once personal situations arise. And without a buy-sell agreement, you may be forced to sell the company to pay out a departing partner or their heirs, end up in litigation with a disgruntled partner, or find yourself in business with the ex-spouse of a partner.

BUILD-YOUR-BUSINESS WORKSHEET

Questions to Ask Potential Partners

Use the questions in this checklist to discuss the terms of your partnership.

☐ Why are you going into business?

☐ What past experiences have prepared you for going into business?

☐ What are your personal goals for this business?

☐ How much money do you need now? How much money will you need over the next 12 months? 24 months? 36 months?

☐ How much money are you able and willing to invest in the company, if any?

☐ What kind of credit rating do you have?

☐ How big would you like the company to one day be?

☐ What would you like to see as the eventual exit strategy?

☐ How much time do you have to devote to the business?

☐ What other obligations do you have, both business and personal, that will affect your commitment of time, money, and attention?

☐ How do you see decisions being made? By whom?

☐ What areas of responsibility do you feel capable of taking on?

☐ What areas of responsibility do you want to be in charge of?

☐ How formal/informal do you like to be about such things as work hours, dress code, and so on?

☐ What are your business values and what kind of corporate culture do you want to create?

☐ Is your family supportive of this commitment?

☐ Have you ever been in a partnership before? What happened?

☐ What are your fears in this partnership?

☐ How will you resolve differences? What if one of the partners wants to sell or leave the business?

☐ Are you willing to sign a buy-sell agreement?

if what you're creating is purely the compilation of facts, you won't be able to copyright that.

Under U.S. and Canadian laws, the rights to your creation are yours at the moment you create it. Theoretically, you don't have to do anything to ensure your copyright. But that's putting you at some risk.

You should take at least some steps to protect your asset. The easiest thing to do to protect your copyright is to add a simple copyright notice whenever you produce something. Just add the word "copyright," the © symbol, the date, and your name.

However, this does not enable you to challenge someone who illegally copies your work and it does not, conclusively, establish authorship. Instead, it's wise, for greater protection, to register your copyright with the U.S. Copyright Office (www.copyright.gov); it's inexpensive and easy. In Canada, register your copyright with the Canadian Intellectual Property Office (www.cipo.ic.gc.ca).

Patents

Unlike copyrights, **patents** are designed to protect new inventions rather than creative works. A patent is a government-issued right, protecting your invention from competition from other imitators. It enables you to—in the words of U.S. patent law—"exclude others from making, using, offering for sale, or selling" or importing into the United States your invention (or copies of your invention). The three types of U.S. patents are:

- **Utility patents:** for inventing or discovering any new and useful process, machine, article of manufacture, composition of matter, or any new and useful improvement of the above.

- **Design patent:** for inventing a new, original, and ornamental design for something manufactured (made).

- **Plant patent:** for inventing or discovering and artificially reproducing a distinct and new variety of plant.

To qualify for a patent, your new invention or process must be both unique and "nonobvious." If someone infringes on your patent, it is your responsibility—not the government's—to pursue legal action.

Copyrights are easy to get; patents are very tough to acquire. Copyrights cost little or nothing; patents are typically expensive. Copyrights are yours the instant you create the work; patents can take years to get issued. Patents are also difficult and costly to enforce—if someone violates your patent and starts selling a knockoff of your product, it may take a lot of money (in legal fees) and time to put a stop to it. And if the perpetrator is overseas, enforcement will be even harder. So if you're building your business around a new invention, process, machine, recipe, or formula that needs to be patented, it will be tough going.

Shhhhh!

Trade secrets are more difficult to protect and defend in court than are patents or trademarks. One company that has managed to protect its trade secret well is Coca-Cola. For more than 120 years, the company has zealously guarded its formula for mixing its flagship product. Trade secrets are not limited to products, though. Many manufacturing firms have business processes that allow them to operate more efficiently than other firms, and they classify those processes as trade secrets.

Is registration of my mark required?

No. You can establish rights in a mark based on its legitimate use. But in the United States, owning a federal trademark registration on the Principal Register secures the following advantages:

- Constructive notice to the public of the registrant's claim of ownership of the mark

- A legal presumption of the registrant's ownership of the mark and the registrant's exclusive right to use it nationwide on or in connection with the goods and/or services listed in the registration

- The ability to bring an action concerning the mark in federal court

- The use of the U.S. registration as a basis to obtain registration in foreign countries

- The ability to file the U.S. registration with the U.S. Customs Service to prevent importation of infringing foreign goods

If, however, your invention is likely to be worth a good deal of money, you'll want to pursue the patent process. You'll need a competent patent attorney. An experienced one will warn you of the costs and pitfalls before you get too far down the road.

Trademarks

One of the most valuable IP assets a company can develop is the brand name of its company, products, or services. You'll work hard to get customers to look for and trust your brand names, so you certainly want to keep others from offering similar goods using your names. That's where trademark laws come in. There are two primary kinds of **trademarks**:

- **Trademark.** A word, phrase, symbol, or design (or a combination of these) that identifies and distinguishes the maker of a product from makers of other, similar, products.

- **Service mark.** The same as a trademark, except that a **service mark** identifies and distinguishes the provider of a service rather than a product. (In Canada, a trademark can be used for either a product or a service.)

When your company acquires the rights to a trademark or a service mark, other companies are legally prevented from using your trademark or service mark, whether expressed in a name, logo, tagline, or other distinctive marker, on their *competing* products or services. Note the emphasis on the word "competing": Two companies that operate in completely different business spheres can have the same name. It's only when there's possible confusion between two entities that trademark law becomes relevant.

There are limits to what you can trademark. You may be surprised—and frustrated—to learn that you can't trademark the simplest names. That's because the U.S. Patent and Trademark Office requires a mark to be "distinctive" and not simply "descriptive." For instance, you can't get a trademark for a health resort called Spa, because it's merely descriptive.

You may run into difficulty if you use a name that's similar to that of a bigger, better-known company, even if you think you can get a trademark for that name. McDonald's, for instance, has been very effective in keeping others from using the "Mc" as a prefix for many different kinds of products and companies. A national juice bar company whose name started with the letter "J" was able to keep other, small juice bars from using names starting with the letter "J" just by taking them to court. Often, it's the company with the biggest bank account and most aggressive lawyers, rather than the ones with the law on their side, that controls a name or trademark.

DOING A TRADEMARK SEARCH

When deciding on a name for your company, product, or service, first check for trademarks to determine whether anyone else is already using the name you're considering. To begin a trademark search, go to the website of the U.S. Patent and Trademark Office, or USPTO (www.uspto.gov/), find the section for trademarks, and follow the links to "Search." In Canada, you can do a trademark search on the website of the Canadian Intellectual Property Office (www.cipo.ic.gc.ca).

To see the various results, try the different ways offered to search. Begin by searching as broadly as possible—singular and plural forms of your words, similar words, alternate spellings, and so on. Results may show both "live" and "dead" marks. Dead marks are those that previous owners have let lapse.

Keep in mind that even if a particular name or mark doesn't show up as being taken, that does not necessarily mean you will be able to trademark the name or mark. Some names may already be in use in interstate commerce but not yet officially registered. Other names or marks may not be allowed to be registered as trademarks. So don't print up hundreds of brochures quite yet!

If you're going to spend a great deal of money investing in a name and trademark, you might consider using a professional trademark search firm or hiring a trademark attorney to conduct a more complete search.

IP agreements

In addition to copyrights, patents, and trademarks, the following two agreements may help protect your intellectual property as well:

- **Nondisclosure agreements.** One of the simplest ways to protect your ideas is to get a signed **nondisclosure agreement** or confidentiality agreement before discussing your concepts with others, including partners, contractors, employees, and the like. This is a standard business procedure, and you'll often be asked to sign NDAs if you're trying to do business with another company. But be forewarned: Venture capitalists will refuse to sign NDAs, because they see far too many new business ideas.

- **Noncompete agreements.** Once a **trade secret** is learned, it can't be unlearned. So sometimes the biggest fear you'll have is that a valuable and knowledgeable employee or a partner will leave you and go to work for a competitor or set up their own business. To guard against this, you may want to have employees sign an agreement limiting their ability to work for a competing firm (or start their own competing company) for a given period. However, not all noncompete agreements are enforceable (they must be reasonable and not keep someone from making a living), and the State of California, for one, doesn't allow them at all except in very limited circumstances. Make certain an attorney reviews any noncompete agreements before you put them into effect.

When can I use the trademark symbols ™, ˢᴹ, and ®?

"Any time you claim rights in a mark, you may use the 'TM' (trademark) or 'SM' (service mark) designation to alert the public to your claim, regardless of whether you have filed an application with the USPTO. However, you may use the federal registration symbol '®' only after the USPTO actually *registers a mark*, and not while an application is pending. Also, you may use the registration symbol with the mark only on or in connection with the goods and/or services listed in the federal trademark registration."

– from the U.S. Patent and Trademark Office

Sample Document: NDA

Re: (Company Name)

Nondisclosure Agreement

I agree that any information disclosed to me by _____ Company in connection with my review of the company will be considered proprietary and confidential, including all such information relating to the Company's past, present, or future business activities, research, product design or development, personnel, and business opportunities.

"Confidential Information" means any information disclosed, either directly or indirectly, in writing, orally, or by inspection of tangible objects (including business plans, research, product plans, products, services, customers, markets, software, inventions, processes, designs, drawings, engineering, marketing, or finances).

Confidential Information shall not include information previously known to me or the general public or previously recognized as standard practice in the field. It will also not include information that becomes generally available in the public domain through no action or inaction of myself, my employees, or others associated with me.

I agree not to use any Confidential Information for any purpose except to evaluate and, if applicable, implement a potential business relationship with _____ Company. I agree not to disclose any Confidential Information to third parties or to anyone except those who are required to have the information in order to evaluate or engage in discussions concerning the contemplated business relationship.

I agree that for a period of five years, I will hold all confidential and proprietary information in confidence and will not use such information except as may be authorized by the Company and will prevent its unauthorized dissemination. I acknowledge that unauthorized disclosure could cause irreparable harm and significant injury to the Company. I agree that upon request, I will return all written or descriptive matter, including the business plan and supporting documents, to the Company.

Accepted and Agreed to:

_____

Signature

_____

Printed Name

_____

Company/Title

_____

Date

Contracts

A contract is an agreement between parties. Although the days of doing business with only a handshake may not be entirely over, having a written contract or signed letter of agreement is a normal, advisable business practice in virtually every instance.

As a business owner, you should get used to drawing up contracts or written agreements as a routine part of doing business, whether with customers or clients, vendors, employees, partners, distributors or retailers, landlords, and anyone else with whom there may later be the potential of misunderstanding or disagreement over the nature and terms of your relationship.

With a contract or letter of agreement, you:

- Spell out all terms, such as what each party will pay or be paid

- Detail the nature of the work to be performed as well as the deadlines for performing it

- Describe the conditions under which the work will be performed

- Elucidate ownership of and rights to any and all work created under the contract

- List all other considerations that are important to all parties

What's the difference between a contract and a letter of agreement? Nothing, legally. Once you have a letter of agreement signed between two parties, you've entered in to a contract. The term "contract" tends to refer to a more formal document. It usually includes more detailed provisions, such as which state or country law applies, but you could include that in a letter of agreement as well.

In most businesses, you'll find that you have a number of types of agreements or contracts that you use repeatedly. For instance, if you're a consultant, you may have a standard consulting agreement. If you're a distributor, you may have a contract you use with manufacturers to detail the conditions under which you distribute their products and the commissions or prices you charge. A lawyer can help you draw up standard agreements or contracts, to have them on hand. Attorneys should also be used to help you negotiate and draw up contracts for significant deals.

From the start of your business, get in the habit of drawing up contracts or letters of agreement and having them signed by all parties. Failure to get a written agreement leaves you at risk. Ours is a litigious society, and the best way to avoid ending up in court—or in hot water—is to *get things in writing*. You may be tempted to forgo written agreements—they seem so formal!—but when you're in business, it's normal, expected, and prudent to get everything in writing and signed and dated.

Types of legal agreements

The many types of legal agreements you may need include:

- **Contracts**
- **Letters of agreement or engagement**
- **Leases**
- **Employment contracts**
- **Distribution agreements**
- **Project proposals**
- **Statement of work (SOW)**
- **Work-for-hire agreements**
- **Nondisclosure agreements**
- **Noncompete agreements**

Sample Document: Letter of Agreement

[DATE] December 1, 2012

[NAME/CONTACT OF CONTRACTOR] Aaron Hill
3456 University Drive
Chapel Hill, North Carolina 27516

[SALUTATION] Dear Aaron:

[BRIEF OPENING PARAGRAPH]

I am delighted that you will be assisting Telescope Financial Services in launching our new company website, and I look forward to working with you on this project. Listed below are the details of our work together. I have enclosed two signed copies of this letter. Please sign and return one copy to me. I am excited about getting this project under way.

PROJECT: Content writing for Web pages for the relaunch of the Telescope Financial Services website.

SCOPE OF WORK: Aaron Hill ("Contractor") will write copy for the new Telescope Financial Services' ("Client") website based on materials provided by Telescope Financial Services and interviews with Telescope executives and staff. The Contractor will be responsible for editing and rewriting copy on approximately 50 existing Web pages and writing new copy for approximately 30 new pages.

TIMELINE AND DUE DATES: The project will begin on January 1, 2013, and continue through May 30, 2013, with the Contractor expected to devote approximately 20 hours per week to the project during that period, for approximately 160 hours. Client acknowledges, however, that significant revisions of the text requested of Contractor after completing initial drafts may result in the project's extending beyond the due date and add additional hours.

FEES AND EXPENSES: Contractor will be paid a rate of $60 per hour. Contractor will be reimbursed for the following expenses: overnight courier services. Contractor will not be paid for travel time to Client's offices nor be reimbursed for any other expenses.

TERMS AND CONDITIONS: Contractor is engaged by Client as an independent contractor and is not deemed an employee of Client in any manner. Contractor acknowledges that this is a work-for-hire relationship in which all work, including but not limited to the content of the Web pages, is created for Client and is the sole property of Client. Contractor further acknowledges that all information provided by Client shall be deemed Confidential and agrees not to disclose such information unless necessary in the scope of the work for Client and with Client's prior approval.

Upon signing, Client will make a nonrefundable deposit of $1,000, which will be applied against the first month's billing. Contractor will then invoice Client for fees at the end of each month. Invoices are due upon receipt. Either Client or Contractor can terminate this relationship by giving at least 30 days' notice.

The above is accepted and agreed to by:

_____   _____

For Telegraph Financial Services (Client)   By Aaron Hill (Contractor)

_____

Title

_____

Date   Date

Licenses, Permits, and More

You may be ready to start your business, but, in some cases, you must make sure you have the proper licenses or permits. As frustrating as it may seem, you can't just rent an office or a building and set up shop. Although establishing a business in the United States or Canada is far, far easier than in most parts of the world, you still have to deal with a bit of paperwork.

The bureaucratic things you'll deal with fall into three general categories:

1. **Identification numbers.** To keep track of your dealings with government authorities. Example: identification numbers for income tax authorities, such as the Employer Identification Number (EIN) in the United States or the Business Number (BN) in Canada.

2. **Licenses or certifications.** Required to engage either in any business (in a specific locality) or in certain types of businesses or professions. Examples: a city business license, a contractor's license, a license to sell alcoholic beverages, an optometrist certification, a beautician certification.

3. **Permits.** Required for particular, often more limited, actions. Examples: construction permits, special event permits. The requirements vary greatly, depending on the type of business you're opening and the state, county, or city in which you plan to do business.

Sometimes these terms are used interchangeably, such as "permit" instead of "license" or vice versa. To make matters more complicated, you may need to acquire licenses, permits, or identification numbers from different levels of government. In the United States, for example, these may include:

- Federal

- State

- County

- City

Primarily, you'll be dealing with state and local licensing and permit regulations. The federal government generally doesn't regulate local or state businesses. There are exceptions, of course, especially if you're involved in interstate transportation (such as interstate moving companies or trucking). And there may be federal requirements regarding your production, especially if you use hazardous materials. That's why it's important to ask your attorney about these types of licenses.

How to get a federal tax ID number online

Most new businesses can apply for an EIN on the Internal Revenue Service (IRS) website (www.irs.gov). Navigate to "Business Topics" and look for "Employer ID Numbers." Answer a handful of questions, wait for validation, and the site will generate and confirm your new number, which you can use immediately.

In Canada, if you run a business with simple registration requirements, go to the Canada Revenue Agency (CRA) website (www.cra-arc.gc.ca). Find "Businesses" and look for "Business Number (BN) registration" under topics.

Federal tax ID numbers

One number you'll be asked for repeatedly in the United States is your Federal Employer Identification Number. This ID number may also be referred to as your Employer Identification Number, or Tax ID number, or a variety of different abbreviations: FIN, TIN, FEIN, and so on. Getting a Tax ID number is very easy.

You'll need a federal tax ID number if your business has employees, or is formed as a corporation, LLC, or partnership. Don't be misled by the word "Employer" in the name—you do *not* need to have employees to get a "Federal Employer Identification Number."

Even if you're not required by law to have a Federal Tax ID number—for instance, if you're operating as a sole proprietor—you may still want to get one. That's because many of your customers, especially if they are other companies, institutions, or government entities, will ask for your Tax ID number. It's more professional (and safer) to provide a Tax ID number than to give out your Social Security number.

State licenses, certifications, and ID numbers

Individual U.S. states may also assign you an identification or account number, for various reasons. The usual IDs are: corporation number for incorporated businesses, employer account number for employer businesses, and certificate numbers and license numbers to operate certain businesses (such as a contractor's license number).

It's a good idea to ask your own attorney about the types of licenses, certifications, and permits you need in your community and for your type of business. You might also consult with a local Small Business Development Center (SBDC).

Reseller's license

There's one government permit you won't mind getting—a reseller's license or reseller's permit. If you're a manufacturer, wholesaler, or retailer, and your state collects sales tax, you may qualify for a reseller's license.

Such a license enables your company to purchase goods or materials for manufacture or sale without paying sales tax, since you're not the ultimate consumer—your customer is. In other words, if you own a chain of sporting goods stores, you can buy golf clubs from the manufacturer without paying sales tax because you'll charge your customers the tax. If you're going to use the clubs yourself, you do need to pay the sales tax, since the exemption is allowed only on goods you will resell.

Once again, each state has its own requirements and terminology. So check your own state's rules. Some states don't even require a license for you to get an exemption from sales tax—just a signed statement of intent to resell goods.

County and city licenses and permits

Most cities or counties require some form of basic business license, no matter what kind of business you're in. If you want to open up shop—whether a retail store, a manufacturing plant, a high-tech start-up, or even just a consulting practice—you have to get a business license from your county or city.

In addition to basic business licenses, cities frequently require permits to operate certain types of businesses, install various kinds of business equipment, or make changes in buildings or facilities. The more likely you are to be dealing with any kind of food, chemicals, equipment, manufacturing, construction, and such, the more likely you are to need additional certifications, licenses, or permits.

If you use a **fictitious business name**—in other words, any name other than your own personal name—you may also be required to file a **DBA** ("doing business as…") or fictitious business name statement with your county, city, or state authorities. In other words, if your bakery is called "All You Knead," you'll most likely have to file a fictitious business name statement stating who the real owner of "All You Knead" is.

The distinction between an actual and a "fictitious" name is important because with the latter, the world can't tell who is legally responsible for the business. This lack of transparency in ownership has the potential to give rise to shady business practices. This is why many local governments require companies operating with fictitious names to file a DBA.

Taxes

Paying taxes is a part of operating a business, and understanding key tax concerns is critical for most businesses. No matter what business structure you choose—sole proprietorship, partnership, or corporation—there are taxes you need to pay, and pay on time, or face penalties. Be certain to keep track of when taxes are due, and give yourself enough time to prepare them.

New entrepreneurs should plan on spending some time with their accountants, talking about taxes. Ask them to help you understand which taxes you're liable for, when your taxes are due, and how various transactions and expenses are taxed. Have your accountant also help you plan how to minimize your tax liability.

Payroll taxes and withholding

Payroll taxes are the U.S. state and federal taxes that you, as an employer, are required to either pay or withhold from employees' payroll checks on their behalf. Payroll taxes fall into three basic categories:

- Taxes employees pay
- Taxes employers pay
- Taxes *both* employees and employers pay

Business Licenses and Permits

Use this worksheet to list the licenses and permits you'll need, including where and how to apply, requirements, and fees.

License Type	Agency and Contact Info	Requirements	Fees
Local Licenses			
Local Permits			
County Licenses/ Permits			
State Licenses			
DBA Required			
Federal Certification			
Other:			

You—and your employees—have federal as well as state obligations. In some states, there are also local payroll taxes for cities, counties, or school districts. The types of payroll taxes you and your employees face are:

- **Income taxes.** Employees pay the entire portion of their federal and state income taxes. As their employer, you do not pay any of these taxes. However, federal and state governments require you to withhold these income taxes from your employee' paychecks and submit these amounts, as required, to meet federal and state deadlines. In some places, employers may be required to withhold state income tax, or even city income tax.

- **Social Security and Medicare.** FICA is the combination of Social Security and Medicare taxes that are paid and deducted from payroll to help ensure an employee's future retirement and health care. These are federal taxes. Both the employer and the employee pay a portion of these taxes. There's an annual maximum on Social Security tax, an amount that usually increases every year. Check www.ssa.gov for current and annual limits. There is no annual limit for Medicare.

- **Unemployment taxes.** On a federal level, only employers pay for unemployment insurance—or what's referred to as FUTA (Federal Unemployment Tax Act) on payroll slips. You're also responsible for state unemployment insurance, though rates for that tax vary (and several states don't require any state income tax at all). Some states require employees to also pay a portion of state unemployment taxes.

Income tax

You're required to pay tax on the profits you generate in your business. How your company is legally structured determines how your income tax liability will be handled.

Most small businesses have **pass-through taxation**. In other words, the company or corporation doesn't pay the income taxes, but instead the tax liability passes through to its owners. This is true for sole proprietorships, LLCs, S corporations, and most partnerships. Say you have a small company, structured as an S corporation, that generates $100,000 in annual profits. The corporation files an income tax return, but the profits are deemed distributed to you, the owner, so you pay the tax on those profits as part of your own income tax return.

One exception to the pass-through treatment is C corporations. Such corporations are treated as separate entities whose income tax on profits must be paid by the corporations. Any profits distributed to C corporation owners or stockholders are also subject to income tax on those individuals' tax returns. Because of this, this type of income tax treatment is sometimes referred to as double taxation. For example, if you were the sole owner of a C corporation that had profits of $100,000, the corporation would pay income tax on $100,000. If, after paying the corporate income tax, the corporation then distributed the remaining amount to you—let's say $80,000—you would

U.S. taxes you may be required to pay include:

- Payroll and other employment-related taxes (Social Security, Medicare, workers' compensation, unemployment, etc.)
- Income tax (federal, state, county, perhaps even local)
- Sales tax
- Personal property tax and use taxes
- Property tax
- Special taxes (hotel, food, transportation, etc.)
- Import/export, custom taxes, duties
- Transfer taxes
- Capital gains taxes
- Inventory taxes

States with no personal income tax

- Alaska
- Florida
- Nevada
- New Hampshire*
- South Dakota
- Tennessee*
- Texas
- Washington
- Wyoming

Residents are required to pay income tax on dividends and interest income, but not on wages.

then also pay tax on that amount on your individual tax return, though perhaps at a lower tax rate than on other, earned income.

After your first year in business, you will generally be required to make estimated income tax payments four times a year—commonly referred to as **quarterlies**, because they're paid each quarter of the year. These are estimates of how much you're likely to owe at the end of the year, typically based on how much you made the previous year. So, while employees who receive wages or salaries subject to withholding only have to worry about April 15 (in the United States) as tax day, business owners have tax payments due more frequently. Be sure to ask your tax advisor how to handle your quarterly tax payments.

DEDUCTIONS

A tax deduction is a business expense the government allows you to subtract from your overall revenues, resulting in a reduction, or deduction from income, in the total tax you pay. This is obviously desirable, and you want to make certain you take advantage of each and every deduction you are legally allowed.

For example, if you generated $10,000 a month selling your new gizmo, and it cost you $5,000 to pay your employees to sell, manufacture, and ship your gizmo, plus you had another $1,000 in overhead expenses, you would be able to deduct $6,000 in expenses and only pay taxes on $4,000 of that income. You'd probably also be able to deduct, or "write off," a portion of the cost of your equipment, lowering even more the amount you'd pay taxes on.

You'll likely make some decisions—or alter them—based primarily on tax implications. Some business expenses are fully deductible. Some are only partially deductible, and others have to be depreciated over a number of years. And still others are not deductible at all. You should have at least a fair understanding of those issues as you make choices in your business. If you purchase a very expensive piece of equipment, for instance, and expect to deduct the total cost of it from your income this year, you may be surprised to discover that the expense has to be spread out (depreciated) over as many as five to 10 or even 20 years.

Because all these issues are so complicated, it's advisable to get a reliable accountant to work with your business and to consult with on financial matters.

Sales Tax

As a business, you may pay sales tax on products you purchase for your use, though inventory and raw materials purchased for resale are usually exempt from sales tax in most jurisdictions. Still, you'll likely be required to collect sales tax on most of the products and perhaps (in limited cases) some services that you sell.

Most U.S. states and some counties and cities tax the sale of most goods and some services. Sales tax rates and rules vary from state to state, even from city to city, and there are an enormous number of laws and taxing authorities. These taxes can go by various names: sales tax, franchise tax, transaction privilege tax, use tax, and more. Some are the responsibility of the seller, others of the buyer. But the government typically makes it the responsibility of the business to collect the tax at the time of sale.

Generally, if you're going to collect sales tax, you must get a license from your state. On each taxable transaction, you calculate the applicable sales tax, collect it from the buyer, keep tax records, and then file a tax return and pay the total taxes to your state. You'll pay monthly, quarterly, or annually, depending on your level of sales.

Each state makes its own rules as to which sales are taxable. Although most products sold to end-users are taxable, major exemptions include:

- Prescription drugs

- Food, especially groceries and nonprepared food

- Animal feed, seed, and many agricultural products

- Products for resale—raw materials, inventory, and other items that are going to be sold, rather than used, by your customer

Many states also exempt services from sales tax. But that varies greatly from state to state, and even within a state the rules as to what is taxable and what is not seem very inconsistent.

As to collecting sales tax on sales from out of state, the U.S. Supreme Court has twice ruled that states can't require a business to collect sales tax unless it has a physical presence—or **nexus**—in the state. This is obviously important to consider if you sell goods or services over the Internet. Although one of the lures of ecommerce, at least at the beginning, was that goods could be purchased tax free, that is frequently no longer the case.

The sales tax clearinghouse

Founded in 1999, the Sales Tax Clearinghouse (STC) provides tools and data to help U.S. sellers navigate the complicated landscape of calculating sales and use taxes in more than 7,000 taxing authorities (states, counties, and cities).

STC offers two forms of sales tax calculations: manual, in which subscribers can use either an online or a desktop calculator, and automatic, in which an automated service allows businesses to connect their business software systems directly to the STC's servers to calculate rates automatically. Find more information at www.thestc.com.

Giving Away Facebook

For a bunch of seemingly smart kids, the guys involved in Facebook's founding did some pretty stupid things—at least from a legal point of view. This resulted in years of lawsuits and billions of dollars in settlements.

Most new start-ups are in the position of having to give up some degree of ownership in return for early-stage financing. After all, investors want to get something for their money, and that is typically a percent of the equity—or ownership—of the company. And they *deserve* a big payout for taking a chance on an entrepreneur, for risking their money before anyone else. Nevertheless, those decisions shouldn't be made lightly or without considering the legal consequences, even when a "business" is still in the idea stage. Or when it's just being discussed in your college dorm.

The exact facts revolving around the founding of Facebook remain in dispute. But some things are agreed upon. A site called "TheFacebook. com" was launched in 2004, by Mark Zuckerberg, Dustin Moskovitz, Chris Hughes, and Eduardo Saverin while they were students at Harvard University. Saverin, a wealthy student, provided Zuckerberg with $15,000 to purchase the servers for TheFacebook. In return, Zuckerberg allotted Saverin 30 percent of the company.[1] That was generous—extremely so. And it was a decision that would come back to haunt Zuckerberg.

In the meantime, while getting ready to launch TheFacebook, Zuckerberg was also working for twins Cameron and Tyler Winklevoss and for Divya Narendra, who had hired him to work on their own social networking site. Their site had essentially the same concept that would become Facebook. The decision not to tell his employers that he was working on a competing site was another problem that would come back to haunt Zuckerberg and Facebook.

Those are the facts that are agreed upon. Other issues remain in dispute and have eventually ended up in court.

Like many teams in a start-up venture, some founders—notably Zuckerberg and Moskovitz—stayed more closely involved with growing the venture, while others, particularly Saverin, had other demands on their time. When founders don't clearly delineate their responsibilities and what consequences will happen for failing to live up to their responsibilities (if any), this inevitably creates tensions and disagreements, which is exactly what happened in the case of Facebook.

Zuckerberg moved the new company to Palo Alto, California (from Cambridge, Massachusetts). To help finance Facebook's growth, Zuckerberg brought in other investors, notably Peter Thiel, cofounder of PayPal. As a result of this investment, Saverin's 30 percent ownership was diluted substantially. Saverin alleged this was done unfairly, and later sued the company. Although the exact terms of the suit were not revealed, Saverin

challenge

To launch and finance a new company, the founders promised large shares of ownership to those who helped get it off the ground

solution

Lawsuit after lawsuit after lawsuit, with huge sums of money involved

---

1. "Facebook's Complicated Ownership History Explained," by Ben Parr. *Mashable.com*. April 13, 2011.

eventually received 5 percent of the ownership of Facebook. His $15,000 investment ended up being worth many billions.

Another complication came about because Zuckerberg failed to disclose that he had a conflict of interest while working on the Winklevosses' project. He launched Facebook a few days before their intended launch, and they immediately alleged that he had stolen their idea and intentionally delayed the launch of their project so he could launch his. The Winklevosses later sued, winning a lawsuit against Facebook for more than a million shares of Facebook stock and $20 million in cash.

Zuckerberg's legal complications continued. Another person, Paul Ceglia, alleged that he hired Zuckerberg to work on his company, Street-Fax.com, at the same time that he was working on what would become Facebook. In 2010, Ceglia sued, producing a document showing that Zuckerberg gave him 50 percent of the company in return for a $1,000 investment. Facebook's lawyers assert the document is a fake.[2]

Of course, it's true that every extremely successful company is likely to encounter legal challenges. After all, once millions or even billions of dollars are involved, many people will want a piece of ownership. But many of the problems and huge settlements encountered by Facebook were avoidable.

Zuckerberg was accepting money to work on the Winklevosses' social networking program while simultaneously developing his own competing program. This was a clear scenario for conflict. It was inevitable that his motives would come into question—especially when he launched a competing site a mere few days before his employers planned to. It may have seemed to Zuckerberg like a mere gig for him to pick up a few extra dollars, but whenever you're working on another company's projects, you are responsible for maintaining its trade secrets. Moreover, it's likely that Zuckerberg was laboring on a "work-for-hire" basis, meaning that anything he produced while working for them—such as computer code—in fact belonged to them. That could have been another area of conflict.

But perhaps the biggest problem was that in his eagerness to raise the money he needed to launch, Zuckerberg gave away a huge percentage of the company. He failed to get any kind of legal advice that might have helped him structure an agreement that would have delayed putting a percentage value on Saverin's investment (such as until the first round of financing) or that would have made clear how Saverin's percentage would be diluted.

As the Facebook example proves, simple college-dorm agreements can later become the basis for extremely serious stock ownership battles.

Even though most of those involved with Facebook's founding eventually got fabulously rich, the complications arising from their lack of legal foresight created tremendous problems, strained friendships, and led to legal battles and settlements worth millions—even billions. ■

questions

1. Can you know if you have a potentially hugely successful company on your hands when you first launch it?

2. Should all companies take the precautions Facebook *failed* to take? Or can some companies be more relaxed about such legal issues as partnerships and ownership? Why or why not?

3. What types of agreements and contracts do you think Mark Zuckerberg, his partners, and Facebook's early investors should have drawn up?

4. What contracts do you think the Winklevoss twins and Divya Narendra should have drawn up when they hired Zuckerberg to work for *their* company?

---

2. "The Guy Who Says He Owns 50% of Facebook Just Filed a Boatload of New Evidence—And It's Breathtaking," by Henry Blodget. *Business Insider*. April 12, 2011.

GET IT IN WRITING

Goal:

Create a strong partnership agreement with a built-in "exit" strategy.

What to Do:

Working with one other person, imagine that you are two entrepreneurs considering pooling your talents and resources to create a consulting firm specializing in setting up websites for business clients. You each bring different skills to the table. You need to create a partnership agreement that makes sense for both of you.

One of you will put more money into the operations; the other will put in more time. Neither of you will take a salary until you begin to make a profit.

1. First, list all the resources you're committing to the company. Include funds, time, and all other resources you'll contribute.

2. List the respective roles and responsibilities each of you will undertake. Who will be responsible for which activities in the company?

3. Determine how you will make decisions. Will either of you be able to make decisions without the other?

4. Specify how much time each of you will put into the business each week. What happens if one of you doesn't put in the time you've committed to?

5. Establish how you'll handle the company's money. Who will be able to make spending decisions? Who will be able to make withdrawals or transfers from bank accounts?

6. Make decisions regarding the following issues:

   a. Have you agreed upon a business plan? A future growth strategy? Are you in agreement on how big you want the company to be?

   b. What happens if one of you decides to leave the company?

   c. What happens if one of you doesn't perform adequately?

   d. What happens if you no longer want to work together? How will you dissolve the company? What happens with any remaining assets—including the customer list and active accounts?

   e. Can one of you buy the other out? If so, how will the value of the company be determined? Will you have a buy-sell agreement in place?

7. Finally, draw up a partnership agreement that spells all this out.

8. Discuss all the other steps you'll take, both individually and jointly, before you sign the agreement. Include getting an attorney to review the agreement.

9. Be prepared to explain why you think you've created an agreement that works for both of you.

CHAPTER 17

Social Entrepreneurship and Social Responsibility

learning objectives

In this chapter, you'll learn how to:

- Distinguish between social responsibility and social entrepreneurship

- Consider the benefits and obligations of companies acting in a socially responsible manner

- Understand the triple bottom line (people, profits, and planet)

- Identify opportunities in social entrepreneurship

Charity is still important

Smart businesses have always supported their communities. It might have been something as simple as a hardware store buying uniforms for a Little League team or a large corporation helping fund the city's symphony, yet companies have long known that actively engaging with society helps them both survive and thrive.

"Old-fashioned" corporate charity—donating money as well as expertise—is still important. Approximately 5 percent of all charity dollars comes from corporations, and charities depend on these funds. Corporations derive many benefits from giving, in addition to the satisfaction of helping their communities: They may receive tax deductions and earn a "halo" in their city.

Doing Well by Doing Good

Entrepreneurs change the world. In some cases, they change the world by inventing new products or services that meet people's needs and desires. Many times, they change the world by creating good jobs in communities where few existed before. They help to create positive change in the world when they make sure the sources supplying their inventory or raw materials are treating the planet and its people well. Entrepreneurs change the world—one person at a time—by treating employees with respect and paying them fairly so they, in turn, feel pride in their work and have the ability to go home and support their families.

All those things change the world, even when the principal goal of the company is to sell a product or service at a profit.

Increasingly, however, entrepreneurs want to have a more direct positive impact. There's been an enormous movement among entrepreneurs—and investors as well—to create businesses that, as a main focus, try to address some of the problems facing our world, and do so while still embracing a profit motive.

Entrepreneurs today believe they can make a huge difference by applying entrepreneurial thinking and innovative approaches to the problems plaguing the planet and its people. Given the significant breakthroughs entrepreneurs have made in developing new products and services—and creating astounding wealth in the process—there's great hope that the same kind of thinking can create significant breakthroughs in addressing our world's most pressing needs.

Social responsibility vs. social entrepreneurship or social ventures

In trying to be a responsible business or to help address larger societal issues, you may hear the terms **social responsibility**, **social entrepreneurship**, and **social ventures**. These names are often used interchangeably. Moreover, sometimes these designations are applied solely to for-profit companies, while at other times they'll also be applied to not-for-profit organizations.

Although these are not exact designations, as most people use them, and as used in this chapter, these terms can be distinguished in this way:

- Social responsibility refers to the commitment any business has made to society at large, regardless of its products, services, or mission. Another term occasionally used for this is "good corporate citizenship."

- Social entrepreneurship or social ventures refer to companies whose primary mission is to address a social problem or concern, using entrepreneurial approaches, while still maintaining a profit motive.

As used in this chapter, the terms "social ventures" and "social entrepreneurship" are being applied only to for-profit companies.

Certainly, not-for-profit agencies (often referred to as NGOs—or non-governmental organizations, especially in global endeavors) often consider themselves to be social ventures or social entrepreneurs when they embrace entrepreneurial thinking and innovation in pursuing their social goals. So the terms can get a bit murky.

The distinction is that not-for-profit agencies have different governing structures than do for-profit companies, as well as not having an overall profit motive. They are typically funded by donations rather than sales, and their governing bodies are (usually) volunteer Boards of Directors rather than shareholders. Some not-for-profit agencies have for-profit components that they use to help support their mission.

en·tre·pre·neur·ship key terms

Social entrepreneurship (or social ventures)

Companies that have a specific and direct social purpose as part of the core mission of the business. The chief goal of social entrepreneurship is to bring the same sense of innovation, purpose, and drive that entrepreneurs bring to other fields to the cause. This does not preclude making a profit, but the chief goal of social entrepreneurship is to advance social goals.

Social responsibility

The obligation of a company to be concerned about the social and environmental impact of its operations and management; a company's commitment to the larger community, environment, and people as part of its ongoing business operations.

Stakeholder

Anyone who is affected by a company's actions, not just people who have directly invested money in the business. This includes employees, customers, suppliers, members of the community in which a business operates, and all others who feel the impact of a company's decisions—in addition to stockholders, who have a financial piece of the ownership of the company.

Sustainability

Developing a product, goods, services, or companies themselves in such a way that their ongoing development can be continued—theoretically forever—in ways that don't deplete the resources, natural or otherwise, that they consume. In particular, sustainability has come to mean substantially minimizing both the damage done by and the nonrenewable resources used for business or personal activities.

Triple bottom line

In addition to measuring a company's success by the "bottom line" of its financial statements (in terms of monetary profits or losses), the triple bottom line measures a company's success by its impact on the "three Ps"—profits, people, and planet.

Social Responsibility Is for *All* Businesses

As you start your business, you'll have many goals. You'll be focused on developing your business concept, perfecting your product or service, getting funded, finding outstanding team members, and making money. You'll hardly have time to worry about how your business activities affect the larger world around you. Nevertheless, social responsibility is something to consider right from the start. Being a good corporate citizen should be part of your company's DNA.

Just as individuals have responsibilities to their communities, companies likewise have responsibilities and obligations to society at large. Why? Isn't it enough to make money, create jobs? Yes, there's no question that those activities make a huge contribution. But companies have a big impact on both society and the environment—whether it's the waste they create, the energy they use, their treatment of employees and contractors, and much more. Just as individuals need to consider the impact of their actions to contribute to a healthy society, so must companies.

Moreover, corporations are unique entities with many rights and privileges. Society, through its laws, grants corporations special and favorable benefits, such as limiting the personal liability of a corporation's shareholders. Imagine, if you can, if every shareholder in a corporation was personally liable for that company's actions. No one would want to invest in companies, and there certainly wouldn't be much of a stock market. Every business, whether it realizes it or not, relies on society's continuing support.

Yet being socially responsible isn't merely an obligation; it also plays an important part in the overall well-being of your company.

First, by being socially responsible, you help to foster and support a healthy local and national economy. Few businesses thrive when the economy of which they are a part suffers. Positively contributing to the well-being of your community increases the likelihood that your own business will prosper.

Feeling a sense of social responsibility also helps to establish your company's values and foster your corporate culture. Businesses that act with integrity and honesty are more likely to see their employees act with integrity and honesty toward the company and their fellow workers alike.

An ethical and honest company, moreover, is less likely to get into trouble with regulatory agencies and taxing authorities, or to face lawsuits or fines.

In addition, employees themselves gain value from being part of an organization that's committed to enhancing the social good. Programs that allow employees to involve themselves in community causes as part of their company activities are viewed as a valuable employee benefit. Prospective employees often look at a company's values and social commitment when comparing job offers. Being able to attract and retain the kind of people you want is critical to the success and growth of your business, so your social commitment helps build the long-term value of your company.

Customers, too, increasingly want the companies they patronize to be a good corporate citizen. While only a certain segment of the market may actively seek out socially responsible companies, most customers want to feel good about the products and services they use. When you actively consider the social and environmental impact of your actions, especially when customers can perceive or learn that you are doing so, their sense of commitment and engagement with you increases. For example, many customers may not particularly go out of their way to seek out a coffee shop that uses recycled napkins and fair-trade coffee, but they're likely to feel better about patronizing a company whose management is thoughtful enough to make those choices.

Over the years, the concept of a company's social responsibility has broadened. Consumers now expect companies to be conscious of their actions on a wide array of issues—including treatment of employees, animals, the environment, and more. Now, large corporations must even take care about the actions of their contractors and subcontractors. Large companies have faced public outcries even when their subcontractors have treated employees badly, paid less than minimum wage, used child labor internationally, abused animals in testing products, dumped toxic waste, and on and on.

What's in it for you?

Most young entrepreneurs today want to be socially responsible simply because it is the right thing to do. They're idealistic, so they value both the planet and the people who live on it, and they want to do the right thing by both. But the even better news is that being socially responsible can help you as a business. In a wide-ranging survey in 20 developed countries, an international research firm, Environics, found that a company's commitment to social responsibility accounted for a significant portion of how the company is perceived. Some 42 percent of North America consumers (United States, Canada, and Mexico) have refused to buy products from companies they perceive as socially irresponsible.

Your business derives a number of benefits from being committed to social responsibility and making sure you act with integrity with regard to issues such as the environment, labor practices, and your relationship to your local community. Among the direct benefits that accrue to your company:

- **Visibility.** Being socially responsible earns your company greater visibility in the community and your industry. This can be particularly helpful to small, new companies because community activities can be a highly effective way to become known, at less cost than other marketing methods.

- **Positive corporate image.** Being seen as a good corporate citizen helps foster positive feelings about your company in the community and in potential customers, employees, and funders.

Community service

Being a good member of the community can work wonders for your marketing efforts. Whether this involves volunteering at the local homeless shelter or animal rescue center, being an active member of the chamber of commerce, or running for the school board, being visibly involved in your community puts you, personally, in a positive light; creates positive feelings about your business; and increases word of mouth about you and your company, and what you do.

- **Recruitment tool.** Social responsibility can aid your company's effectiveness in attracting employees. Potential employees often choose to apply to those companies whose values and social commitment they respect.

- **Stronger team.** Having shared values and shared activities helps develop cohesiveness and commitment among all your employees and management.

- **More satisfied employees.** A commitment to social responsibility enhances the work experience of employees, not only by allowing them to be involved directly or indirectly in community or social affairs, but also by letting them know they work for a company that acts with integrity in all its dealings. Employees will never have to lie for a socially responsible employer.

Socially responsible certifications

If you position your company or its products as socially responsible, many of your customers will want to know that you truly practice what you promote. To that end, some organizations and governmental or quasi-governmental entities can certify you in specific areas of social responsibility. Many consumers look for such certification before deciding which companies to do business with or which products to purchase. So investigate the types of certifications available in your industry and for the social goals you wish to achieve.

A few of the types of certifications you can get are:

- **Organic:** for food products and produce

- **LEED:** green building certification (stands for Leadership in Energy and Environmental Design)

- **Fair trade:** to ensure fair labor treatment, especially in international agriculture

- **Humane certified:** to ensure that farm-raised animals are treated in a humane and decent manner

- **Energy Star:** known best for lower energy consumption electronics and appliances (although buildings themselves can be certified as Energy Star compliant)

The Triple Bottom Line

One reflection of the widespread commitment to social responsibility and social entrepreneurship is the increased emphasis on meeting what's become known as the **triple bottom line**. Its three components are usually referred to as *people*, *planet*, and *profit*.

The "bottom line" in business refers to the actual bottom line of an income statement (or "profit & loss statement"), and is traditionally defined as how much money you've earned (your profit) or lost. The triple bottom line expands on that concept by measuring the success of an organization across three parameters: economic, environmental, and social.

As defined by business consultant and author John Elkington in the mid-1990s, the major premise behind the triple bottom line is that a business's responsibility is to **stakeholders** rather than shareholders. In other words, companies must answer to everyone who's affected by their actions, not just people who have directly invested money in the business. This includes members of the immediate community in which a business operates, as well as customers, suppliers, the industry as a whole, and a host of other individuals and organizations.

People

The "people" part of the triple bottom line means that the business will behave fairly and ethically, first toward its employees and also toward the community in which it conducts its business and any person who could be affected by its actions around the globe.

Thus, a company would take care to deal honestly with its suppliers and customers to ensure that its decisions affect positively the towns and cities where it does business. Likewise, a company would refuse to employ children or sweatshop workers overseas because that would exploit vulnerable populations, even if the financial bottom line would benefit from such actions.

What goes into being socially responsible in relationship to people? A number of key practices:

- **Employees.** Make sure you act responsibly and fairly with regard to wages, working conditions, benefits, and equal treatment. Are you paying a living wage—one with which a person working for you full time could sustain themselves and their family? Or are you paying the minimum you can get by with? What are your working conditions like—are they safe, healthy? Do you have appropriate and consistent work hours, so that employees can maintain a reasonable and salubrious schedule? Do your benefits include health care, adequate vacation, and family leave time? Do you treat employees fairly or do you play favorites, discriminate, or apply rules capriciously?

  You may be staying within the law in terms of how you treat employees, but you may not, in fact, still be socially responsible. For example, some companies purposefully schedule employees so they won't qualify for benefits or health insurance—or even be able to maintain a reasonable schedule to arrange for child care, school, or other activities. This may be within the law but is hardly socially responsible. The best companies have a commitment to their employees, viewing them as partners in their

REAL-WORLD RECAP

Your commitment to people

Social responsibility means dealing fairly with all those who may be affected by your business:

- **Employees**
- **Business partners/suppliers**
- **Customers**
- **The community/the world**

long-term success. They value *all* employees—not just executives or key personnel—and treat none as interchangeable or disposable.

- **Business partners/suppliers.** Being socially responsible means acting ethically and with honesty in all your dealings and interactions, even with your suppliers. Treat them fairly; don't take or give bribes—even when it's common practice in some locales. Don't use overly aggressive tactics to press unfair terms or conditions on vendors.

  Also, make sure your suppliers are themselves acting in a socially responsible manner. Ensure that they treat their employees well, pay decent wages, and maintain healthy working conditions. Control your supply line so that you work only with ethical companies.

- **Customers.** Provide them with a quality product and service, and treat them with respect both during and after the sale is complete. Be honest in all your dealings—don't mislead or misrepresent to make a sale. Take complaints and disagreements seriously, and work to resolve them. Don't pay or receive bribes or other improper incentives. Stand behind your product or service. And deliver what you promise.

- **The community/the world.** Your company has an impact on a number of people, in addition to those who make, sell, or buy your product or service. The local community, for example, is positively benefited by the jobs you create and, if you're a large employer, can be devastated by those you eliminate. Your business may create traffic, trash, noise, or air pollution. Be aware of your impact on the people in your community—and in a larger sense, the world—and take steps to ensure that you have a positive rather than a negative impact.

Planet

By considering the planet as a whole to be a stakeholder in the business, a "triple bottom line company" will make every attempt to engage in sustainable environmental practices. At the very least, such companies will try to do no harm, through actions such as by paying close attention to the natural resources they consume and working to reduce their environmental footprint. They also won't manufacturer or trade in products that could harm the planet, such as toxic materials.

- **Maintain sustainable operations.** This includes reducing your carbon footprint whenever possible, and using scarce resources like water, electricity, and oil products as sparingly as possible.

- **Support responsible animal stewardship.** Animals, likewise, are a valuable resource, as well as living beings. Being socially responsible toward animals means, first, recognizing that they have a right to share our planet and that we humans have a responsibility toward ensuring both their future and their humane treatment. It includes maintaining humane and decent conditions for animals being raised for food, eliminating or reducing testing on animals for products, and harming no animals during testing. It also means being conscious of the importance of maintaining habitats for wild animals and making sure that your actions—and the actions of your suppliers—do not destroy precious habitats that animals depend upon.

■ **Manage the entire life cycle of a product or service.** Socially responsible companies realize that their impact on the environment doesn't end when they ship a product out the door. That product will affect the planet in all sorts of ways, depending on how it's used and how it's disposed of. Some states, in fact, now require that manufacturers take back their equipment at end-of-life and dispose of it in environmentally sound ways.

■ **Encourage and enable "greener" behavior among employees, customers, and suppliers.** The biggest environmental footprint your employees may have is before they walk through your door—commuting to work. So reduce individual commuting by car through ride-share and carpooling programs, reimbursement for use of public transportation, even locating your company near transportation hubs. Remind employees of their need to use energy and resources carefully—especially equipment and consumable supplies.

■ **Do business with other companies that practice sustainability.** Your actions as a customer help to create a positive chain of behavior. By using suppliers that are committed to **sustainability**, you, in turn, help create demand for sustainable products and thus—over time—lower prices and improved industry standards. For example, as more and more companies demanded recycled office paper, costs were lowered substantially and entire forests were saved.

■ **Understand that waste costs money.** Generating excess waste is more than environmentally unfriendly behavior. It also costs you money. By seeing where you're spending money that leads to waste, you can become more planet-friendly while improving the traditional bottom line. For example, some "superstores" realized they were wasting enormous amounts of electricity by maintaining bright lights in their huge stores—commonly believed to enhance the merchandise. They took actions such as adding windows and skylights, turning down the brightness of the lights, and making sure that lights were actually turned off at night—all leading to using less electricity and a lower carbon footprint, but also saving millions of dollars in utility bills.

Profit

You know what profit is—the money you've made after all your costs have been subtracted from your income. Profit is *critical* for businesses. After all, without it, companies can't stay in business long—they, too, are not sustainable. Every company must concern itself with its ability to make—and continue to make—a profit. And when thinking of the "triple bottom line," no

REAL-WORLD RECAP

Your commitment to the planet

Triple bottom line companies attempt to engage in sustainable environmental practices by:

- Maintaining sustainable operations
- Supporting responsible animal stewardship
- Managing the entire life cycle of a product or service
- Encouraging "greener" behavior among employees, customers, and suppliers
- Doing business with other companies that practice sustainability
- Understanding that waste costs money

business can afford to forget the original bottom line: Can you make money, remain in business, and continue to create and provide jobs?

Traditionally, however, profit has been the sole "bottom line" that's mattered to companies. Triple bottom line companies, by contrast, view profit in economic terms but take a broader perspective by considering the economic impact on society at large—measuring whether their actions lead to a sustainable business in the long term. For example, a company that racked up financial profits, but that did so at the expense of cutting thousands of jobs, would have a disastrous overall economic impact on the community, or even the national economy if the company was large enough. In such a case, the company might, in fact, be reducing the potential market for its products and services in the long term.

Your triple bottom line

How will *you* measure your profitability? In financial terms alone? Or also by your impact on the world you live in—its people and the planet itself? Responsible companies today include all three prongs of the triple bottom line when planning and operating their businesses.

Start by considering your social responsibility right as you develop your business plan. Identify "success" in terms broader than simply numbers on a financial statement. Be specific about how you'll measure your success. For example, a business plan for a socially responsible diner wouldn't just project how much income it would make, but might include how much trash it would generate, how much energy it would use—and how it would mitigate those negative impacts, as well as how it might have a positive impact, perhaps by participating in groups that take unused food to low-income food banks or homeless shelters.

Writing social responsibility directly into your business plan ensures that all stakeholders are on board. You want your investors or stockholders to understand your priorities so that they will support—rather than hinder—your socially responsible actions.

Social Entrepreneurship

All of us, whether entrepreneurs or not, want our work to be meaningful. We'd like to feel that at the end of the day   the end of our life   we've made a positive impact on the world we live in. Of course, we don't have to set out to solve the world's problems to make a difference—how we behave in our everyday lives and in our normal businesses can contribute to the overall well-being of the world.

Nevertheless, there's been a growing commitment by entrepreneurs to trying to tackle some of the world's most pressing problems. They want to use their talents, intelligence, skills, and entrepreneurial approaches to help solve a number of important issues facing the planet and its people.

One reason so many people want to apply entrepreneurial approaches to solving social ills is that they know that entrepreneurs believe in innovation and optimism. Entrepreneurs, by definition, look at a need and see an opportunity. In most cases, they try to turn that opportunity into a money-making business: providing a consumer or business product or service. Increasingly, though, they look at the needs of the planet and its people and see an opportunity—an opportunity to meet those needs, solve those problems, and perhaps make a profit at the same time.

Another reason that so many young people are emerging from business schools to found social ventures is that they view the horizon as virtually limitless. The world faces so many problems, from shrinking supplies and inadequate distribution of critical resources like water and oil, to global climate change, to hunger, to disease, to poverty.

Social entrepreneurship is somewhat different than social responsibility. All companies today should strive to be responsible. This doesn't mean they all have to make the social good the primary driver of their existence. This is what social entrepreneurs do. They have a specific social purpose behind the companies they create.

Social entrepreneurship and nonprofit agencies

Of course, for generations, not-for-profit organizations have addressed some of the same issues to which social entrepreneurs are lately turning their attention, although social entrepreneurs differ from not-for-profits.

Social entrepreneurs wish to solve critical problems. But they also want to be profitable. They believe that by using entrepreneurial approaches—including having a profit motive—they can make substantial changes.

There's a significant difference between a nonprofit and a for-profit social entrepreneurship venture. Not-for-profits have traditionally been seen as slow-moving organizations, often saddled by bureaucratic decision-making structures, hampered by lack of funds, and reliant on donations (frequently from older, more hidebound donors).

By contrast, for-profit companies have traditionally been viewed as strictly focused on their bottom line—dedicated solely to increasing profits, regardless of the impact their actions have on the society around them, and entirely intent on producing unimportant or trivial products or services.

Obviously, both these characterizations are stereotypes; myriad nonprofits are innovative, and huge numbers of for-profit businesses typically produce goods and services that people both need and desire (after all, that's how they stay in business).

What will you use your talents for?

"A lot of our best minds are going to sports or entertainment or finance...the allocation of IQ to Wall Street is higher than it should be.... How do we get the brightest people onto the biggest problems?"
— *Microsoft founder Bill Gates*

BUILD-YOUR-BUSINESS WORKSHEET

Social Responsibility

Describe the attributes of your social responsibility plan in the space below.

CORPORATE CITIZENSHIP

Describe the ways you will ensure that your company:

Obeys the laws: _____

_____

Treats employees fairly/with respect: _____

_____

Deals honestly with customers/suppliers: _____

_____

Is honest in its advertising and marketing: _____

_____

Considers the impact of its actions on the community: _____

_____

Acts with integrity in all its dealings: _____

Other: _____

ETHICS

How will your company handle issues such as:

Gifts from or to suppliers/potential suppliers/vendors: _____

_____

Special favors, recreational outings, meals from or to suppliers/vendors/customers: _____

_____

Conflicts between laws in different countries where your company operates: _____

_____

Selecting suppliers based on their ethics: _____

_____

Ensuring that subcontractors act ethically: _____

_____

Personal use of company property (e.g., company cars, phone, email): _____

_____

Expense accounts: _____

_____

SOCIAL RESPONSIBILITY ACTIVITIES/PROJECTS

What are your business goals?

☐ Visibility in community

☐ Visibility in industry

☐ Aid in recruiting employees

☐ Enhancing employee morale/employee involvement

☐ Developing contacts with other companies

☐ Other:_____

In what ways will you participate?

☐ Donate money from operating budget

☐ Participate as a company in community events

☐ Donate a set percentage of profits/sales

☐ Donate in-kind products/services

☐ Allow employees to be active in projects on paid time

☐ Formulate socially responsible operations practices (e.g., waste disposal management)

☐ Encourage employees to be active on a volunteer basis/after-hours

☐ Encourage company personnel/management to serve on agency boards

☐ Donate company facilities for use by community

☐ Formulate socially responsible purchasing groups practices (e.g., environmentally-friendly-only products or type of vendor)

☐ Donate product overruns

☐ Other: _____

What period of time are you willing to commit for? (e.g., day, week, year):_____

What types of concerns do you want to be involved with?

☐ Animal Welfare

☐ The Arts

☐ Children

☐ Community Enhancement and Improvement

☐ Economic Empowerment

☐ Education

☐ Environment

☐ Gender Equality/Issues

☐ Health Issues

☐ Recreation/Athletics

☐ Safety

☐ Other:_____

Entrepreneurial approaches for social ventures

Having seen the success of entrepreneurial thinking and approaches in other areas, entrepreneurs increasingly want to apply those same skills and attitudes to helping solve critically important problems for the world.

Some aspects that social ventures want to embrace are as follows:

■ **Innovation.** Old problems won't be solved by old thinking. Significant social problems require "out-of-the-box" thinking, creative use of new technologies, and innovative approaches. Social ventures are willing to experiment with fresh management and organizational concepts, as well as with unique or unusual solutions to problems.

■ **Fast.** Get out there and do something. Then iterate. The Google mantra "experiment, expedite, iterate" is being applied to social problems as well as to other entrepreneurial ventures. Recognize that it is OK to try something and fail, that failure isn't permanent. The important thing is to keep making improvements quickly.

■ **Profit motive.** Yes, having an interest in making a profit can actually be harnessed to achieve positive social goals. Instead of being overly reliant on donors, the idea in social ventures is to find a business model that's sustainable through income. By creating an ongoing income stream, the social ventures can continue to work on the problems they've been established to address, rather than having to spend their time on fundraising from a broad donor base.

■ **Competitive.** The act of competing can be a force for good, by letting a company keep an eye on what others in the same space are doing—then attempting to improve upon and build on their efforts. Competition can also add a sense of urgency, motivating people in the social venture to move quickly.

■ **Cooperative.** In fact, cooperation is not in conflict with competition. The best entrepreneurs learn and share with one another. An "open source" mentality has helped build many gigantic industries and widely profitable companies. By sharing with others, the goal is to find better, more workable solutions to social problems.

■ **Empowering.** Most successful entrepreneurial ventures enable employees to quickly make independent decisions rather than maintaining a "command-and-control" decision-making structure from company headquarters. Social ventures want to bring the same process of pushing decision making down to those who are closest to the problem—whether it be company employees or the people most directly affected by the social problem.

Social issues for social ventures

The types of issues that social entrepreneurs tackle include the following.

PLANET

Most issues around environmental concerns deal with sustainability—the concept that you should build companies, create organizations, and solve problems in ways that enable them to continue to survive healthfully, and indefinitely, rather than needing a constant influx of new resources, while at the same time eliminating or minimizing damage that the planet incurs as a result of personal or business activities. A term that's often used to apply to many issues dealing with the environment and sustainability is "green," and over the last few decades green social enterprises have been flourishing.

■ **Waste.** Not only is waste an environmental issue, it also represents resources not consumed. That squanders resources and money. Many entrepreneurial businesses have come up with innovative ideas for recycling waste into useful products or reusing what previously would have been considered waste. Others have tried to reduce wasteful carbon emissions or pollutants from entering our air and water supplies.

Social venture example: BioLite came up with a unique, market-based approach to addressing the fact that more than half the world's population still cooks on wood fires. The smoke from these fires is wasted—contributing to climate change. At the same time, these wood fires are responsible for approximately two million deaths annually from respiratory disease caused by breathing the fumes. BioLite designed a very low-cost stove for use in rural areas and developing countries that captures the energy—or waste heat—from the fires' fumes and uses that heat to generate electricity. The stoves use 50 percent less fuel, create some 90 percent less carbon dioxide and smoke, and, as importantly, transfer the captured heat to generate enough electricity to power cell phones or other small electric devices. BioLite sells a market-rate version in developed countries, which enables campers to charge their cell phones while camping, and at the same time creating a sustainable income source for the company. *www.biolitestove.com*

■ **Energy.** Demand for energy is increasing worldwide as more people enter the middle class in developing countries. The earth's supply of fossil fuels can't indefinitely support this increasing desire for energy—to power cars, homes, and businesses. Additional and alternative sources of energy must be found and supplied.

Social venture example: AllEarth Renewables is a Vermont-based company that manufactures and installs solar panels that change position to follow the sun throughout the day. Using GPS, the solar panels move orientation to maximize the amount of the sun's energy reaching the panels. This unique solution increases both the energy produced and the electrical output of solar installations, making it more cost efficient for

Five strategies for achieving social goals

1. **INVENT SOMETHING.** Create something new to meet a social goal.

2. **BRING SOMETHING TO MARKET.** Take a new product that has been developed by someone else and create a distribution, retail or sales company to market that product.

3. **CREATE NEW SERVICES.** Develop new services that haven't been offered before to meet a social goal.

4. **PROVIDE SERVICES.** Offer established services that meet a social goal.

5. **ADAPT AN EXISTING PRODUCT.** Take an existing product but slightly change its properties or use so that it can achieve social goals.

consumers to turn to solar energy instead of other, nonrenewable, resources. *www.allearthrenewables.com*

- **Water.** More than 880 million people in the world lack access to clean water, and 3.6 million people per year die from waterborne diseases. Clean water is a highly limited resource, and one that must be managed responsibly as the world population increases, middle class demand soars, and global climate conditions suggest increasing drought and dry conditions. Both the scarcity and the quality of water represent immense challenges for this most precious (and limited) resource. Social technology ventures are sometimes referred to as "bluetech" (as opposed to greentech for environmental companies).

Social venture example: Bilexys, based in Brisbane, Australia, has pioneered a method for converting wastewater in city wastewater treatment plants into valuable chemicals. This for-profit company helps solve several issues: It reduces the amount of chemicals put back into the environment, capturing them for reuse, often by the treatment plant itself; it helps communities turn more wastewater into clean water while providing income for their treatment facilities; and it reduces the expensive energy needed to treat wastewater. *www.bilexys.com*

- **Animals.** Worldwide, animals are in distress. Whether it be animals in the wild facing the double threat of habitat loss and poaching, or animals raised for food under inhumane conditions in agribusiness, or domestic animals in developed countries facing inhumane treatment and abandonment, animals need human support and intervention if they're to survive and to live without pain and suffering. In the United States alone, approximately 4 million cats and dogs are put to death each year because they don't have homes. A century ago, India had more than 45,000 tigers living in the wild; today, estimates range that there are only 800 to 1,400 on the entire subcontinent, and only about 3,000 left worldwide—indeed, within a few years there may be no wild tigers left anywhere on the planet.

Social venture example: Beijing-based International Center for Veterinary Services is serving the needs of the growing number of Chinese residents who are ready and willing to own pets. The center provides a full for-profit veterinary hospital and clinic, but uses part of the profits to run various programs to help the Beijing pet population and better educate folks about the importance of protecting and respecting other species. ICVS instituted the country's first "trap–neuter–release" program—an effective method of reducing the number of stray cats and dogs. *www.icvsasia.com*

PEOPLE

Most of the issues around human concerns deal with the concept that all humans have the right to live a healthy, decent, productive life, and that all humans are equally valuable. As the business world becomes ever more global, entrepreneurs have grown increasingly aware of the plight of those living in poverty: hunger, disease, deficient education, and challenges of human and political rights.

- **Poverty reduction.** According to the World Bank, in 2008 over 1.2 billion people in the developing world lived on less than $1.25 a day—the global standard for extreme poverty—or more than 22 percent of the population in those countries. And the United Nations Development Programme reports that almost half the people in the world—that's more than 3 billion people—live on less than $2.50 a day. Many social ventures focus on helping people escape poverty and communities build infrastructure that will reduce poverty long-term. Whether through providing education, jobs, proper nutrition, or housing, these initiatives try to break the self-perpetuating cycle by giving hope to families and communities that have lived without hope for generations. And these ventures don't all happen in the Third World.

  Social venture example: Drishtee is a for-profit venture focusing on supporting microentrepreneurs in rural India. The company has created a network supporting over 14,000 rural entrepreneurs—primarily women. The company uses a franchise model to train rural residents to operate "routes" conveying a variety of needed services, including health care, education, job training, and infrastructure (including IT support). Moreover, it provides direct support for rural entrepreneurs in the form of microloans and the distribution and sale of handmade arts and crafts. *www.drishtee.com*

- **Health care.** The opportunities for improving the health of people around the world are enormous, so it's no wonder that a significant proportion of social entrepreneurs focus on health care ventures. There's tremendous potential for significantly reducing disease and infection, increasing lifespan, and improving overall well-being—and also tremendous potential for making money while doing so.

  Social venture example: Dimagi means "smart guy" in Hindi, and is also the name of a software company in Cambridge, Massachusetts, that releases open-source software—that is, free software—designed to improve health care in underserved populations around the world. Past initiatives have included creating mobile apps for clinicians treating tuberculosis patients, to a national medical record system used in Zambia for HIV care. The company became profitable in its very first year. *www.dimagi.com*

- **Hunger and food production.** Approximately 1 billion people worldwide go to bed hungry or malnourished every night, according to the United Nations Food and Agriculture Organization. In 2010, nearly 15 percent of Americans were "food insecure" at some point in the year, according to the U.S. Department of Agriculture. The world *does* produce enough food— yet poverty, war, and inadequate distribution and storage all contribute to world hunger. Even among those who have adequate access to food, there's increasing concern over the quality of food grown and methods used in

B corporations

Traditional corporations have the fiduciary responsibility to maximize returns for shareholders. This has come to be seen as maximizing *financial* returns and has left for-profit companies that make decisions for social reasons open to the possibility of shareholder lawsuits. To respond to this, a new type of legal entity—a benefit (B) corporation—was established and is now recognized in a growing number of states.

If registered as a B corporation, a company is required by law to create general benefits for society as well as for shareholders. It can make decisions to achieve both social goals and financial returns. It's held to higher standards of reporting and transparency, based on third-party standards.

agriculture. Issues around food production and distribution, hunger, and famine all present social entrepreneurs with an opportunity to make a significant impact, and a profit too.

Social venture example: When entrepreneur Lauren Walters saw severely malnourished children in Rwanda and learned that they could be treated with a simple 500-calorie nutrition pack, he vowed to do something to help. He teamed up with another entrepreneur, Will Hauser, and together they launched Two Degrees—a nutrition bar company. Following the lead of Tom's Shoes (for every pair of shoes you buy, it donates a pair of shoes to an impoverished child), Two Degrees donates one nutrition package for every nutrition bar a customer buys. The firm's first donation was over 10,800 packs to a village in Malawi. Moreover, they have their nutrition packs manufactured in that African nation, using local ingredients and helping provide jobs for low-income people there. *www.twodegreesfood.com*

■ **Human rights.** Standing up for the rights of humans around the planet regardless of their race, ethnicity, religion, gender, or sexual orientation is another banner cause for social entrepreneurs. Many of them focus their work on developing technologies that can rouse people at the grassroots level and get their voices heard in the corridors of power.

Social venture example: Change.org, a "B" corporation, is a social media platform enabling individuals to rally and organize others to help address problems they've identified. Change.org has adapted for the Internet age the traditional petition—formerly taken door to door, shopping mall to shopping mall, for signatures. Anyone with access to the Web can start a cause and recruit their families, friends, and associates to join their cause—and bring the power of the masses to bear on a critical social issue. Change.org raised $2 million from "angel" investors in its first year of operation and has been profitable since early 2011. *www.change.org*

■ **Politics and civic life.** Another category of social ventures includes one that attempts to improve the political process, and to empower greater numbers of people by helping them become more engaged in their communities.

Social venture example: The software firm Azavea creates data-based applications that help communities understand and solve problems they face. For example, Azavea has developed a crime analysis system that provides communities with "early warnings" of crime waves through identifying patterns, using statistical analysis. Another of the company's applications helps citizens participate electronically in the process of redrawing legislative districts—a vital activity that previously took place out of sight in the proverbial smoke-filled back rooms. *www.azavea.com*

Your Company's Mission

Whether you establish your entrepreneurial venture to address a critical social issue—say you're a social venture—or even if you're merely determined to run a socially responsible business, the payoffs can be significant. Of course, if your venture can truly help solve a real-world problem, the results—regardless of your bottom financial line—will have made a tremendous difference. But even if you just run a more sustainable operation because you're committed to environmentally sound practices and reducing waste, you'll likely save money.

Social entrepreneurship and social responsibility gives you more than profits: It pays benefits in terms of increased job satisfaction for you and all your colleagues and employees. It enhances and deepens engagement and commitment with your customers, suppliers, and community. And it gives you a sense of purpose and drive.

After all, entrepreneurs change the world.

REAL-WORLD CASE

Go Green, Make Green: New Leaf Paper

challenge

Improve the footprint of one of the world's most environmentally unfriendly industries— paper production

solution

Focus the corporation on solving serious environmental problems rather than on profitability

Until 2010, the primary goal of all for-profit corporations had been, well, profit. This is codified in federal and state law, as well as in articles of incorporation for "C" corporations, LLCs, and other entities. Under the law, if corporate executives failed to focus exclusively on maximizing profit, shareholders could sue them for breach of their fiduciary responsibilities.

But a number of states have been busy creating a new kind of corporation, the benefit corporation[1]—or "B" corporation—that is designed to have a broader mission. B corporations are not singularly concerned about maximizing profit for shareholders. Instead, the purpose of these new kinds of businesses is "to create a material positive impact on society and the environment." In fact, B corporations are *required* to solve social and environmental problems.[2] Each B corporation has an "expanded fiduciary duty" that actually requires that management consider nonfinancial interests when making decisions. Additionally, its overall social and environmental performance must be assessed against a third-party standard, not simply its own internal goals. B corporations are now legally certified in several states, and many more states have B corporation legislation in process of becoming law.[3] We're entering the era of the benefit corporation.

Jeff Mendelsohn, a socially conscious student of international relations at Cornell University, was following all this with great interest. Always intrigued by the relationship between business and government, Mendelsohn chose to have the environmentally focused paper company he founded—called New Leaf Paper—certified as one of the first B corporations.[4]

Mendelsohn founded New Leaf Paper in 1998 with the environmentally activist mission of becoming the leading national source for environmentally responsible, economically sound paper. He wasn't after a renegade audience, either: He hoped to attract regular businesses, both large and small, to his products because those products met business needs. He also wanted to inspire—through old-fashioned commercial success—"a fundamental shift toward environmental responsibility in the paper industry."[5]

1. www.bcorporation.net.
2. Ibid.
3. "California Law to Protect Socially Conscious Firms," *SFGate.com*, Nov. 17, 2011.
4. www.newleafpaper.com/about/founding-b-corp.
5. www.newleafpaper.com/about/mission-history.

At that point, the paper industry was in crisis. Although some environmentally sensitive people actually worked in the paper business, it was a group in need of a leader. Mendelsohn fully understood the complexity of the challenge. He knew that paper production was a dirty business. It polluted waters. It was responsible for the loss of native forests and biodiversity. In fact, paper production is the third largest industrial energy consumer in the world and one of the biggest emitters of greenhouse gasses.[6] Mendelsohn also knew that the industry was gridlocked and resistant to change.

The statistics are dismal, and Mendelsohn was smart enough not to fight them. According to the Better Paper Project of Green America, paper accounts for some 40 percent of the solid waste clogging up U.S. landfills, and is deeply poisoning the environment.[7] The U.S. Environmental Protection Agency (EPA) Toxic Release Inventory has documented that paper production is a leading industrial source of dioxin—a chemical that's a major contaminant of water, soil, and, ultimately, our food supply. Dioxin has been found in fish, seabirds, and mammals, and is associated with many types of cancers and birth defects.[8]

New Leaf Paper products are all based on environmental specifications, use the highest percentages possible of recycled and sustainably harvested fibers, and are processed without any use of toxic chemicals. The company's 100 percent postconsumer recycled paper, bleached without chlorine, has become the market standard. Competitors have since followed suit, and manufactured their own environmentally sound paper products, creating a ripple effect of positive environmental change.

New Leaf Paper products are used by organizations you'd expect, like the Sierra Club, but also by the less-expected, such as Dell Computer and Old Navy. Recognized for its truly innovative and inspiring approach to paper production, it has won many environmental awards, including the U.S. EPA Power Leadership Club, the Forbes Top 30, and the Sustainable Business Institute's "Seal of Sustainability." Turning over a new leaf, New Leaf Paper proves that a dedicated, well-run company can be both profitable and good for the earth. ■

questions

1. Do you feel that B corporations have a place in the business world? Why, or why not? How common do you think this relatively new corporate structure will be a decade from now?

2. Jeff Mendelsohn realized that his industry needed a leader, if any positive social change were to occur. What other social problems do think face this same lack of leadership?

3. Do you believe industries that pollute the environment have an obligation to clean up the mess? Why, or why not? If not, who *is* responsible? The government? Consumers?

---

6. www.newleafpaper.com/paper-and-environment/your-choice-matters.
7. "Recycled Paper Facts," *Better Paper Project.*
8. Ibid.

HELP SOCIETY, HELP YOURSELF

Goal:

Come up with a new product or service that improves the quality of life on earth as well as has the potential to be profitable.

What to Do:

1. Working alone or in groups, brainstorm a list of challenges and problems that society faces at present. Be specific! For example, don't just say "we generate too much greenhouse gas." Specify what's causing that (we drive our cars when we could walk, bike, or take public transport). Come up with a list of at least 10 (this shouldn't be difficult).

2. Now, for each challenge on your list, come up with as many obstacles as you can that prevent the challenge from being easily resolved. (For example, if too many people drive cars, one obstacle to reducing that number is the lack of adequate public transit in many U.S. cities, towns, and rural areas.)

3. Look over your challenges and obstacles. Pick just one challenge. Brainstorm a solution for it that could also be a viable (profitable) business.

4. Write an outline of the business model:

   a. Where would the revenues come from?

   b. Who is your target audience?

   c. What are the costs (both startup and ongoing operational)?

   d. What are the risks?

   e. What are the long-term opportunities?

   f. How will it solve the problem you've selected?

   g. How do you know if will be profitable?

5. Present your social entrepreneurship idea to the class.

CHAPTER

18 Globalization

learning objectives

In this chapter, you'll learn how to:

- Recognize opportunities globally

- Demonstrate cultural sensitivity when conducting business internationally

- Identify potential partners in other countries

- Research international markets

- Determine target countries, regions, and customers in foreign markets

- Assess the financial considerations of a global operation

- Define a plan for international marketing and sales

- Determine which tasks and operations may be suitable for offshoring

- Manage, motivate, and communicate with a foreign-based staff

- Distinguish which aspects of a company's operations, by moving overseas, will reap the greatest benefits

- Conduct business abroad while adhering to both domestic and foreign laws

- Demonstrate good corporate global citizenship

Go Global, Grow Global

The world has grown smaller and more connected. Today, every aspect of an entrepreneurial business can potentially benefit from embracing a broad geographic vision. Regardless of industry or location, any company, even a small one, can now be global. By looking beyond your borders, you can become more competitive, more innovative, and more successful.

By going global, you may find new markets and new customers. International markets may be far more underserved than your home market and offer greater potential for profits than competing in your own country. Looking abroad, you may also find new suppliers and manufacturers, investors and partners, service providers, and perhaps even employees.

If you're selling a digital product—software, content, graphics, and the like—delivered over the Internet, you face fewer barriers to entry to foreign markets than you do when selling a physical product or service. Even language may pose no barrier, especially for B2B (business-to-business) products, as many foreign companies are used to conducting some of their business in English. But if it's just a matter of translation to make your product useful in another country or region, the cost may be minimal in comparison to the opportunity.

You can also **export** your knowledge and services. The world is hungry for services such as engineering, management consulting, architecture, design, marketing, pollution control—the whole range of business services, particularly ones that can be performed on a consulting basis.

Seasonal businesses have the opportunity to become year-round companies by expanding from one hemisphere to the other as the seasons switch in the southern and northern hemispheres—summer in the north is winter in the south, and vice versa. If you sell ski clothes, for example, in the United States, you have just a few months to earn your entire year's income. But what if you also sell to Argentina and Brazil? You can stretch your sales window almost year-round and improve your cash flow.

Even if you don't plan on being a worldwide company when you launch your business, going global should be part of your long-term vision. As you become successful in your home market, other countries present you with new market opportunities, allowing you to leverage your investment in products, services, personnel, and infrastructure across a broader geographic area.

Culture and Norms

One of the most important—but perhaps most subtle—issues when doing business internationally is developing an understanding of the cultural norms in the countries you're in. As you do business globally, take time to try to understand cultural practices and business norms as much as possible. You won't become an expert, but even a little bit of sensitivity can help you succeed internationally.

Significant differences in how people communicate can lead to real problems. In the United States and Canada, for example, it's typical for a customer who disagrees with you or an employee who doesn't understand something

10 reasons to go global

1. Your product or service is appropriate for other markets.
2. New markets in developing countries are opening.
3. Competition in your home market is entrenched.
4. Sales in your home market have stalled.
5. Unique inventory or supplies are available.
6. Supplies, manufacturing, or services cost less.
7. Customers in countries outside of yours will pay for your expertise.
8. Year-round cash flow can be developed.
9. Dependence on one market is reduced.
10. Operational costs may decrease.

en·tre·pre·neur·ship key terms

Export
Selling goods and services to a country overseas. Exported goods can include raw materials, parts for other products, and finished products.

Foreign agents
Representatives in a foreign country who call on accounts there and secure orders for your business.

Import
Receiving goods and services produced in a country overseas. Importing goods may impute a tariff or duty (see *tariff*).

Licensing
The granting of permission by one company to another to use its products, trademark, or name in a limited, particular manner.

Living wage
A wage paid to workers that enables them to afford to live decently in their own country if they work full time.

Offshoring
Using outside vendors located in a country overseas or transferring your own company's operations to a country overseas, usually to reduce costs.

Outsourcing
Having certain tasks, jobs, manufacturing, and so on produced by an outside company on a contract basis, rather than having the work done by one's own company "in-house."

Tariff (or Duty)
A tax levied on goods coming into one country from another. Governments put tariffs into place to protect their country from foreign competition and to generate revenue.

Cultural norms to consider

- Physical contact and personal space
- Gift giving
- Dress
- Topics of conversation
- Level of formality
- Management styles

to speak up. In many other countries, they would say nothing. This might leave you with the impression that your customer agrees to certain terms or a contractor understands your requirements when, in reality, they don't. Once you're aware of the cultural attitude that stands in the way of their overtly disagreeing with you, you will take the time to make sure you have reached a true understanding, and you'll be more likely to spell out terms in writing.

Something as simple as a business card can signal cultural awareness. In the United States and Canada, giving and getting a business card is expected in a meeting, but in some parts of the world, business cards have even greater importance. In China, for example, business cards are given and received with a bit more ceremony—presented and received with both hands, and it's considered impolite if you fail to look at a business card when you receive it. If you do a lot of business in a country or region where a language other than English is spoken, have business cards printed in that language, or with English on one side and the second language on the reverse. Even if you conduct most of your business in English, the fact that you've shown the consideration to print your cards in the recipient's language will be much appreciated.

You won't become an expert overnight on the cultural norms of the country with which you intend to do business. Still, the important part of being a global entrepreneurial company is to develop an *attitude of cultural learning*. Instead of barging ahead in a country overseas, expect that things will be different, so ask and learn. Read up on the country and its business practices and norms before you go. Ask questions of locals and others who've done business in that country. Additionally, a number of business culture websites (see page 479) can give you an overview of your specific countries.

Most important, learn the words for "please" and "thank you" in the language of the countries where you do business, and use them. Remember, you don't have to learn it all. Most people appreciate your attempt to be culturally considerate and aware.

CULTURAL NORMS EXAMPLES

NORM	U.S./CANADIAN EXAMPLE	INTERNATIONAL EXAMPLES
Names and titles	First name expected (e.g., "Mary" not "Ms. Smith")	In Germany, using first names is considered rude (e.g., "Ms. Smith" is correct, not "Mary")
Business hours, pace, and timeliness	Eight-hour workdays; eating lunch at desk while working	Long and fast workdays in China; business done more slowly in Arab countries
Socializing and meals	Business lunches common; business discussed over meals; negotiations done and deals closed during meals	In Spain, sharing meals is important, but discussing business over meals is considered extremely rude

International Partners

As you think about expanding your business internationally, one approach can come from finding existing companies "on the ground" to partner with in your potential markets. This makes your entry into countries outside your borders far easier, faster, and more successful. It also helps you to understand local business customs and practices, and to better serve your market. Local partners already know the market and may already have a sales presence there, even customers.

As you develop your global business plan, consider the different types of international partners you can work with.

- **Importers, distributors, and wholesalers.** These companies **import** your product—typically physical goods—into the receiving country and take on the responsibility of selling your goods in that country. Working with a distributor (or sales representative) is a great way to explore how much demand there might be for your products abroad without investing a great deal of money in infrastructure or employees. For example, if you manufacture athletic shoes, an international shoe distributor might import your finished goods, maintain them in its warehouse, and sell them to retailers, who in turn sell your shoes to end-users.

- **Sales representatives and foreign agents.** Similar to sales reps operating in your home country, international sales reps and **foreign agents** call on accounts to try to secure orders for you—in their countries. In the case of the athletic shoes, your sales rep in Brazil might call on sporting goods stores there, show samples of your shoes, and take orders that you fulfill directly from your home country. This requires even less of an investment.

  Make certain to obtain any distribution or sales rep agreements in writing, and be aware that some countries limit your ability to terminate these agreements without cause. So check with a knowledgeable attorney before signing any documents or sending any products.

  With both sales reps and distributors, you must make sure you comply with all import regulations of the country where you sell your products.

- **Licensees.** A very cost-effective way to sell your product or intellectual property is to **license** it to a company in another country. You may or may not allow that company to adapt your offerings to meet the needs of the local market, or you may allow them to market your offerings under either your name or their own company name. Once again, using the example of athletic shoes, instead of physically making the shoes in your facility and distributing them to international customers, you can simply design them in-house, hopefully build a brand name through marketing, and then license the manufacturing and distribution in other countries— typically to your exact specifications. In other words, a Brazilian shoe company could license your design and then manufacture and sell the

Global logistics

One key issue to address when doing business internationally is logistics—how will you fulfill orders if you sell internationally? How will you ship goods you buy or produce internationally? Before entering into any significant deal or starting your marketing overseas, develop a logistics plan.

product either under your name or under a different name that has greater local appeal.

Not only can you license physical property, but many companies also license intellectual property for sale and distribution in international markets.

- **Joint ventures or investors.** A variety of types of partners can help you establish a global presence by investing or co-investing in your developments abroad. Often these investors bring more than merely money—they bring connections, plus an understanding of the country in which you want to do business. If you're fortunate, you might also find an international investor to help fund your activities in your home country.

Remember, you don't have to go it all alone. By partnering with others on the ground, you can more effectively and efficiently serve countries outside your own. Just take care to maintain those relationships well, as they're critical to your global success.

Target Markets and Customers

As you consider launching your entrepreneurial venture, look beyond your own borders to assess market opportunities. Surprisingly, it may be easier to launch a product or service in an international market, rather than in your home country, especially if your home country is the United States. After all, the country is a huge and highly developed market, making it expensive and challenging to get a foothold in many categories, and often difficult and expensive to carve out even a small market share. Or, perhaps the life cycle of your product has run its course domestically, but is still viable elsewhere. If you have a highly niche product, your customers may be widely scattered internationally. Finally, if you manufacture your products overseas, targeting markets closer to your production facilities might make sense. And if you're in a knowledge industry—such as engineering, design, or consulting—you may find you have less competition abroad, particularly in emerging markets.

Determining target countries

When thinking about reaching global markets, you need to determine which countries you will serve. Think also about "regions," not simply individual countries. For instance, you may want to target a number of countries in Latin America since they share the same language, or a number of European countries because of their geographical proximity.

If you make your product or service available globally—especially on the Web—you may be tempted to view the entire world as your geographic target market. But that may not be realistic, considering the costs of shipping or **tariff (duty)** barriers. Even online, you'll face limitations on which geographic areas make good candidates as your primary target markets.

Although your first thoughts should turn toward the countries likely to have the greatest demand, that may be difficult to determine. If you and members of your team come from several countries and possess language or cultural skills that make it easier for you to do business in certain countries or regions, you may want to target those countries first.

Determining target customers

It won't do to say that you'll sell in Costa Rica, Cambodia, or Cameroon; you still need to decide which customer segments in those countries you want to reach—consumers or businesses? If businesses, how big are they and what industry are they in? If consumers, what are their characteristics (for example, gender, age, income group, and educational level)?

One purpose of your global business plan is to specify *exactly* the countries or regions you will target and which customers within those markets you hope to reach. Even if you don't plan on developing a global market, you should think about how you'll serve international customers who find *you*, especially online.

Money

Whenever you cross a country's border, you cross financial borders as well. You already recognize that the whole world may not do business in your currency, so you know you need to plan accordingly. But you must take into account many other financial issues when developing your global business plan. You don't have to be an economics major, though a little bit of knowledge can help a lot.

For instance, suppose you sell your products on the Internet in the United States and Canada and want to do so overseas as well. It's typical for American and Canadian consumers to pay by credit card. But in many parts of the world, a large percentage of customers don't regularly use credit cards. How will you accept payment then? Figuring out how you'll get paid, and making sure that happens, are absolutely critical issues.

Whenever contemplating doing business in another country, do a little homework on its currency first. Currency fluctuations can greatly affect your profits and costs, whether you're buying or selling, so take into account historic patterns of currency exchange rates in your target countries. Be particularly cautious with countries facing political instability or high inflation rates.

When possible, try to fix your prices—especially for B2B sales transactions—in your home country's currency. If you're selling to consumers abroad, or if you can buy at much better prices in foreign currencies, fixing your prices may not be practical. Again, be mindful of currency fluctuations.

Ideally, when selling to businesses or making sales in large amounts, it's ideal to get the funds wire-transferred in advance, especially for new customers—this way, the money is deposited into your bank before you send the goods or

When choosing target countries, focus on:

- Demand
- Language
- Culture
- Legal issues or tariffs
- Product or service fulfillment
- Political stability
- Economic and currency stability

provide the service. Of course, your customer may not be willing to do this, as they are taking the full risk on you. In the United States and Canada, in B2B sales, it's typical to extend credit on "open account" with "30 day net" payment terms. You may not want to do that overseas, particularly with new accounts or where currencies or the political environment are unstable.

Letters of credit are a time-honored way of doing business internationally. That is a method in which the customer's bank agrees that it will deposit the funds in your bank once the transaction has been completed.

One way to reduce your risk is to purchase export credit insurance, which covers losses if your foreign purchaser fails to pay you. If you're a small American business selling products abroad (less than $5 million in annual sales), you can get a special credit insurance policy from the Export-Import Bank of the United States (www.exim.gov/products/insurance/index.cfm).

Confer with an accountant knowledgeable in foreign business operations to help you plan your financials when conducting considerable business abroad. Be certain to ask about the tax ramifications, as tax issues when dealing with international operations and sales can be complicated.

Marketing and Sales

Just as in your own country, international sales don't magically happen—you must devise a marketing and sales plan. How will you make potential customers aware of your offerings, build a brand, and emphasize your competitive advantages? And how will you actually make sales and get and take orders?

When marketing and selling your product or service, local input really helps. Because you may find it difficult to grasp the nuances and sensitivities of other markets, it's often a good idea to recruit locals to your marketing team or hire local marketing companies (public relations or advertising firms, for example) that better understand the market. For instance, in some countries, comparison advertising (such as taste tests of Coke versus Pepsi) is not done. In many Asian countries, red is a symbol of good luck; in other countries, red implies energy or danger. You may need to know about laws relating to advertising or marketing as well.

Marketing

Even if you only market through trade shows or sales representatives, you'll need marketing collateral materials (such as brochures or signs) written in the local language and sensitive to the cultural norms.

As you build your global marketing plan, keep in mind the following marketing vehicles:

- **Website.** As you build or redesign your website, keep international prospects in mind and make your website friendly for your global customers. For example, you may want to offer a choice of languages,

BUILD-YOUR-BUSINESS WORKSHEET

Global Financial Considerations

Choose a country in which your company (either real or fictitious) will conduct business, then answer the following questions regarding foreign currencies, international operations, and selling your products or services internationally.

Which country or countries have you chosen, and how will you conduct business there? _____
_____
_____

Have you accounted for the way exchange rates will affect your financial analysis and projections? _____
_____
_____

How stable are the foreign currencies you will be dealing with? Are they historically consistently stable or do rates fluctuate greatly? Is there political or social unrest that could affect the value of the currency in the areas where you plan to operate? _____
_____
_____

Are there any unique start-up costs associated with doing business in some regions? Are there unique tax or tariff considerations you should be aware of in the countries where you plan to operate? _____
_____
_____

What seasonal factors will affect financial projections or cause revenue fluctuations in the regions in which you plan to operate? _____
_____
_____

Will you be paying any staff in a foreign currency? If so, what are the average pay rates for the positions you plan to fill? Are there expected region-specific benefits you need to be aware of? _____
_____
_____

What are the average costs of supplies, goods, or services that you may purchase locally if working internationally? Would it be more economical in some cases to purchase goods in your home country and ship them to your international locations? _____
_____
_____

Importing 101

If you plan on importing a product, instead of placing a large order, buy only a few samples or prototypes; go back to your home country and secure orders there; and only then place your import order. That way you'll be exposed to far less risk.

display prices in currencies other than your own, use the metric system for measurements, and provide customer support for the various time zones and in local languages. You can also build special areas or landing pages for each country or region you market to.

- **Search engine marketing.** As in your home country, you can create online ads aimed at users in countries outside your borders. Most search engines allow you to target particular countries, so your ad appears only when a searcher from that country types in the keywords associated with your products or services. Keep in mind that in some countries, search engines other than the ones you use may be dominant—such as Baidu in China.

- **Social media.** Participating in blogs and other social networking sites—populated mostly by users who live in your target countries—is another way to make yourself known.

- **Advertising.** Remember the power of traditional advertising vehicles, such as print (newspaper, magazines), radio, and television.

Sales

Once you have determined that a healthy demand exists in other parts of the world for your products or services, you need to evaluate how you'll actually make sales and take orders.

If you have an international retail operation, you'll make your sales at your physical location. But most companies won't open retail stores abroad. You may work through distributors or sales reps who make sales on your behalf. Or, you may take orders directly from your website, especially if yours is a digital product.

Recognize that conducting sales abroad may differ from what you're used to in your home country. For instance, consumers may not have credit cards, or regulations may impose limits on the interest rates you can charge even your commercial customers. Payment terms will also likely differ from those in your home country, as may typical commissions you'll have to pay sales reps if you use them. As you make your sales plans and projections, you'll need to understand those differences.

An excellent way to both market and sell in global markets is by participating in international trade shows. Such shows offer an efficient means to reach a large number of international customers and partners in a short time span, as these events bring together many parties in an industry to show their products to potential customers and, typically, to take orders. They also offer great public relations opportunities for hot products or new services.

BUILD-YOUR-BUSINESS WORKSHEET

International Marketing

Identify the issues associated with marketing in another country. If you haven't yet selected a product or service to sell, answer the following questions for a sporting goods product of your choice.

Which countries are your best prospects, and why? _____

_____

_____

_____

How will you create or adapt globally friendly websites? Choose from below and then give specific examples.

— Support multiple languages in product info _____

— Use social media _____

— Buy adwords targeted to specific countries _____

— Partner with international marketing firms_____

— Participate in international trade shows _____

— Open international locations _____

— Other: _____

_____

_____

_____

How will you adapt your website to accommodate international customers? Choose from below and then give specific

examples.

— Support multiple languages _____

— Indicate prices in other currencies _____

— Provide customer service in different time zones_____

— Provide measurements in metrics _____

— Adjust website content to be sensitive to cultural norms_____

— Use visuals (e.g., photos) that reflect international orientation _____

— Other: _____

_____

_____

_____

BUILD-YOUR-BUSINESS WORKSHEET

Sales

Focusing on the products or services you want to sell globally, answer the following questions.

What concerns, if any, could you face with fulfillment (shipping, customs, tariffs, etc.)? _____

_____

_____

Which specific products or services in your line are most appropriate for international sales?_____

_____

_____

When selling internationally, will you be selling through a third party or through direct sales? _____

_____

Will you open a sales office in the country or countries you will target? _____

_____

_____

Will you hire sales reps in the countries you will target? _____

_____

What are the typical commissions in the countries where you'll be selling? _____

_____

_____

What are the typical terms of sale in the countries where you'll be selling?_____

_____

_____

What other concerns with selling internationally have you identified? (If you chose to sell beverages, for example,

what are the rules, regulations, and tariffs regarding selling alcohol?)_____

_____

_____

Management and Labor

Thanks to developments in technology, it's possible for even new and growing companies to have employees or contractors work at great distances from the main office. In fact, they no longer have to work in the same city or even the same country as you do. That creates the possibility that, as an entrepreneurial business, your company may have to deal with an international workforce.

Companies are now **offshoring** many tasks. Finding workers—especially sales, manufacturing, technology, or customer service labor—in countries outside your own may offer significant cost reduction. Of course, managing a distant labor supply has challenges, and you must think those through as you plan the global aspects of your business.

When deciding on which functions to offshore, first make certain you'll gain an actual advantage and have a compelling business reason to move those functions abroad. Advantages include significant cost reductions, a closer proximity to your markets or customers, and access to talent or resources you can't find at home. Next, clearly define those functions or projects and create clear-cut standards. This makes it easier for your overseas staff to meet your goals. Finally, make certain that the necessary resources will be readily available to your offshored personnel in a cost- and time-efficient manner. If, for instance, you plan on having your product assembled in a Latin American country, determine where the components will come from and how reliable and expensive shipping will be.

Managing across borders

The more you operate in countries abroad, the more challenging it is to manage those operations solely from your home base. Sure, when you're just starting out and your customers or suppliers are few and not critical to your success, you may be able to do most of your routine international business from a distance, visiting in person from time to time. But as your global activities increase—with customers, suppliers, manufacturers, partners, and the like—you'll find you need foreign-based staff and eventually foreign-based management.

Keep in mind that foreign-based contractors and employees often require greater management time than most of your domestic-based contractors or employees. Why? Because, owing to language, cultural, and time zone differences, and possibly differences in skill sets, your domestic managers may have to give more-detailed direction, provide more feedback, and spend more time on quality control and supervision. Plan for that extra time when considering which staffing functions to locate abroad.

Issues to consider when offshoring labor

- Communication and language
- Fulfillment, shipping, and logistics
- Taxes, duties, and customs
- Import or export limitations
- Measurements and standards
- Quality control
- Differing work hours and habits
- Decent working conditions

Staff responsibilities often located abroad

- Customer service calls and email
- Call center staffing and management
- Software development and programming
- International marketing
- Sales reps and distributors
- Manufacturing staff and management
- Telemarketing

Communication

When locating some of your staff internationally—whether as employees or contractors—it's imperative that you maintain clear, continual communication. At a minimum, once every two weeks (if not more frequently) hold a conference call with your key people abroad, even if you send frequent emails. Remember, emails can be misinterpreted.

You want everyone who's working for you—even those working abroad—to feel that they're part of the same company team. Copy overseas personnel on routine emails sent to locally based staff, so they stay in the loop on what's happening back home with the "mother ship."

The most effective way to both ensure quality and motivate overseas staff is to visit them in person now and then. Doing business face-to-face reduces misunderstandings and boosts motivation. Successful management requires the personal touch to keep your staff the most productive.

Global Operations Options

Virtually any aspect of your operations can have a global component today, regardless of the size of your business. In addition to finding some of the following operational sources yourself, you may want to turn to brokers who know providers in specific industries or countries, and who can help you locate suppliers, manufacturers, and others.

- **Inventory sources.** Importing goods for resale is perhaps the most typical aspect of conducting business globally. If you're a retailer or wholesaler, you'll almost certainly want to look abroad for at least some of your inventory. Making overseas buying trips enables you to discover a broader range of goods, negotiate better prices, or have goods custom made to your specifications.

- **Supplies and raw material.** If you produce goods, at least some of your materials will likely come from countries other than your own. Consider sourcing material and inventory globally as you grow your company. Once again, taking buying trips gives you more choices at better prices. When considering using global sources for supplies and materials, though, make sure you have a consistent supply source along with consistent quality. Consider also the cost and time of shipping.

- **Manufacturing and production.** Some industries (such as electronics or apparel) have many established contract manufacturers, and working with such companies can enable you to get up and running faster—and usually more cheaply—than you might be able to do at home. Be certain to visit the manufacturing facilities regularly to ensure they maintain both your product quality and ethical workplace standards.

- **Technology development.** The easiest types of products to "ship" internationally are digital products. If you develop software, mobile applications, websites, or cloud-based services, or if you need programming as part of your product development or marketing, you have a world of providers to choose from. When using overseas techies, however, build additional time and money into your global business plan for home-based staff to manage and communicate with your foreign-based tech workforce.

- **Customer service and support.** Call centers, tech support, and customer service functions can often be handled less expensively overseas. Having international customer service also enables you to better serve international customers, keep your customer support center staffed 24/7, and serve customers in different time zones.

- **Back-office functions.** Today it's possible to locate even critical business functions—such as accounting, legal, human resources, and administrative tasks—internationally. You may do this by hiring staff directly or using an **outsourcing** company. Keep in mind that you may be putting sensitive, confidential, or even mission-critical information into the hands of individuals or companies you don't interact with in person on a day-to-day basis, located overseas, and whose security systems you may not be in a position to monitor. So move cautiously.

Legal Issues

The thought of dealing with international legal issues can be daunting. After all, once you start working in another country or do business with companies across borders, you have to deal not only with domestic laws regarding importing and exporting but with foreign laws, too. However, if you get some basic legal advice, you shouldn't let that scare you.

Once you start working globally, educate yourself about the basic legal requirements and issues that can affect your business. Better yet, find an "in-country" lawyer or one who's familiar with the laws of the countries you deal with.

Keep the following basics in mind:

- **Contract law.** If you enter into international deals, make sure to get all agreements in writing, making certain the terms are clear and your means of recourse are spelled out. Contract law can differ substantially from one country to another. Importantly, determine where any disputes or lawsuits will be settled. If at all possible, make sure that any disputes are adjudicated under the laws of your home country and your state or province. The cost of trying to litigate in a foreign country can be prohibitive.

- **Intellectual property (IP).** If you sell products that entail significant intellectual property—such as software, electronics, new products, or branded consumer goods—make certain that the countries where you'll sell your products provide adequate legal protection against piracy. Piracy is frequently cited as the number one problem that companies have when doing business internationally.

REAL-WORLD RECAP

Global operations

Operations suitable for a global component include:

- Inventory sources
- Supplies and raw materials
- Manufacturing and production
- Technology development
- Customer service and support
- Back-office functions

Export help

If you're considering exporting from the United States, a good place to start is Export.gov (www.export.gov) or the U.S. Commerce Department's website, Exporting Basics (www.bis.doc.gov/licensing/exportingbasics.htm). And, of course, the country where you ship your goods from may also limit your imports or place duties on them. (See page 478 for more resources to help you with importing or exporting.)

REAL-WORLD RECAP

Global legal issues to consider

Once you begin to conduct business globally, educate yourself about the following issues:

- Contract law
- Intellectual property (IP)
- Exporting
- Importing
- Foreign ownership

- **Exporting.** When you sell abroad, you help your home country's balance of trade—the value of exports versus imports. Nevertheless, several laws cover exporting, including some limitations on what you can export and to which countries. The U.S. government, for example, prohibits American companies from exporting items that might potentially have a military use, even if they can also be used for nonmilitary purposes. These include things such as electronics, computers, chemicals, marine products, and more. So before you begin to sell abroad, put your legal paperwork in order.

- **Importing.** As with exporting, you may face some limitations on what you can import, or you may have to pay a tax—also known as a duty or tariff—on the goods you bring into your country. In a few instances, there may be prohibitions on imports from certain countries (for example, no Cuban cigars in the United States). In most cases, you'll have to indicate the country of origin if you resell imported goods in the United States or Canada. If you are new to importing, it's often advisable to work with a customs broker to help you navigate the duties and other legal issues.

- **Foreign ownership.** If you want to purchase property, manufacture goods, or acquire companies abroad, be on the lookout for some countries' limits on the activities and ownership rights of foreign companies. Many countries, for instance, require companies in certain industries to be at least majority-owned by locals. They may also limit foreign ownership of land. Be sure to understand those limits before investing heavily in an international market.

Social Responsibility

The best international companies are good global citizens. When doing business internationally, you'll likely encounter a number of issues relating to what type of corporate—and world—citizen you are or want to be, whether dealing with labor issues, human rights, the environment, or corruption.

- **Laws and ethics.** The first component of social responsibility is to obey the laws of both your home country and the other countries in which you do business. In some countries, "greasing the wheels" of commerce by giving bribes or gifts to government officials may be viewed as "business as usual." But it's not. Moreover, it's also against the law in the United States and Canada. In the United States, the Foreign Corrupt Practices Act prohibits any American company or its personnel from giving money or *anything* of value to a foreign official to ease or enhance business dealings. In Canada, the Corruption of Foreign Public Officials Act works similarly.

- **Working conditions, fair pay, and child or slave labor.** As an employer in a country abroad—or as a customer or client of such an employer—exercise care to make certain that all those who work for you are treated and paid fairly. In good conscience, you don't want to play any part in promoting or enabling such activities as child labor or slave or forced labor.

Make certain the working conditions of those who work on your behalf, either directly for you or indirectly through suppliers, are healthy. Ensure that anyone who works for you or a supplier is paid at least the minimum wage in their country, but ideally, that they're paid a **living wage**—a wage that lets them afford to live decently in their own country if they work full time. Choose your suppliers carefully, and visit them frequently to observe conditions. You can also hire monitoring companies to conduct inspections.

■ **Discrimination.** It may be common practice—even legal—in some countries to discriminate against potential employees or contractors based on gender, religion, race, or sexual orientation. How will you handle that situation? Will you go along with what's usual or try to do what's right and fair? Keep in mind that your employees, customers, or partners in your home country may find such discrimination odious.

■ **Environment and sustainability.** No matter where you do business, you'll want to consider the impact of your actions on the environment. Ideally, you'll want to do as much as you can to conserve energy, reduce waste, use the fewest natural resources, and generally operate your business—and purchase your goods—in an environmentally sustainable fashion.

BUILD-YOUR-BUSINESS WORKSHEET

Global Social Responsibility

If you are developing an international social venture, identify the social issues you plan to address:

Environmental goals

☐ Energy reduction

☐ New energy sources

☐ Waste reduction

☐ Water purification and access

☐ Food purification and access

☐ Improved production and agricultural processes

☐ Other: _____

Labor goals

☐ Living-wage pay scales

☐ Gender equality

☐ Ethnic, religious, or other equality

☐ Eliminating child labor

☐ Healthy working conditions

☐ Ensuring fair trade practices

Other international social goals

☐ Improving human rights

☐ Improving the treatment of animals

☐ Reducing censorship

☐ Eliminating bribery and corruption

Would You Like Dim Sum with That? The Global Expansion of Yum! Brands

challenge

Find acceptance for traditional American products in global markets

solution

Adapt products to local preferences

You may not be familiar with the Yum! Brands name, but the chances are excellent that you and maybe everyone you know has eaten at a Yum! Brands restaurant. The company owns and operates KFC (formerly Kentucky Fried Chicken), Pizza Hut, Taco Bell, Long John Silver, and A&W, among other notable restaurant chains, making it the world's largest quick-service restaurant (QSR) company. Today Yum! Brands boasts nearly 37,000 outlets in more than 110 countries around the globe, and its international units are generating the majority of its revenues.[1]

When Yum! Brands was spun off from Pepsico in 1997, it generated most of its revenue and profit from the United States. Yes, it had an international division, but it performed poorly compared to its American cousin.

Yum!'s management understood there were literally billions of additional potential customers in the rest of the world. In 2010, Yum! Brands operated 42 units for every million consumers in the United States, but just seven units for every million consumers in China, and 12 per million consumers in the rest of the developed world.[2] Yum! management realized this represented an opportunity to build an international operation capable of supporting significant growth for decades to come.

But would Chinese customers really buy Kentucky Fried Chicken? Would people in India actually eat burritos from Taco Bell? This was far from certain.

Yum! management faced some serious challenges. How could they drive sustainable and profitable expansion in markets where there existed significant cultural gaps from U.S. tastes? And they didn't just want to open a few token units—they wanted to become fast-food market leaders in rapidly developing countries. They faced a big challenge.

Sure, they had proven formulas in the United States and Canada, but to lead internationally meant adapting to the realities of global markets. One of the main ways Yum! does this is through "localization," or the process of offering food choices that would be compatible with and unique to each country's taste.[2]

---

1. *Yum! 2010 Annual Report*. Feb. 14, 2011.
2. "Yum! Brands Set to Dominate the Global Fast Food Market," by Andrew Burchett. *Elite Inside Trader*. May 10, 2011.

For example, in China, Yum!'s KFC outlets—known worldwide for chicken—still sell chicken. But those yummy mashed potatoes you're used to getting with your fried chicken? Chinese customers aren't really into them. Instead, the standard side dish is rice, and Chinese KFC outlets offer a variety of other Chinese dietary favorites. If you go to a Pizza Hut in Beijing, you can get pizza, of course, but you can also get traditional Chinese dim sum.

Yum! Brands provides unique menu offerings throughout the developed and emerging countries it serves worldwide. In South Africa, Yum! found it had to expand its menus to compete with local restaurants. Pizza Huts there offer a broad range of pastas and lasagna as well as the traditional pizzas found in U.S. outlets.

Going global has enabled the unprecedented growth of Yum! Brands. The company may lag far behind other fast-food outlets in the United States, but go to China and you'll see many KFC outlets all over every big city. In fact, the growth of its international business is changing the very nature of the company. Look at how the distribution of its units and revenue has shifted: In 2006, the United States represented 60 percent of outlets and 48 percent of Yum!'s revenue, and China merely 6 percent of units and 17 percent of revenue. By 2011, KFC had about 5,200 American outlets and more than 15,000 outside the United States.[3] By 2015, by Yum!'s own forecasts, China will represent 60 percent of Yum's revenues, while the United States will deliver just 18 percent. This presents a complete reversal of the importance of the global market vis-à-vis the United States in terms of Yum! Brands' revenue and growth potential.[4]

Yum! is focusing on continued international expansion of its strongest brands—KFC, Pizza Hut, and Taco Bell. Yum! hopes to replicate this success in other untapped international markets, using the same strategy of localizing its American menu options with a wide range of regional favorites.

An unexpected benefit of going global for any company is what it learns from its international operations and brings back home to a domestic market. So don't be surprised if the Vegetarian Zinger Burger they sell at KFC in India shows up one day at the KFC nearest you.

"Yum," indeed. ■

questions

1. What type of products do you think sell best internationally?

2. What type of products, if any, do you think would *not* sell well internationally?

3. Besides localization, what factors do you think helped enable Yum! Brands to successfully expand internationally?

4. For a start-up, do you think focusing on global sales dilutes attention from first building a successful company domestically?

3. "About Us," www.kfc.com.
4. *Yum! 2010 Annual Report*.

THE WORLD IS YOUR CLINIC

Goal:

Understand the challenges of markets culturally different from your own.

What to Do:

You want to create a social enterprise—a business that achieves a positive social impact while still making a profit. One of the areas of interest you've focused on is providing affordable health care to low-income individuals in developing countries.

The model of "urgent care" provided in walk-in clinics has been launched successfully in the United States and has recently expanded to a number of other developed countries. Now, you'd like to consider bringing this concept to India, a rapidly developing country with an expanding middle class.

These walk-in, urgent care clinics provide onsite, immediate care for non-life-threatening illnesses, such as minor injuries, the flu, and minor broken bones, as well as health screening procedures such as blood tests.

1. Think through the issues you would have to research in order to assess whether this concept would work in India.

2. Develop questions you would need to research regarding:

   a. The business model, operations, and profitability of urgent care businesses in the United States

   b. The nature of the health care market in India, questions such as where most Indians get their health care

   c. The cultural attitudes toward doctors and health care in India

   d. Payment for health care and the health insurance system in India

   e. The regulatory climate for opening medical care facilities in India

3. Discuss whether you think the idea would work in India. If not, why not? If so, what aspects of the U.S. business model would you have to change to make it viable there?

CHAPTER 19 Growing the Venture

learning objectives

Why Grow, and When?

It may be hard to think about growing your business when you're just starting out. But if you plan carefully, execute well—and have a little luck—pretty soon you'll find yourself dealing with the issue of growth in your company.

Most entrepreneurs, of course, hope that one day their fledgling business will get bigger. Growth brings many benefits: more cash coming in, an expanding customer list, additional employees to help you build your company, greater brand recognition, and often more options of how to spend your money. But more cash coming in doesn't necessarily mean more profits. That's because growth also brings many challenges.

Many of these challenges are the same as when you're first starting out, but as you grow, these issues can grow too: cash flow management, the urgent need for quality employees, tremendous demands on management's time and attention, potential lack of focus, and much more. Most important, rapid expansion often means the size of your risk increases as the size of your business grows. To finance your growth, you'll likely take on more debt or seek more investment financing. And you'll have to meet a larger payroll, have a greater number of people dependent on you for their livelihood, and have bigger and more urgent demands coming from your major customers.

Being aware of the challenges of growth can help you better manage those issues. But don't let them scare you off—after all, you almost certainly want your business to grow, perhaps grow very big. That can happen, if you plan for growth, manage it well, and have a little luck on your side.

When is it time to grow?

Growth is a choice. Even if customers are beating a path to your door, you must make an active decision to hire employees, add locations, extend product lines, and so on. What makes the decision more difficult is that growth rarely occurs in a straight line; you can go along for years with a healthy 20-person business, when suddenly business booms, and you're faced with choosing how to handle it.

There are times in the life of a business when it's particularly important to sit down and consider growth. You'll need to actively work toward growth when you:

- Are first starting out and need to reach a sustainable size

- Want to seize a significant opportunity

- Want a company that will be a market leader

- Want a business you can sell, take public, or have acquired in the future

- Are facing aggressive competitors going after your customer base

- See your industry consolidating and realize you'll need to grow to compete

- Have more work than you can handle

- Need to add products, services, or locations to retain your current customer base

- Want to take your business in new directions

- Want to or need to substantially increase your company's revenues

Grow or die

In rapidly consolidating industries, it's often difficult to stay small and survive. When a handful of companies are establishing market domination (and becoming huge) by acquiring all their midsize competitors, your only option for survival may be growth—that, or acquisition by a soon-to-be market 800-pound gorilla.

en·tre·pre·neur·ship key terms

Annual plan
A yearly business plan or business planning session, during which critical members of a company's team gather to outline specific goals and objectives for the coming year.

Event
A specific milestone in an entrepreneurial company's development. Investors may particularly speak of "events" at which a company's value can be established, such as a funding round, an acquisition, or an IPO.

Exit strategy
The options envisioned for being able to make the investment in an entrepreneurial venture "liquid"—in other words, to turn equity ownership into cash or other easily sold assets, such as stock.

Go public
To issue an IPO (see next column).

Initial public offering (IPO)
The first time the company's stock is sold to the general public (other than by a limited offering) through stock market or over-the-counter sales.

Liquidity
Having assets that are able to easily and quickly be turned into cash, such as stocks, bonds, and bank accounts. Investors in companies look to have an event that will enable them to convert their illiquid equity into liquid assets.

White label
To bring about a product (or, far less frequently, a service) to be marketed under the brand name of another company. In other words, the product has no branding of its own: It has a "white label."

You grow, too

With any growth comes a transition period in which you have to redefine your own job responsibilities and learn to delegate more and more authority to other people. This can be both challenging and rewarding. You—as an entrepreneur—will be growing along with your company.

Growing companies often experience natural turning points in their growth. The first occurs when you hire your first employee. When you're just starting out, this is a major step. Ideally, it's a step that helps you grow substantially, as you now have someone else helping to grow your company. But it also puts more pressure on you to grow. Before your first hire, your "company" consists of only you and any others who work with you (on an equity or volunteer basis) to launch your business. Yes, you may be generating revenues and have customers, and you may be using independent contractors. But once you hire your first employee, you have to meet payroll, and someone else's paycheck hinges on you.

The next critical juncture comes when your company reaches roughly 10 to 20 employees. At this point, many customers may not have direct contact with you, the founder and entrepreneur. At this stage you can no longer supervise or regularly interact with all your employees, so you need managers. This can feel like a major loss of control. Many entrepreneurs consciously choose to stop their growth at around this point because they want to run a business where they know and manage everyone who works for them, and in which the income can be significant enough to meet their personal goals.

The next transformation comes at approximately 100 employees. This milestone is often the point where a company needs substantial professional financial and operational management. And it's often a stage at which a company reaches a decision point—is this size sustainable? After all, you're now big enough for major competitors to start taking notice of you. Will you be able to compete against *them*?

Once you get beyond 500 to 1,000 employees, you have other growth issues. You almost certainly start to grapple with the issue of **liquidity**—in other words, how can you turn the value of your equity ownership into assets that are easily sellable? This is particularly important if you have outside investors. After all, your company is now probably worth a substantial sum, but if you continue to hold it as a private company, you limit your ability to realize that value. Will you want to issue stock and **go public**? Or get acquired?

Why grow?

You may reach a point in your business where you're quite satisfied with the size of your company. You feel that you have the amount of control you want, your income is steady, and you're meeting your personal and professional goals. Why not merely rest on your laurels? After all, growth is challenging. It means changing roles—taking on different, and often more, responsibilities in your own company. It also typically means taking on more risks and, often, more debt. So why grow?

If you don't work toward growth, your business will inevitably shrink. As someone once said, "If you just sit there in the middle of the road, you'll get run over." Some of the reasons:

- **Natural loss of customers.** Every year, you'll lose some customers, no matter how good a job you do. After all, some of them will move away, or their needs will change. Nobody's client base stays the same forever.

- **New competition.** Inevitably, you'll face new competitors or fresh types of competition. If you have a healthy market, new competitors will enter to get a piece of the action. Even in a troubled market, some new, creative competitors may see opportunities.

- **New competitive forces.** The competition may not come in the form of a specific company but rather in new distribution channels, new technology, or globalization.

- **Changing demographics or preferences.** You may lose customers due to the inevitable evolution of customers' buying patterns or changes in the demographic makeup of your customers and prospects.

- **Increasing costs.** Prices inevitably rise. Increasing prices mean shrinking profit margins when your sales remain stable.

- **Economic forces outside your control.** Economic conditions may threaten the future financial health of your company regardless of how well you manage it. Growing now, and managing cash carefully, may enable you to build up financial reserves that will see you through downturns.

Your Vision of Growth

What do you want your business to look like in three, five, or 20 years? The first step in growing a venture is to determine what your vision of success looks like.

What do you want in the future, both for yourself and for your company? You probably have a vision of what your company may be in years to come. The vision may not be well-formed, perhaps something like "One day I want this company to be known for making the very best product of its type." Or the vision may be very specific, set by you or your investors; it might be a goal such as "Sales of $10 million within three years."

In founder-led companies, the personal goals of the entrepreneurs inevitably shape and affect the growth vision for the business. Otherwise, inherent tensions undermine the success of the business. There's little likelihood that you'll build a billion-dollar company when what you really want is to be on the ski slopes for months at a time or be home every day at 3 p.m. That's simply not a realistic fit.

Keep in mind that the greater your vision for growth, the greater the risk.

The vision that you and the other decision-makers hold for your company shapes the nature of your day-to-day activities and should determine the priorities for how you expend your resources as you reach toward growth. Always grow toward your vision.

In the table below, consider which of the following visions you have for your company.

VISION AND GROWTH

VISION	DESCRIPTION	GROWTH AND RISK POTENTIAL
Steady Provider	Maintain a stable level of profit; earn a good, reliable income; maintain personal control over many day-to-day aspects of the business.	Low
Quality Leader	Produce the service or product everyone would buy if price were no object; develop a reputation for excellence; take pride in creating the best, regardless of cost.	Low to moderate
Niche Leader	Carve out a narrow place in the market that your company dominates; specialize; do only one thing, but do it extremely well.	Low to moderate
Innovator	Produce entirely new and different products or services; change the way the market views a product or service; act on your new ideas and creativity.	Moderate to high
Global Competitor	Sell or distribute products or services to a global audience or to an international region.	Moderate to high
Exploiter	Build on the successes of others; take advantage of the trends of the moment; take risks for quick rewards.	Moderate to high
Market or Industry Leader	Dominate the market in terms of sales and products; have a well-known name and run a large operation.	High

Growth Strategies

Once you've decided to grow, you have to decide on which growth strategies will best take your company toward your long-term goals. Developing an overall strategy gives you the basis for deciding on the priorities for specific actions and expenditures of funds.

You can pursue a number of key strategies to reach your goals. These include:

- **Expansion.** Add products or services to existing lines, open additional locations, or increase production capacity or distribution systems in an effort to increase sales.

- **Sales Growth.** Significantly intensify marketing and sales efforts to substantially increase the sales of your current product or service lines.

BUILD-YOUR-BUSINESS WORKSHEET

Company Vision

Describe the vision you hold of your company for the next decade.

Overall Long-Term Development: _____
_____
_____
_____

SPECIFIC GOALS	One Year	Five Years	Ten Years
Number of Employees	_____	_____	_____
Number of Locations	_____	_____	_____
Annual Sales	_____	_____	_____
Profits or Profit Margin	_____	_____	_____
Number of Products or Services	_____	_____	_____
Awards or Recognition Received	_____	_____	_____
Ownership Allocation	_____	_____	_____
Other:	_____	_____	_____

_____
_____

BUSINESS STRATEGIES

One year:_____
_____
_____
_____

Five years: _____
_____
_____
_____

Ten years: _____
_____
_____
_____

- **Diversification.** Add new product or service lines to boost overall sales.

- **Acquisition.** Buy other companies to rapidly expand the size and sales of your company and add new markets and customers.

- **Franchise.** License your business model and operations to others to quickly expand and increase income.

- **Globalization.** Find and exploit a foreign market instead of, or in addition to, your own. Even if you don't plan on being a global company at launch, consider the long-term international opportunities. (See Chapter 18 for more on globalization.)

- **Refocus.** Modify the essential nature of the company in terms of market, products, or services, so it can respond to changing conditions or substantial business reverses.

Priorities

To implement your strategies, you must undertake specific actions. For instance, if your strategy is to substantially increase sales, you'll need to use your resources, of both money and time, on your marketing and sales efforts. If, by contrast, your strategy is to diversify, you want to accumulate resources to expend on researching and developing new product lines.

To clarify how your chosen activities relate to your long-term goals, develop a set of priorities for how you'll expend your resources. A list of priorities is a *critical* tool for every business. Use the worksheet "Priorities" to specify the relative importance of each activity.

Strategic partnerships

One highly effective way to grow your company is by securing strategic partnerships and alliances with other companies to achieve your objectives. These mutually beneficial relationships with other companies bring opportunities such as distribution, product development, promotion, or add-on sales.

Generally, partnerships differ from selling outright to another company. The relationship may involve your sharing income or paying commissions, but it may also mean that the partner pays *you.*

Let's say you have a new company, making motors for motorcycles. You could partner with a company that already sells to motorcycle manufacturers to have their sales representatives include your motors in their product line and take a commission on the sales they make; or you could jointly market through trade shows and advertisements and each pay part of the costs; or you could have them market your motors under their brand name, and they pay you a commission for each motor they sell.

BUILD-YOUR-BUSINESS WORKSHEET

Priorities

Rate each area's priority for the expenditure of funds, in hierarchical order (1-2-3, with 1 being the highest priority). Describe the specific priorities or amounts in each area.

Priorities	Specifics	Rating
Add Employees		
Add New Lines		
Increase Marketing		
Add Locations		
Add Capacity		
Increase Salaries		
Increase Inventory		
Increase Profits		
Retire Debts		
Increase Reserve		
Acquire Other Companies		
Other:		

Some types of typical strategic partnerships are:

- **Distribution.** This is an arrangement whereby one company sells another company's product line or services to retailers or other sales outlets. This relieves the original company from having to maintain a large sales force and increases its sales reach. Typically, the distributor takes a percentage of the sale as its commission. For example, a toy distributor might sell puzzles for a puzzle manufacturer.

- **Licensing.** In this arrangement, a company grants permission to another to use its brand name, trademark, license, or even the product itself. Examples abound in the entertainment industry where, for instance, toy manufacturers will license a movie's brand and create toys around the movie's main characters. Professional athletes often also license their names and likenesses for promoting sporting goods.

- **White labeling.** Instead of selling your product or service directly, you might license it to another company to sell under its name and brand. The omission of your branding—hence the term **white label**—is common in many kinds of manufacturing businesses, especially electronics and consumer goods. For instance, major appliances, such as refrigerators, washing machines, and televisions, are often made by only a handful of companies, and various brand names are then attached.

- **Cooperative advertising.** This type of advertising occurs when two companies are mentioned in an advertisement for which each company pays part of the costs. This is a frequent practice in many industries. Manufacturers frequently offer co-op advertising packages for their retailers. For example, a food company might pay part of the cost of an ad for a grocery store.

- **Bundling.** This is a relationship between two companies where one company includes another company's product or service as part of a total package. You keep your own identity, but get the advantage of being included in their package. For example, this could be a company's software that comes preinstalled on the second company's laptops.

Securing a major company as a key partner not only can give your company specific competitive advantages, but also can add credibility with customers and funders alike.

Planning for Growth

Now that you've decided that you want to grow, and you've determined the size to which you want to grow, you need to plan for that growth.

Milestones

How will you know that you're making sufficient progress toward your goals? If your goal is to reach sales of $3 million in two years, how many customers must you have on board by the end of Year One one to be on the path to reach that goal? If you want to get a patent within 18 months, when do you need to have a prototype completed?

In the daily press of business, it can often seem that you're making no progress at all when, in fact, you've accomplished quite a lot. Or, in the giddiness of landing some customers, you may not realize you're falling behind in reaching other key objectives.

Milestones enable you to better measure your progress on your road toward achieving your vision of growth. A list of milestones sets out clearly delineated objectives for your business growth and gives you a tool by which to measure your success.

Importantly, if you have investors, they'll want to know that you are reaching your milestones—that you're making timely progress in accomplishing what you forecast in your business plan. This is especially important in a "pre-revenue" company—that is, one before it's made any sales—because measuring progress can often be difficult. For example, it may take nine months and $100,000 to get a working prototype of your new mobile application. If you've chosen that time frame to achieve that milestone, your investors won't become impatient if you're not done in six months and you've gone through $50,000. And they'll be pleasantly surprised if you're ahead of your milestones and finish it in eight!

By creating a list of milestones you plan on achieving, you and your financing sources have a clearer idea of what you plan to accomplish. Your milestone list should focus on the specific objectives you intend to achieve and the dates by which you expect to accomplish them. These must be concrete—in other words, either specific actions (file for patent, complete prototype, finish first funding round) or specific quantitative goals (quarterly sales of $250,000, secure five enterprise customers, raise $1 million in angel financing).

A milestone list sets out clear objectives. Fill out the worksheet "Milestones" to outline your key steps in your company's growth.

Annual business plan for growth

As you grow your business, one useful tool is an annual business plan. Developing one will give you a clear sense of where you're going and how you should spend money to get there. An **annual plan** aligns your long-term goals with your near-term objectives, enabling you to set priorities for the expenditure of your resources—time, money, and personnel.

Developing an annual plan can be a fairly formal process, involving gathering information for weeks in advance, hiring an industry consultant, and spending a few full days in planning sessions. Yet an annual planning process can even be much simpler, especially in a small or newer business. Set aside a few hours or a day to work exclusively on your goals and objectives for the coming year. Get away from your offices—conduct the meeting offsite. Include everyone who's critical to the growth of your company in your planning process.

Mark progress on your road to success

"Milestone: A stone marker set up on a roadside to indicate the distance in miles from a given point. An important event...a turning point."
— *American Heritage Dictionary*

BUILD-YOUR-BUSINESS WORKSHEET

Milestones

State your specific future objectives and when you plan to achieve each one.

Event	Specifics	Goal Date
Incorporation		
Lease Signed		
Key Employees Hired:		
Initial Financing Secured		
Product Design Completed		
Market Testing Completed		
Trademarks/Patents Secured		
Strategic Partnerships Secured		
First Product Shipped		
Level of Sales Reached ($)		
Level of Sales Reached (units)		
Level of Employees Reached		
Profit Level Reached		
Second Product Line Developed		
Second Product Line Tested		
Second Product Line Shipped		
Additional Financing Secured		
Debts Retired		
Additional Location Opened		
Other:		

The steps to a successful annual planning process range from setting overall goals to devising a specific plan of action.

- **Evaluate the past.** Before going in new directions, see what's worked for you—and what hasn't. In particular, identify which activities have been the most successful in terms of profit, not just income.

- **List your goals.** Write down all your goals: how much money you want to make, products or services you'd like to add, new marketing approaches, changes in operations. Include personal goals that affect your work life.

- **Get specific and include numbers.** Turn general goals into extremely specific, quantifiable objectives. Let's say one of your goals is to increase your business next year. Decide whether that means more customers, more income per customer, or both. Describe the exact type of customers you want. Then, with each goal, add a specific number: the number of customers, average dollar sale per customer, total sales for each product line or sales channel. Numerical goals are hugely powerful motivators.

- **Develop steps.** Identify the steps necessary to achieve objectives. For instance, to attract more customers, you'll need to increase marketing. List the ways you'll do this: advertising, trade shows, direct mail, mobile marketing, and so on. Then, write down numerical targets for each step. How many trade shows will you attend? How many ads will you run?

- **Estimate costs.** Put a dollar figure next to each step. If you don't know exact costs (and you won't!), write down your best estimate. Everything you do has a financial cost; it's important to understand those costs as you develop your plan.

- **Estimate time expenditure.** Activities don't just take money, they take time. Estimate how much time each step might take. For instance, writing a newspaper ad may take two hours, while exhibiting at a trade show may take 40 hours of preparation and five days to attend the show and travel to and from it.

- **Decide on responsibilities.** Determine who'll be responsible for each step and how many people are needed. This means that someone will be in charge of following through on each goal or step.

- **Prioritize.** By now, the items on your to-do list require more money, more time, and more people than you have. So prioritize your goals and steps. Start with your bread-and-butter business—the things that keep your doors open. Next, choose those with the highest probability of success. Eliminate some goals entirely rather than attempting them all halfway.

- **Conduct a reality check.** Look over your list. Does it fit with how you and your employees truly behave? If your plan seems overly ambitious, it probably is. Go back and reprioritize.

Areas to examine

As you develop your annual plan, some of the topics you should evaluate are:

- **Strategic position and company vision**
- **Product or service development**
- **Budget**
- **Marketing**
- **Getting organized**

- **Gain consensus.** Discuss the plan with all affected parties. Do they agree it's realistic? Are they willing to commit to it? Getting everyone on board improves the chances that you'll actually achieve your goals.

- **Set deadlines.** List target dates beside each step to create real-life deadlines.

- **Write it all down.** You now have an action plan with goals, deadlines, and job assignments.

Managing Fast Growth

Frequently, successful entrepreneurial ventures start slowly and then gather speed rapidly. While growing fast is the kind of problem many businesses would *love* to have, it's a challenge nonetheless. It's easy—in fact, typical—to be overwhelmed. You have a lot to juggle: finding and training staff, managing cash flow, and serving customers. And decisions must be made quickly.

How will you acquire the staff you need? And train them? And pay them? Where will you even put them? How will you ensure quality in your product or service as you turn it out rapidly? If you're able to handle growing quickly, you'll likely create a stronger, sustainable company—*and* make a lot more money. Handled poorly, fast growth can bring down an otherwise healthy business.

Fast growth presents many challenges:

- **Staffing.** This is the toughest problem. Some of the biggest problems that fast-growing companies face deal with employees: hiring, motivating, and training them. Keep in mind that you'll be tremendously busy scrambling to turn out work. How will you find enough good people, and then manage them?

  Many fast-growth companies turn to independent contractors, especially until they see whether it looks like the growth is sustainable. But consider hiring an HR director or consultant early on.

- **Leadership.** As your company grows, you will find that you can't handle all the management responsibilities yourself. No matter how hard you work or how many hours you put in, it's impossible for the founder or founders of a company to manage all aspects of a rapidly expanding company.

  You'll have to learn to delegate and hire other managers. You might first delegate along functional lines—marketing, operations, finance, and the like. But you may find you need a second-in-command to handle overall management, too.

- **Financing and cash flow.** Even when sales increase substantially, it's tough to finance fast growth from income alone. Typically, you face substantial cash flow management issues. You'll often need to spend money faster than it comes in: hiring staff, purchasing materials or inventory, renting facilities, buying equipment.

The first approach to handle your cash flow needs may be to secure a line of credit. But as you grow, you may find you need greater financial resources than you can get from a bank or that you feel comfortable borrowing. To seize growth opportunities, it may be time to consider an investor as well.

■ **Strategy.** As you grow, you'll have lots of decisions to make, especially how to direct your future growth path: which opportunities to pursue, which to let go? You'll also face investment decisions: which activities to build, which to abandon? Or do you want to stash away money you're making in case the growth doesn't last?

To help with these issues, you may want to form an Advisory Committee or hire a management consultant.

■ **Systems.** Fast growth can easily lead to a certain amount of chaos. When things move quickly, it's virtually inevitable that you'll have a harder time communicating with team members, managing deadlines, and ensuring accountability. Your growth may outpace your ability to scale up your infrastructure—your data management, your IT systems, and your collaboration and communication systems.

You'll want to find people fairly quickly who can help you plan management systems that can scale in accordance with your growth.

■ **Corporate culture.** In all the confusion, you still want to build a corporate culture that attracts and retains great employees. So be certain to communicate, pay fairly, and thank and reward staff for jobs well done. Pay attention to the kind of business you're building—not merely its size or your profits.

Exit Strategies

If you're fortunate, plan well, and work hard, you may grow a company of considerable worth. While creating annual income is a major motivation for many entrepreneurs, ideally your company will achieve worth beyond its annual profits. Eventually, you may want to be able to extract some of that value from the company—and benefit from that worth.

If you have investors, they will certainly want to be able to realize the return on their investment. After all, the value of your company may be extremely high on paper, but how do you turn that value into actual cash?

Even without investors, if there's more than one partner or principal in the business, creating a clear **exit strategy** can reduce the friction that comes from having unspoken exit assumptions. One founder may dream of building a company worth millions with the aim of selling it in the next few years, while the other founder may hope to build a modest business to run for many years to come. Those differences may make for significant disagreements over the company's direction.

A number of options let you exit from a company, but if you're dealing with investors, they may be interested in only two or three of those options. Gen-

REAL-WORLD RECAP

Top challenges of fast-growth companies

- Staffing
- Leadership
- Financing and cash flow
- Strategy
- Systems
- Corporate culture

An exit plan doesn't mean *you* exit

Just because you're developing an exit strategy doesn't mean you necessarily intend to, or need to, leave your company. Many exit scenarios permit the entrepreneurs to stay in control of the company, yet turn all or some of their value liquid.

erally, sophisticated investors look for companies that can go public (sell stock that will be traded to the general public on stock exchanges or "over the counter") or that are candidates for acquisition by other companies. Investors prefer these exit strategies because they get out of the company cleanly, usually with substantial rewards, based on just one of two **events**: either an **initial public offering (IPO)** that happens when the stock is first publicly traded, or the sale of the company.

These two strategies, especially acquisition, can mean that all or some of the top management, including the founders, may end up having to leave or having far less control over the company. This may be an acceptable option, given the nature of the financial rewards involved.

Novice entrepreneurs often imagine being able to buy out their investors, though this is not usually a realistic option. In highly successful companies, the investor has little motivation to sell, and in any case the amount of money needed to purchase their stock could be prohibitive. In less successful companies, the investors may want to get out, but the entrepreneur is unlikely to have the extra cash necessary to buy them out.

The table below, "Exit Plan Options," briefly outlines the major exit strategies and their advantages and disadvantages. The disadvantages assume that

EXIT PLAN OPTIONS

OPTION	DESCRIPTION	ADVANTAGES	DISADVANTAGES
Go Public	Sell shares in the company to the public, traded on a stock exchange "over the counter."	Stock easily convertible to cash, liquidity; current management stays.	Must be large company: highly regulated; management can be replaced by stockholders.
Acquisition	Bought by another existing company.	Receive cash and/or stock; current management has continuing role.	Must be appropriate fit for existing company; management leaves or has new boss.
Sale	Bought by individuals.	Receive cash.	Must find willing buyer; management goes.
Merger	Join with existing company.	Combined resources; current management may stay; may receive stock or some cash.	New partners or bosses; usually little or no cash; less control.
Buyout	One or more stockholders buy out the interests of another.	Seller gets cash; others stay in control of company.	Must have sufficient cash; seller must be willing.
Franchise	Sell concept to others to replicate.	Receive cash; current management stays; future potential.	Concept must be appropriate; legally complicated.
Hand Down	Give company to next generation.	Stays in family; current management may continue.	Family tensions; no cash; tax implications.
Close	End operations.	Relatively easy; feeling of being finished.	No financial reward; feeling of loss.

the current management would like to have a continuing role in the company, which may or may not be true in your situation.

Positioning for acquisition

The question that acquirers ask when considering whether to acquire a company is "Build versus Buy?" In other words, is it cheaper and faster for them to purchase your company to gain whatever you can bring them, or should they try to develop it themselves? Many novice entrepreneurs think they have a terrific idea that's worth many millions. But unless your idea is carefully protected, others can be inspired by your idea, take it, and run with it. They don't need to buy—they can build.

You have to create something that an acquiring company can't easily "build" themselves if you want them to open their wallet to purchase your business.

Three things are paramount when *technology* companies go looking for an acquisition:

- **Market.** Many acquisitions are driven by the desire to grab a new or bigger market. If you have a large, valuable, or desirable customer base, that can be a compelling motivation for an acquisition. You don't need to have millions of customers to be attractive to an acquiring company on the hunt. Perhaps by owning you, an acquirer immediately expands geographically or is able to serve a new industry.

- **People.** Great ideas are easy to come by, but great people are much harder to find. Companies often look for talent acquisition, and when they spot a terrific team, one that works well together and is capable of building and growing a company, that's an especially appealing target. If you hope to be acquired one day, don't compromise on the quality of the people you hire.

- **IP (intellectual property).** If you have managed to create a new technology or invention and develop it to a point where you have proved the concept, you'll be more interesting to an acquirer. This is especially true if you have ensured good patent protection. Even without cutting-edge technology, if you've developed something impressive, an acquiring company may want to acquire you to get to market sooner. They may say to themselves, "We want this property. We could build it ourselves and have it in a year, or we could buy it and go to market tomorrow."

If your company is growing dramatically, an acquisition might be driven by the acquirer's mix of fear and opportunity—the opportunity to grow and the fear that if they don't acquire you, your hot start-up might eat their lunch.

Keep this in mind, though: If your guiding principle is "I want to be acquired," it's unlikely you'll be a good target. Instead, focus on building a great company. Because the things you do to build a great company are the very things that will get you acquired.

Recipe for Growth: Zingerman's Deli

Founded in 1982 by Paul Saginaw and Ari Weinzweig, Zingerman's Deli is considered an institution in the bustling college town of Ann Arbor, Michigan. Although barely clearing $100 in sales on its first day of business in its cramped, 1,200-square-foot premises, Zingerman's Deli quickly grew into one of the city's most popular places to eat and buy amazingly delicious food.[1]

challenge

A popular delicatessen wanted to grow without franchising or adding new locations

solution

Branch out into a series of related businesses with an innovative ownership structure

With their growing success, Saginaw and Weinzweig wanted to build a true, local business with the highest-quality products, service, and reputation. To do that, they fervently believed they had to stay a one-of-a-kind entity. They didn't want to see a chain of Zingerman's Delis, run by half-hearted salaried managers, or worse, franchise their concept and have strangers eventually erode the quality and standards they set.

"We knew we wanted to have just one store and that we were not going to grow by replicating ourselves," said Saginaw. "For us, by definition, if there was more than one store, it wasn't unique anymore. This wasn't a political belief or ideology; it was a lifestyle we wanted to live."

What did Saginaw mean by "lifestyle"? He and Weinzweig wanted to spend their time actually working at the store, getting to know the employees and customers intimately, and being committed members of the Ann Arbor community.

According to an interview in the *New York Times*, Zingerman's founders have had "dozens and dozens of opportunities to franchise, sell the name, take the check, and walk away."[2]

Instead, they rejected conventional business-school wisdom, and chose to grow "deep" by adding related businesses. Their first was Zingerman's Bakehouse. The Bakehouse began by making the breads and pastries sold in the deli, but soon began selling to other restaurants, retailers, and consumers.

Over the years, the "Zingerman's Community of Businesses" grew to include a catering firm, a mail order food business, a coffee company, a creamery, and a full-service restaurant. They even have a training company to help teach other small businesses the Zingerman's secrets of customer service and management.

Saginaw and Weinzweig start a new business when someone they know and trust—typically, a current employee—comes to them with what they consider a promising idea. They must develop a complete business plan and also have a hands-on role in leading and managing the business. There are no absentee owners in the Zingerman's family.

---

1. "Community Food Enterprise: Local Success in a Global Marketplace." The Wallace Center at Winrock International Business Alliance for Local Living Economies.

2. "A Corner Deli with International Appeal," by Micheline Maynard, the *New York Times*. May 3, 2007.

Each of the Zingerman's companies is a separate legal entity, owned by one to three partners. One of the partners is always Dancing Sandwich Enterprises, the 50/50 partnership of Saginaw and Weinzweig, which holds their joint financial interests in all Zingerman's companies.

Although each of the companies is independently owned and operated, all businesses are part of "ZingCOB," Zingerman's Community of Businesses. All partners of all Zingerman's-related companies agree to a set of guiding principles. They make all major governance decisions across the companies by consensus. With regularly scheduled meetings every other week, the partners work closely together, troubleshoot problems, and make strategic and tactical plans.

"The other businesses don't control you, but you want their support," said Saginaw. "It's your decision to make, but at least make a decision that everyone can live with. This is why we meet every other week, as all decisions are by consensus."

One Zingerman's business not visible to the public is Zingerman's Service Network. The network provides all ZingCOB companies with services related to financial leadership and management, payroll and benefits, human resources, information technology, marketing, and graphics.

Growing the business in this unique way wouldn't be possible without exceptional employees. Yet Zingerman's employees weren't necessarily "exceptional" when they were hired. Zingerman's invests heavily in training, and emphasizes continual training for each employee in every ZingCOB company. The training is not merely in rote job skills, but training to be able to make independent decisions, even as to how to clear tables or take out garbage.

Saginaw believes that "leadership" is a quality that every employee is capable of. This, too, goes against conventional wisdom that says employees in "low-skill" jobs like food service should merely be trained in completing routines, not acting independently.

Zingerman's also provides highly competitive benefits that include health care, food discounts, and generous vacations that add up to as much as six paid weeks off. Employees are involved when setting goals for each of the companies every year and get bonuses if the goals are exceeded.

Whenever a new employee is hired, the first-day orientation is always provided by either Saginaw or Weinzweig. "It's the last thing we would ever delegate," said Saginaw. "It's very important that you hear from the founders what it is we are trying to accomplish as an organization. I tell people that if you want to stake a career here, I have a responsibility to work with you and see that it happens."

It's certainly working. Today, the Zingerman's Community of Businesses has annual revenues in excess of $36 million and employs more than 500 people. Revenue has grown, on average, at more than 10 percent per year. Most telling of all, the "family of businesses" has become a model for other local businesses that want to grow up without selling out. ∎

questions

1. In addition to the areas described here, into what other types of businesses can Zingerman's expand?

2. In the case of baked goods, by spinning off a new business to create them, Zingerman's can better control the quality, the timing, the cost, and so on, of the final product. Can you think of other types of businesses that could move processes or production in-house? In what type of business would it make sense to continue to buy supplies, or to outsource manufacturing, to a third party?

3. Can you think of other jobs traditionally considered "low skill" that could be approached in a creative way to empower employees? Which ones, and how?

GROWING BIG WITHOUT SELLING OUT

Goal:

Come up with a plan to grow your local business without selling out.

What to Do:

Imagine that you have a local gym that's doing very well and that has amassed an extremely loyal clientele. You want to grow the business—but not by adding franchising or by becoming a chain. You want to retain the personal feel that made you a success.

1. Brainstorm various ways to grow the business in ways similar to Zingerman's Deli. Consider:

   a. Other products you can develop and sell

   b. Other lines of services you can offer

   c. Other complementary companies you can start

   d. Any other ways you could grow

2. Identify which aspects of your corporate culture will help make you successful in your approach.

3. Present your ideas to the class. Be prepared to defend the ways your plan will grow the business substantially, while keeping the main gym unique.

20 Resources

Online U.S. Government Resources

U.S. Census Bureau

www.census.gov

Because Census Bureau data covers such a huge number of people and businesses, and because it is so detailed, Census Bureau data is considered among the most reliable information you can use.

AMERICAN FACTFINDER

http://factfinder2.census.gov

This site's easy-to-use interactive menu allows you to find a range of demographic information about the American people—down to city or census tract level.

CENSTATS

http://censtats.census.gov

This site provides access to databases, including Census Tract Street Locator, County Business Patterns, International Trade Data, and more.

COUNTY BUSINESS PATTERNS

www.census.gov/econ/cbp/index.html

Provides annual reports on the number of business establishments—detailed by industry, business size, and payroll—throughout the United States and Puerto Rico, available on national, state, county, metropolitan area, and zip code levels.

CURRENT INDUSTRIAL REPORTS

www.census.gov/manufacturing/cir/index.html

The Census Bureau publishes more than 100 Current Industrial Reports, providing very detailed data on tens of thousands of manufactured products. These reports provide information on production, shipping, inventories, consumption, and the number of firms manufacturing each product. The data is reported monthly, quarterly, and annually.

ECONOMIC CENSUS

www.census.gov

If you are looking for information about specific industries or types of businesses, from the Census Bureau's home page, go to "Data" and click "Economic Census." From there, choose the link to the latest results (left-hand column) or the years you're interested in. A full Economic Census of the United States is conducted every five years; the last one covered the year 2007.

STATE DATA CENTERS

www.census.gov/sdc

The U.S. Census Bureau maintains links to individual U.S. states data and statistics programs. This will help you locate statewide economic statistics.

Edgar Database—U.S. Securities and Exchange Commission

www.sec.gov/edgar.shtml

You can find annual, quarterly, and other financial reports required from publicly traded companies by selecting the "Edgar" filings. You need the name of the corporation, not the brand name of the product, to find reports.

FedStats

www.fedstats.gov

This main gateway to national statistics has links to statistics compiled by over 100 government agencies as well as government statistical agencies. It is a very good entry-point to all U.S. statistics.

Government Printing Office

www.gpo.gov

Information from the U.S. Government on federal laws, governmental departments, and the like.

Internal Revenue Service

www.irs.gov/taxstats/

Tax statistics are generally harder to maneuver than Census Bureau statistics. However, if you have a specific income or tax-related statistic you are seeking, this might be a source of that data.

Library of Congress

www.loc.gov/rr/news/stategov/stategov.html

This guide to state websites provides links for every state. Some states have more comprehensive links than others. Also includes links to other sites with state and local government information, such as the easy-to-use and privately run www.statelocalgov.net.

NAICS Codes

www.census.gov/eos/www/naics

NAICS is the abbreviation for North American Industry Classification System. It replaces the older Standard Industrial Classification (SIC) codes. Each industry—and subsector of each industry—is assigned a specific NAICS number.

Small Business Administration (SBA)

www.sba.gov

The SBA maintains this portal to government (both federal and state-by-state), legal, and regulatory information. You'll also find information on starting and managing a business, loans and grants, locations of SBA offices near you, and more.

Small Business Publications

http://publications.usa.gov/USAPubs.php?CatID=10

Small business publications include topics such as trademark, copyright, health care, and federal programs for the Americans with Disabilities Act.

Canadian Resources

BMO Capital Markets

www.bmonesbittburns.com/economics

BMO Capital Markets is a good, nongovernmental source of Canadian and North American economic statistics, including economic outlooks.

Canada Business Network

www.canadabusiness.ca/eng/

This site provides a single access point to all the Canadian government services and information helpful to those wishing to start, run and grow a business in Canada.

Canadian Census

www12.statcan.gc.ca/census-recensement/2011/rt-td/index-eng.cfm

Canadian Industry Statistics

www.ic.gc.ca

This well-organized site makes readily available the resources and data of Industry Canada, a Canadian government department.

Statistics Canada

www.statcan.gc.ca

This is the primary entry point for statistical information about all aspects of Canada, including demographics and economic conditions.

International Resources

State Department Country Background Notes

www.state.gov/r/pa/ei/bgn

The U.S. State Department prepares background papers on virtually every country in the world. Background papers on this site include statistics and overviews of each country's economy, as well as useful links.

U.S. Census Bureau List of Foreign Statistical Websites

www.census.gov/aboutus/stat_int.html

The U.S. Census Bureau maintains links for users to locate statistical sites of countries around the world.

The World Bank

www.worldbank.org

This international organization compiles data worldwide. It offers free data by topic or country, contains links to online databases, and publishes its own economic reports.

General Business and Industry Resources: Online

The Advertising RedBooks

www.redbooks.com

This directory contains detailed profiles of nearly 13,500 U.S. and international advertising agencies, including accounts and brand names represented, fields of specialization, gross billings, and contact information on agency personnel.

Business & Company Resource Center

www.galegroup.com/BusinessRC

This premier online research site that is of special use to entrepreneurs has its own content as well as a search engine that lets users look up detailed information about potential competitors; free access is often available at public libraries.

Dialog

www.dialog.com

Paid database and research service. Highly used in business.

LexisNexis

www.lexisnexis.com

This service provides a wealth of information and should be the first place you start when you are ready to pay for information. It offers access to hundreds of databases, thousands of worldwide publications, public and legislative records, data on companies and executives, and more. Payment for access to the LexisNexis database is available by the article, or by day, week, or subscription.

Louisiana State University

www.lib.lsu.edu/gov

LSU maintains a very well-organized index to research and data available on the Web, including government sources and subject-specific search engines.

Mintel

www.mintel.com

A global supplier of consumer, media, and market research. You can use these custom reports to find out what's going on in a broad range of markets and industries.

Plunkett Research Online

www.plunkettresearchonline.com

This site provides market research, company profiles, analysis, trends, statistics, data, and business information. Plunkett is an excellent resource for researching potential business competitors.

ProQuest

www.proquest.com

Offers abstracts and full-text articles from leading publications. By searching through this database you can find out virtually anything that's been published about a particular market or industry in a major business or trade magazine.

Risk Management Association

www.rmahq.org

This association that serves the banking industry produces the most relied-on study of financial performance and ratios of over 600 industries. Its annual studies are available online on a per-industry basis for a small fee.

SRDS or Standard Rate and Data

www.srds.com

Reliable source of information on all publications and media outlets, including business publications, consumer magazines, online advertising, direct marketing lists, radio, cable, and television. You must subscribe to get information online, but copies of its books are in larger public libraries.

Standard & Poor's NetAdvantage

www.netadvantage.standardandpoors.com

A comprehensive repository of in-depth business and investment information. One of the top business databases, this provides independent research, data, and commentary on stocks, bonds, funds, and industries—all of which helps entrepreneurs get the "big picture" of what's going on in their chosen markets or industries. Note: available only through libraries.

Technology Industry Resources

For statistics and trends in technology-related industries, the following two websites are sources for fee-based research reports and data:

FORRESTER

www.forrester.com

GARTNER GROUP

www.gartner.com

General Business and Industry Resources: Offline

InfoTrac

Many libraries subscribe to an online database service called InfoTrac (published by Gale Group), which allows you to search for magazine and journal articles, as well as gain access to substantial proprietary information.

Predicasts F&S Forecasts

Provides an index to articles, as well as to the full text of brief articles and excerpts, in nearly 1,000 journals, newspapers, research studies, and the like, that cover all manufacturing and service industries as well as a wide range of business-related subjects.

Predicasts PROMT

Provides summaries and full text of articles from trade and industry publications. It is especially useful for finding detailed information on specific companies, industries, products, and brands.

Standard & Poor's Industry Surveys

While designed for investors, this can be a source of significant insights about your overall industry and major competitors. It provides overviews of trends and reports company revenues for over 50 industries.

Wilson Business Full

This provides full-text access to articles from business publications. If your library has access to the Wilson Business database, it may be an inexpensive way to get archived articles from publications.

Publications

GALANTE'S VENTURE CAPITAL AND PRIVATE EQUITY DIRECTORY

This directory lists over 2,000 American and international venture capital and angel investors. It is extremely expensive to purchase, so check for availability at a good library.

PRATT'S GUIDE TO PRIVATE EQUITY AND VENTURE CAPITAL SOURCES

www.prattsguide.com

This long-standing annual directory lists more than 20,000 venture capital sources around the world. It lists contact information, recent investments, and capital under management, and is cross-referenced by investment preferences, investment stage, and other key information. It is extremely expensive to purchase—either in print or through Web access—so check for availability at a good library.

You can also find information about industries, trends, and companies from a number of publications, which may charge a fee for the full text of archived stories. A few to try:

BUSINESS WEEK
www.businessweek.com

THE ECONOMIST
www.economist.com

FORBES
www.forbes.com

RED HERRING
www.redherring.com

WALL STREET JOURNAL
www.wsj.com

Credit and Other Information on Specific Companies

Dun & Bradstreet

www.dnb.com

D&B maintains credit reports and financial information on tens of thousands of companies. You can purchase a report about a competitor, a customer, or a supplier. You can also buy targeted marketing lists and industry reports.

Hoover's Online

www.hoovers.com

From this site you can get free, basic information on individual companies, particularly public ones, as well as more detailed information for a fee. Look at Hoover's Publications for more information relating to your industry. Hoover's also has links to other sources of specific information on companies, mostly fee-based.

Human Resources/Personnel Issues

Advanced HR

www.advanced-hr.com

Provides salaries and stock options for pre-IPO companies. Fee based. But offers free limited access for start-ups.

American Management Association

www.amanet.org

Offers reports and studies on general business and industry-specific issues, including best practices in selected industries.

Society for Human Resource Management

www.shrm.com

Leading organization of HR directors and staff. Excellent, deep site on human resource topics. It also has some excellent links to general business resources on the Internet.

Manufacturing

ASQ

www.asq.org

Worldwide organization that provides tools, best practices, and experts to ensure quality.

ISO 9001 International Quality Standards

www.easy9001.com

National Association of Manufacturers

www.nam.org

This large industry association provides substantial information to manufacturing companies, as well as collects data about manufacturing.

Thomas Register

www.thomasnet.com

ThomasNet, the ultimate resource for locating suppliers and vendors, lists suppliers by product category. A number of suppliers offer detailed product/part/equipment lists as well, some with prices.

Marketing

Advertising Age

www.adage.com

American Marketing Association

www.marketingpower.com

Social Responsibility Resources

BSR

www.bsr.org

A national association of over 250 member companies interested in implementing responsible corporate policies and practices. BSR provides information on corporate leadership practices, conducts research and education workshops, develops practical business tools, and provides consulting services and technical assistance to its member companies.

Computer Professionals for Corporate Responsibility

www.cpsr.org

Social Venture Network (SVN)

www.svn.org

www.svneurope.com (Social Venture Europe)

A membership organization of successful business and social entrepreneurs dedicated to changing the way the world does business. Provides opportunities for entrepreneurs to exchange ideas, share problems and solutions, and collaborate on an ad hoc basis with their peers.

Social Venture Partners

www.svpi.org

VolunteerMatch

www.volunteermatch.org

A nonprofit organization dedicated to increasing volunteerism through the Internet.

Entrepreneurs' Sources

PlanningShop

www.PlanningShop.com/associations

PlanningShop, publisher of this book, maintains a list of major trade associations on its company website.

ASAE, The Center for Association Leadership

www.asaecenter.org

This national association of directors of trade, industry, and professional associations also provides a "Gateway" on its site that can help you locate associations related to your business.

Better Business Bureaus/Better Business Bureau Online

www.bbb.org

www.bbb.org/online

A long-respected organization of businesses that agree to adhere to certain standards. BBBOnline offers a certification program for Internet sites to increase users' confidence in sites' reliability or privacy policies.

Columbia Books National Trade and Professional Associations of the United States

Available in most major libraries.

Edward Lowe Foundation

http://edwardlowe.org

A nonprofit organization dedicated to assisting entrepreneurs. Extensive website of resources and articles.

Entrepreneurship.org

www.entrepreneurship.org

Run by the Ewing Marion Kauffman Foundation, a nonprofit organization dedicated to assisting entrepreneurs. Extensive website of resources.

FEW (Forum for Women Entrepreneurs)

www.fwe.ca

Founded in 1993, the Forum for Women Entrepreneurs serves entrepreneurial women who are building or leading high-growth technology and life-science companies. Started and headquartered in the San Francisco Bay Area, FWE has chapters in Seattle, San Diego/Orange County, and Los Angeles, as well as in Paris.

Gale's Encyclopedia of Associations

This publication lists over 135,000 membership organizations worldwide. You may be able to find it at a good library.

Inc. Magazine and Website

www.inc.com

Leading magazine for growing businesses. Website offers substantial archive of articles on business issues.

Intuit Community

www.community.intuit.com

Resources and peer-to-peer information sharing on small business topics, created by Intuit, maker of QuickBooks.

NASE (National Association for the Self-Employed)

www.nase.org

Membership organization providing a number of services to self-employed and small businesses, including insurance and discounts.

NAWBO (National Association of Women Business Owners)

www.nawbo.org

Membership group of women-owned businesses, with many local chapters around the country.

SBDCs

www.asbdc-us.org/searchResults.php

Small Business Development Centers and subcenters maintain a library of reference materials, and can usually direct you to sources appropriate to your planning process. They may be able to help you identify local resources for your particular business, and they often conduct workshops on business topics and skills. SBDC centers are located in many American communities, often at community colleges or universities.

SCORE (Service Corps of Retired Executives)

www.score.org

Provides retired business owners as counselors for assistance to individual entrepreneurs, and conducts workshops on business skill topics.

Software Developers' Forum

www.sdforum.org

Long-standing, well-regarded Silicon Valley group of entrepreneurs—primarily but not exclusively in high tech. Sponsors or cosponsors many seminars and programs on general entrepreneurship and start-up issues. Conducts one-on-one meetings with venture capitalists.

Trade Show News Network (TSNN)

www.tsnn.com

A database listing more than 15,000 trade shows worldwide.

Women in Technology International

www.witi.com

An organization devoted to increasing the number of women in executive roles in technology and technology-based companies. More oriented to employees than to entrepreneurs, but still a good source of information and excellent conferences. Has regional chapters.

Funding Sources

Angel Investors

ANGEL CAPITAL ASSOCIATION

www.angelcapitalassociation.org

Directory of groups of angel investors throughout the United States and Canada.

THE ANGELS' FORUM LLC

www.angelsforum.com

Business Plan Competitions

MIT ENTREPRENEURSHIP COMPETITION

http://mit100k.org

Since 1989, MIT has awarded cash prizes to student teams of entrepreneurs competing in its annual business plan competition. Many of the participants go on to build extremely successful companies.

NEW YORK TIMES BUSINESS PLAN COMPETITION GUIDE

www.nytimes.com/interactive/2009/11/11/business/smallbusiness/competitions-table.html

The New York Times regularly updates this comprehensive list of business plan competitions, including information on prizes and deadlines.

STANFORD UNIVERSITY

http://bases.stanford.edu

Stanford conducts both an entrepreneur's business plan competition and a social entrepreneur's business plan competition for socially conscious for-profit and nonprofit companies.

International Sources

BRITISH VENTURE CAPITAL ASSOCIATION

www.bvca.co.uk/home

PRIVATE EQUITY AND VENTURE CAPITAL ASSOCIATION

www.evca.eu

Loans and Venture Capital Sources

DOW JONES FINANCIAL INFORMATION SERVICES

www.fis.dowjones.com

Provides news on venture capital and capitalists, both in the United States and abroad.

THE GARAGE

www.garage.com

A for-profit company intended to help start-up companies interact with and secure funding from potential investors.

INVESTORS' CIRCLE

www.investorscircle.net

A network of investors making private investments to socially responsible companies. It circulates proposals (for a fee) to their members, and twice a year it holds venture fairs where socially responsible businesses can present for funding.

MID-ATLANTIC VENTURE ASSOCIATION

www.mava.org

THE NATIONAL ASSOCIATION OF GOVERNMENT GUARANTEED LENDERS

www.naggl.org

NAGGL is the association of banks and lending institutions that are active in offering SBA loans.

NATIONAL ASSOCIATION OF SEED AND VENTURE FUNDS

www.nasvf.org

An organization of private, public, and nonprofit groups helping to create networks of investors in early-stage companies; also provides seminars for entrepreneurs.

NATIONAL VENTURE CAPITAL ASSOCIATION

www.nvca.org

A leading organization composed of venture capitalists and private equity investors. An excellent list of association members is available for a fee. The list includes names of venture capital firms, addresses, phone numbers, and persons to contact, as well as geographic and industry preferences and stages of companies funded.

PACT—GREATER PHILADELPHIA ALLIANCE FOR CAPITAL AND TECHNOLOGIES

http://philadelphiapact.com

SMALL BUSINESS INVESTOR ALLIANCE

www.nasbic.org

This group of private investors provides funding to small- and medium-size businesses.

U.S. SMALL BUSINESS ADMINISTRATION (SBA)

www.sba.gov

The SBA maintains lists of banks and other lending institutions most active in making loans to small businesses in each geographical area. It also provides a loan guarantee program (not actual loans) to existing businesses, and direct loans limited to special categories such as Vietnam-era veterans and the disabled.

VENTURE CAPITAL INVESTING CONFERENCE

www.vcinvestingconference.com

WESTERN ASSOCIATION OF VENTURE CAPITALISTS
www.wavc.net

This association of more than 140 members represents virtually all the professionally managed venture capital firms in the western United States.

WESTLAKE SECURITIES
www.westlakesecurities.com

Provides a full range of investment banking and financial advisory services to emerging growth companies as well as established privately held and publicly traded companies.

Global Business Resources

General International Business Information

GLOBAL EDGE, MICHIGAN STATE UNIVERSITY
http://globaledge.msu.edu

U.S. COMMERCIAL SERVICE
http://trade.gov/cs

In-person counseling in more than 100 U.S. cities.

U.S. SMALL BUSINESS ADMINISTRATION INTERNATIONAL TRADE PORTAL
http://www.sba.gov/about-offices-content/1/2889

Import/Export

COMMERCIAL NEWS USA
http://thinkglobal.us

EXPORT.GOV
www.export.gov

The main U.S. Web portal for export resources.

FEDERATION OF INTERNATIONAL TRADE ASSOCIATIONS
www.fita.org/index.html

GLOSSARY OF IMPORT/EXPORT TERMS
www.usaexportimport.com/glossary.php

U.S. EXPORT ASSISTANCE CENTERS
www.sba.gov/aboutsba/sbaprograms/internationaltrade/useac/index.html

In-person assistance in exporting for small and medium-size business in major U.S. cities.

Country Information

CIA WORLD FACT BOOK
www.cia.gov/library/publications/the-world-factbook/index.html

COUNTRY INFORMATION OF THE U.S. STATE DEPARTMENT
http://travel.state.gov

THE WORLD BANK: COUNTRY AND REGION INFORMATION
www.worldbank.org

Financial

EXPORT/IMPORT BANK OF THE UNITED STATES
www.exim.gov

SBA EXPORT FINANCE PROGRAMS
www.sba.gov/category/navigation-structure/starting-managing-business/
managing-business/exporting-importing

YAHOO FINANCE INTERNATIONAL
http://finance.yahoo.com/international

Legal

INTERNATIONAL LAW ADVICE
www.worldlawdirect.com

WORLDWIDE NETWORK OF LAW FIRMS
www.globalaw.net

Business Cultures and Norms

CANADIAN GOVERNMENT CENTRE FOR INTERCULTURAL LEARNING
www.dfait-maeci.gc.ca/cfsi-icse/cil-cai/index-eng.asp

INTERNATIONAL ETIQUETTE GUIDE
www.kwintessential.co.uk/resources/country-profiles.html

INTERNATIONAL BUSINESS ETIQUETTE AND MANNERS
www.cyborlink.com

WORLD BUSINESS CULTURE
www.worldbusinessculture.com

Social Responsibility

FAIRTRADE LABELING ORGANIZATIONS INTERNATIONAL
www.fairtrade.net

U.S. ENVIRONMENTAL PROTECTION AGENCY
www.epa.gov/oecaerth/international/importexport.html

Notes:

Index

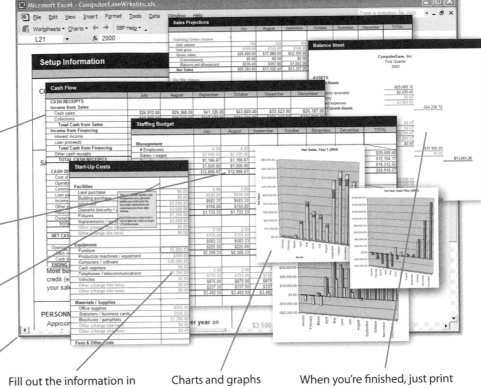

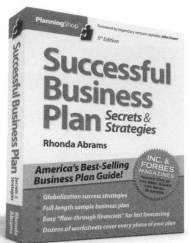